MYTH, RULERSHIP, CHURCH

Frontispiece   Professor Nicholas Brooks

Myth, Rulership, Church and Charters
Essays in Honour of Nicholas Brooks

Edited by

JULIA BARROW
University of Nottingham, UK

and

ANDREW WAREHAM
Roehampton University, UK

Routledge
Taylor & Francis Group
LONDON AND NEW YORK

First published 2008 by Ashgate Publishing

2 Park Square, Milton Park, Abingdon, Oxon OX14 4RN
711 Third Avenue, New York, NY 10017, USA

Routledge is an imprint of the Taylor & Francis Group, an informa business

First issued in paperback 2016

Copyright © Julia Barrow and Andrew Wareham 2008

Julia Barrow and Andrew Wareham have asserted their moral right under the Copyright, Designs and Patents Act, 1988, to be identified as the editors of this work.

All rights reserved. No part of this book may be reprinted or reproduced or utilised in any form or by any electronic, mechanical, or other means, now known or hereafter invented, including photocopying and recording, or in any information storage or retrieval system, without permission in writing from the publishers.

Notice:
Product or corporate names may be trademarks or registered trademarks, and are used only for identification and explanation without intent to infringe.

British Library Cataloguing in Publication Data
Myth, rulership, church and charters: essays in honour of Nicholas Brooks
1. Great Britain – History – Anglo-Saxon period, 449–1066
  I. Brooks, Nicholas II. Barrow, Julia III. Wareham, Andrew,
  1965–
  942'.017

Library of Congress Cataloging-in-Publication Data
Myth, rulership, church and charters: essays in honour of Nicholas Brooks; edited by Julia Barrow and Andrew Wareham.
  p. cm.
  Includes bibliographical references and index.
  ISBN 978-0-7546-5120-8 (alk. paper)
1. Great Britain–History–Anglo-Saxon period, 449-1066. 2. Great Britain–History, Military–449–1066. 3. Anglo-Saxons. I. Barrow, Julia. II. Wareham, Andrew, 1965–III. Brooks, Nicholas.

DA152.M98 2007
942.01–dc22

2007008134

ISBN 978-0-7546-5120-8 (hbk)
ISBN 978-1-138-26475-5 (pbk)

Contents

List of Figures   *vii*
Notes on Contributors   *ix*
Acknowledgements   *xi*
List of Abbreviations   *xiii*

1	Introduction: Myth, Rulership, Church and Charters in the Work of Nicholas Brooks *Julia Barrow*	1
2	Nicholas Brooks at Birmingham *Christopher Dyer*	11
3	Anglo-Saxon Origin Legends *Barbara Yorke*	15
4	A Nearly, but Wrongly, Forgotten Historian of the Dark Ages *James Campbell*	31
5	Anglo-Saxon Charters: Lost and Found *Simon Keynes*	45
6	Reculver Minster and its Early Charters *Susan Kelly*	67
7	Stour in Ismere *Margaret Gelling*	83
8	Was there an Agricultural Revolution in Anglo-Saxon England? *Alex Burghart and Andrew Wareham*	89
9	'The Annals of Æthelflæd': Annals, History and Politics in Early Tenth-Century England *Pauline Stafford*	101
10	The First Use of the Second Anglo-Saxon *Ordo* *Janet L. Nelson*	117

11	Where English Becomes British: Rethinking Contexts for *Brunanburh* Sarah Foot	127
12	Archbishop Dunstan: A Prophet in Politics? Catherine Cubitt	145
13	A Mass for St Birinus in an Anglo-Saxon Missal from the Scandinavian Mission-Field Alicia Corrêa	167
14	The Saint Clement Dedications at Clementhorpe and Pontefract Castle: Anglo-Scandinavian or Norman? Barbara E. Crawford	189
15	England and the Norman Myth Nick Webber	211
16	What Happened to Ecclesiastical Charters in England 1066–c.1100? Julia Barrow	229
Nicholas Brooks: A List of Publications		249
Index		*255*

List of Figures

Frontispiece Professor Nicholas Brooks

14.1	Map of medieval churches dedicated to St Clement in England	190
14.2	Plan of collegiate and monastic precincts in medieval York, with the site of St Clement's priory on the west bank of the River Ouse. From D.M. Palliser, T.R. Slater and E.P. Dennison, 'The topography of towns 600–1300', in *The Cambridge Urban History of Britain*, I: *600–1540*, ed. D.M. Palliser (Cambridge, 2000), 179	195
14.3	Map of routes and rivers in southern Yorkshire	199
14.4	Plan of Phases 1 and 2 at Pontefract Castle from Ian Roberts, *Pontefract Castle* (Wakefield, 1990), 402	204
14.5	The east end of St Clement's Chapel, Pontefract Castle	206

Notes on Contributors

Julia Barrow is Reader in Medieval Church History at the University of Nottingham. She has published editions of the charters of twelfth and thirteenth-century bishops of Hereford and of St Davids and is the author of numerous articles on clergy, bishops and charters.

Alex Burghart is a researcher and editor for the *Prosopography of Anglo-Saxon England* project, and has written a doctoral thesis on 'The Mercian Polity, 716-918'.

James Campbell was a Fellow of Worcester College, Oxford from 1957 to 2002 and Professor of Medieval History 1996-2002; he is the author of *Essays in Anglo-Saxon History* (1986) and of *The Anglo-Saxon State* (2000), and the editor of *The Anglo-Saxons* (1982).

Alicia Corrêa is a freelance indexer and copy-editor of academic publications; she has edited the Durham Collectar and is the author of several articles on liturgical texts.

Barbara E. Crawford is Honorary Reader in Medieval History at the University of St Andrews and is continuing to pursue her researches into the history and archaeology of the Scandinavian settlements in Scotland and contacts across the North Sea in the Middle Ages. She is the author of *Scandinavian Scotland* (1987), and in 1999 published the results of her own excavation of a medieval farm site belonging to the kings of Norway on the island of Papa Stour in Shetland.

Catherine Cubitt teaches early medieval history at the Department of History and Centre for Medieval Studies at the University of York. She has published widely on the history of the Anglo-Saxon church, including *Anglo-Saxon Church Councils c. 650 – c. 850* (1995). She is currently writing a book on penance entitled *Sin and Society in Tenth- and Eleventh-Century England*, to be published by Ashgate.

Christopher Dyer is the Professor of Regional and Local History at the University of Leicester. He works in medieval economic, social and landscape history, especially in the English midlands. His most recent books are *Making a Living in the Middle Ages: The People of Britain 850–1520* (2002), and *An Age of Transition? Economy and Society in England in the Later Middle Ages* (2005).

Sarah Foot is Regius Professor of Ecclesiastical History at the University of Oxford. She is the author of *Veiled Women*, 2 vols (Ashgate, 2000) and of *Monastic Life in Anglo-Saxon England, c. 600–900* (2006)

Margaret Gelling is Honorary Reader in English Place-Name Studies at the University of Birmingham. Her publications include *Signposts to the Past: Place-Names and the History of England* (1978; 3rd edn 1997), *The West Midlands in the Early Middle Ages* (1992) and (with Ann Cole) *The Landscape of Place-Names* (2000).

Susan Kelly is Senior Research Fellow in the Department of Medieval History, University of Birmingham. Recent publications include editions of the pre-Conquest charters of Abingdon Abbey, Malmesbury Abbey, St Paul's Cathedral in London, Bath Abbey and the cathedral of Wells in the British Academy Anglo-Saxon Charters series.

Simon Keynes is Elrington and Bosworth Professor of Anglo-Saxon, University of Cambridge, and Fellow of Trinity College, Cambridge; he is the author of *The Diplomas of King Æthelred 'the Unready'* (1980), and of articles on various aspects of Anglo-Saxon history from the seventh century to the eleventh century.

Janet L. Nelson is Professor Emeritus of Medieval History, King's College, London; her publications include *Politics and Ritual in Early Medieval Europe* (1986), *Charles the Bald* (1992), *The Frankish World, 750–900* (1996), *Rulers and Ruling Families in Early Medieval Europe: Alfred, Charles the Bald, and Others* (Ashgate, 1999) and *Courts, Elites and Gendered Power in the Early Middle Ages: Charlemagne and Others* (Ashgate/Variorum, 2007).

Pauline Stafford is Professor Emerita of Medieval History, University of Liverpool. She is the author of books and articles on early medieval women and queens, and on tenth- and eleventh-century England, most recently a collection of essays, *Gender, Family and the Legitimation of Power: England from the Ninth to Early Twelfth Century* (Ashgate, 2007).

Andrew Wareham is Reader in English Social History and Director of the British Academy Hearth Tax Project at Roehampton University London. His research has been focused upon the central middle ages, and publications include *Lords and Communities in Early Medieval East Anglia* (2005) and *Negotiating Secular and Ecclesiastical Power* (1999) (co-editor). He is currently working on the development of the fiscal state in England across the medieval and early modern periods.

Nick Webber studied under Nicholas Brooks both as an undergraduate and a postgraduate, and presently works in research support at the University of Birmingham. His doctoral thesis was adapted for publication as *The Evolution of Norman Identity* (2005).

Barbara Yorke is Professor of Early Medieval History at the University of Winchester. Her books include *Kings and Kingdoms of Early Anglo-Saxon England* (1990), *Wessex in the Early Middle Ages* (1995), *Nunneries and the Anglo-Saxon Royal Houses* (2003) and *The Conversion of Britain: Religion, Politics and Society c. 600–800* (2006).

Acknowledgements

The editors are very grateful to Chris Wickham and Peter Jackson for advice, to Tom Gray, Barbara Pretty and Anne Keirby at Ashgate for their assistance and encouragement; and to Keith Tritton for help.

List of Abbreviations

ANS	*Anglo-Norman Studies*
ASE	*Anglo-Saxon England*
BCS	W. de Gray Birch, *Cartularium Saxonicum* (3 vols and index, London, 1885-1899) – cited by charter number
BL	British Library, London
BM	Bibliothèque Municipale
BN	Biblothèque Nationale, Paris
Bodl.	Bodleian Library, Oxford
CCCC	Corpus Christi College, Cambridge
De moribus	*De moribus et actis primorum Normanniae ducum auctore Dudone sancti Quintini decano*, ed. Jules Lair, Société des Antiquaires de Normandie (Caen, 1865)
Dudo	Dudo of St Quentin, *History of the Normans*, tr. Eric Christiansen (Woodbridge, 1998)
EHD, I	*English Historical Documents*, I, *c. 500–1042*, ed. Dorothy Whitelock, 2nd edn (London, 1979)
EHR	*English Historical Review*
EME	*Early Medieval Europe*
GND	*The Gesta Normannorum Ducum of William of Jumièges, Orderic Vitalis, and Robert of Torigni*, ed. and tr. Elisabeth M.C. van Houts, OMT (2 vols, Oxford, 1992–1995)
GRA	William of Malmesbury, *Gesta regum Anglorum*, ed. and tr. R.A.B. Mynors, completed by R.M. Thomson and Michael Winterbottom, OMT (2 vols, Oxford, 1998–1999)
HBS	Henry Bradshaw Society
HE	*Bede's Ecclesiastical History of the English People*, ed. Bertram Colgrave and R.A.B.Mynors, OMT (Oxford, 1969)
MGH	Monumenta Germaniae Historica
ODNB	*Oxford Dictionary of National Biography, in Association with the British Academy. From the Earliest Times to the Year 2000*, ed. H.C.G. Matthew and B. Harrison, 61 vols (Oxford 2004)
OMT	Oxford Medieval Texts
Origins	*The Origins of Anglo-Saxon Kingdoms*, ed. Steven Bassett (Leicester, 1989)
pd	printed
PL	*Patrologia cursus completus, accurante J.-P. Migne. Series latina* (221 vols, Paris, 1844–1865)
S	P.H. Sawyer, *Anglo-Saxon Charters: an Annotated List and Bibliography*, Royal Historical Society Guides and Handbooks, 8 (London, 1968) – cited by charter number

s.a.	*sub anno* (*annis*)
s.v.	*sub verbo*
tr.	translated
TRHS	*Transactions of the Royal Historical Society*
Vatican	Biblioteca Apostolica Vaticana, Vatican City
Vita Æthelwoldi	Wulfstan of Winchester, *Vita Sancti Æthelwoldi*, ed. Michael Lapidge and Michael Winterbottom, OMT (Oxford, 1991)

Chapter 1

Introduction: Myth, Rulership, Church and Charters in the Work of Nicholas Brooks

Julia Barrow

Nicholas Brooks has, for more than 40 years, been reshaping our understanding of the Anglo-Saxons. The four principal themes of this book, myth, rulership, the Church and charters, are all central to his scholarship and all represent areas within which he has been able to open up new lines of enquiry and to establish new bases of knowledge. The aim of this introduction is to provide an overview of Nicholas' contribution to each of these four themes and to link this up with the papers which follow, showing how he has inspired and influenced his friends and pupils.

Myth, our opening theme, was not one of Nicholas' earliest interests, but had become one of his areas of study by the mid-1980s, by the time he moved from St Andrews to take up the chair of Medieval History at Birmingham.[1] For a scholar whose work has been rooted in the history of Kent and its early kingdom, the issue of the creation and development of myth was inescapable: Hengist, Horsa and Vortigern occur in many different sources and an important task for historians of early Kent is to confront them.[2] Nicholas' solution was to work out the development of the myth from the differences appearing in each retelling of the story, leading him to suggest that the original story could have been invented for Æthelberht of Kent to bolster the identity of his kingdom and give his ancestry a much longer and grander past than those of contemporary Anglo-Saxon dynasties.[3] In providing a pair of adventurous brothers as the co-founders of the kingdom of Kent, the creator of the myth made use of a widely-found motif in Indo-European origin myths and, by naming them 'Stallion' and 'Horse', linked them up with the cult of Woden, in which horses seem to have played a role.[4] In this collection of essays Barbara Yorke makes use of this approach to re-examine all the Anglo-Saxon origin myths to see if further light can be shed on the circumstances of their production, and she also

---

1 Dyer, this volume.

2 Nicholas Brooks, 'The Creation and Early Structure of the Kingdom of Kent', in *The Origins of Anglo-Saxon Kingdoms*, ed. S.R. Bassett (Leicester, 1989) 55–74; repr. in Nicholas Brooks, *Anglo-Saxon Myths: State and Church 400–1066* (London and Rio Grande, 2000), 33–60, at 37–46.

3 Nicholas Brooks, 'The English Origin Myth', in Brooks, *Anglo-Saxon Myths*, 79–89, at 85.

4 Ibid., 88–9.

surveys burial evidence to show how that, too, allowed those who buried the dead to make statements about their identity.[5]

Nicholas' earliest published comments about myth are to be found in his inaugural lecture at Birmingham, given in 1986: at the start of this he referred to the thesis of his predecessor at Birmingham, R.H.C. Davis, that the Normans deliberately created a myth to give themselves an identity, and proceeded to illuminate this with an insight from one of his own areas of study, the iconography of warriors in the Bayeux Tapestry. The Normans shaved the backs of their heads in a conscious attempt to look different from their neighbours.[6] Norman identity was the subject undertaken by Nicholas' pupil Nick Webber for his doctoral thesis;[7] his paper in this volume deals with the role of England in the Norman myth, and shows that although England occurs frequently in the narrative of Norman history from the time of Dudo of St-Quentin onwards, it was not 'incorporated into *Normannitas*' until the twelfth century.[8]

Anglo-Saxon kingship, of which origin myth was a vital component, has been one of Nicholas Brooks' main areas of research from the outset. In particular it is the range of resources available to Anglo-Saxon rulers and the ways in which they could enforce demands for these on their subjects that have aroused his interest: above all the three 'common burdens' of fortresses, bridges and army service. Already in 1964 Nicholas had begun to work on the identification of the forts of the Burghal Hidage;[9] much more recently, for a Manchester Centre for Anglo-Saxon Studies conference on 'The Defence of Wessex' (published in 1996), he returned to the subject to explore the administrative problems faced by Alfred and his successor in setting up the system.[10] These were also problems for Alfred's daughter Æthelflæd in the West Midlands in the early tenth century, the subject of Pauline Stafford's article below, on which more shortly.[11] More generally on the topic of Anglo-Saxon reactions to Viking attacks in the ninth century, in 1978 Nicholas delivered a powerful rebuttal of Peter Sawyer's thesis that the size of Scandinavian fleets and armies in the ninth century had been greatly exaggerated by contemporary chroniclers and subsequent generations of historians: rather, as Nicholas demonstrated, the smaller Viking fleets

---

5   Yorke, this volume.
6   Nicholas Brooks, *History and Myth, Forgery and Truth* (Birmingham, 1986), repr. in Brooks, *Anglo-Saxon Myths*, 1–19, at 3.
7   Nick Webber, 'The Evolution of Norman Identity, 911–1154', Ph.D. thesis, University of Birmingham (2002), now published as *The Evolution of Norman Identity, 911–1154* (Woodbridge, 2005).
8   Webber, this volume.
9   'The Unidentified Forts of the Burghal Hidage', *Medieval Archaeology*, 8 (1964), 74–90, repr. in Nicholas Brooks, *Communities and Warfare 700–1400* (London and Rio Grande, 2000), 93–113.
10 'The Administrative Background to the Burghal Hidage', in *The Defence of Wessex: the Burghal Hidage and Anglo-Saxon Fortifications*, ed. David Hill and Alexander Richard Rumble (Manchester, 1996), 128–50, repr. in *Communities and Warfare 700–1400*, 114–37.
11 Stafford, this volume.

of the earlier ninth century had amalgamated to form the large fleet carrying the 'Great Army', leaving most of the Anglo-Saxon kingdoms unable to cope.[12]

The second of the three common burdens, bridge-building, became one of Nicholas' interests rather more recently, when he was invited to contribute to a volume on the history of Rochester Bridge (published in 1993). Here a charitable trust founded in the late fourteenth century took over the task of building and maintaining a bridge which earlier in the middle ages had been a responsibility shared out among local landowners; a document copied into the twelfth-century *Textus Roffensis* explains how manpower was organised in the Anglo-Saxon period to work on each of the piers.[13] From the Medway, Nicholas' bridge-inspecting remit has extended across Europe to other examples of bridges with ancient pasts and continuity of use.[14] In this volume, Barbara Crawford examines the significance of the cult of St Clement to comment on the Anglo-Saxon and Anglo-Norman fear of dangerous river-crossings: at Pontefract (as its name suggests, a 'broken' and thus a failed bridge in a part of England where Anglo-Saxon royal administration was markedly less efficient than it was in the area south of the Humber) a dedication to Clement may reveal William the Conqueror's gratitude for a successful passage over the River Aire.[15]

The last of the three common burdens, army service, has been a particular interest of Nicholas throughout his academic career. Nicholas' interest in armour and weapons was aroused when he was a pupil at Winchester College. Together with his history teacher at Winchester, H.E. Walker, he explored the evidence of the Bayeux Tapestry for body armour and weapons, in the process comparing the portrayal of Anglo-Saxon byrnies in the Tapestry with a fragment of relief sculpture, probably dating to the reign of Cnut, from Old Minster, Winchester, and this was published in an early volume of the proceedings of the Battle Conference on Anglo-Norman Studies.[16] Also in the late 1970s, through analysis of heriots recorded in wills and those stipulated in law codes, he was able to show that Æthelred greatly increased the quantity of military equipment that earls, bishops and king's thegns

---

12 'England in the Ninth Century: the Crucible of Defeat', *Transactions of the Royal Historical Society*, 5th ser. 29 (1979), 1–20, delivered 3 February 1978, repr. in *Communities and Warfare 700–1400*, 48–68; for Peter Sawyer's thesis on Viking numbers, see *The Age of the Vikings* (London, 1962), and its 2nd edn (London, 1971).

13 Nicholas Brooks, 'Rochester Bridge, AD 43–1381', in *Traffic and Politics: the Construction and Management of Rochester Bridge AD 43–1993*, ed. Nigel Yates and James M. Gibson (Woodbridge, 1994), 1–40, repr. in *Communities and Warfare 700–1400*, 219–65; idem, 'Church, Crown and Community: Public Work and Seigneurial Responsibilities at Rochester Bridge', in *Warriors and Churchmen in the High Middle Ages: Essays Presented to Karl Leyser*, ed. Timothy Reuter (London, 1992), 1–20.

14 'Medieval European Bridges: a Window onto Changing Concepts of State Power', *Journal of the Haskins Society*, 7 (1997 for 1995), 11–29, repr. in *Communities and Warfare 700–1400*, 1–31.

15 Crawford, this volume.

16 N.P. Brooks and H.E. Walker, 'The Authority and Interpretation of the Bayeux Tapestry', *ANS*, 1 (1978), 1–34 and 191–9, repr. in *Communities and Warfare 700–1400*, 175–218.

were expected to provide;[17] subsequently, in the millenary volume for the Battle of Maldon, he provided an explanation for this – references to Anglo-Saxon weapons and armour in the *Battle of Maldon* suggest that the Anglo-Saxons were ill-equipped, and above all ill-protected, and it was probably as a delayed reaction to this that Æthelred insisted in the early eleventh century that the higher-ranking members of the Anglo-Saxon forces should own helmets.[18] The study of heriots is only one of several areas (bridges form another) in which Nicholas has pointed to closely contemporary parallel developments across in Europe;[19] similarly he has always encouraged his pupils to look at Anglo-Saxon developments within a comparative European framework.[20]

More generally on the three common burdens it is to Nicholas that we owe a full understanding of the significance of the charter issued by Æthelbald of Mercia at the Synod of Gumley in 749, the earliest Anglo-Saxon charter to reserve a king's right to the common burdens even when granting immunity from other duties to churches: thanks to Nicholas we can see that Offa introduced the three common burdens into Kentish charters once he had finally taken power in Kent and then, in the ninth century, the system was adopted by the kings of Wessex, some time after they in their turn had brought Kent under their rule, once they recognised the necessity of building fortifications.[21] Discussion of the theme of the three common burdens has an ancient history and James Campbell looks at the insights or, better, foresights, into this topic and into many other features of Anglo-Saxon kingship that were achieved by the nineteenth century historian Eben Robertson.[22] Royal authority could exploit a range of natural resources, in particular timber and salt, but to some extent metal as well;[23] in doing this kings relied on a developing system of estate management, thanks to which manpower and money could be supplied for army service, fortification, bridges and weapons, and Nicholas has analysed the acquisition and intensifying exploitation of lands by the Church of Canterbury over the period from the eighth century to 1066 in his *Early History of the Church of*

---

17 'Arms, Status and Warfare in Late-Saxon England', in *Ethelred the Unready: Papers from the Millenary Conference*, ed. David Hill, British Archaeological Reports, British Series 59 (Oxford, 1978), 81–103, repr. in *Communities and Warfare 700–1400*, 138–61.

18 'Weapons and Armour', in *The Battle of Maldon, AD 991*, ed. Donald Scragg (Oxford, 1991), 208–19, repr. as 'Weapons and Armour in the *Battle of Maldon*', in *Communities and Warfare 700–1400*, 162–74.

19 'Arms, Status and Warfare', in *Communities and Warfare 700–1400*, 139–41; 'Medieval European Bridges'.

20 For example, Andrew Wareham, 'The Aristocracy of East Anglia c. 930–1154: a Study of Family, Land and Government', Ph.D. thesis, University of Birmingham (1992); see also Andrew Wareham, *Lords and Communities in Early Medieval East Anglia* (Woodbridge, 2005).

21 Nicholas Brooks, 'The Development of Military Obligations in Eighth- and Ninth-Century England', in *England before the Conquest: Studies in Primary Sources Presented to Dorothy Whitelock*, ed. Peter Clemoes and Kathleen Hughes (Cambridge, 1971), 69–84, repr. in *Communities and Warfare 700–1400*, 32–47.

22 Campbell, this volume.

23 Nicholas Brooks, *Church, State and Access to Resources in Early Anglo-Saxon England*, 20th Brixworth Lecture, 2002 (Brixworth, 2003).

Canterbury (a lack of surviving genuine early charters precludes detailed study of the estates in the period before the late eighth century).[24] Literacy was vital to the Canterbury community in keeping track of its possessions, and Nicholas has shown how a decline in Latinity and in scribal skills at Canterbury in the 870s led to a crisis when it was difficult for the church to supply a scribe capable of drafting a charter; by the start of the tenth century, however, Archbishop Plegmund had reversed this situation.[25] Literacy had further uses to landowners, however, as Alex Burghart and Andrew Wareham argue in their paper below:

> during the tenth and eleventh centuries manuals of estate management began to be written and such writings could well have played an important role in disseminating advice, comparable (though on a much smaller scale) to that played in the eighteenth century by journals advising on improved agricultural techniques.[26]

Rulership also depends for its success on the projection of a suitable image and, this in turn, depends on the development of appropriate propaganda and ceremonial. We have already noted the role of origin myths in the creation of dynastic identities for rulers; the writing of history also needs to be considered in this regard. Pauline Stafford's exploration of the context of composition of the group of annals known as the Mercian Register, which she argues was designed to project the achievements of Æthelflæd, Lady of the Mercians, supplies an important tool for our understanding of historical writing in England in the early tenth century and, at second remove, of the compilation of the *Anglo-Saxon Chronicle*.[27] Nicholas' 1999 Jarrow lecture explored Bede's use of 'Saxon' and 'Angle' to construct a particularly Christian image for the latter, with vital consequences for future generations: 'What we can, I believe, be quite certain about is that we should not think of ourselves as "English" today had Bede not written the *Ecclesiastical History*'.[28] Sarah Foot's paper examines the claims made for Æthelstan as ruler of Britain in the *Brunanburh* poem.

By the end of the eighth century, religious ceremonial was coming to be the means by which rulership was legitimated, and over the course of the ninth and tenth centuries Anglo-Saxon England followed Francia in insisting that unction and coronation were needed for kings to become kings. This subject is central to the question of the relationship between Anglo-Saxon kings and the church of Canterbury from the time of Offa onwards: Nicholas has carefully analysed the fluctuations in relations between Mercia and Canterbury in his exploration of how Offa, insistent that his own son Ecgfrith should be anointed in his own lifetime, fell out with the then archbishop of Canterbury, Jaenberht, and had Lichfield raised to metropolitan

---

24 Nicholas Brooks, *The Early History of the Church of Canterbury* (Leicester, 1984), esp, chs. 5, 7–11; on the lack of early charters, see ibid., 100–103.

25 Ibid., 173–4, 214. See also Brooks, 'England in the Ninth Century', in *Communities and Warfare*, 62–3.

26 Burghart and Wareham, this volume.

27 Stafford, this volume.

28 *Bede and the English*, Jarrow Lecture 1999 (Jarrow, 2000), especially 15–16; the quotation is on p. 22.

status so that an archbishop would be available to anoint Ecgfrith.[29] Coronation continued to play a vital role in the relations between archbishops of Canterbury and Anglo-Saxon kings: it was a rite for which an archbishop was essential, and archbishops with a serious interest in their role might well devote thought to the creation of new coronation *ordines* or orders of service to underline particular aspects of kingship, for example the use of the coronation ring or the crown itself. In his *Early History of the Church of Canterbury* Nicholas suggested, for example, that the Second English *Ordo* might well have been designed by Archbishop Athelm of Canterbury for the coronation of Æthelstan in 925, though later, in his chapter for *The History of Canterbury Cathedral*, he left the identity of the archbishop more open, between Plegmund and Athelm.[30] Janet Nelson, who had previously argued that the Second *Ordo* was designed by Plegmund for Edward the Elder at Pentecost 900, has now accepted the case for Athelm and in her article in this volume establishes why Athelm, and not Plegmund, must have been the author.[31]

Through coronation and the role of the archbishops of Canterbury in supporting Anglo-Saxon kings we arrive at the third theme of this volume, the church. Nicholas' work on church history grew out of his doctoral thesis on the charters of Christ Church Canterbury. This led to the definitive study of pre-Conquest Canterbury, *The Early History of the Church of Canterbury*, in 1984, a book which impressed all its reviewers, and a whole generation of readers, by its scope and not least by the range of source material that had been mastered to write it: as many of them commented, it is a truly interdisciplinary work, in which close knowledge of the topography and archaeology of Canterbury are woven together with the written sources.[32] This book, the best work to date on the history of a single Anglo-Saxon church, succeeds in fixing Christ Church in its topography, in exploring the role of Rome in its foundation and in its later history, in demonstrating the continuing political importance of Canterbury throughout all the fluctuations of the Anglo-Saxon kingdoms and in showing the tenacity of Christ Church as an institution by tracing the development of the cathedral estates. In Nicholas' book the ninth century emerges as a key period in the development of Canterbury cathedral, partly because of the role of its archbishops in Anglo-Saxon synods, and partly because it was in that period that Canterbury took over several Kentish minsters, absorbing their estates

---

29 *Early History of the Church of Canterbury*, 117–18.

30 Ibid., 215; Nicholas Brooks, 'The Anglo-Saxon Cathedral Community, 597–1070', in *A History of Canterbury Cathedral*, ed. Patrick Collinson, Nigel Ramsay and Margaret Sparks (Oxford, 1995), 1–37, repr. as 'The Cathedral Community at Canterbury, 597–1070', in Brooks, *Anglo-Saxon Myths*, 101–54, at 129.

31 Nelson, this vol.

32 Reviewers of *The Early History of the Church of Canterbury* included Martin Brett in *Archaeologia Cantiana*, 101 (1984), 389–91; David Rollason in *History*, 69 (1984), 447–8; C.H. Lawrence in *English Historical Review*, 100 (1985), 618–19; C.N.L. Brooke in *Antiquaries' Journal*, 65 (1985), 188–9; A.D. Frankforter in *Speculum*, 60 (1985), 950–2; Rosamond McKitterick in *Journal of Ecclesiastical History*, 36 (1985), 484–6; Frank Barlow in *Southern History*, 7 (1985), 183–4; Patrizia Lendinara in *Schede medievali*, 10 (1986), 166–7; M.T. Gibson in *Journal of Theological Studies*, 38 (1987), 227–9; M.M. Gatch in *Albion*, 19 (1987), 211–13; Tim Reuter in *Deutsches Archiv*, 43 (1987), 698–9.

into its own and supervising their pastoral care, a process which greatly strengthened archiepiscopal control of the diocese.[33] This development is mirrored, as far as we can see from admittedly very fragmentary evidence, in several other Anglo-Saxon sees, and shows growing episcopal authority over lesser churches.[34] One of the minsters taken over by Canterbury was Reculver, on the northern Kentish coast, and the full history of pre-Conquest Reculver, traceable in a lengthy sequence of charters, is the subject of Susan Kelly's article below.[35] Canterbury also, unsurprisingly for a major church, acquired its own range of saints' cults (though curiously slowly, almost grudgingly)[36] and played a prominent role in liturgical developments within England;[37] Nicholas' overview of the hagiographical sources associated with Christ Church and his study of its manuscript collection has helped to illuminate both these aspects.[38] Alicia Corrêa in her paper in this volume shows how receptive Canterbury was to the cult of a saint associated with another major church, Saint Birinus of Winchester.[39]

Subsequently Nicholas has looked further at the relations between Canterbury and Rome[40] and has tackled the pre-Conquest history of Kent's other medieval cathedral,

---

33 Brooks, *Early History of the Church of Canterbury*, 129–206; on the takeover of minsters, see 175–206.

34 Cf. I.N. Wood, 'Anglo-Saxon Otley: an Archiepiscopal Estate and its Crosses in a Northumbrian Context', *Northern History*, 23 (1987), 20–38, at 36–7; Patrick Sims-Williams, *Religion and Literature in Western England, 600–800* (Cambridge, 1990), 169–76; Julia Barrow, 'Survival and Mutation: Ecclesiastical Institutions in the Danelaw in the Ninth and Tenth Centuries', in *Cultures in Contact: Scandinavian Settlement in England in the Ninth and Tenth Centuries*, Dawn Hadley and Julian Richards (eds) (Turnhout, 2000), 155–76, at 157; Francesca Tinti, 'The Costs of Pastoral Care: Church Dues in Late Anglo-Saxon England', in *Pastoral Care in Late Anglo-Saxon England*, ed. Francesca Tinti (Woodbridge, 2005), 27–51, at 42–3.

35 Kelly, this volume.

36 On Canterbury's relative slowness to develop saints' cults in the tenth century see Alan Thacker, 'Cults at Canterbury: Relics and Reform under Dunstan and his Successors', in *St Dunstan: His Life, Times and Cult*, ed. Nigel Ramsay, Margaret Sparks and Tim Tatton-Brown (Woodbridge, 1992), 221–45. It was much more go-ahead after the Conquest: cf. Richard Pfaff, 'Lanfranc's supposed Purge of the Anglo-Saxon Calendar', in *Warriors and Churchmen in the High Middle Ages: Essays Presented to Karl Leyser*, ed. Timothy Reuter (London, 1992), 95–108; Richard Sharpe, 'Eadmer's Letter to the Monks of Canterbury Concerning St Dunstan's Disputed Remains', in *The Archaeology and History of Glastonbury Abbey: Essays in Honour of the Ninetieth Birthday of C.A. Raleigh Radford*, Lesley Abrams and J.P. Carley (eds) (Woodbridge, 1991), 205–15; Jay Rubenstein, 'The Life and Writings of Osbern of Canterbury', in *Canterbury and the Norman Conquest: Churches, Saints and Scholars, 1066–1109*, ed. Richard Eales and Richard Sharpe (London, 1995), 27–40.

37 On Canterbury and liturgy cf. *The Leofric Missal*, ed. Nicholas Orchard, HBS, 113–14 (London, 2002), I, 20, commented on by Nelson, this volume.

38 Brooks, *Early History of the Church of Canterbury*, 227–31, 251–2, 261–78.

39 Corrêa, this volume.

40 Nicholas Brooks, 'Canterbury, Rome and the Construction of English Identity', in *Early Medieval Rome and the Christian West: Essays in Honour of Donald A. Bullough*, ed. Julia M.H. Smith (Leiden, 2000), 221–47; Nicholas Brooks, 'Rome and Canterbury: the limits

Rochester.[41] He has also undertaken biographical studies of several archbishops of Canterbury, notably Archbishop Dunstan of Canterbury, whose early career he has skilfully re-evaluated.[42] In this volume, Catherine Cubitt looks at Dunstan's role as a prophet, and in particular his use of liturgical curses to try to achieve the political results he desired.[43] Nicholas organised the millenary conference for Oswald, archbishop of York and bishop of Worcester, at Worcester in 1992[44] and novocentenary study days in honour of Saint Wulfstan of Worcester at Worcester in 1995.[45] With Wulfstan, we arrive at the period of the Norman Conquest and the difficult period of adjustment undergone by the English church in the decades that followed, the subject of Julia Barrow's chapter.[46]

Charters, the final theme in this volume, have been one of Nicholas Brooks' main areas of study since he began work on his thesis on the charters of Christ Church Canterbury.[47] The charters of Christ Church and particularly the light they shed on the estates and community of the church of Canterbury provided the backbone for Nicholas' book on Canterbury. The long-awaited edition of Christ Church charters for the British Academy Anglo-Saxon Charters series, jointly being prepared by Susan Kelly and Nicholas Brooks, is now near completion.[48] Appropriately enough, therefore, charters figure prominently in this volume. The charters concerning Reculver, which were preserved in the archive of Christ Church, provide the main source material for Susan Kelly's chapter.[49] In his work on charters Nicholas consistently stresses their use as a source for the landscape and its exploitation by people living and working on it;[50] for example, his paper on the Micheldever forgery,

---

and myth of Romanitas', in *Roma fra Oriente e Occidente*, Settimane di Studio, 49 (Spoleto, 2002), 797–830.

41 Nicholas Brooks, 'Rochester, A.D. 400–1066', in *Medieval Art, Architecture and Archaeology at Rochester*, ed. Tim Ayers and Tim Tatton-Brown, British Archaeological Association Conference Transactions, 28 (Leeds, 2006), 6–21.

42 Nicholas Brooks, 'The Career of St Dunstan', in *St Dunstan: his Life, Times and Cult*, ed. Nigel Ramsay, Margaret Sparks and Tim Tatton-Brown (Woodbridge, 1992), 1–23; repr. Brooks, *Anglo-Saxon Myths*, 155–80. See also Nicholas Brooks, 'Honorius [St Honorius], (d. 653), Archbishop of Canterbury', 'Justus [St Justus] (d. 627x31), Archbishop of Canterbury', 'Laurence [St Laurence] (d. 619), Archbishop of Canterbury', 'Mellitus' and 'Wulfred' *ODNB*, respectively XXVII, 910; XXX, 845–6; XXXII, 691; XXXVII, 751–2; LX, 552–4.

43 Cubitt, this volume.

44 Published as *St Oswald of Worcester: Life and Influence*, ed. N.P. Brooks and Catherine Cubitt (London, 1996); cf. also Nicholas Brooks, 'Oswald [St Oswald] (d. 992), Archbishop of York', *ODNB*, XLII, 79–84.

45 Published as *St Wulfstan and his World*, ed. Julia Barrow and Nicholas Brooks (Aldershot, 2005).

46 Barrow, this volume.

47 N.P. Brooks, 'The Pre-Conquest Charters of Christ Church Canterbury', unpublished D. Phil. thesis, University of Oxford, 1968.

48 *Charters of Christ Church Canterbury*, ed. N.P. Brooks and S.E. Kelly, British Academy Anglo-Saxon Charters Series, in preparation.

49 Kelly, this volume.

50 cf. Nicholas Brooks, 'Romney Marsh in the Early Middle Ages', in *Romney Marsh: Evolution, Occupation, and Reclamation*, ed. Jill Eddison and Christopher Green, Oxford

a charter in the archives of Winchester College, traces an Anglo-Saxon boundary clause that can still be walked today.[51] In his work on topography, Nicholas has often benefited from discussion of place-names with the place-name expert Margaret Gelling,[52] and her chapter in this volume takes a new look at the charter of Æthelbald of Mercia for Cyneberht concerning Stour in Ismere, issued in 736, and in particular at the identification of the places mentioned in the text.[53]

In 1973, on the eve of the inauguration of the British Academy Anglo-Saxon Charters series, Nicholas surveyed the work that had been done in the field of Anglo-Saxon charter studies over the previous 20 years,[54] and a quarter of a century later he supplied a sequel to cover the years down to 1998.[55] By then he had been a member of the Anglo-Saxon Charters committee for 15 years, and its chairman for seven (since 1991), and could comment with satisfaction on the progress being made by the series. Three of the chapters in this volume deal with groups of charters from more than one archive and, thus, provide overviews of particular aspects. Simon Keynes, the secretary of the British Academy Anglo-Saxon charters committee, explains how and where searches might be undertaken for lost pre-Conquest charters.[56] Alex Burghart and Andrew Wareham look at the development of the lease from the ninth century onwards and link this to the development of estate management in Anglo-Saxon England,[57] while Julia Barrow compiles a list of charters issued by bishops and by abbots in the three and a half decades between the Norman Conquest and the coronation of Henry I, and uses this as the basis for a commentary on the impact of the Conquest on the production of charters by ecclesiastics and on the merger of Anglo-Saxon and French charter features in the late eleventh century.[58]

At this point in the proceedings the author of this introduction can emerge from the purdah of the third person singular and reveal a first person face. My own acquaintance with Nicholas began when I was a student at St Andrews; it is thanks to him and his colleagues that I developed an interest in the earlier middle ages and, thanks to Nicholas in particular, that I was enthralled by the Anglo-Saxons. However unfashionable it is to admit this, I shall always be grateful that the St

---

University Committee for Archaeology, Monograph 23 (Oxford, 1988), 128–59, repr. in *Anglo-Saxon Myths*, 275–300.

51 Nicholas Brooks, 'The Oldest Document in the College Archives: the Micheldever Forgery', in *Winchester College: Sixth-Centenary Essays*, ed. Roger Custance (Oxford, 1982), 189–228, repr. as 'The Micheldever Forgery' in *Anglo-Saxon Myths*, 239–74.

52 Nicholas Brooks, with Margaret Gelling and David Johnson, 'A New Charter of King Edgar', *Anglo-Saxon England*, 13 (1984), 137–55, repr. in *Anglo-Saxon Myths*, 218–37; Margaret Gelling supplied the analysis of the place-names.

53 Gelling, this volume.

54 Nicholas Brooks, 'Anglo-Saxon Charters: the Work of the Last Twenty Years', *ASE*, 3 (1974), 211–33, written in 1973; for details of the reprinted version, see the following note.

55 Nicholas Brooks, 'Anglo-Saxon Charters: Recent Work', in Brooks, *Anglo-Saxon Myths*, 181–215, a reprint of the 1974 article with a postscript on work published 1973–98 on pp. 202–15.

56 Simon Keynes, this volume.

57 Burghart and Wareham, this volume.

58 Barrow, this volume.

Andrews medievalists in the 1970s made their fourth-year students study English constitutional documents, but I am even more grateful that it was possible to choose to study those for the earlier middle ages: under Nicholas' tutelage this meant a course in Anglo-Saxon and post-Conquest English law, with the continuities over the whole period from Edward the Elder to Magna Carta made clear. It took a long time for me as a scholar to look back from the twelfth century to the tenth century and earlier, but not the least of Nicholas' gifts as a teacher is the ability to inculcate ideas that take time to develop in the minds of his pupils. This quality is one that is recognised and valued by all the contributors to this volume and also by the wider community of Anglo-Saxonists.

Chapter 2

Nicholas Brooks at Birmingham

Christopher Dyer

The Birmingham History Department, or School of History, saw only three occupants of the Chair of Medieval History in the second half of the twentieth century, Harry Cronne, Ralph Davis and Nicholas Brooks. During that time the department, or grouping of medieval historians, grew in distinction and reached a peak of scholarly achievement in Nicholas Brooks's time as professor.

When Ralph Davis retired a distinguished field of candidates applied for the post, proof of Birmingham's reputation as a centre of historical endeavour, but also because it was known to contain a congenial group of people with whom a newcomer would be able to work. Nicholas was the obvious choice as he had an excellent record of his research already completed and an exciting programme of future projects. He had established a reputation as a leading historian of the early middle ages, which complemented the existing expertise in the Department, and his broad interests extended through the later middle ages into modern times.[1] He was also known to be an amiable and humane colleague, who had shown himself at St Andrews to be an able administrator.

When he arrived in 1985 he made an immediate personal impact, taking care to get to know everyone, and ensuring that no-one felt left out of his circle. He developed a friendly relationship with Rodney Hilton, who, though retired, was still a strong presence in the Department. The smooth running of the School of History depended on a close community spirit between medieval, modern and American history (the three departments making up the School), and he established a good personal rapport with John Grenville and Alec Campbell (the professors in charge of the modern and American departments). In his own department he took an interest in everyone's professional and personal lives and both Nicholas and Chloë took particular pleasure in entertaining colleagues in their home.

He quickly showed that, for all his quiet manner, he could take tough decisions. In one of the first examining boards that he attended a case of plagiarism was revealed and Nicholas volunteered to telephone the student to explain the disastrous degree classification that followed from the discovery of this dishonesty. His inaugural lecture revealed him to have an expansive, even flamboyant tendency, which was normally hidden from view. The lecture began with a great rhetorical flourish, in Latin, and then proceeded to explore the theme of forgery in the broadest terms,

---

1 N.P. Brooks, 'The Organization and Achievements of the Peasants of Kent and Essex in 1381', in *Studies in Medieval History Presented to R.H.C. Davis*, ed. Henry Mayr-Harting and R.I. Moore (London, 1985), 247–70. This was written shortly before his move from St Andrews to Birmingham.

including discussion of the likely identity of the perpetrator of 'Piltdown Man'.[2] Throughout his time at Birmingham he encouraged research and publication among his colleagues, and he played an important part also in writing up the School's achievements for the Research Assessment Exercise. His experiences on the RAE panel also helped in the presentation of the School's work to the assessors and Birmingham was awarded a coveted '5' in three successive rankings.

He was very skilful in joining in the existing academic seminars at Birmingham, recognising their merits and realising that individuals were committed to them. He held back from introducing his own schemes until the moment was right. He was a stalwart supporter of the two main research seminars, the Medieval Society and the 'Friday Night' Seminar. The latter enjoyed great success from 1969 to 1997 as an informal gathering, with wine, in the houses of staff and students, but when it faltered Nicholas realised that a new formula was needed, and set up a postgraduate seminar which became a very effective forum for discussion. He led a contingent of research students from Birmingham to the Medieval Congress at Leeds, which even took him on to the dance floor. He showed a generous interest in all of the research students in the department, and supervised a succession of students specialising in early medieval England, including Aysu Dincer, Nigel Dorrington, Alan MacKinley, Colin Peterson, Lewis Skidmore, David Symons, Robert Thomas, Christine Wallis, Andrew Wareham and Nick Webber. They include contributors to this book.

Another early initiative of his was to encourage a group of colleagues to begin a series of conferences on urban themes, which spanned the late Roman, medieval and early modern periods and united the disciplines of archaeology, geography and history. Two of the conferences yielded published volumes on 'death in towns' and 'urban decline' – the conferences, contrary to the impression that these themes might suggest, were very cheerful occasions.[3] He also responded to the conference organised with typical care and dedication by his colleague Steve Bassett on the beginnings of Anglo-Saxon kingdoms and contributed two major essays on Kent and Mercia to an important subsequent publication.[4]

Nicholas Brooks put great enthusiasm into his teaching: he brought to Birmingham a Special Subject on Northumbria which he had developed in St Andrews, and which attracted students steadily at a time when interest in medieval courses was sometimes faltering. An integral part of the course was a tour of sites across northern England and the Scottish borders which Nicholas clearly enjoyed as much as the students. In his sensitivity to student interests he also taught a course on warfare and, when a new syllabus was adopted, he joined with a modern historian, John Breuilly, in teaching a thematic course on the state which brought medieval and modern history together.

Nicholas always took a broad view of his place in the University and was anxious to make a contribution in the Faculty and Senate. He was a popular choice to serve as dean of the Arts Faculty between 1992 and 1995, and then later temporarily

---

2 N.P. Brooks, *History and Myth, Forgery and Truth* (Birmingham, 1986).

3 *Death in Towns. Urban Responses to the Dying and the Dead, 100–1600*, ed. S.R. Bassett (Leicester, 1992); *Towns in Decline AD 100–1600*, ed. T.R. Slater (Aldershot, 2000).

4 N.P. Brooks, 'The Creation and Early Structure of the Kingdom of Kent'; 'The Formation of the Kingdom of Mercia', in *Origins*, 55–74, 159–70, 250–4, 275–7.

resumed the role in an emergency. The historians (who were sometimes criticised by outsiders for being excessively wrapped up in their own affairs) were sorry to lose him to this grand office, though he maintained links and continued to do some teaching throughout his term. He steered the Faculty through various changes and difficulties. He was particularly proud of the staff who were chosen when he was chairing appointment committees, and he took a personal interest in their subsequent careers.

Management skills are also useful in research, and Nicholas has played an important part in the development of his subject by chairing the British Academy committee with the task of publishing all of the texts of the Anglo-Saxon charters, in which his own volume on the Canterbury charters will soon appear. At Birmingham he found that his own interest in urban topography, which had resulted in an article on the development of the town of St Andrews,[5] fitted well with the research of Terry Slater in the School of Geography, and could also benefit from the 'new blood' appointment in medieval urban history, Gervase Rosser. Their application to the Leverhulme Trust resulted in a grant which enabled Nigel Baker and Dick Holt to be employed to explore the topography of the towns of Gloucester and Worcester, which resulted in a notable volume published in 2004.[6] Seminars and symposia held in conjunction with the research stimulated discussion among Birmingham staff and outsiders, and culminated in a volume of essays on the role of the church in urban development.[7]

Anglo-Saxonists are always quick to notice the anniversaries of battles, or of the demise of kings and bishops, which provide an opportunity to hold a conference reappraising the reputation of such figures as Alfred or Dunstan. Nicholas was invariably invited to contribute papers on these occasions.[8] In 1992 and 1996, on the 1000th and 900th anniversaries respectively of two famous bishops of Worcester, Oswald and Wulfstan, Nicholas was instrumental in bringing scholars together at Worcester and eventually arranging for the papers to be published.[9] The books appeared in the series edited by Nicholas originally for Leicester University Press as 'Studies in the Early History of Britain', and later published by Ashgate as 'Studies in Early Medieval Britain', to which Birmingham-based authors were able to contribute;

---

5 N.P. Brooks and Graeme Whittington, 'Planning and Growth in the Medieval Scottish Burgh: the Example of St Andrews', *Transactions of the Institute of British Geographers*, new series, 2 (1977), 278–95.

6 Nigel Baker and Richard Holt, *Urban Growth and the Medieval Church. Gloucester and Worcester* (Aldershot, 2004).

7 *The Church in the Medieval Town*, ed. T.R. Slater and Gervase Rosser (Aldershot, 1998).

8 For example N.P. Brooks, 'Weapons and Armour in the Battle of Maldon', in *The Battle of Maldon*, ed. D.G. Scragg (Manchester, 1991), 208–19; N.P. Brooks, 'The Career of St Dunstan', in *St Dunstan: Life and Times*, ed. N.J. Ramsay, Margaret Sparks and Tim Tatton Brown (Woodbridge, 1992), 1–22.

9 *St Oswald of Worcester: Life and Influence*, ed. Nicholas Brooks and Catherine Cubitt (Leicester, 1996); *St Wulfstan and his World*, ed. Julia S. Barrow and N.P. Brooks (Aldershot, 2005).

by encouraging publication in the whole field by a range of contributors, the series helped to give Nicholas a reputation as the hub of a wide circle of scholars.

His colleagues at Birmingham were always conscious of Nicholas's enthusiasms, and once he took up an idea he pursued it, talking to all those who had something to contribute, and eventually producing an exciting publication. One such passion was his interest in bridges, which led him to reinterpret the history of Rochester bridge, then to write more generally about bridges in Europe and the role of the state in sponsoring transport and construction.[10] Later he took up the idea of ethnogenesis and explored the Englishness of the English to great effect.[11] In all of these interests his commitment to using both archaeological and documentary evidence, which went back to his own undergraduate days, fitted in well with a Birmingham department where such a multi-disciplinary approach was widely practised, notably by Steve Bassett, Chris Wickham and the author of this contribution. He helped to develop contacts between disciplines over the whole University, and through his influence the historians enjoyed closer relations with scholars from archaeology, Byzantine studies, continuing studies, English, geography and other disciplines. Nicholas valued in particular the presence at Birmingham of Margaret Gelling, the place-name specialist.

Having begun this appraisal of Nicholas Brooks's time at Birmingham with the positive way that he interacted to the people already in post, one should not end it without mentioning the many people who came to Birmingham because of Nicholas's presence. Not least among these mention must be made of Chloë, who played an important role in keeping him organised, and in providing hospitality for his colleagues and visitors, and his daughter Ebba and son Crispin. In addition we gained various colleagues, if only temporarily – Alicia Corrêa who worked on the Canterbury charters, Katy Cubitt who provided replacement teaching when he was Dean, Julia Barrow, one of the earliest British Academy postdoctoral research fellows, Susan Kelly who worked on the British Academy charter project – and many others who came on briefer visits.

Nicholas Brooks was clearly stimulated by the people he encountered in the School of History and the University at Birmingham. His wide interests connected with others, and resulted in many fruitful discussions, which are reflected both in his work and the writings of his colleagues, on such subjects as the church, developments in continental Europe and the Byzantine Empire parallel to those in early medieval England, and anthropology, in addition to those already mentioned. All of those who engaged with him at Birmingham are very conscious of the many gifts he contributed in his time as Professor of Medieval History.

---

10 N.P. Brooks, 'Rochester Bridge, AD 43–1381', in *Traffic and Politics: The Construction and Management of Rochester Bridge, AD 43–1993*, ed. Nigel Yates and James M. Gibson (Woodbridge, 1993), 1–40, 362–9; N.P. Brooks, 'Medieval European Bridges: a Window onto Changing Concepts of State Power', *Journal of the Haskins Society*, 7 (1995), 11–29.

11 N.P. Brooks, 'The English Origin Myth', in *Anglo-Saxon Myths. State and Church, 400–1066* (London, 2000), 80–9.

Chapter 3
Anglo-Saxon Origin Legends

Barbara Yorke

In 1989 Nicholas Brooks published a paper on the early history of the kingdom of Kent which contained a masterly exposition of what he described as 'The Kentish Origin Myth'.[1] The study established the dividing line between Kent's mythical origins and the point at which the traditions of its royal house entered the historical horizon with Irminric, the father of Æthelbert. With this paper Nicholas contributed to the assault made by a number of writers on the historical validity of Anglo-Saxon sources purporting to come from the fifth and sixth centuries,[2] and helped to establish that they should no longer be accepted as straightforward records of what might actually have occurred during that timespan. That is not to say, as Nicholas himself stressed, that the sources have no contribution to make to our knowledge of the early middle ages, but simply that they should not be taken at face value for the period they purport to describe. What certain people in Kent and elsewhere wanted to believe about the origins of their kingdoms is potentially very valuable information for our basic understanding of ethnogenesis and kingdom formation, and one that can be revisited in the light of recent work, not least by Nicholas himself, on early medieval identities.[3] It may therefore be useful to examine the origin legends that have survived from early Anglo-Saxon England as a distinctive type of early medieval record in order to establish their common features and to consider the circumstances that may have lain behind their construction, and in the hope that this will be a suitable tribute to an inspirational historian and friend.

The use of such myths to explain the origins of new people (and their rulers) was widespread in early medieval Europe, and parallels can also be found in many other parts of the world.[4] What origin legends did in essence was to provide a new start;

---

1 Nicholas Brooks, 'The Creation and Structure of the Kingdom of Kent', in *Origins*, 55–74, at 58–64; reprinted in Nicholas Brooks, *Anglo-Saxon Myths: State and Church 400–1066* (London, 2000), 33–60.

2 See, in particular, David Dumville, 'Sub-Roman Britain: History and Legend', *History*, 62 (1977), 173–92; Patrick Sims-Williams, 'The Settlement of England in Bede and the Anglo-Saxon Chronicle', *ASE*, 12 (1983), 1–41.

3 Nicholas Brooks, *Bede and the English*, Jarrow Lecture for 1999 (Jarrow, 2000).

4 There is a large literature on the use of myth as part of the wider debate on medieval ethnogenesis initiated by Reinhard Wenskus, *Stammesbildung und Verfassung. Das Werden der frühmittelalterlichen gentes* (Köln-Graz, 1961; 2nd ed. Köln-Wien, 1977). For useful summaries of the debate for the middle ages and later see Susan Reynolds, 'Medieval *Origines Gentium* and the Community of the Realm', *History*, 68 (1985), pp. 375–90; Anthony Smith, *The Ethnic Origins of Nations* (Oxford, 1986); Patrick Geary, *The Myth of Nations. The Medieval Origins of Europe* (Princeton, 2001); Walter Pohl, 'Ethnicity, Theory and Tradition; a Response' in *On Barbarian Identity. Critical Approaches to Ethnicity in the Early Middle*

they drew a line under previous political arrangements and explained the formation of new ones through the claim of migration by a homogeneous people. The mongrel nature of new regimes was disguised by the myth of a common origin in which old identities could conveniently be subsumed. Such reordering of the past had its origins in oral tradition and can also be seen in the manipulation of genealogical evidence.[5] So successful was the Anglo-Saxon propagation of this myth that in the nineteenth century it was regarded as literally true that Anglo-Saxons arriving from Germany had replaced the British in much of the former Roman province.[6] A wider appreciation of historical and ethnographic parallels during the twentieth century has led to the current understanding that the processes that led to the formation of the 'Anglo-Saxons' and their kingdoms must in fact have been more complex and varied. What is also undoubtedly complex is the interplay between oral and written tradition in the development and propagation of origin myths. From the point where Tacitus recorded the myth that the *Germani* were descended from the three sons of Mannus,[7] we have evidence of a continual interdependence of oral and classical traditions about the origins of medieval peoples into which biblical tradition was eventually woven as well.[8]

The main collection of Anglo-Saxon origin legends is to be found in the *Anglo-Saxon Chronicle* where they have been fitted into the annalistic format for the fifth and sixth centuries.[9] Although Bede's information about the two brothers Hengist and Horsa who led the Anglo-Saxon *adventus* indicates the currency of traditions concerning them by the early eighth century, the exploits of the others are only known to us through the late-ninth-century *Chronicle*. However, Ine's genealogy with descent from Cerdic, Cynric and Woden was included in what is known as the 'Anglian' collection of royal genealogies, regnal, papal and episcopal lists that was

---

Ages, ed. Andrew Gillett (Turnhout, 2002), 221–39. Nicholas has advocated the value of the comparative approach and for some time at Birmingham taught a comparative course on origin myths.

5   Hermann Moisl, 'Anglo-Saxon Royal Genealogies and Germanic Oral Tradition', *Journal of Medieval History*, 7 (1981), 215–48; David Dumville, 'Kingship, Genealogies and Regnal Lists' in *Early Medieval Kingship*, ed. Peter Sawyer and Ian Wood (Leeds, 1977), 72–104.

6   The relatively measured discussion of the evidence for invasion by John Mitchell Kemble, *The Saxons in England* (London, 1849) gave rise to increasingly strident claims for replacement of native British by Anglo-Saxons in works such as Charles Kingsley, *The Roman and the Teuton. A Series of Lectures Delivered before the University of Cambridge* (Cambridge, 1864) and John Richard Green, *The Conquest of England* (London, 1883). For a useful historiographical review see Sims-Williams 'Settlement of England', 1–5, and for the growth of racial Anglo-Saxonism, Reginald Horsman, *Race and Manifest Destiny. The Origins of American Racial Anglo-Saxonism* (Cambridge, Mass., 1981).

7   Moisl, 'Anglo-Saxon Royal Genealogies', 217–8.

8   Reynolds, 'Medieval *Origines Gentium*'; Geary, *The Myth of Nations*.

9   *Two of the Saxon Chronicles Parallel*, ed. John Earle and Charles Plummer (2 vols, Oxford, 1892), 12–17; *The Anglo-Saxon Chronicle*, ed. Dorothy Whitelock, with David C. Douglas and Susie I. Tucker (London, 1961), 10–12.

probably assembled in Mercia or Northumbria in the late eighth century.[10] There is therefore an implication that Cerdic and Cynric had been established as founders of the West Saxon dynasty before the end of the eighth century. The *Chronicle* text includes legends for Kent (Hengist and Horsa), the South Saxons (Ælle and his three sons), the *Wihtwara* of the Isle of Wight (Stuf and Wihtgar) and the 'Jutish' people situated opposite them in southern Hampshire (Port and his two sons), as well as for the West Saxons themselves (Cerdic and Cynric). The annals depict, in effect, each of these people as having had their origins with a small fleet of ships that arrived off the south coast under the leadership of the founders of their ruling houses who established kingdoms in the areas through defeating their British inhabitants.[11] The accounts in the form in which they have come down to us are clearly as much about the origins of royal houses as of specific peoples, and would appear to be concerned to present the two as closely linked.[12] The origin legends that have survived are restricted to this group of southern Saxon and Jutish provinces bordering the Channel. Memories were preserved of the first members of the Bernician and East Anglian dynasties to have established themselves in Britain,[13] and these could be a faint indication that similar legends were produced in Anglian areas, but we lack certain proof.[14] Perhaps the bringing together of the origin-legend material within the *Anglo-Saxon Chronicle* can be seen as a manifestation of the hegemony that the West Saxons had established by the ninth century over these formerly independent peoples of the south coast in a way that is analogous to the bringing together in the so-called Anglian collection of genealogies and regnal lists of provinces which were subject to the overlordship of Northumbria and Mercia.[15]

Although superficially similar in the way they are presented, the Saxon and the non-Kentish Jutish origin legends in the *Chronicle* in fact differ in various ways from each other and from that of Kent. Cerdic and Cynric, like Hengist and Horsa, follow the well-known Indo-European model of a founding pair with alliterating names, but are represented as father and son rather than a pair of brothers.[16] Cynric 'the kin-ruler' has an appropriate name for the founder of a Saxon dynasty, but Cerdic seems to have a name that is not even Germanic in origin, for it is derived ultimately from

---

10 David Dumville, 'The Anglian Collection of Royal Genealogies and Regnal Lists', *ASE*, 5 (1976), 23–50.

11 Barbara Yorke, 'The Jutes of Hampshire and Wight and the Origins of Wessex', in *Origins*, 84–96.

12 Barbara Yorke, 'Political and Ethnic Identity: a Case Study of Anglo-Saxon Practice', in *Social Identity in Early Medieval Britain*, ed. William Frazer and Andrew Tyrell (London, 2000), 69–90.

13 David Dumville, 'A New Chronicle Fragment of Early British History', *EHR*, 88 (1973), 312–4, especially 314, n. 2.

14 Barbara Yorke, 'The Origins of Mercia', in *Mercia: An Anglo-Saxon Kingdom in Europe*, ed. Michelle Brown and Carol Farr (London, 2001), 13–22.

15 Dumville, 'The Anglian Collection'.

16 In some versions of the West Saxon royal pedigree Cynric is presented as the son of Creoda son of Cerdic, but in the annals he is designated as Cerdic's son e.g. s.a. 534: *Saxon Chronicles*, ed. Plummer, 16–17.

the British *Caraticos*.[17] It would appear that at some stage it was important for the leaders of the Gewisse to lay claim to British origins, or at least to link themselves to a great hero/ruler from the island's past whose precise ethnic identity may not have been known to them. Other *Chronicle* origin legends are more diverse still in their form. Ælle arrived with not one, but three sons, Cymen, Wlencing and Cissa, whose names appear to be preserved in Old English place-names in the South Saxon province.[18] On the other hand, Port appears to have derived his name from the Latin word *portus* that was utilised in various Old English place-names in the vicinity of Portsmouth Harbour.[19] His two sons, Bieda and Maegla, appear to have acceptable Germanic names, though no exact parallels have been found in other Anglo-Saxon sources.[20] In these two cases the number of sons seems to have dictated the number of ships, for Ælle arrived with three and Port with two. With Stuf and Wihtgar we return to the convention of two kinsmen, probably intended as brothers,[21] and three ships, but without the alliterating names. Stuf may be a Germanic name, but that of Wihtgar derives from *Wihtgara*, 'the people of Wight', and the first element comes ultimately from the Latin name for the island *Uecta*.[22] The two Jutish founders, Port and Wihtgar, both have names derived from Latin names for significant features of their provinces. Ælle's sons, in contrast, apparently have places named after them (in Old English), and several place-names incorporating Cerdic are cited, though only *Cerdices ford* in the annal of 519 can be identified with a modern place-name.[23] The derivation of names of characters from place-names is a feature of oral tradition that is found also in the Hengist and Horsa annals. Thus *Wippedesfleot* in the annal for 465 is said to have taken its name from a British leader slain by Hengist and Oisc (Æsc), just as *Natan leaga* (modern Netley in Hampshire) is said to be derived from that of Natanleod, reputedly a British ruler of the area defeated by Cerdic and Cynric in 508.[24] There may well once have been more fully developed sagas of the activities

---

17 Richard Coates, 'On Some Controversy Surrounding *Gewissae/Gewissei, Cerdic* and *Ceawlin*', *Nomina*, 13 (1990), 1–11; David Parsons, 'British *Caraticos, Old English Cerdic', *Cambrian Medieval Celtic Studies*, 33 (1997), 1–8.

18 The lost *Cymensora* where the family landed according to the annal for 477 (*Saxon Chronicles*, ed. Plummer, 14–15), Lancing and Chichester respectively.

19 Margaret Gelling, 'Latin Loan-Words in Old English Place-Names', *ASE*, 6 (1977), 1–13, at 10–11.

20 Sims-Williams, 'Settlement of England', 40.

21 The entry s.a. 534 refers to them as *nefas* of Cerdic and Cynric; *Saxon Chronicles*, ed. Plummer, 16–17.

22 Yorke, 'Jutes of Hampshire and Wight', 85–6. I am grateful to Andrew Wareham for drawing to my attention to the use of the name Wihtgar by a ninth-century Kentish family who were ancestors of Wulfstan of Dalham: for fuller details see Andrew Wareham, *Lords and Communities in Early Medieval East Anglia* (Woodbridge, 2005), 33–5.

23 Charford in Hampshire; Richard Coates, *The Place-Names of Hampshire* (London, 1989), 51.

24 For a different view see Andrew Breeze, '*Natanleod*' in Richard Coates and Andrew Breeze, *Celtic Voices, English Places. Studies of the Celtic Impact on Place-Names in England* (Stamford, 2000), 97–9.

of Cerdic and the rest as we know there must have been for Hengist and Horsa from the more detailed material concerning them in the *Historia Brittonum*.[25]

With the exception of the material relating to Hengist and Horsa, we cannot trace the development of the *Chronicle* legends before their appearance in this ninth-century text. At the time the *Chronicle* was produced in the reign of Alfred, there was an undoubted interest in the king's earlier Germanic ancestors, which also manifests itself in the first two chapters of Asser's *Life of Alfred*, for instance, in which Alfred's paternal and maternal descent is discussed. Alfred's mother Osburh apparently claimed descent from Stuf and Wihtgar,[26] and this helps to explain their prominent role in the early annals, but not necessarily the complete invention of a separate tradition concerning the foundation of Wight, not to mention that for the even more obscure Jutish province in southern Hampshire that presumably can be linked with Port and his sons. The *Chronicle* annals covering the provinces of Wight and southern Hampshire have been produced in such a way as to give the West Saxons ancestral claims to an area that does not in fact seem to have been fully under their control until after the conquests of Caedwalla (685–88), the point after which they became known as West Saxons instead of the Gewisse.[27] The South Saxons and Kent were incorporated into Wessex in the ninth century. The *Chronicle* makes no case for prior claims in these areas, but does provide a common origin in battle against a common foe for the south-eastern areas that had become part of the enlarged Wessex by the time of Alfred. All the origin legends in the *Chronicle* may have originated before the ninth century, but they probably underwent considerable adaptation and manipulation in order to fit into the *Chronicle*'s annalistic format and to comply with what may have been its over-arching aims. The use of repeated formulae helps to unify them with each other and the text as a whole.[28]

Whatever the putative origins of the rest, the only legend that can be traced back further in a written text is that of Kent. Hengist and Horsa make their first appearance in *Historia Ecclesiastica* I, 15 as one of the additions Bede made to his summary of ch. 23 of Gildas's *De Excidio Britanniae*. Gildas's text appears to suggest that the basic features of the Germanic origin legend were already known in Britain by the time he composed his work, probably within the first half of the sixth century.

'A pack of cubs burst forth from the lair of the barbarian lioness, coming in three 'keels' (*cyulis*) as they call warships in their language. The winds were favourable; favourable too the omens and auguries, which prophesied, according to a sure portent among them,

---

25 Brooks, 'Kingdom of Kent', 60–4; Brooks, *Anglo-Saxon Myths*, 79–90

26 *Alfred the Great. Asser's Life of King Alfred and Other Contemporary Sources*, ed. and tr. Simon Keynes and Michael Lapidge (Harmondsworth, 1983), 68, 229–30; Janet Nelson, 'Reconstructing a Royal Family: Reflections on Alfred from Asser, Chapter 2', in *People and Places in Northern Europe 500–1600. Essays in Honour of Peter Hayes Sawyer*, ed. Ian Wood and Niels Lund (Woodbridge, 1991), 47–66.

27 Harold Elliot Walker, 'Bede and the Gewisse: the Political Evolution of the Heptarchy and its nomenclature', *Cambridge Historical Journal*, 12 (1956), 174–86; Yorke, 'Jutes of Hampshire and Wight', 92–6.

28 Jacqueline Stodnik, 'Reading the *Anglo-Saxon Chronicle* as List', in *The Anglo-Saxon Chronicle*, ed. Alice Cowan (forthcoming).

that they would live for three hundred years in the land towards which their prows were directed, and that for half the time, a hundred and fifty years, they would repeatedly lay it waste'.[29]

This one event is made to stand for the whole incursion of Saxons settlers into the eastern part of the island, even if Gildas does refer subsequently to the arrival of re-enforcements. Not the least noteworthy thing about this passage is the implication that the information must have come ultimately from an Anglo-Saxon source. The text explicitly states that it is citing Saxon traditions, and includes the word *cyulis* (OE *ceol*), which is identified as a Germanic term for warships, '*ut lingua eius exprimatur*'. It also refers to the consultation of auguries. The importance of this custom among the Germanic peoples of North Sea areas is well-attested by other early medieval writers, and is graphically described by Sidonius among a group of Saxon raiders.[30] The arrival of the founders of a new nation in a small number of ships is also a standard element of Germanic ethnogenesis, and it was in three ships that the founders of the Goths set out from their Scandinavian homeland according to Gildas's near contemporary Jordanes.[31]

If this passage from *De Excidio* is accepted as part of Gildas's original text it carries the implication that origin legends were being developed among the Germanicised communities of eastern England by the first half of the sixth century – or even earlier if revisionist dates for the composition of *De Excidio* in the latter part of the fifth century are accepted.[32] Such conclusions might seem surprising and, indeed, a case for seeing the extract from ch. 23 referring to the keels and the portent as a later Anglo-Saxon interpolation has been presented recently by Alex Woolf.[33] He points out that the 150 years during which, according to the Anglo-Saxon prophecy, the island was to be laid waste would have begun in 447 (when Aëtius was consul for the third time) and ended in 597, the year of the arrival of the mission despatched by Pope Gregory. He suggests that the interpolated passage could have originated as a marginal or interlinear gloss, made at some point between 672 (the council of Hertford) and 747 (300 years after the consulship of Aëtius), most probably at

---

29 Gildas, *The Ruin of Britain and Other Documents*, ed. Michael Winterbottom (Chichester, 1978), 26, ch. 23.3.

30 Ian Wood, 'Pagan Religions and Superstitions East of the Rhine from the Fifth to the Ninth Century' in *After Empire. Towards an Ethnology of Europe's Barbarians*, ed. Giorgio Ausenda (Woodbridge, 1995), 253–79, at 260–63.

31 Patrick Sims-Williams, 'Gildas and the Anglo-Saxons', *Cambridge Medieval Celtic Studies*, 6 (1983), 1–30, at p.23.

32 The question of the date of composition of Gildas's *De Excidio* is explored in some detail in *Gildas: New Approaches*, ed. Michael Lapidge and David Dumville (Woodbridge, 1984) where a mid-sixth-century date is generally preferred. A late fifth-century date is suggested by Michael Herren, 'Gildas and Early British Monasticism', in *Britain 400–600: Language and History*, ed. Alfred Bammesberger and Alfred Wollmann (Heidelberg, 1990), 65–78, and Nicholas Higham, *The English Conquest. Gildas and Britain in the Fifth Century* (Manchester, 1994). The judicious conclusion of Sims-Williams, 'Gildas and the Anglo-Saxons', 3–5, is that the best one can do is to regard it as a sixth-century work.

33 Alex Woolf, 'An Interpolation in the Text of Gildas's *De Excidio Britanniae*', *Peritia*, 16 (2002), 161–7.

Canterbury, and subsequently copied into a manuscript of *De Excidio* that became the ancestor of all other surviving versions, all of which include the contested passage.

One of the problems for reaching a definitive view on whether the passage is an interpolation or not is that the surviving manuscript versions of the full text date from the tenth century or later, and none of the earlier works which make use of excerpts from the text cite this particular passage,[34] including Bede's *Historia Ecclesiastica* I, 15. In fact even Bede would not have appreciated that 150 years after the appeal to Aëtius brought one to 597, for his calculations had produced the date of 445/446 for Aëtius' third consulship.[35] One cannot help thinking that if the prophecy had been inserted into Gildas's text in order to draw attention to the significance of the arrival of St Augustine, then that purpose would have been better served if the reference was more explicit and the mathematics easier to compute. If it was an interlinear or marginal gloss that was incorporated into a manuscript during copying, it was a remarkably literary and expansive gloss, and one which had been couched as if written by Gildas for his British audience as the phrases 'in their language' and 'a sure potent among them' indicate. There may be factors which raise suspicions about the passage, but its inclusion does not look accidental – it is either part of Gildas's original text or was deliberately composed to appear as if it was, and if the latter was the case the purpose behind it was not made immediately obvious to a reader.

The case for the existence of origin legends among the Anglo-Saxons by the sixth century does not have to rest purely on Gildas's testimony, for there is evidence for a preoccupation with origins and a manipulation of evidence concerning them in the archaeological record. What we seem to see in burial customs in eastern and southern England around the turn of the fifth century is a marked adherence to the funereal rituals of the North Sea homelands. The people practising these customs may not have defined them as distinctively 'Germanic', but they were presumably aware that they were ancestral, and continual contact across the North Sea, among the settlers on the eastern coasts at least, would have kept this awareness alive.[36] The most conservative and uniform of Anglo-Saxon burial customs was cremation, where many facets such as the burning of the human bodies with those of animals, the transfer of remains to urns, often with the inclusion of miniature grave-goods, and burial in communal cemeteries are extremely close to rites practised in northern Germany and southern Denmark,[37] and remarkably consistent up to the end of the practice of cremation burial in the early seventh century. As Howard Williams has stressed, cremation is not simply a by-product of migration, but represents a conscious choice by the communities which practised it to follow a labour-intensive and

---

34 Woolf, '*De Excidio*', 166–7.

35 In *HE*, 44–7 (Book I, ch. 13) Bede, utilising the *Chronicle* of Prosper of Aquitaine, states that Theodosius became emperor in 423 and that Aëtius was consul for the third time in the twenty-third year of his reign.

36 John Hines, *The Scandinavian Character of Anglian England in the Pre-Viking Period*, British Archaeological Reports, British Series 124 (Oxford, 1984); John Hines, 'The Scandinavian Character of Anglian England: an Update', in *The Age of Sutton Hoo*, ed. Martin Carver (Woodbridge, 1992), 315–29.

37 Catherine Hills, 'Did the People of Spong Hill come from Schleswig-Holstein?', *Studien zur Sachsenforschung*, 11 (1998), 143–54.

complex rite that must have been regarded as a significant component of their group identity.[38] Adherence to a common ancestral rite carried the same basic assumptions as the simple origin legend, namely 'we came from overseas as a group'.

The other burial rite practised in eastern and southern England in the fifth and sixth centuries was inhumation. With inhumation a much greater variation between and within cemeteries and over time is found, but there are also some aspects where there is a remarkable uniformity. The typical male weapon-burial is one of these and Heinrich Härke has argued that many of its features could be interpreted as a manifestation of the basic characteristics of the Anglo-Saxon origin legend, particularly as presented in the *Chronicle* annals, where a group of men arrives from overseas and wins land for itself by successfully defeating the existing inhabitants.[39] The selection of weapons for burials is clearly symbolic. Only rarely do those interred have a full weapon-set and many of those buried were too old, too young or too ill to have wielded weapons at the time of their death. Härke argues that these were not weapons to equip warriors for an afterlife where current lifestyles were to be continued, but were designed to convey to observers, perhaps both human and divine, that the dead man was a free Anglo-Saxon warrior. For whatever may have been the actual ethnic origins of those buried, a controversial issue which may only be settled by scientific analysis of the skeletons, the uniformity of the male weapon-burial gave them a common origin as free Anglo-Saxon warriors – which in its simplest form was what the Anglo-Saxon origin legends of the *Chronicle* also conveyed.

Further facets are displayed in the more complex and variable costumes and jewellery of women who were probably from the same social group as the men buried as warriors.[40] The costumes can be studied most easily through inhumations, but cremated remains suggest they were also worn by women who followed that burial rite as well. Female burial rites seem to convey multiple messages, some of which may be designed to indicate family or very localised origins,[41] but with such variations contained within broader conventions that signalled, firstly, a common Germanic identity and, secondly, an allegiance to a particular Anglo-Saxon grouping

---

38 Howard Williams, 'An Ideology of Transformation: Cremation Rites and Animal Sacrifice in Early Anglo-Saxon England', in *The Archaeology of Shamanism*, ed. Neil Price (London, 2001), 193–212; Howard Williams, 'Remains of Pagan Saxondom? The Study of Anglo-Saxon Cremation Rites', in *Burial in Early Medieval England and Wales*, ed. Sam Lucy and Andrew Reynolds, Society for Medieval Archaeology Monograph Series, 17 (London, 2002), 47–71; Howard Williams, 'Material Culture as Memory: Combs and Cremation in Early Medieval Britain', *EME*, 12 (2003), 89–128.

39 Heinrich Härke, '"Warrior graves"? The Background of the Anglo-Saxon Weapon Burial Rite', *Past and Present*, 126 (1990), 22–43; Heinrich Härke, 'Material Culture as Myth: Weapons in Anglo-Saxon Graves', in *Burial and Society: the Chronological and Social Analysis of Archaeological Data*, ed. Claus Kield Jensen and Karen Høilund Nielsen (Aarhus, 1997), 119–28.

40 Gale Owen-Crocker, *Dress in Anglo-Saxon England* (Manchester, 1986), 19–64.

41 Sam Lucy, 'Burial Practice in Early Medieval Eastern Britain: Constructing Local Identities, Deconstructing Ethnicity', in *Burial in Early Medieval England and Wales*, ed. Lucy and Reynolds, 72–87.

that had developed since arrival in Britain. Kentish female dress, for instance, seems to reflect a carefully calculated choice from a number of possible ingredients, some of which reflect the southern Scandinavian origin contained in their claim to a Jutish identity, while other component parts were borrowed from contemporary Frankish dress.[42] Conventions for elite female dress in what by Bede's day would be defined as Anglian and Saxon areas also appear to have been developed within Britain, but with reference to more distant Germanic origins, even if much greater variation in practice is seen than in the male weapon-burial rite.[43] So perhaps rather surprisingly, facets of the elite women's costume among the Anglo-Saxons can be seen as conforming to the presentation of the *adventus Saxonum* in *Historia Ecclesiastica* I, 15 where the contingents of the three warships are said to have come from 'three very powerful Germanic tribes, the Saxons, Angles and Jutes'.[44] Although it is hard to understand exactly how they may have functioned, these three dominant confederations may have controlled eastern and southern England in the sixth century.[45] Female costume may have encoded the myth of a common origin that helped to enforce group identities within these broad provinces. Within this context, it is interesting to note Tania Dickinson's proposal that elements of Saxon brooch decoration may be drawn from a Romano-British repertoire,[46] for the claim that the West Saxon royal house was descended from Cerdic seems to embody a willingness to claim descent from a former British hero and so acknowledge a British contribution to West Saxon identity. It might appear illogical for such claims to co-exist with the Germanic origins embodied in the *Chronicle* tradition of Cerdic and Cynric coming to Wessex from overseas,[47] but what we probably have is a layering of different traditions created at different periods and for different purposes. The *Chronicle* itself was one stage in a long history of West Saxon myth creation in which, recent archaeological

---

42 Birte Brugmann, 'Britons, Angles, Saxon, Jutes and Franks', in *The Anglo-Saxon Cemetery on Mill Hill, Deal, Kent*, ed. Keith Parfitt and Birte Brugmann, Society for Medieval Archaeology Monograph Series, 14 (1997), 110–24. Work on a distinctive costume in the Jutish areas bordering the Solent is currently being undertaken by Nicholas Stoodley.

43 John Hines, 'The Becoming of the English: Identity, Material Culture and Language in Early Anglo-Saxon England', *Anglo-Saxon Studies in Archaeology and History*, 7 (1984), 49–59. For specifically Anglian dress, see Hines, *Scandinavian Character*, and for Saxon, see Tania Dickinson, 'Material Culture as Social Expression: the Case of Saxon Saucer Brooches with Running Spiral Decoration', *Studien zur Sachsenforschung*, 7 (Hildesheim, 1991), 39–70; Tania Dickinson, 'Early Saxon Saucer Brooches: a Preliminary Overview', *Anglo-Saxon Studies in Archaeology and History*, 6 (Oxford, 1993), 11–45.

44 Presumably one tribe per ship is meant, as in the *Chronicle* origin legends where there is often a correlation between the number of named leaders and the number of ships.

45 Barbara Yorke, 'Anglo-Saxon *Gentes* and *Regna*', in *Regna and Gentes. The Relationship between Late Antique and Early Medieval Peoples and Kingdoms in the Transformation of the Roman World*, ed. Hans-Werner Goetz, Jurgen Jarnut and Walter Pohl (Brill, 2003), 381–407, especially pp. 395–402.

46 References as in n. 43 above.

47 Not only is it the case that myths do not have to be logical, but there are other instances in the early *Chronicle* annals where illogicalities exist; see, for instance, David Dumville, 'The West Saxon Genealogical Regnal List and the Chronology of Early Wessex', *Peritia*, 4 (1985), 21–66.

analyses suggest, visual display had been a significant element in its propagation and an important aspect of early Anglo-Saxon culture.

In the early seventh century there were major changes in the burial rites, the explanations for which remain controversial.[48] Cremation disappeared as a widely practised rite and female burial dress changed dramatically and became more Romanised in appearance with necklaces and pendants taking the place of the former *peplos* gown fastened with 'Germanic' brooches.[49] Inhumations generally became simpler with fewer grave-goods, apart from the very richest burials, which grew increasingly elaborate, with the Sutton Hoo ship-burial in mound 1 as the apogee of the princely burial-rite. The cemetery evidence implies major changes within society and the written sources suggest that the changes coincided with the development of kingdoms, a conclusion which the elaboration of the so-called princely burials would support. The kingdoms emerged from the dissolution of the dimly understood Anglian and Saxon confederations (though that of the Jutes seems to have survived for longer and Bede's correspondents were able to provide him with some observations concerning it).[50] In such circumstances the costumes which had signalled Anglian or Saxon allegiance not only became irrelevant, but could also have sent out dangerous messages of opposition to the new regimes. With the emergence of kingdoms the Anglo-Saxons moved away from the socio-political traditions of the North Sea homelands to take their place alongside other Germanic peoples who now ruled parts of the former Roman empire, and that shift may help to explain how women's costume came to favour elements of 'imperial' style.

Of course, the growth of kingdoms and increasing contacts with areas of the former Roman empire led ultimately to the introduction of Christianity, something that might be expected in itself to have had an impact on burial custom, though the general consensus seems to be that many of the changes in burial practice pre-date the period in which Christianity was sufficiently widespread to have had this type of effect. It may be that instead the decline of many aspects of communal burial can be linked with a different type of mythic transfer, one in which the royal court became a ceremonial *locus* for the reinforcement of shared identities. In such a scenario the decline of aspects of the ritual of cremation and inhumation in the communal cemeteries could be directly related to the elaboration of the burials of the leaders and their families, though the latter may be only one aspect of identity-ritual sponsored by the royal courts. Burial under mounds (whether newly created or pre-existing prehistoric ones) helped create a visual focus for a new dynasty that tied it to the land it claimed to rule, but also evoked the memory of those who may have ruled it in the past.[51] Perhaps the claim that a past ruler, Caraticos/Cerdic, had been

---

48 Helen Geake, *The Use of Grave-Goods in Conversion Period England c.600–c.850*, British Archaeological Reports, British Series 261 (Oxford, 1997).

49 Owen-Crocker, *Dress in Anglo-Saxon England*, 85–106.

50 Yorke, 'Anglo-Saxon *Gentes*', 401–405.

51 Howard Williams, 'Ancient Landscapes and the Dead: the Re-use of Prehistoric and Roman Monuments in Early Anglo-Saxon Burial Sites', *Medieval Archaeology*, 41 (1997), 1–32; Martin Carver, 'Reflections on the Meanings of Monumental Barrows in Anglo-Saxon England', in *Burial in Early Medieval England and Wales*, ed. Lucy and Reynolds, 132–43.

the founder of the Gewissan dynasty could be interpreted as part of this annexation of past ancestors, while the creation of Port and Wihtgar from existing place-names might represent an analogous idea of claiming ancestors who were *genii locorum*.

The creation of new kingdoms and dynasties and the provision of mythic support for these is not, of course, something peculiar to the Anglo-Saxons in the sixth century, but part of a much wider movement in both the North Sea homelands and in other former Roman provinces of Europe. The use of origin legends as a support for the process may have been a fairly basic reflex action, born out of a common Indo-European inheritance, but one might expect also to find some more specific borrowing of ideas for which there may be evidence from Kent. One aspect of this is the descent from Woden claimed for Hengist and Horsa in their genealogy cited by Bede in *Historia Ecclesiastica* I, 15. Although Bede had presumably been able to convince himself that Woden was in reality a human ancestor who had been mistakenly labelled as a god, as Bishop Daniel advised Boniface to argue with any similar cases that he encountered,[52] we, of course, know that Woden is one of the best attested deities of the Germanic world. It seems a not unreasonable presumption that Woden's association with the royal house of Kent dated back to before the conversion of the province to Christianity,[53] even if the composition of a genealogy in which he became a progenitor of the Kentish dynasty dated to after the conversion of the province.[54] Some archaeological finds from Kent have close affinities with material from Scandinavia that has been linked with the cult of Odin and with the development of cults to help support royal power.[55] A striking example is the male dancing figure wearing a bird-headed helmet and carrying spears depicted on a belt-buckle from grave 95 from a cemetery at Finglesham (Kent) which closely parallels similar figures on helmet-plates found in Sweden that have been interpreted as representing rituals associated with the cult of Odin.[56] Kent has also produced examples of the wearing and burial of bracteates that have been associated in Scandinavia with Odin's cult, though only D-bracteates have been found in Kent that lack the more explicit iconography of some of the other series.[57]

Adherence to Woden/Odin not only links with the supposed southern Scandinavian origins of the Jutes of Kent, but associates them with a broader group of Germanic peoples. Scandinavian origins and descent from Odin were also claimed

---

52 *Die Briefe des heiligen Bonifatius und Lullus*, ed. Michael Tangl, MGH Epistolae Selectae, I (Berlin, 1916), 38–41, no. 23.

53 For a different view see Richard North, *Heathen Gods in Old English Literature* (Cambridge, 1997).

54 That is, genealogies may be a literary form introduced after conversion, but the material incorporated in them may have a much older origin even if it was not necessarily envisaged in quite the same way.

55 Lotte Hedeager, 'Myth and Art: a Passport to Political Authority in Scandinavia During the Migration Period', in *The Making of Kingdoms*, ed. Tania Dickinson and David Griffiths, Anglo-Saxon Studies in Archaeology and History 10 (Oxford, 1999), 151–6.

56 Sonia Hawkes, Hilda Davidson and Christopher Hawkes, 'The Finglesham Man', *Antiquity*, 39 (1965), 17–32.

57 Charlotte Behr, 'The Origins of Kingship in Early Medieval Kent', *EME*, 9 (2000), 21–52.

by the Lombards, Burgundians and Heruli (as well as by various Scandinavian dynasties) who shared as well the use of animal-style art and bracteates.[58] The out-of-Scandinavia myth seems to have originated with the Goths, or at least with their literate commentators, and has been a major battleground between those who see myths as simply stories and others who believe them to have had a major role in negotiating identities.[59] Our main source of evidence for Gothic origin traditions is the *Getica* of Jordanes that was written in Constantinople in about 550, but which drew upon earlier accounts that have not survived. Jordanes was himself of Gothic descent and probably used genuine Gothic oral traditions, but these were combined with the classical ancestry already provided for the Goths by Cassiodorus at the court of Theodoric in the 520s and which equated them with various other 'barbarian' peoples who came out of the north in a long classical tradition.

Some specific parallels can be found between Gothic foundation myths and those of the Anglo-Saxons. Arrival in three ships is a basic feature of both accounts. Jordanes refers to the founding ancestors of the Goths, two brothers with alliterating names, as *Ansis* which he translates as *semideos* 'demi-gods'.[60] The Kentish foundation legend appears to incorporate two pairs of founding brothers with alliterating names, Hengist and Horsa and Oisc and Oeric; according to Bede, Oisc was the *cognomen* of Oeric, son of Hengist.[61] The name Oisc, and possibly that of Hengist, is derived from the same root, Germanic **ans*, as Jordanes's *Ansis*. Oisc is likely to be cognate with the name of **Anschis* whom the ninth-century Ravenna Cosmographer believed to be the *princeps* who brought the Saxons to Britain.[62] In the Kentish genealogy the divine nature of Hengist and the rest is suggested by descent from Woden, but Jordanes has a more developed account in which the Gothic founders were raised to semi-divine status through the bestowal of *fortuna* by the god of war,[63] and it may be the case that the Kentish origin legend originally contained something similar.

---

58 Lotte Hedeager, 'Cosmological Endurance: Pagan Identities in Early Christian Europe', *European Journal of Archaeology*, 1 (1998), 382–96.

59 Leader of the sceptical tendency is Walter Goffart, *The Narrators of Barbarian History (AD 550–800); Jordanes, Gregory of Tours, Bede and Paul the Deacon* (Princeton, 1988), 20–111, especially 30–31 and 87–96. That the Gothic legends had a contemporary significance beyond the literary was argued by Herwig Wolfram, *The History of the Goths* (Berkeley, 1988), with further support from, among others, Moisl, 'Anglo-Saxon Royal Genealogies and Germanic Oral Tradition'; Pohl, 'Ethnicity, Theory and Tradition'; and Peter Heather, *Goths and Romans 332–489* (Oxford, 1991), especially 9–61 and Peter Heather, 'Theoderic, King of the Goths', *EME*, 4 (1995), 145–73.

60 Moisl, 'Anglo-Saxon Royal Genealogies', 220–222.

61 *HE*, 150–151 (Book II, ch. 5). Bede may have been drawing on two different origin traditions; see Brooks, 'Kingdom of Kent', 58–60. One wonders if there could be a connection with the division into two provinces of east and west Kent, each of which had its own ruler in the seventh century and may have had different origins; Barbara Yorke, 'Joint Kingship in Kent c.560–785', *Archaeologia Cantiana*, 99 (1983), 1–19.

62 Sims-Williams, 'The Settlement of England', 22–3.

63 Moisl, 'Anglo-Saxon Royal Genealogies', 220–223, and for something rather similar among the Lombards, ibid., 226–7.

Hengist, Horsa and Oisc are presented primarily as successful warleaders, like the Gothic founders.

It is not impossible that there could have been direct knowledge of Gothic foundation myths in sixth-century Kent. Gregory of Tours has a reference to a 'Saxon' army that had been in Italy, and many of his references to 'Saxons' seem to refer to people who were from or had close links with the areas of England that claimed to be Jutish.[64] One testimony to the interest in the Goths in sixth-century Kent may be the name of King Æthelbert's father, Irminric, which he shares with one of the most famous of Gothic leaders. But contact might also have been more indirect. Kent participated in the long-distance trade-networks that united elites of many different areas of Germanic Europe and helped spread common manifestations of status such as gold and garnet jewellery and the wearing of necklaces which seem to have been adopted earlier in Kent than elsewhere in Anglo-Saxon England.[65] Myths were another means of supporting status, sometimes alluded to directly in the iconography of prized artefacts, and knowledge of them may have travelled along the same routes.

Whether other Anglo-Saxon provinces adopted the Gothic out-of-Scandinavia myth independently of Kent is difficult to say. A case can be made for its use by the emerging royal house of the East Angles. The distinctive naked, dancing figure with spears of the Finglesham belt-buckle is also to be found on panels of the helmet from mound 1 at Sutton Hoo, and is only one example of a strong Swedish influence on items buried there.[66] Unfortunately we do not possess an origin legend for the East Angles, unless we accept the case for *Beowulf* having originated in the province and preserving traditions that its royal house was of Geatish descent.[67] Nor was Kent the only dynasty that may have sought to boost prestige through the adoption of a Gothic name in the latter part of the sixth century, for one of the sons of Ida of Northumbria was called Theodric. It is not necessarily the case that all the Anglo-Saxon dynasties originally followed the same pattern of claiming Scandinavian or Gothic links and a connection with Woden. The *Chronicle* origin legends for various southern provinces (excluding Kent) may have had different traditions behind them. But by 735 Bede was identifying Woden as one '*de cuius stirpe multarum provinciarum regium genus originem duxit*' ('from whose stock the royal families of many kingdoms claimed their descent').[68] It would appear that by the time Bede wrote descent from Woden was a *sine qua non* for any family that wished to be considered as royal.[69] Anglo-Saxon kingdoms evolved along similar lines and regularly seem to have borrowed ideas from one another, so their origin legends too may have evolved towards a

---

64 Barbara Yorke, 'Gregory of Tours and Sixth-Century Anglo-Saxon England', in *The World of Gregory of Tours*, ed. Kathleen Mitchell and Ian Wood (Leiden, 2002), 113–30.

65 Hedeager, 'Myth and Art'.

66 Rupert Bruce-Mitford, *The Sutton Hoo Ship-Burial*, II: *Arms, Armour and Regalia* (London, 1978), 186–220.

67 Sam Newton, *The Origins of Beowulf and the Pre-Viking Kingdom of East Anglia* (Woodbridge, 1993).

68 *HE*, 50–51; I, 15.

69 Eric John, 'The Point of Woden', *Anglo-Saxon Studies in Archaeology and History*, 5 (1992), 127–34.

common norm though this may also be expressive of a growing sense of unity among the 'English' fostered by overlordship and the concept of a common English church.

H.M. Chadwick's vision of a Germanic Heroic Age has few supporters these days,[70] and the emphasis is rather on the late eighth and ninth centuries as the period in which ideas were developed within western Europe of a common Germanic past as a type of literary exercise.[71] England shared in this ninth-century interest, as suggested by Asser's claim that Alfred had Gothic forbears and by the elaboration of Germanic heroes in the West Saxon genealogy.[72] However, the Anglo-Saxon evidence also indicates that the interest did not begin at this point, but was just a further stage in the development of a concern with origins that may go back to the fifth century and even then drew upon much older practices among Germanic peoples that helped explain the emergence of new polities.[73] Like heroic verse the Anglo-Saxon origin legend was not simply the product of either book-learning or oral tradition, but of complex interaction between them as we would expect to find in a society like that of the Anglo-Saxons where the two forms co-existed.[74]

An interest in maintaining and proclaiming aspects of culture that stemmed from their North Sea homelands can be seen to be a feature of early Anglo-Saxon communities in Britain, and the nurturing of a core origin myth that was common to many Indo-European societies is likely to have happened in such an environment. *De Excidio* ch. 23 may provide the first instance of the transfer of an Anglo-Saxon origin legend from oral tradition into a written text. The *De Excidio* text may have helped frame Bede's presentation of the *adventus*, but is unlikely to have been the starting-point for all the Anglo-Saxon foundation accounts. Our surviving, developed, Anglo-Saxon origin legends seem to stem from the period of the formation of kingdoms and the desire of their ruling houses (or some of them at least) to identify themselves with their peoples' origins. Development of the Kentish legend of Hengist and Horsa, the most detailed one to survive, seems itself to have been influenced by traditions of other Germanic peoples, some of which, such as those of the Goths, may have drawn ultimately upon classical texts. The legend of Hengist and Horsa may itself have affected how the origin legends of other southern peoples were presented in the *Chronicle*, but these accounts seem to have followed originally a rather different format in which leaders embodied their people by deriving their names from the places they occupied or, in the case of Gewisse, traced descent from a past leader.

---

70 Hector Munro Chadwick, *The Origin of the English Nation* (Cambridge, 1907).

71 Goffart, *Narrators of Barbarian History* passim; Roberta Frank, 'Germanic Legend in Old English literature' in *The Cambridge Companion to Old English*, ed. Malcolm Godden and Michael Lapidge (Cambridge, 1991), 88–106; Matthew Innes, 'Teutons or Trojans? The Carolingians and the Germanic Past' in *The Uses of the Past in the Early Middle Ages*, ed. Yitzak Hen and Matthew Innes (Cambridge, 2000), 227–49.

72 Kenneth Sisam, 'Anglo-Saxon Royal Genealogies', *Proceedings of the British Academy*, 39 (1953), 287–346; Malcolm Godden, 'The Anglo-Saxons and the Goths: Rewriting the Sack of Rome', *ASE*, 31 (2002), 47–68.

73 See n. 4, and also Nick Webber in this volume.

74 Matthew Innes, 'Memory, Orality and Literacy in an Early Medieval Society', *Past and Present*, 158 (1998), 3–36.

The most influential literary embellishment of the Germanic origin myth was, of course, that of Bede, drawing perhaps on developments that had already been made by clerics in Kent. It was Bede, it would appear, who married the Germanic origin legend with an even more powerful one drawn from the Bible, that of a Chosen People with a destiny to fulfil[75] – a Christian prophecy to take the place of an earlier pagan one recorded by Gildas. In so doing Bede produced a potent image which would inspire much proliferation of links between the migrations of the Anglo-Saxons and the Children of Israel,[76] and would lead ultimately to a further stage of ethnogenesis – that of the English people.[77]

---

[75] Herbert Cowdrey, 'Bede and the English People', *Journal of Religious History*, 11 (1981), 501–23; Brooks, *Bede and the English*, see also Alan Thacker in this volume.

[76] Nicholas Howe, *Migration and Mythmaking in Anglo-Saxon England* (New Haven, 1989).

[77] Patrick Wormald, '*Engla Lond*: the Making of an Allegiance', *Journal of Historical Sociology*, 7 (1994), 1–24; Sarah Foot, 'The Making of *Angelcynn*: English Identity before the Norman Conquest', *TRHS*, 6th series, 6 (1996), 25–50. The author is very grateful to the editors of the volume for their helpful comments and advice.

Chapter 4

A Nearly, but Wrongly, Forgotten Historian of the Dark Ages

James Campbell

Eben William Robertson was born in 1815, came to Worcester College, Oxford, in 1833, graduated in Classics in 1837 and, after a period at Lincoln's Inn, lived as a country gentleman in Leicestershire. He published two books: *Scotland under her Early Kings* (1862)[1] and *Historical Essays* (1872).[2] That these are among the most important nineteenth-century works on Anglo-Saxon history is demonstrable. Their influence, or at least their acknowledged influence, has been slight. Robertson was largely neglected in his own day (though not by Stubbs)[3] and almost completely in ours. He is used by Maitland exceedingly lightly; his works do not appear in the bibliographies of the textbooks by Stenton,[4] Loyn[5] and Sawyer.[6] They do not appear even in Rosenthal's full-scale bibliography.[7]

Some of the neglect of Robertson among Victorian historians is explicable. The old *Dictionary of National Biography* says of him: 'His style was dry and unadorned'.[8] An understatement: his style was gnarled, sometimes to the point of impenetrability. His books are arranged on idiosyncratic principles, one of which is that titles should not provide an adequate guide to contents. Thus, those who seek the clearest summary of his crucial views on the relationships between land tenure and

---

1   E.W. Robertson, *Scotland under her Early Kings* (2 vols, Edinburgh, 1862).

2   E.W. Robertson, *Historical Essays in Connection with the Law, the Church etc* (Edinburgh, 1872).

3   William Stubbs had, plainly, read both of Robertson's works carefully. He often found him tending to 'far too much latitude of conjecture', e.g. *The Constitutional History of England* (3 vols, Oxford 1880), I, 92, n. 4, but sometimes 'highly instructive and suggestive', e.g. I, 131, n. 4.

4   F.W. Maitland, *Domesday Book and Beyond* (Cambridge, 1897), 227n, 486, 519; F.M. Stenton, *Anglo-Saxon England*, 3rd edn (Oxford, 1971).

5   H.R. Loyn, *Anglo-Saxon England and the Norman Conquest,* 2nd edn (London, 1991).

6   P.H. Sawyer, *From Roman Britain to Anglo-Saxon England*, 2nd edn (London, 1998).

7   J.T. Rosenthal, *Anglo-Saxon History: An Annotated Bibliography* (London, 1985).

8   Thomas Seccombe, 'Robertson, Eben William', *Dictionary of National Biography*, ed. L. Stephen and S. Lee (63 vols, London, 1885–1900), s.v.. The version of this revised by Nilanjana Banerji in *ODNB*, s.v., abbreviates its predecessor, but adds information on Robertson's will and reproduces a miniature by Sir William Charles Ross.

state formation need to know that it lurks in the introduction to the densely expressed learning of an essay on 'Irish measurements'.[9]

If his learning was counterbalanced by his stylistic self-indulgence both were equalled by the originality and importance of his interpretations. Two examples follow. First, the question of whether the free peasantry of the Danelaw were by origin Scandinavian. This fascinating subject has long kept scholars on both sides of the North Sea in gainful employment. Its modern English study begins with Stenton's lecture of 1927. He makes no reference to Robertson. Yet it was in fact Robertson (very characteristically, in his book on Scotland) who first put forward the theory of the major Scandinavian influence on the social structure of the Danelaw, based on Domesday statistics and reinforced by a survey of the place-name evidence.[10]

More important, and more certain, was Robertson's discovery of the basic units of early Dark Age organisation in much of this island. The investigation of such units and of related systems of authority has attracted much attention in recent decades. Scholars working from different angles have come to the same conclusion: that in wide areas there was an early system of organisation such that the countryside was divided up into units of, not infrequently, the order of 100 square miles, each owing services to a royal vill; the settlements in each such unit sharing areas of common grazing. The work of in particular Barrow, and Rees following on that of Maitland and Jolliffe has strongly suggested that the lathes of Kent, the small shires of Northumbria and Scotland, the sokes of the Danelaw, the *maneria cum appendiciis* of other areas represent a widespread system with considerable elements of uniformity and sometimes Celtic origins.[11] Beyond doubt the most fundamental discoveries in these matters were made by Robertson. In *Scotland under her Early Kings* he revealed the small shire system of Northumbria and southern Scotland, demonstrated its extraordinary regularities, brought out its integration with ecclesiastical organisation and, not least, proved its existence north as well as south of the Forth thus presenting identical features in areas which had once been part of England and areas which had not.[12] Furthermore, he elsewhere drew attention to the likely existence of similar units in southern England. Thus he suggested that the Domesday indications of a unit of six hundreds centred on Wallop with common grazing suggested 'some forgotten shire' in Hampshire.[13] He also made the crucial observation that charter evidence suggests that some early tenurial arrangements

---

9 Robertson, *Essays*, 152–154.

10 Robertson, *Scotland*, II, 272, 432–435; F.M. Stenton, 'The Danes in England', *Proceedings of the British Academy*, 13 (1927), 203–246, reprinted in *Preparatory to Anglo-Saxon England*, ed. D.M. Stenton (Oxford, 1970), 36–65; R.H.C. Davis did acknowledge Robertson's priority, 'East Anglia and the Danelaw', *TRHS*, 5th ser., 5 (1955), 23–37 at 23, reprinted in R.H.C. Davis, *From Alfred the Great to Stephen* (London and Rio Grande, 1991), 15–32, at 15.

11 In particular G.W.S. Barrow, *The Kingdom of the Scots* (London, 1973), 7–69; Della Hooke, *The Landscape of Anglo-Saxon England* (Leicester, 1998); W. Rees, 'Survivals of Ancient Celtic Custom in Medieval England' in *Angles and Britons*, no editor (O'Donnell Lectures, Cardiff, 1963), 148–168.

12 Robertson, *Scotland*, I, 101–106; Robertson, *Essays*, 127–128.

13 Robertson, *Essays*, 126.

in the West Midlands resembled those of medieval Wales. One modern scholar writing on such matters has certainly acknowledged indebtedness to Robertson. This is G.W.S. Barrow, who in a seminal publication of 1973 developed Robertson's account of the small shire and fully substantiated some of the most important and surprising of Robertson's conclusions: that as soon as these northern units come into documented light in Scotland, some had at their head a thane whose status was more official than proprietary.[14]

Fundamental to Robertson's approach on these and other matters was a wide comparative view, a determination to see English and Scottish developments in the context extending from Ireland to Bavaria with equal concern to integrate the study both of local structures and of socio-legal developments into a context of state formation. In both ways he anticipates and adds to modern work.

Robertson draws into relationships laws from different areas and periods: the early Kentish laws, the thirteenth-century *Sachsenspiegel*, laws of the Carolingian period, Irish laws, later evidence from Frisia and much else are all deployed in complicated argument. The reader can be tempted to abandon the struggle with Robertson's prose, consoling himself with the thought that there must be too much guesswork and anachronism here. Doubtless Robertson bit off more than even he could chew. But he makes repeatedly illuminating comparisons on the basis of extensive learning. One example among many is his discussion of Ine's law, distinguishing between the penalties for participating in the unlawful activities of groups defined as 'thieves' if up to the number of seven, a 'band' if between seven and 35, a '*here*' if more than 35.[15] He refers to a parallel in the mid-eighth century Bavarian laws which distinguish between the activities of a body numbering 42 or more, a *heriraita*, and one numbering less. The significance of this comparison is that it is an indication of the likelihood that provisions such as of Ine are not in essence new English laws, nor laws more or less invented to buttress royal power, or simply for prestige, but rather that they may represent the writing down of regulations derived from a common Germanic inheritance. He develops this point in suggesting that the 'more than 35' of Ine's laws suggests the importance of 36, three times 12, while the Bavarian 42 is three times 14.[16] Why is this? He shows that in more than one early legal system, units of three villages mattered, for example that early Scottish laws take account of a *visnet* or neighbourhood composing three vills.[17]

Or again, he compares the early English laws with the Carolingian *Lex Saxonum*. In Ostphalia a widow had no claim on the moveable goods of her husband, in Westphalia

---

14 Barrow, *The Kingdom of the Scots*, 7–69. A fundamental study of these matters is provided by Alexander Grant in his 'Thanes and Thanages from the Eleventh to the Fourteenth Century', in *Medieval Scotland. Crown, Lordship and Community. Essays presented to G.W.S. Barrow*, ed. Alexander Grant and Keith Stringer (Edinburgh, 1993), 39–81.

15 *Die Gesetze der Angelsachsen*, ed. Felix Liebermann (3 vols, Halle, 1903–1906), I, 95 (Ine, c. 13).

16 Ibid.; *Lex Bavariorum*, ii, 23 and 24, translated by T.J. Rivers, *Laws of the Alamans and Bavarians* (Philadelphia, 1977), 133; Robertson, *Essays*, 137.

17 Ibid.

she was entitled to half of them, and so she was in early Kent.[18] The significance of such discoveries as this is that legal archaeology may be as important as spade archaeology in determining Anglo-Saxon origins. English speaking historians have, since Robertson, found discretion the better part of valour and avoided entanglement in the infinitely difficult web of parallels and possible connections between Anglo-Saxon and Continental laws. There is one major exception: the work of G.C. Homans, in particular on the Frisians in East Anglia.[19] There he demonstrates relationships and equivalences between the system of local government and administration in medieval Frisia and those of early East Anglia which are too close for coincidence to be the explanation of choice. The connection between Frisia and England has a particularly strong claim to attention because the historic, geographical and linguistic links are plain. Robertson boldly called on Frisia in his comments on Bede's *Letter to Egbert*.[20] He was the first to see the importance of this *Letter* for the history of land-tenure. Like Eric John he argues that, until tenure by charter was introduced, noble land-tenure was largely precarious or non-hereditary.[21] Robertson compared the arrangements still surviving in his day in a part of Frisia, Theel-Land. There men of a certain status received allocations of a kind of public land on a basis of life tenure. At a minimum he thus shows how such a system could work.

Recent work on English history has given life to other comparisons between England and Germany long regarded as dead. Consider, for example, the 'mark theory'. This first appeared in the work of Grimm, and was elaborated with many variations later. It had many variants, but its essence was a contention that the early Germans lived in free associations in areas known as *Marken*, characterised by some kind of communality of property among the free, and in particular by each mark's possessing common woodland and grazing. Traces of this system were seen as surviving in north Germany until recent times as stretches of woodland, controlled by *Markgenossenschaften*. Kemble introduced the mark theory to England and related it to his interpretation of place-names in *-ingas* and the like.[22] Mark theory or theories became *idées reçus*. W.J. Ashley was marvellously scathing about this in his account of Oxford teaching in the 1870s.

> ...the mark theory became in an amazingly brief period the accepted tutorial doctrine. It appealed to many of the strongest feelings of academic man. It was new, and therefore enlightened: on the other hand, the example of Dr Stubbs showed that it was compatible with great learning and unimpeachable Conservatism. Moreover it was admirably adapted to the exigencies of the modern tutorial method, which tempts the teacher to put his

---

18 Ibid., 61 n. referring to Ethelbert, c. 78 and Hlothere and Eadric, c. 6 (*Gesetze*, ed. Liebermann, I, 8, 10). Liebermann draws attention to related Continental laws in his commentary.

19 G.C. Homans, 'The Frisians in East Anglia', *Economic History Review*, 10 (1957–1958), 189–206.

20 Robertson, *Essays*, pp. xlv–xlvi; Robertson, *Scotland*, II, 253–254.

21 Eric John, *Orbis Britanniae* (Leicester, 1966), 64–117.

22 J.M. Kemble, *The Saxons in England* (2 vols, London, 1849), I, 35–71.

instruction into the form of neat tips, and leaves him scant time or inclination to revise his system.[23]

Maitland treated mark theory with delicately suggestive agnosticism;[24] and since then it has been treated by most English historians as an historiographical blind alley to the extent that they say nothing of it.[25]

So, it is with interest and, indeed, surprise that we turn to some recent work on the origins of the early Anglo-Saxon kingdoms, in particular to a study by Steven Bassett published in 1989. He sees the essential units of the earliest Anglo-Saxon polity as tribal areas in which each 'early group' had a 'well defined settlement area'. He believes that the land was held in common by 'the tribe' with 'each separate nuclear unit using the tribe's land freely subject to the control of a patriarch'. He thinks that many such tribal divisions should be recognised as 'embryonic kingdoms'.[26] Characteristic of such units were areas of common grazing. Steven Bassett has come close to reinventing the mark theory seven generations after Kemble though without reference to nineteenth-century predecessors. His hypotheses may be too bold; not least because his small units, which are often probably identical with those of the small shire type, may often or always have been components of larger wholes. Be that as it may, his work strengthens Robertson's case for examining early England in a German context.[27]

Comparison between the early political systems of England, Wales and Ireland is at present high on the historical agenda after many generations of neglect. In the early Dark Ages organisation of all three areas presented resemblances which could have been more than superficial. We see many small units of independent or quasi-independent authority, shifting hierarchies of authority between dynasties, a tendency for wide areas of hegemony to be created and then to collapse. A key question is that of why England moved in a different direction from Wales and Ireland towards large units of authority ruled in an important sense directly by one dynasty rather than by the establishment of the superiority of one dynasty or line over others. Thomas Charles-Edwards explains this in large measure by differences in the succession systems. In Ireland the success of a dynasty was expressed in the establishment of several branches of a royal family each with territorial power.[28] In

---

23 W.J. Ashley, *Surveys, Historic and Economic* (London, 1900), 40–41; see also 161–6.

24 Maitland, *Domesday Book and Beyond*, 354–356. Maitland admitted, however, the possible significance in this context of a Domesday reference to the common pasture of a whole hundred, 355.

25 J.N.L. Myres, *The English Settlements* (Oxford, 1986), 37 is an exceedingly cautious exception in saying 'the mark theory, at least in its more extreme form' has been 'generally abandoned by historians'.

26 S.R. Bassett, 'In Search of the Origins of Anglo-Saxon Kingdoms', in *Origins*, 17–23.

27 For a review of German scholarship on *Marken* see the article by A. Cordes, 'Mark, Markgenossenschaft', *Lexikon des Mittelalters* (9 vols, Munich and Zürich, 1977–1998), VI, 298–299.

28 Thomas Charles-Edwards, 'Early Medieval Kingships in the British Isles', in *Origins*, 28–39.

England, at least after the seventh century, dynastic success was largely expressed in the accumulation of conquered lands under the control of one dominant line.

Robertson observed the same phenomenon and concerned himself with several aspects of it. One which particularly interested him was the means which rulers in England and elsewhere used to establish control over newly acquired lands: by establishing provincial agents who acted on behalf of the king in return for a proportion of royal revenues; in several countries this proportion was a third.[29] He was the first to point out the relevance in this regard of the Hwiccian charters in which can be glimpsed the depression of a family from quasi-royal to quasi-ministerial status. He also took note of the way in which the laws of Ine treat as officials the ealdormen who, seen from an older viewpoint could almost certainly have appeared as sub-kings.[30] Robertson saw such process happening not only in England, but also in Norway and Scotland.[31] The case of Scotland is particularly interesting, for there Robertson and Barrow have established the presence of a royal officer or delegate in each of the at least 60 or 70 small shires north and south of the Forth. This speaks of extensive royal authority based on something more direct than the subordination of lesser dynasties.[32]

Let us pause to take note of what Robertson lacked. Remarkably for a Leicestershire squire he had little interest in topography. But it is notable how far recent landscape studies have deepened our knowledge of the remote past in ways which do not replace, but, on the contrary, vindicate interpretations of a Robertsonian kind. One of the most remarkable of these was that put forward by J.E.A. Jolliffe. Published in a *Festschrift* of 1934 it is little referred to.[33] How far Jolliffe was consciously dependent on Robertson is unknowable; the essay is innocent of footnotes, but it is very Robertsonian. Building on his research on Kentish and Northumbrian institutions Jolliffe gives an account of units of the 'small shire' type over much of England. He was the first since Robertson to do so, and anticipated Davis and Barrow in seeing traces of such units in the Danelaw in the eleventh century (and contending, vainly, against the then fashionable views of Stenton on the Danelaw). Like Robertson, Jolliffe saw this system of organisation as associated with the existence of significant free classes in direct contact with kings.[34] 'Manorialisation' he argued to have been over much of England an intrusive and incomplete process which did not comprise the whole of the countryside. In his view the organisation of innumerable medieval manors bore clear traces of an older system organised by relation to units of the small shire type, to royal vills, and ultimately, to rulers. Jolliffe was clear that this

---

29 Robertson, *Scotland*, I, 101–106; Robertson, *Essays*, 152–153.

30 Robertson, *Scotland*, II, 455.

31 Ibid., II, 299

32 Ibid., I, 106; II, 444–71; Barrow, *The Kingdom of the Scots*, 41–59. Thomas Charles-Edwards suggests that the remarkable success of the kings of Dal Riata may be partly explained by their expansion into the areas east of Druim Alban where local royal centres probably already existed: 'Early Medieval Kingships', 39.

33 J.E.A. Jolliffe, 'The Era of the Folk in English History', *Oxford Essays in Medieval History Presented to Herbert Edward Salter*, no editor (Oxford, 1934), 1–32.

34 Discussion of such matters has recently been revived and enlarged by Rosamond Faith, *The English Peasantry and the Growth of Lordship* (London, 1998).

did not apply to the Midlands.[35] He said 'the apparently solid mass of the Midland manorial villages with their ingrained servitude and all pervading lordship' is 'the most formidable obstacle to the acceptance of organised freedom as the sole basis of English history'. He said 'It is hard to look upon a Midland manor as the product of evolution'. 'For the moment I see no prospect of fitting this strange anomaly in our countryside into any intelligible course of history'. We may set beside these statements recent discoveries about the history of the English countryside. It has been powerfully argued that over wide areas its layout is much older than the Saxon invasion. Thus one of the most eminent exponents of such views, Oliver Rackham, distinguishes between what he calls the 'modern countryside', stretching in a broad swathe from south-west to north-east, and the 'ancient countryside', occupying large areas in the south and east and the north and west.[36] His 'modern countryside', by which he means the countryside whose layout of fields and roads is post-prehistoric, is largely that of the manorialised Midlands which Jolliffe found alien to his normal pattern and where it seems more and more likely that the villages and fields were created deliberately in and after the tenth century.

The apparent extreme antiquity of the lay-out of large areas of England raises questions about the antiquity of units of land organisation. How old was the small shire system? Robertson was confident that it went back into the pagan period and that it might have Celtic as well as Germanic origins. Here we should note some of the most surprising of the conclusions of G.W.S. Barrow. He pointed out that a not inconsiderable number of Scottish small shires have names likely to be older than the ninth century and that the surprisingly regular appearance of an *eccles* name in each small shire not infrequently relating to an abandoned or lost site suggest to him 'that the shires were there when the first missionaries came'.[37] There is no doubt who first opened these amazing views of antiquity: Robertson.[38]

Robertson also displayed innovatory interest in the appearance from about the later eighth century of immunity clauses such that excluded from the immunity are what a tenth-century scribe termed *trimoda necessitas*: *fyrd* service, *burh* service, and bridge-building. The problems which arise are notoriously difficult; for the considerable sources are readily capable of more interpretations than one. At the same time the matter cannot be neglected, for it has to do with the essence of royal power and with possible major changes in this. Robertson dealt with these matters in *Scotland under Her Early Kings*. His account is, characteristically, squirreled away as a footnote to an appendix entitled 'The Kin'.[39] He assembled most of the relevant documents and concluded that military service was incumbent on all, or some, English monasteries from their earliest times, but not services to do with fortresses

---

35 Jolliffe, 'Era of Folk', 27–29.

36 Oliver Rackham, *The History of the Countryside* (London, 1986), 1–5. Cf. Carenza Lewis, Patrick Mitchell-Fox and Christopher Dyer, *Village, Hamlet and Field: Changing Medieval Settlements in Central England* (Manchester, 1997), 77–157.

37 Barrow, *Kingdom of the Scots*, 63–64. For a suggestion to the contrary, see John Blair, *The Church in Anglo-Saxon Society* (Oxford, 2005), 251 n.

38 For example Robertson, *Essays*, 130.

39 Robertson, *Scotland*, II, 337 n.

or bridges. These he argued to have been introduced under Æthelbald of Mercia in accordance with a royal edict mentioned in a record of a synod held at Gumley in 749. Stubbs made judicious use of Robertson's account of the *trimoda necessitas*.[40] But there was no further detailed discussion of these matters until W.H. Stevenson published a major (if rather petulant) article in 1914.[41] In it he argues against some of Robertson's main conclusions, maintaining that the burdens to which exclusions from exemptions relate were not new in the eighth century. In 1943 Stenton dealt with these matters with informed evasion.[42] There the matter rested until Eric John's contribution in 1958.[43] In this he contended that English monasteries had always enjoyed immunity from *expeditio* (*fyrd* service), that Æthelbald enforced their performance of fortification and bridge-building services, and that immunity from *fyrd* service was removed somewhat later by Offa. He maintains that Stevenson had been unfair to Robertson, above all in his arguments against the authenticity of the document which contains a crucial reference to Æthelbald's imposition of bridge and *burh* work.[44] The arguments were further and importantly pursued by Nicholas Brooks in 1971.[45] This considered the issues with learned agility. His comprehensive account brings forward considerations not mentioned by his predecessors, in particular that early exemptions could have varied from one monastery to another, and that the uniform obligation towards the 'common burdens' having originated in Mercia seems to have spread to other kingdoms only somewhat later. Brooks's discussion is very much longer than Robertson's; it is noticeable that their arguments resemble one another (very broadly) and that Robertson had assembled nearly all the relevant documents. In this, as in many other major questions he laid the foundations for later discussion, and firm foundations they were.

Robertson also anticipated other modern directions in research. Recent work on the late Anglo-Saxon church, for example that of John Blair, has centred round the process whereby the large parishes associated with 'minster' churches became split up into smaller ones associated with individual estate units. But Robertson was there, at least in regard to the north, by 1872. The parish of a minster church was 'often shorn of its original limits by the erection of other churches upon private property or *boclands*'. 'Field churches' were established. The addition of a burial ground raised them to the position of small parish churches which, in the course of time, gradually ceased to be dependent on the representative of the old minster.[46]

---

40 Stubbs, *Constitutional History*, I, 87, n.1.

41 W.H. Stevenson, 'Trinoda Necessitas', *EHR*, 29 (1914), 689–703.

42 F.M. Stenton, *Anglo-Saxon England* (Oxford, 1943), 286–289.

43 Eric John, 'The Imposition of the Common Burdens on the Lands of the English Church', *Bulletin of the Institute of Historical Research*, 31 (1958), 117–129, reprinted in Eric John, *Land Tenure in Early England* (Leicester, 1964), 64–79.

44 S 92; BCS, I, no. 178; John, *Land Tenure*, 66–67. The case for the authenticity of this key document has been greatly strengthened by Nicholas Brooks, 'The Development of Military Obligations in Eighth- and Early Ninth-Century England', in *England Before the Conquest. Studies in Primary Sources Presented to Dorothy Whitelock*, ed. Peter Clemoes and Kathleen Hughes (Cambridge, 1971), 69–84, at 76, n. 1.

45 Brooks, 'The Development', 69–84.

46 Robertson, *Essays*, 124–127; Blair, *Church*, chapters 7 and 8, 368–504.

Another important area of recent discovery has been the use of charters to open a prosopographical view of the politics of the tenth and eleventh centuries. One might think of the scholars concerned as following in the footsteps of Syme and later of Namier. In fact they have been following, unconsciously, Robertson. For Robertson used Kemble's *Codex Diplomaticus*[47] to illuminate late Anglo-Saxon history in a way unmatched for over 100 years. His essay 'The King's Kin' established and emphasised the extent to which the great men of tenth-century England were related to one another and to the royal house.[48] He realised, as no one else before Simon Keynes, that the regularities of precedence in the witness lists reveal something about political circumstances, for example the collapse and destruction of the old high nobility between 1005 and 1017, in particular the fall of men once high in favour as Eadric Streona rose to power.[49] His interpretation of the 'anti-monastic reaction' of 975–978, largely in terms of the rivalries of the great ealdormen, anticipates most of what has been said on the subject since Fisher wrote in 1952.[50] Robertson's essay on the king's kin was supported by three others, one on royal wives, one on the policy of Dunstan, and one on coronation. He took all three subjects to a level of sophistication not otherwise reached until recently.

Some examples of his perception follow. He uses charter witnessings to show the fluctuating status of queens and queen mothers and to bring out, for example, the great importance of Edgar's second wife as compared to his first.[51] He analyses the career of Dunstan with regard to his political significance, and brings out the important extent to which he was not a 'reformer'.[52] He noticed, as historians have hardly done until recently, the sheer forcefulness of the tenth-century kings, for example, showing how the forfeiture to the king for disobedience involves lands held from others than the king, and pointed out how Cnut's law in this regard anticipated medieval practice.[53] And he saw how the violence of authorities would go further down, quoting Edgar: 'if any generate man neglect his lord's tribute ... be obdurate and think to resist it ... the lord's anger will so greatly increase, that he will neither grant him property, nor life'.[54]

---

47 *Codex Diplomaticus Aevi Saxonici*, ed. J.M. Kemble (6 vols, London, 1839–1848).

48 Robertson, *Essays*, 177–189.

49 Robertson, *Essays*, 180, 182–183, 185–188. Cf. Simon Keynes, 'Cnut's Earls', in *The Reign of Cnut: King of England, Denmark and Norway*, ed. Alexander Rumble (London, 1994), 27–42.

50 Robertson, *Essays*, 175–182; D.J.V. Fisher, 'The Anti-Monastic Reaction in the Reign of King Edward the Martyr', *Cambridge Historical Journal*, 10 (1950–1952), 254–270.

51 Robertson, *Essays*, 166–171. For more recent work on queens and queenship see, in particular, Pauline Stafford, *Queens, Concubines and Dowagers. The King's Wife in the Early Middle Ages* (London, 1983), and Pauline Stafford, *Queen Emma and Queen Edith. Queenship and Women's Power in Eleventh-Century England* (Oxford, 1997).

52 Robertson, *Essays*, 189–200. Cf. N.P. Brooks, 'The Career of St. Dunstan', in *St. Dunstan, his Life, Times and Cult*, ed. Nigel Ramsay, Margaret Sparks and Tim Tatton-Brown (Woodbridge, 1992), 1–24. See also Cubitt, this vol.

53 Robertson, *Essays*, p. lvi.

54 IV Edgar, 1, 2; *Gesetze*, ed. Liebermann, I, 206. An extreme example of legislative violence is that of the brutality of laws of Edgar, chiefly known from an episode in an account

Robertson's account of the tenth century is marked not only by a strong sense of likely political reality, but also by an equally strong awareness of institutional change and of the relevance of Continental parallels. Thus he constantly emphasises the importance of the change from a small shire based to a hundredally based system of local government in the tenth century, and fully appreciated the significance of the failure to extend the hundredal and frankpledge systems to the far North and North-West.[55] He repeatedly signals the relationship between the means and rhetoric used to establish unified regimes in Germany and England.[56]

Some of the almost impossibly intricate parts of Robertson's *Essays* reflect his deep interest in numismatics and in the history of measurement. He sometimes seems almost obsessed in his wish to show how wergeld and status, land measurements, the appropriate endowment of men of different statuses, all sorts of units, rules and assumptions, were related to one another over much of Europe. A number-dominated approach can be too easily dismissed. Most striking is his demonstration of how often the small shires of Northern England and of Scotland consisted of 12 vills.[57] This seems too artificial to be true, but Robertson's argument is supported by the work of Barrow.[58] What Robertson reminds us of is that to look at almost any of the evidence we have for the socio-legal systems of early Europe is to be faced with innumerable and interrelated regularities which should not automatically be assumed to be merely notional. With social systems as with languages it may be that the older the system, the more complex and rigid the rules. In their social arrangements, as in their poetry and art, pattern was a dominating theme for such peoples as the Anglo-Saxons. We cannot get away from hides and carucates, from hundreds large and small, from shires large and small, from intricate palimpsests of patterns of tens and twelves, fives and sevens. The aversion from the tedious semi-scrutable complications of these systems is summed up in astonishing omissions from *English Historical Documents*, vol. I: those of the 'Tribal Hidage' and the 'Burghal Hidage'. These documents are fundamental to the understanding of Anglo-Saxon government and society. Robertson was a pioneer in showing why this should be so.

It is not difficult to find other instances of Robertson's imaginative learning. An example is this. Many owe to Lynn White's book of 1962 the notion that the introduction of the stirrup and the horseshoe may, by changing the possibilities of cavalry warfare, have transformed the organisation of states and societies.[59] Robertson wrote as follows 90 years previously: 'Without the stirrup and the horse shoe the mounted man at arms ... who used his spear as a lance in rest and wore down opposition by the weight of his charge would never have been called into existence'.[60]

---

by Lantfred of the translation and miracles of St Swithun: Patrick Wormald, *The Making of English Law*, I, *Legislation and its Limits* (Oxford, 1999), 125–127.

55 Robertson, *Scotland*, II, 338–339; Robertson, *Essays*, 130.
56 Robertson, *Essays*, 179, 214–215.
57 Robertson, *Essays*, 122–123.
58 Barrow, *The Kingdom of the Scots*, 32–33.
59 Lynn White Jr., *Medieval Technology and Social Change* (Oxford, 1962), esp. 14–38.
60 Robertson, *Essays*, pp. xiii–xiv. Here Robertson discusses the significance of weaponry in a manner which among modern historians only Nicholas Brooks has paralleled, in particular

The greatest of Robertson's gifts was the power of integration of socio-legal changes and political development. He said: '... in the regulation of the code, and under the forms of the cartulary, often lie hidden the real causes of events'.[61] He had the capacity, shared by none of his successors, not even, to the same extent, by Maitland, to relate legal to social change and both to state formation. He believed that through much of the Dark Ages a widely prevailing succession system in north-western Europe was one which joined family inheritance to individual possession which was not necessarily permanent. A characteristic was that land was held by a family within a certain number of degrees of kinship, that the family had some kind of elected head or representative, and that the death of one member of the possessing family would be followed by a reallocation of property.[62] This is the kind of system which we see among the nobility in tenth-century Germany, in parage tenure in northern France, very probably in the system on which early Anglo-Saxon kings succeeded. It was characteristic of many forms of peasant tenure.[63] Robertson saw the processes of state formation and in particular of state centralisation changing this system, once more or less universal among the significantly free, for a variety of reasons. One was that the maintenance of the unity of the state depended upon a different system of royal inheritance. This is Thomas Charles-Edwards's argument put in a somewhat different way.[64] The creation of provincial authorities who were not subordinated princely families, created a kind of relationship and a quasi-tenure for which what we might loosely call a parage system (for the want of a better current word) was inappropriate. Robertson saw feudal tenure as tending to go with primogeniture, and the effect of feudalism and the centralising state to have been such as to reduce to the lower region of society systems in which the inheritance units were extended families.[65]

> Wherever the adoption of the benefice had introduced the principle of settled military service, the representatives of the earlier freemen had invariably sunk into a class of agricultural peasantry, free, but occupying an intermediate station between the noble and the læt or serf.[66]

He argued that the persistence of extended family systems of land tenure in – for example – Ireland was not something specifically Celtic. Rather it was a more general system which persisted in Ireland in consequence of the absence of effective

---

in his 'Arms, Status and Warfare in Late-Saxon England', in *Ethelred the Unready: Papers to the Millenary Conference*, ed. D.H. Hill, British Archaeological Reports, British Series, 69 (Oxford, 1978), 81–103; and 'Weapons and Armour in the *Battle of Maldon*', in *The Battle of Maldon*, ed. D.C. Scragg (Manchester, 1991), 208–219, reprinted in Nicholas Brooks, *Communities and Warfare* (London and Rio Grande, 2000), 138–161, 162–174 respectively.

61 Robertson, *Essays*, p. ix.
62 Robertson, *Essays*, pp. lxii–lxviii, 152–153; Robertson, *Scotland*, I, 101–102, 237, 241–244; II, 455, 465.
63 Robertson, *Essays*, pp. lvii–lxx.
64 Cf. above at n. 28.
65 Robertson, *Essays*, pp. vii–lxix, esp. lxix.
66 Robertson, *Scotland*, I, 244; Robertson, *Essays*, 152–153.

large-scale central authority there.[67] He is particularly interesting in arguing how the relationship between the old *Landrecht* and the newer *Lehnsrecht* in the *Sachsenspiegel* shows the interaction, in the thirteenth century, between an older, extended-family-centred system and one introduced by centralising authorities.[68] Robertson's case is very similar to that now widely accepted on the progress from *Sippe* to *Geschlecht*, from inheritance in terms of the extended family to inheritance in terms of something like the nuclear family.[69]

Where did Robertson's learning come from? Like all the great Victorian medievalists he could not have studied his subject as part of an undergraduate course. It is, however, important that in his day Anglo-Saxon could form part of the elementary studies of the educated classes and that interest in Anglo-Saxon history was fairly widespread. Thus in the 1830s Stubbs was taught Anglo-Saxon at an undistinguished school at Knaresborough.[70] In the same period the daughter of an eminent lawyer could be taught, at home, 'a little Anglo-Saxon' (apart from five other languages).[71] Such a bibliographical survey as that by John Petheram (1840) is indicative of the scope and scale of Anglo-Saxon interests among the educated.[72] During Robertson's time at Oxford there were Anglo-Saxonist scholars there who could have influenced him. It is too true that the terms of appointment to the Rawlinson chair of Anglo-Saxon made it appear as something of a joke before their reform in 1858.[73] Nevertheless some of the holders were distinguished. Among them was James Ingram (1803–1808), who continued his devotion to Anglo-Saxon studies at Oxford until his death in 1850.[74] His successor, J.J. Conybeare, did distinguished work on Anglo-Saxon poetry. He also had some distinction in geology and chemistry.[75] His intellectual career, like Robertson's, indicates how far application could take an intelligent man when the subjects of his interest laboured under less secondary literature than now they do. (Gladstone's Homeric and other studies tell the same tale.) So, Robertson's time at Oxford could have helped foster his Anglo-Saxon interests and his scholarly career fits into a pattern not too uncommonly found among a nineteenth-century elite.

The works of Kemble and most nineteenth-century historians of Anglo-Saxon England were in some degree contributions to a debate about freedom. This is true of Robertson; though his views on the political bearing of his studies were unusual.

---

67 Robertson, *Essays*, 160.

68 Robertson, *Essays*, 153.

69 For example. Robert Fossier, *Enfance de l'Europe. Aspects économiques et sociaux* (2 vols, Paris, 1982), I, 319–322; II, 912.

70 James Campbell, 'William Stubbs', *ODNB*, s.v.

71 Ursula Ridley, *Cecilia. The Life and Letters of Cecilia Ridley 1819–1849* (London, 1958), 16.

72 John Petheram, *An Historical Sketch of the Progress and Present State of Anglo-Saxon Literature in England* (facsimile reprint, Edinburgh, 2000, introduction by Karen Thomson).

73 Tenure was for five years only; the holder had to be unmarried, not a Fellow of the Society of Antiquaries, and never to become one: Charles Harding Firth, *The School of English Language and Literature* (Oxford and London, 1909), 10.

74 W.A. Greenhill, revised by J.D. Haigh, 'Ingram, James', *ODNB*, s.v..

75 H.S. Torrens, 'Conybeare, John Josias', *ODNB*, s.v..

The free Germans were idolised by some of his contemporaries; Robertson saw them as dominated by a fiercely exclusive nobility and yeomanry. To quote: 'The theory that every man is born into this world with equal rights may, or may not, be correct, but it is a theory which would have been repudiated by every member of a free community, whether *Adaling* or *Friling*, with contempt'.[76] He saw feudalism as liberating, because it broke the mould of exclusivity and opened careers to talent.[77] But it is hard to find that politically related concerns were at the root of Robertson's driving energy as a historian.

I think he sought to know the truth about the past in a prematurely professional way. In this it is likely that some of the principal influences on Robertson were Scottish. Not only did he write on Scotland, he was very conscious of Scotland as 'land of my forefathers'. The covers of his books bore a lion rampant, and Robertson had himself painted in full Highland fig.[78] The great eighteenth-century Scottish historian William Robertson was a collateral ancestor. Medieval history in Scotland was on a better basis than it was in England. There was a stronger tradition of exact scholarship. This is represented by, for example, *The Annals of Scotland* published by David Dalrymple, Lord Hailes, between 1776 and 1779. This is a narrative of the history of medieval Scotland such that every fact is attested by reference to an original source. England had nothing like it. Furthermore, the historians of medieval Scotland remained in some important ways ahead of their English counterparts, not least in the publication of texts, until the collapse of Scottish historiography in the later nineteenth century.[79] The intellectual tradition of the Scottish enlightenment was such as to put history into a sociological context and to stimulate comparative studies. For example, a major review bringing out the significance of Frisian institutions for the study of those in England appeared in the *Edinburgh Review* in 1819.[80]

The very nature of Robertson's position as a Scot interested in early English history could well have affected his intellectual development and attitudes independently of his likely share in the legacy of the Scottish enlightenment. Students of Anglo-Saxon England are too apt to forget that until c. 1000 England extended to the Forth. The English of the Lothians became culturally dominant both in language and in law in what by dynastic accident came to be called the land of the Irish: Scotland. To look at southern England from the English lands between the Forth and the Tees is to gain a perspective not normally to be gained from Oxford or Reading. Robertson was the first, and with one exception, the only historian[81] to have sought to make serious comparisons between those step-sisters, Scotland and England. It was he who made the crucial observation that the structures of local authority north of the

---

76 Robertson, *Essays*, p. v.
77 *Essays*, xx–xxi, lxviii.
78 Banerji, 'Robertson, Eben William'.
79 Marinell Ash, *The Strange Death of Scottish Historiography* (Edinburgh, 1980).
80 *Edinburgh Review*, 32 (1819), 1–16, an anonymous account of Tileman Dothias Wiarda's *Neueste Ostfriesische Geschichte* (Berlin, 1818).
81 The exception is G.W.S. Barrow, 'Kingship in Medieval England and Scotland', in his *Scotland and its Neighbours in the Middle Ages* (London and Rio Grande, 1992), 23–54, originally published as 'Das mittelalterliche englische und schottische Königtum: Ein Vergleich', *Historisches Jahrbuch*, 102 (1982), 362–89.

Danish kingdom of York remained those which had probably once existed in most of southern England, but which had been largely transformed by the reforms of the tenth-century English kings.[82]

Such insight marks Robertson as the most creative of historians of Anglo-Saxon England; he anticipated much written since by historians some of whom have not known his works, and the value of what he wrote is anything but exhausted. His was an astonishing achievement for a short Victorian life. Robertson died in 1874 at the age of 59. Even the only modern historian to do him justice, Geoffrey Barrow describes him, a shade unkindly, as 'exasperatingly over-learned' though 'remarkably perceptive'.[83] But then, not too many of us would resent such an epitaph.

---

82 Robertson, *Essays*, 120; cf. F.W. Maitland, 'Northumbrian Tenures', *EHR*, 5 (1890), 625–632.

83 Barrow, *The Kingdom of the Scots*, 7.

Chapter 5

Anglo-Saxon Charters: Lost and Found

Simon Keynes

The corpus of Anglo-Saxon charters was first defined by John Mitchell Kemble (1807–1857), in his six-volume *Codex Diplomaticus Ævi Saxonici* (1839–1848); and although his work had many limitations it remains by any standards a remarkable achievement.[1] Kemble's edition was soon superseded by Walter de Gray Birch's three-volume *Cartularium Saxonicum* (1885–1893), at least for the period to 975.[2] Within two years of the publication of Birch's third volume, two noted scholars had expressed their view, 'It cannot be said that the O.E. charters have yet been edited';[3] and, two years after that, another ventured his conviction that a century from his time there would be 'a critical edition of the Anglo-Saxon charters in which the philologist and the palaeographer, the annalist and the formulist will have winnowed the grain of truth from the chaff of imposture'.[4] There matters stood for many years. The value of charters as evidence for understanding of the Anglo-Saxon period, in all its aspects, was fully appreciated;[5] but although the students of H.M. Chadwick, in Cambridge, produced editions of the vernacular documents,[6] a further call for a new edition appears not to have been heard.[7]

---

1 J.M. Kemble, *Codes Diplomaticus Ævi Saxonici* (6 vols, London, 1839–1848), cited as KCD (with number). Light is thrown on Kemble's working methods by his materials for a seventh volume of the *Codex Diplomaticus*, now in Yale University, Beinecke Library, Osborn MS fd.57. For Kemble himself, see the entry on him in *The Blackwell Encyclopaedia of Anglo-Saxon England*, ed. Michael Lapidge, John Blair, Simon Keynes and Donald Scragg (Oxford, 1999), 269, with references; see also *John Mitchell Kemble (1807–57)*, ed. S. Keynes and Jonathan Smith (forthcoming).

2 BCS was published in parts, initially by Whiting & Co. The publisher failed in 1892, and parts 29–32, completing vol. III, were published by C.J. Clark between August 1892 and March 1893. The new publisher announced a change of plan to the subscribers, on the inside cover of part 29, whereby vols. I–III were deemed to constitute a 'First Series' and a 'Second Series' was projected in three further volumes, depending 'on the support which may be extended to Mr. de Gray Birch'. Evidently no such support was forthcoming.

3 *The Crawford Collection of Early Charters and Documents now in the Bodleian Library*, ed. A.S. Napier and W.H. Stevenson (Oxford, 1895), p. viii.

4 F.W. Maitland, *Domesday Book and Beyond* (Cambridge, 1897), 520.

5 F.M. Stenton, *The Latin Charters of the Anglo-Saxon Period* (Oxford, 1955); Whitelock, in *EHD*, I, 369–82.

6 *Select English Historical Documents of the Ninth and Tenth Centuries*, ed. F.E. Harmer (Cambridge, 1914); *Anglo-Saxon Wills*, ed. Dorothy Whitelock (Cambridge, 1930); *Anglo-Saxon Charters*, ed. A.J. Robertson (Cambridge, 1939), 2nd edn (Cambridge, 1956); F.E. Harmer, *Anglo-Saxon Writs* (Manchester, 1952).

7 David Knowles, *The Prospects of Medieval Studies*, Inaugural Lecture, 25 October 1947 (Cambridge, 1947), 10–11.

The study of Anglo-Saxon charters was put on a new footing by the 'Leicester' series of regional calendars, initiated in 1953,[8] and this series must have contributed significantly to the emergence of a fresh view, in the 1960s, of the challenge facing historians of the Anglo-Saxon period. In 1964–1965 a committee formed of representatives of the British Academy and of the Royal Historical Society met several times to consider the possibility of producing a new edition of the entire corpus of charters. A minority of four of its members felt there was no need for a new edition, except of the Latin charters of the period 975–1066; but a majority of six recommended that a joint committee be set up to tackle the problem.[9] The first meeting of a formally-constituted 'British Academy – Royal Historical Society Joint Committee on Anglo-Saxon Charters' was held on 8 July 1966. It was quickly decided that the charters would need to be edited in a series of separate volumes, each of which would contain texts formerly preserved in the archives of a particular religious house (or group of houses), though (interestingly) the decision to adopt this procedure was more a matter of practicality than an expression of any detailed appreciation, at this stage, of the view that charters should be edited and criticized in the context of the history, endowment, and muniments of each of the houses in question.

The re-awakened scholarly interest in Anglo-Saxon charters, in the 1960s, found expression in other ways. Nicholas Brooks embarked upon a close study of the pre-Conquest charters from the archives of Christ Church, Canterbury, demonstrating just how much could be gained from close palaeographical and diplomatic analysis of the material.[10] Never before had the surviving pre-Conquest muniments from the archives of a single religious house been subjected to such close scrutiny; and the benefit to historical knowledge was clear, most notably in the enhanced understanding of the fortunes of the church of Canterbury in the late eighth and ninth centuries.[11] At much the same time, Dr Pierre Chaplais, Reader in Diplomatic in the University of Oxford, published a series of seminal articles on charters, in the *Journal of the Society of Archivists*. In 1965, Chaplais challenged the prevailing supposition that royal diplomas were drawn up by royal scribes, arguing that they

---

8 H.P.R. Finberg, *The Early Charters of Devon and Cornwall* (Leicester, 1953), 2nd edn (Leicester, 1963); Cyril Hart, *The Early Charters of Essex*, 2 pts (Leicester, 1957), 2nd edn (Leicester, 1971); H.P.R. Finberg, *The Early Charters of the West Midlands* (Leicester, 1961), 2nd edn (Leicester, 1972); H.P.R. Finberg, *The Early Charters of Wessex* (Leicester, 1964); C.R. Hart, *The Early Charters of Eastern England* (Leicester, 1966); C.R. Hart, *The Early Charters of Northern England and the North Midlands* (Leicester, 1975); Margaret Gelling, *The Early Charters of the Thames Valley* (Leicester, 1979).

9 The meetings were convened by Sir Goronwy Edwards. The majority report was attested by Dr Pierre Chaplais, Sir Goronwy Edwards, Professor H.P.R. Finberg, Professor V.H. Galbraith, Dr N.R. Ker, and Mr P.H. Sawyer; and the minority report was attested by Professor R.R. Darlington, Dr F.E. Harmer, Professor Dorothy Whitelock and Professor Francis Wormald.

10 N.P. Brooks, 'The Pre-Conquest Charters of Christ Church, Canterbury', unpublished DPhil thesis, University of Oxford (1968).

11 N.P. Brooks, *The Early History of the Church of Canterbury: Christ Church from 597 to 1066* (Leicester, 1984), 111–206.

were drawn up in ecclesiastical scriptoria, and that their authenticity depended not on autograph signatures, or royal seals, but on the trust placed in bishops and abbots by kings and by the beneficiaries.[12] In 1966, he took matters a stage further, arguing that the eleventh-century vernacular writs were also drawn up by ecclesiastical scribes.[13] Thereafter, Chaplais turned back to the earlier period. He examined several of the earliest Anglo-Saxon charters extant in their 'original' single-sheet form, and drew attention to the physical features which suggest that a charter had been used in a ceremony of conveyance, and was thus presumptively authentic.[14] Finally, he challenged the prevailing supposition that charters had been introduced into England by Archbishop Theodore, towards the end of the seventh century, arguing that a better case could be made for St Augustine, at the beginning of the seventh century.[15] The four articles were reprinted, as a group, in 1971;[16] and, by questioning so much that had previously been taken for granted, they exerted a profound influence on the study of Anglo-Saxon charters thereafter.[17]

The new edition was planned from the outset in the knowledge that publication of Peter Sawyer's *Anglo-Saxon Charters: an Annotated List and Bibliography* was imminent.[18] Indeed, it was Sawyer's 'annotated list' which, when published in 1968, provided scholars with the essential work of reference, at once systematic and comprehensive: the corpus of royal diplomas was set out in a chronological series, complemented by separate lists of vernacular writs, wills, and other forms of documentary record. Quite simply, the publication of Sawyer's catalogue transformed the ways in which the extant documentary records could be approached and understood; and it must have seemed that the material had been processed, organised and defined, once and for all. It has to be admitted, on the other hand, that the new edition made a slow start, with only three volumes published between

---

12 Pierre Chaplais, 'The Origin and Authenticity of the Royal Anglo-Saxon Diploma', *Journal of the Society of Archivists*, 3.2 (1965), 48–61.

13 Pierre Chaplais, 'The Anglo-Saxon Chancery: From the Diploma to the Writ', *Journal of the Society of Archivists*, 3.4 (1966), 160–76.

14 Pierre Chaplais, 'Some Early Anglo-Saxon Diplomas on Single Sheets: Originals or Copies?', *Journal of the Society of Archivists*, 3.7 (1968), 315–36.

15 Pierre Chaplais, 'Who Introduced Charters into England? The Case for Augustine', *Journal of the Society of Archivists*, 3.10 (1969), 526–42.

16 *Prisca Munimenta: Studies in Archival & Administrative History presented to Dr A.E.J. Hollaender*, ed. Felicity Ranger (London, 1973), 28–107. Other papers by Dr Chaplais were reprinted in his *Essays in Medieval Diplomacy and Administration* (London, 1981); see also Pierre Chaplais, 'The Royal Anglo-Saxon "Chancery" of the Tenth Century Revisited', *Studies in Medieval History presented to R.H.C. Davis*, ed. Henry Mayr-Harting and R.I. Moore (London, 1985), 41–51.

17 Nicholas Brooks, 'Anglo-Saxon Charters: the Work of the Last Twenty Years', *ASE*, 3 (1974), 211–34, reprinted, with a postscript covering the period 1973–1998, in Nicholas Brooks, *Anglo-Saxon Myths: State and Church 400–1066* (London, 2000), 181–215; see also Margaret Gelling, 'Recent Work on Anglo-Saxon Charters', *Local Historian*, 13.4 (1978), 209–16.

18 Peter Sawyer, *Anglo-Saxon Charters: an Annotated List and Bibliography* (London, 1968).

1973 and 1988,[19] followed in 1991 by a supplementary volume of facsimiles.[20] More recently, by virtue of the sustained support of various funding agencies, and the hard work of several editors, the project has been gathering some momentum. A further eight volumes were published in the decade between 1995 and 2005[21] and several more are currently in advanced stages of preparation.[22] The older abbreviations, such as 'KCD', for Kemble's *Codex Diplomaticus* and 'BCS', for Birch's *Cartularium Saxonicum*, will long remain a necessary part of the jargon; but in addition to 'S', for 'Sawyer', we will soon need to become familiar with a new range of abbreviations, to indicate where an authoritative text of a given charter is to be found among the component volumes of the new edition.[23] And if the project is completed within 50 years of its inception, so by 2016, it will be thanks in no small part to the efforts of Nicholas Brooks himself, who has served as Chairman of the Joint Committee on Anglo-Saxon Charters since 1993.

Of course, the concept of 'completion', whether applied to a catalogue which aims to be comprehensive, or to an edition which aspires to be definitive, should not be taken literally. Sawyer's catalogue helps simply by virtue of its own existence to flush out further items which have escaped attention. The 'new' material which has come to light in the past 40 years includes texts of several charters previously unknown to Anglo-Saxon scholarship and additional or 'better' texts of charters already registered in the catalogue. Much of this material has been found lurking in unsuspected places; and it is supplemented by the discoveries and refinements which

---

19 *Charters of Rochester*, ed. Alistair Campbell, Anglo-Saxon Charters, 1 (London, 1973); *Charters of Burton Abbey*, ed. P.H. Sawyer, Anglo-Saxon Charters, 2 (Oxford, 1979); *Charters of Sherborne*, ed. M.A. O'Donovan, Anglo-Saxon Charters, 3 (Oxford, 1988).

20 *Facsimiles of Anglo-Saxon Charters*, ed. Simon Keynes, Anglo-Saxon Charters, Supplementary Series, 1 (Oxford, 1991).

21 *Charters of St Augustine's Abbey, Canterbury*, ed. S.E. Kelly, Anglo-Saxon Charters, 4 (Oxford, 1995); *Charters of Shaftesbury Abbey*, ed. S.E. Kelly, Anglo-Saxon Charters, 5 (Oxford, 1995); *Charters of Selsey*, ed. S.E. Kelly, Anglo-Saxon Charters, 6 (Oxford, 1998); *Charters of Abingdon Abbey*, ed. S.E. Kelly, 2 pts, Anglo-Saxon Charters, 7–8 (Oxford, 2000–2001); *Charters of the New Minster, Winchester*, ed. Sean Miller, Anglo-Saxon Charters, 9 (Oxford, 2001); *Charters of St Paul's, London*, ed. S.E. Kelly, Anglo-Saxon Charters, 10 (Oxford, 2004); *Charters of Malmesbury Abbey*, ed. S.E. Kelly, Anglo-Saxon Charters, 11 (Oxford, 2005).

22 *Charters of St Albans Abbey*, ed. Julia Crick, Anglo-Saxon Charters, 12 (Oxford, 2007); *Charters of Bath and Wells*, ed. S.E. Kelly, Anglo-Saxon Charters, 13 (Oxford, 2007); *Charters of Bury St Edmunds*, ed. Kathryn Lowe and Sarah Foot; *Charters of Peterborough*, ed. S.E. Kelly; *Charters of Christ Church, Canterbury*, ed. Nicholas Brooks and S.E. Kelly; *Charters of Wilton Abbey*, ed. Rebecca Rushforth; *Charters of Westminster*, ed. Richard Mortimer.

23 Charters are cited below by their number in Sawyer's catalogue, followed (when necessary) by a formulation identifying the text, whether by reference to BCS or KCD, or (and where possible) to the number of the charter in a particular volume of the new series: e.g. S 89 (BCS 154), S 300 (*Charters of St Augustine's*, ed. Kelly, no. 21), S 356 (*Charters of Malmesbury*, ed. Kelly, no. 20), S 367a (*Charters of St Paul's*, ed. Kelly, no. 10), S 745 (*Charters of New Minster*, ed. Miller, no. 23), S 876 (*Charters of Abingdon*, ed. Kelly, no. 124) and S 1036 (KCD 813).

arise from the process of working systematically through already familiar records of a particular religious house, which might range from obits in calendars and lists of benefactors, to cartularies and house-chronicles.[24] A revised, updated and searchable form of 'Sawyer' is already available on the website of the BA-RHS project (itself dubbed 'Kemble' in symbolic appreciation of the pioneer),[25] pending publication of a second edition. It serves not least as a guide to the corpus as a whole, which might otherwise be in danger of breaking down into its separate archival parts; and it aims at the same time to record all references to charters now lost, and to bring together all information bearing on the history of a particular text.[26] Seemingly ephemeral information of this kind can contribute significantly to the perception of larger patterns and might well prove to be of value when assessing evidence of a particular period, region, or religious house, or associated with a particular person. Yet even a 'Revised Sawyer' will never be definitive and my purpose is simply to suggest that for as long as the search continues, it will prove to be worthwhile.

The interest of Anglo-Saxon charters lies in the value of the documents themselves as evidence for the period in which they were produced (whether genuine or forged) and in the study of the use that has been made of them, for historical and other purposes, from the Anglo-Saxon period to present day. The varied practices employed (or not employed) in the care of an abbey's muniments, from the Anglo-Saxon period to the Dissolution of the Monasteries, constitute the first part of a long story, but lie beyond the scope of this review.[27] The next stage is represented by the

---

24 For example, additional material found in the texts of certain charters in the 'White Book of St Augustine's' (Kew, National Archives, E 164/27): see *Charters of St Augustine's*, ed. Kelly, pp. li–liv, with reference to S 501 (*Charters of St Augustine's*, no. 27), dated 944, and S 875 (*Charters of St Augustine's*, no. 30), dated 990.

25 The 'Kemble' website < www.trin.cam.ac.uk/kemble/ > has been developed with support from the AHRC, the British Academy and Trinity College, Cambridge. The initial work on the 'Revised Sawyer' was undertaken by Dr Susan Kelly; and it has been developed further, as the 'Electronic Sawyer', by Dr Rebecca Rushforth and others. In addition to the revised and updated form of Sawyer's catalogue, the 'Electronic Sawyer' incorporates the Latin or vernacular texts of the charters themselves. The 'Kemble' website also provides a classified list of all Anglo-Saxon charters preserved in single-sheet form (with images).

26 For the treatment of 'lost and incomplete' charters in the original edition, see S, pp. vii and 442–83. The guiding principle is that any written document which has left any trace of its existence should be accorded the dignity of a Sawyer-entry and duly indexed.

27 For the post-Conquest period, see Michael Clanchy, *From Memory to Written Record: England 1066–1307*, 2nd edn (Oxford, 1993), 145–84. For the muniments of Glastonbury abbey, see Lesley Abrams, *Anglo-Saxon Glastonbury: Church and Endowment* (Woodbridge, 1996), 14–20; see also J.D. Martin, *The Cartularies and Registers of Peterborough Abbey* (Northampton, 1978), and R.M. Thomson, *The Archives of the Abbey of Bury St Edmunds* (Woodbridge, 1980). An inventory roll in Ghent reveals the presence there, in the fourteenth century, of what would appear to have been a vernacular writ of Edward the Confessor; see Auguste van Lokeren, *Chartes et documents de l'abbaye de Saint-Pierre au Mont Blandin à Gand* (2 vols, Ghent, 1868), II, no. 996, Section 25, no. 18 ('Edewardus rex Anglie anglice scriptum'). A seemingly comprehensive inventory of muniments of the Carthusian priory of Sheen, in Surrey, reveals that single-sheet 'originals' of the charters of King Edgar and King Edward the Confessor granting land at Lewisham and Greenwich to Ghent abbey (S 728 and

variety of evidence bearing on the activities of Henry VIII's agents, as they set about their business in the 1530s and on the fate, not only of the dissolute members of the dissolved religious houses, but also of their lands, buildings, treasures, muniments and books. It would be interesting, in particular, to undertake a detailed study of the mechanisms by which monastic archives were dispersed, in the mid-sixteenth century, and by which charters, cartularies and other records were either retained in the hands of the families who acquired the formerly monastic lands or buildings, or came to be released sooner or later into wider circulation among antiquaries and collectors; but, perhaps understandably, this has not been a priority of historians of the early modern period. Such a study would be of considerable interest for its own sake, and it would also contribute much to our understanding of the surviving muniments themselves.[28] We may or may not regret the passing of the monasteries, founded in the case of so many Benedictine houses long before the Norman Conquest, by kings, queens, bishops, ealdormen and thegns, who thought that their good works (and the credit that would redound to them in respect of those good works) would last for ever. It often proves to be the case that the charters retained their archival identity in the care of the descendants of those who took over the estates in the sixteenth century and, so, by extension in the custody of the county record offices where their family and estate papers are held. It is instructive, at the same time, to try to keep track of the movements of muniments in the seventeenth century and thereafter, and to relate one's understanding of this process to the activities of antiquaries during the same period, and so in turn to the frequently complex tales of the dispersal of their own working papers.

In 1535 Sir John Prise and his servant William Say collected the texts of a number of monastic foundation charters.[29] The collection was thought not to survive; but its recent identification as the origin of a number of sixteenth- and seventeenth-century transcripts has helped to clarify some otherwise intractable textual problems.[30] In January 1536 Thomas Bedyll was at Ramsey Abbey, looking for evidence which might be germane to the king's purposes. He rooted through

---

S 1002) were at Sheen in the late fifteenth century (BL Cotton MS Otho B. xiv, fos 5–149, at 84v); for the charters in question, see Simon Keynes, 'The Æthelings in Normandy', *ANS*, 13 (1991), 173–205, at 179–80. I am grateful in this connection to Richard Sharpe and Nicholas Vincent.

28 Essential guidance is available on the website of the 'English Monastic Archives' project <www.ucl.ac.uk/history/englishmonasticarchives/index.htm>, conceived by Dr Nigel Ramsay and based at University College, London. On the use of the muniments of Glastonbury abbey by the Thynnes of Longleat, see Kate Harris, *Glastonbury Abbey Records at Longleat House: a Summary List*, Somerset Record Society, 81 (Taunton, 1991), pp. vii–x.

29 N.R. Ker, 'Sir John Prise', *The Library*, 5th ser., 10 (1955), 1–24, reprinted in his *Books, Collectors and Libraries*, ed. A.G. Watson (London, 1985), 471–96, at 472–3 and 496; see also Brian Smith, 'The Archives', *Hereford Cathedral: a History*, ed. Gerald Aylmer and John Tiller (London, 2000), 544–56, at 546–7 and the entry on Prise, by Huw Pryce, in *ODNB*, s.v., with further references.

30 For the 'Prise-Say Register', see Nicholas Vincent, 'The Early Years of Keynsham Abbey', *Transactions of the Bristol and Gloucestershire Archaeological Society* 111 (1993), 95–113, at 95–6; *Charters of St Augustine's*, ed. Kelly, pp. lix–lx; and Catherine P. Hall,

the abbey's charters, and wrote at once to his master (Thomas Cromwell) to tell him what he had found: a charter of King Edgar, and a charter of King Edward the Confessor, from which it appeared that the king acted as supreme head of the church of England.[31] Anglo-Saxon (and later) charters were regularly adduced as evidence in the learned discussions which took place at meetings of the Elizabethan Society of Antiquaries, attended by William Camden, Sir Robert Cotton and others.[32] Among their number was Joseph Holland, who seems to have owned at least one Anglo-Saxon manuscript, as well as some charters, cartularies and coins. On one occasion he showed his fellow antiquaries 'a piece of a charter of king Cenulfus', in order to illustrate a point about Anglo-Saxon law;[33] and in a debate about dukes he remarked, 'I have an aunceint Saxon charter made by kinge Edgar, whereunto there are six dukes witnesses', whom he names, presumably with reference to another single sheet in his possession.[34] One can almost see Holland pulling charters from every pocket and sharing his enthusiasm with others. Another of the antiquaries was Francis Tate, who kept a journal of their proceedings, and who seems also to have had some Anglo-Saxon charters in his possession.[35] And these two were only among the first of those who, in the seventeenth and eighteenth centuries, appreciated the potential of charters for various political, religious, legal and antiquarian purposes.

The example set by the antiquaries of the Elizabethan age was followed by those of various persuasions and interests; for while antiquarian studies had long been

---

'Matthew Parker as Annotator: the Case of Winchester Cathedral MS XXB', *Transactions of the Cambridge Bibliographical Society* 10 (1995), 642–5.

31 The original letters are in BL Cotton Cleopatra E. iv, fos 233–4, printed by John Wise and W.M. Noble, *Ramsey Abbey: its Rise and Fall* (Huntingdon, 1881), 140–44. See also David Cozens, 'The Demise of Ramsey Abbey', *Anglo-Saxons: Studies Presented to Cyril Roy Hart*, ed. Simon Keynes and A.P. Smyth (Dublin, 2006), 288–97. The charters were evidently the (lost) single-sheet 'originals' of S 798 (Edgar) and S 1030 (Edward), of which the latter has now come to light at Holkham Hall (below, p. 60).

32 Many of the original papers as read at the meetings of the society are preserved in BL Cotton Faustina E. v, and were published by Thomas Hearne, *A Collection of Curious Discourses Written by Eminent Antiquaries* (London, 1720), cited from the augmented edition prepared by Joseph Ayloffe (2 vols, London, 1771); see also Christina Decoursey, 'Society of Antiquaries', *ODNB*, with further references.

33 Hearne, *Curious Discourses*, I, 9. As printed by Hearne and Ayloffe, this discourse is anonymous; but the autograph manuscript (BL, Cotton Faustina E. v, fo. 5rv) appears to be in Holland's hand (cf., e.g., Faustina E. v, fo. 8). The charter in question was evidently S 1861 (BCS 364) of uncertain provenance, which passed into the Cotton library (Cotton Charter viii. 39).

34 Hearne, *Curious Discourses*, I, 179–80. The charter in question was evidently issued in the late 960s; cf. Simon Keynes, *An Atlas of Attestations in Anglo-Saxon Charters 670–1066* (Cambridge, 2002), Table LVI.

35 An entry in Tate's lexicon of obscure words (Cambridge, University Library, Ff.5.15), under 'mansa', cites a charter of King Eadred granting six hides at Wouldham, Kent, to his thegn Ælfstan, dated 946, which seems to have been an otherwise unrecorded charter from the Rochester archive; and an entry under 'hida' cites a charter of Eadred granting 5 hides at Idmiston, Wilts., to his thegn Wulfric, presumably with reference to S 530 or S 541, from the Glastonbury archive. See also L.A. Knafla, 'Francis Tate', *ODNB*, s.v., with further references.

driven by religious and political controversy, increasingly in the seventeenth century they were driven also by a certain respect for the past, matched by the perception of a need to consolidate the foundations of the new order, and complemented by a developing interest in local and family history. In 1626, three members of the English Benedictine Congregation – David (Augustine) Baker, Wilfrid (Clement) Reyner, and John Jones (Leander a Sancto Martino) – published their collaborative *Apostolatus Benedictinorum in Anglia*. For his part, Roger Dodsworth set to work in the early 1630s transcribing charters for what by the end of the decade had come to be known as his 'Monasticon Anglicanum' (1638–1640);[36] and in 1638 four leading antiquaries – Sir Edward Dering, Sir William Dugdale, Sir Christopher Hatton, and Sir Thomas Shirley – formed the association known as 'Antiquitas Rediviva', defining their respective roles and undertaking to share information with each other.[37] The material collected by Dodsworth was put to good use by Dugdale, who had been no less assiduous in the collection and processing of material;[38] indeed, it was in the first volume of the *Monasticon Anglicanum*, published in 1655, that the evidence of Anglo-Saxon charters was first put to good use on a significant scale, forming the basis for Dugdale's chronological survey of Benedictine foundations.[39] Towards the end of the seventeenth century Thomas Tanner published his *Notitia Monastica* (1695); and one can sense from this book, from the later enlarged editions of it and from several annotated copies, how quantities of charters and cartularies continued to pass from hand to hand in the later seventeenth and eighteenth centuries.[40]

As one might expect, much of the additional material which has come to light since 1968 is connected in one way or another with the activities of the industrious fraternity of antiquaries in the late sixteenth, seventeenth and eighteenth centuries. Pride of place belongs to the early modern transcripts of single-sheet charters now lost. The Ballidon charter was the first wholly 'new' text to be published after the

---

36 Bodl., MS Dodsworth 10 (SC 4152).

37 The agreement was drawn up by Dering, and printed, from the original at Surrenden, by L.B. Larking, 'On the Surrenden Charters', *Archæologia Cantiana*, 1 (1858), 50–65, at 55–8, and thence by Joan Evans, *A History of the Society of Antiquaries* (Oxford, 1956), 21–3. The original document was in the last part of the Surrenden Library, when sold by Puttick and Simpson in 1863 (lot 1156), and was bought by Quaritch for £4. 15s, but is now lost.

38 For example Bodl., MS Dugdale 11 (SC 6501), and his list of cartularies in Dugdale 48 (SC 6536).

39 For Dugdale's surviving papers, see Historical Manuscripts Commission, *Papers of British Antiquaries and Historians* (London, 2003), 59–60. A document dated 10 May 1658, listed in the typescript catalogue of the Dugdale archive at Merevale Hall, Warwickshire, compiled by the Warwickshire Record Office in 1967, pp. 20–21, sets out the respective roles of Dugdale and Dodsworth; see also *The Life, Diary, and Correspondence of Sir William Dugdale*, ed. William Hamper (London, 1827), and Graham Parry, 'William Dugdale', *ODNB*, s.v., with further references.

40 The autograph manuscript of Tanner's *Notitia* and several annotated copies of the 1695 edition (e.g. by Thomas Hearne, Peter Le Neve, James West, and others) are in the Bodleian Library. Wanley's copy, with annotations, is BL Add. 47842. See also Richard Sharp, 'Thomas Tanner', *ODNB*, s.v., with further references.

appearance of Sawyer's catalogue,[41] and remains in the front rank, extending our knowledge of a singularly distinctive group of charters produced between 958 and 963, by a scribe who would appear to have been in King Edgar's service from the beginning of his reign as king of the Mercians and who remained in his service for at least five years.[42] It was joined in the early 1990s by two further charters of King Edgar, helpfully extending our knowledge of the equally distinctive group of 'Dunstan B' charters closely associated with and arguably produced at Glastonbury Abbey.[43] It is a moot point whether King Æthelbald's charter for unspecified minsters and churches, issued from a council of Gumley in 749, had ever existed in single-sheet form, or whether it was circulated from the outset as part of a related set of 'improving' texts.[44] Whatever the case, the copy of the charter entered in Cotton Otho A. i, an eighth-century manuscript all but destroyed in the Cotton fire of 1731, is known from the beautiful facsimile of its opening page made by Humfrey Wanley, in 1698, for inclusion in his 'Book of Specimens', which came to light at Longleat House in 1996.[45]

---

41 Nicholas Brooks, Margaret Gelling and D. Johnson, 'A New Charter of King Edgar', *ASE*, 13 (1984), 137–55, reprinted in Brooks, *Anglo-Saxon Myths*, 217–37, from a manuscript found in the Staffordshire Record Office; see also *Facsimiles*, ed. Keynes, 44.

42 The group comprises a charter of King Edgar, dated 958, granting land in Cheshire to the community of St Werburgh, Chester (S 667 [BCS 1041]); a charter of King Edgar, dated 958, granting land in Herefordshire to his thegn Ealhstan, preserved in its original form in the archives of Wells Cathedral (S 677 [BCS 1040; *Charters of Bath and Wells*, ed. Kelly, no. 31]); a charter of King Edgar, dated 963, granting land in Shropshire to his thegn Wulfric, from the archives of the Old Minster, Winchester (S 723 [BCS 1119]); and the charter of King Edgar, dated 963, granting land at Ballidon, Derbyshire, to his thegn Æthelferth (S 712a). S 677 is translated in *EHD*, I, no. 109. For discussion of the group (before the discovery of the Ballidon charter), see Simon Keynes, *The Diplomas of King Æthelred the Unready* (Cambridge, 1980), p. 69, n. 137; and esp. Brooks, Gelling and Johnson, 'A New Charter of King Edgar', 226–8. Quite apart from their special interest as representing a 'Mercian' perception of the landscape, in 958–63, perhaps pointedly avoiding any reference to shires, they provide an interesting contrast with the work of the scribe known as 'Edgar A', who was active during much the same period.

43 Simon Keynes, 'The "Dunstan B" Charters', *ASE*, 23 (1994), 165–93. One (S 676a) is a charter of King Edgar, dated 958, from an unidentified archive in the West Midlands, probably Coventry, discovered by Professor Nicholas Vincent in the Gloucestershire Record Office; the other (S 794a) is a charter of King Edgar, dated 974, from the archives of Westminster Abbey, noticed among the Madox transcripts in the British Library.

44 S 92 (BCS 178), on which see Nicholas Brooks, 'The Development of Military Obligations in Eighth- and Ninth-Century England', in *England before the Conquest: Studies in Primary Sources presented to Dorothy Whitelock*, ed. Peter Clemoes and Kathleen Hughes (Cambridge, 1971), 69–84, reprinted in Brooks, *Communities and Warfare 700–1400* (London, 2000), 32–47, at 39–41.

45 Simon Keynes, 'The Reconstruction of a Burnt Cottonian Manuscript: the Case of Cotton MS Otho A. I', *British Library Journal* 22 (1996), 113–60. A facsimile edition of the 'Book of Specimens' is in preparation.

No less interesting are complete transcripts or extended excerpts made not from 'originals', now lost, but from copies entered in medieval cartularies, now lost.[46] There are many famously 'lost' cartularies, ranging from the *Liber terrarum* of Glastonbury Abbey, known from the detailed list of its contents in a mid-thirteenth-century manuscript from Glastonbury,[47] to medieval cartularies of relatively minor religious houses, such as Milton Abbas and Buckfast, known only from the barest traces.[48] Especially tantalising is the reference, in a list of books which Humfrey Wanley wished to obtain for the Harley Library, to a cartulary which might have been of singular historical importance: 'Sir Rob. Davers has a Book at one of his Manors in Lincolnshire, wherein are Registred certain Charters of Coenwulf King of the Mercians.'[49] The 'new' material to which attention has been drawn since 1968 has thrown light on the charters of Abbotsbury,[50] St Paul's,[51] St Albans[52]

---

46 The standard reference work is G.R.C. Davis, *Medieval Cartularies of Great Britain: a Short Catalogue* (London, 1958). See Philippa Hoskin, '*Medieval Cartularies of Great Britain*: Amendments and Additions to the Davis Catalogue', *Monastic Research Bulletin*, 2 (1996), 1–12, with further amendments and additions by Nicholas Vincent, et al., *Monastic Research Bulletin*, 3 (1997), 7–38; 4 (1998), 6–13; and 5 (1999), 26–8. See also Claire Breay, 'Godfrey Davis, *Medieval Cartularies*: a Second Edition', *Monastic Research Bulletin*, 6 (2000), 39–40.

47 Cambridge, Trinity College, MS R.5.33, fo. 77rv: see S. Keynes, *Anglo-Saxon Manuscripts ... in the Library of Trinity College, Cambridge*, OEN Subsidia 18 (Binghamton, NY, 1992), 45–7, with pl. xxix (77r), and Abrams, *Anglo-Saxon Glastonbury*, 14–18 and 31–4. It is often instructive to know whether a given 'Glastonbury' charter was included in the *Liber terrarum*, as well as in the fourteenth-century 'Great Cartulary'; so this information will be duly registered in the 'Revised Sawyer'. For a detailed reconstruction of the *Liber Terrarum*, see Simon Keynes, *The 'Liber Terrarum' of Glastonbury Abbey*, unpublished typescript (1992), publication forthcoming.

48 The lost cartulary of Milton Abbas (Davis, *Medieval Cartularies*, no. 668) was probably compiled in the fourteenth century, as part of an attempt to provide necessary documentation after the destruction of the abbey's charters by fire in 1309; what little we know of it is derived from notes made by those antiquaries who saw it in the seventeenth century. Surviving fragments of the lost cartulary of Buckfast Abbey (ibid., no. 85) suggest that we lack parts 1 and 2 of three parts; and excerpts made in connection with a lawsuit in the 1440s suggest that these missing parts might have contained the texts of several Anglo-Saxon charters.

49 Wanley's Memorandum Book (1721), in *The Diary of Humfrey Wanley 1715–1726*, ed. C.E. Wright and R.C. Wright (2 vols, London, 1966), II, 428: see Simon Keynes, *The Councils of 'Clofesho'*, Brixworth Lecture 1993 (Brixworth, 1994), 26.

50 Simon Keynes, 'The Lost Cartulary of Abbotsbury Abbey', *ASE*, 18 (1989), 207–43. According to Wanley's Memorandum Book (1721), in *Diary of Wanley*, ed. Wright and Wright, II, 427, 'James Strangways Esq has the Leiger of Abbotsbury', which suggests that it survived at Melbury into the eighteenth century.

51 Simon Keynes, 'A Charter of King Edward the Elder for Islington', *Historical Research*, 66 (1993), 303–16; A.H.J. Baines, 'Monks Risborough: New Light from Islington', *Records of Buckinghamshire*, 36 (1994), 98–102; *Charters of St Paul's, London*, ed. Kelly, 68–9.

52 Simon Keynes, 'A Lost Cartulary of St Albans Abbey', *ASE*, 22 (1993), 253–79; *Charters of St Albans Abbey*, ed. Crick.

and Athelney;[53] and it is most unlikely that these cases have exhausted all the possibilities.

Early modern and antiquarian transcripts are all very well; but of course one yearns for the re-appearance or discovery of the real thing. In 1968 the Marquess of Salisbury lent a photocopy of a sixteenth-century cartulary of Ilford Hospital, at Hatfield House, to Mr H.H. Lockwood, who realised that it contained (quite apart from anything else) the texts of nine pre-Conquest charters derived from a lost cartulary of Barking Abbey.[54] We may also take heart from the fact that the long 'lost' fifteenth-century cartulary of Athelney Abbey resurfaced on a dark shelf at Petworth House, in Sussex, in 2001, proving to contain (again, quite apart from anything else) fuller versions of the texts known previously from an eighteenth-century transcript, as well as one 'new' text (a charter of King Edgar, dated 962) which had been overlooked when that transcript was made (in 1735).[55] An original single-sheet inspeximus of Henry III, dated 26 October 1259, brings us as close as we are likely to get to the single-sheet original of King Æthelred's charter for Wherwell Abbey, issued in 1004.[56] The inspeximus had sold for £320 when it first appeared at Sotheby's, in 1974, and was taken to Beverly Hills, California; on its return to England, in 1991, it was quickly absorbed into another private collection.[57]

For prospects of the discovery of charters in their original single-sheet form, one has to reach back into the more distant past. No doubt we should abandon hope of finding the long-lost group of charters from Abingdon Abbey, which belonged

---

53 Simon Keynes, 'George Harbin's Transcript of the Lost Cartulary of Athelney Abbey', *Somerset Archaeology and Natural History*, 136 (1992), 149–59, ending with an expression of hope that the exercise of editing the cartulary from the eighteenth-century transcripts 'would then be upstaged by the more dramatic re-appearance of the cartulary itself'.

54 In July 1969 Mr Lockwood showed his photocopy of the manuscript to Professor T.J. Brown, but the discovery did not become more widely known until the mid-1980s. See H.H. Lockwood, 'One Thing Leads to Another – the Discovery of Additional Charters of Barking Abbey', *Essex Journal*, 25 (1990), 11–13, and Kenneth Bascombe, 'Two Charters of King Suebred of Essex', *An Essex Tribute*, ed. Kenneth Neale (London, 1987), 85–96.

55 S 705a. The discovery was made by Mrs Alison McCann, archivist at Petworth House, in June 2001: see Simon Keynes, 'The Cartulary of Athelney Abbey Rediscovered', *Monastic Research Bulletin*, 7 (2001), 2–5, and Oliver Padel, 'The Charter of Lanlawren (Cornwall)', *Latin Learning and English Lore: Studies in Anglo-Saxon Literature for Michael Lapidge*, ed. Katherine O'Brien O'Keeffe and Andy Orchard (2 vols. Toronto, 2005), II, 74–85.

56 S 904 (KCD 707). The charter was printed by Dugdale from an enrolment of the Inspeximus, and by Kemble from Dugdale. The unpublished text in the Wherwell cartulary (BL Egerton 2104A), from the same inspeximus, is significantly better (Keynes, *Diplomas*, 258), but the charter can now be edited from the inspeximus itself.

57 The Inspeximus of 1259 is now in the Schøyen Collection, MS 1354; an image of it is available on the online catalogue of the Schøyen Collection <www.nb.no/baser/schoyen/>, under Palaeography/Latin Documentary Scripts. An original Inspeximus of Henry VII, dated 1489, contains another text of S 904, derived from the Inspeximus of 1259; it appeared at auction in 1997 (Sotheby's, 2 December 1997, lot 40). In 1997–1998 Professor Nicholas Vincent drew my attention to the presence of copies of a number of pre-Conquest texts among the Exchequer Memoranda Rolls and Exchequer Plea Rolls in the PRO (National Archives).

to Henry VIII's physician, Dr George Owen (d. 1558).[58] In the early seventeenth century Sir Henry Spelman complained about the difficulty of obtaining any original Anglo-Saxon charters,[59] but his younger contemporaries were more lucky, or perhaps less scrupulous. The main sources were by now the cathedral archives, at Canterbury, Rochester, Winchester, and Worcester. The major player was Sir Robert Cotton (1571–1631),[60] who pasted most of the Anglo-Saxon charters that came into his hands into a large portfolio, designated 'Augustus II', while others accumulated in a drawer at the foot of the Augustus press (now separately classified among the 'Cotton Charters'). About 60 (or roughly two-thirds) of the charters in the portfolio were from Christ Church, Canterbury, and the rest were derived directly or indirectly from a number of other archives (including Worcester, Evesham, Abingdon, Bury St Edmunds, and Westminster); over 30 more were found in the drawer, including significant groups from the cathedral archives at Rochester and Winchester.[61] It is the case that of all the pre-Conquest single-sheet charters formerly recorded in the Cottonian collection, only three would appear to have been lost or destroyed.[62] Another key player was Sir Edward Dering (1598–1644), of Surrenden Dering, in Kent, who seems also to have been in a position to acquire a quantity of Anglo-Saxon charters from Canterbury, passing some to Cotton and keeping others for himself.[63] On 10 May 1630 Dering wrote to Cotton, promising to send him 'ye

---

58 Owen's charters are known from the transcripts made by Robert Talbot (Cambridge, Corpus Christi College, MS 111, pp. 139–78); see *Charters of Abingdon*, ed. Kelly, I, pp. lxiii–lxiv.

59 'Thus much of deedes before the Conquest which at this daye are so rare as though I have seen diverse yet could I never obteyne one originall.' From Spelman's tract on charters (Bodl., MS Tanner 130, fos 81–113, at 86r), published posthumously in *The English Works of Sir Henry Spelman, Kt, Published in his Lifetime, Together with his Posthumous Works, Relating to the Laws and Antiquities of England* (London, 1723), pt 2, 233–56, at 236; see also Keynes, 'Abbotsbury', 223–4 and 234.

60 C.G.C. Tite, *The Manuscript Library of Sir Robert Cotton* (London, 1994); *Sir Robert Cotton as Collector*, ed. C.J. Wright (London, 1997); Stuart Handley, 'Sir Robert Cotton', in *ODNB*, s.v., with further references.

61 Among the 'Cotton Charters' we also find several of uncertain provenance, some of which may have come to Cotton as a group, perhaps from another collector (S 96 [*Charters of Malmesbury*, ed. Kelly, no. 49], 221, 264, 308 [*Charters of Malmesbury*, ed. Kelly, no. 50], 706, 1460, 1539, 1861 [ex Joseph Holland]).

62 The three 'missing' Cotton charters are: (1) a charter of King Offa (probably not S 106 or S 114), placed by Cotton at the beginning of a tenth-century Irish psalter (BL, Cotton Vitellius F. xi), but evidently removed later in the seventeenth century; (2) Cotton Augustus ii. '23', described by Thomas Smith as 'Charta donationis agri in Allington Ecclesiæ Christi Cantuariæ, Ceolnotho tunc Archiepiscopo, anno 839', to which he added 'per regem Æthelwulfum' in his own copy of his catalogue (Bodl., MS Smith 140, p. 16); and (3) a vernacular lease issued by Lyfing, bishop of Worcester (1038 x 1040), listed by Smith (Augustus D, no. 18) and described in some detail by Wanley, in George Hickes and Humfrey Wanley, *Antiquæ Literaturæ Septentrionalium Libri Duo* (Oxford, 1703–1705), II , 264, but not to be found among the 'Cotton Charters'.

63 S.P. Salt, 'Sir Edward Dering', *ODNB*, s.v., with further references; C.E. Wright, 'Sir Edward Dering: a Seventeenth-Century Antiquary and his "Saxon" Charters', *The Early*

charter of K. John dat att Running Meade', evidently with reference to an original of Magna Carta (liberated from Dover Castle). He added that he would also send 'ye Saxon charters, as fast as I can coppy them; but in ye meantime I will close K. John in a boxe and send him'.[64] A third was Sir Simonds D'Ewes (1602–1650), of Stowlangtoft, Suffolk, who had been inspired to study records at the Tower of London, on 4 September 1623, when he happened upon 'the charter by which Edward the Confessor confirmed Earle Harolds foundacion of Waltham Abbey' and who, in emulation of Cotton, began in 1626 to form a library of his own.[65] D'Ewes managed to acquire several Anglo-Saxon charters, including two from Bury St Edmunds (probably obtained from his neighbour, Sir Edmund Bacon), one from St Albans, and seven from Winchester Cathedral.[66]

The process of the denudation of an archive can be traced in some detail at Worcester. At the beginning of the seventeenth century, there seem to have been at least 130 pre-Conquest charters in the cathedral archives,[67] yet by 1705 all of

Cultures of North-West Europe, ed. Cyril Fox and Bruce Dickins (Cambridge, 1950), 369–93. Dering's charters were later acquired by Thomas Astle and are now among the Stowe Charters in the British Library.

64 Wright, 'Sir Edward Dering', p. 375. The Magna Carta from Dover Castle became BL Cotton Charter xiii. 31a. It was slightly damaged in the Cotton fire of 23 October 1731, prompting David Casley, Deputy Keeper of the Cottonian Library, to organize the production of an impressive script-facsimile, engraved by John Pine, in 1733 (itself the source of facsimiles published in the late eighteenth or early nineteenth century). The charter suffered further damage thereafter, though it was still displayed in the British Museum in the 1820s, alongside the facsimile (Richard Thomson, *An Historical Essay on the Magna Carta of King John* (London, 1829), 394, 423–4 and 454–6). It was damaged further by conservation work in 1834 (Andrew Prescott, '"Their Present Miserable State of Cremation": the Restoration of the Cotton Library', *Cotton as Collector*, ed. Wright, 391–454, at 406–7), and is now illegible. For an illustration of this charter in its present condition, in the context of all other surviving 'originals' issued in the thirteenth century, see N. Vincent, in *The Magna Carta*, sale catalogue, Sotheby's, New York, 18 December 2007, 56.

65 *The Diary of Sir Simonds D'Ewes (1622-1624)*, ed. Elisabeth Bourcier (Paris, 1974), 154; *The Autobiography and Correspondence of Sir Simonds D'Ewes, Bart.*, ed. J.O. Halliwell (2 vols, London, 1845), I, 235. The Waltham charter is S 1036 (KCD 813). It was in 1626 that D'Ewes also commissioned what is now the iconic portrait of Sir Robert Cotton, as collector, which passed via Humfrey Wanley and Lord Oxford into the hands of James West, before its acquisition by an ancestor of the present owner, Lord Clinton: see Keynes, 'Reconstruction of a Burnt Cottonian Manuscript', 144, n. 17, with fig.

66 A.G. Watson, *The Library of Sir Simonds D'Ewes* (London, 1966), 160–1. The charters from Winchester were there in the early 1640s, and were copied as a group, by D'Ewes himself, in BL Harley MS 596, fos 14v–21r. All passed with the rest of his library to Sir Robert Harley; the original of no. 2 (S 668) is not known to survive. The charter from St Albans is S 1379 (*Charters of St Albans*, ed. Crick, no. 8). It is not clear how it came into D'Ewes's hands, but the recent realisation that it came from St Albans has an important bearing on the circumstances of its production (ibid., pp.164–6).

67 The figure arises from collation of various sources: Patrick Young's excerpts from about 40 charters, made in 1622 (BL Cotton Vitellius C. ix, fos 129–31: *Hemingi Chartularium*, ed. Thomas Hearne (Oxford, 1723), 552–68); Sir William Dugdale's list of about 90 charters, made in 1643 (Bodl., MS Dugdale 12, pp. 502–506; ibid., 579–85); William Hopkins' list of

them had gone. At least three charters from Worcester found their way into the Cottonian library, seemingly at different times and by different routes;[68] in the 1640s Sir Christopher, Lord Hatton, acquired a nicely representative selection of at least 16 single-sheet charters, perhaps on the same basis as he 'borrowed' books from the cathedral library;[69] a similarly representative selection, of at least 24 charters, passed into the hands of a person unknown, some time between 1643 and 1680;[70] and four charters found their way by different routes into the collection of Sir Robert Harley (Lord Oxford), including two sold to him by Peter Le Neve and one (the famous 'Altitonantis' charter) 'garbled' from Worcester by Silas Taylor.[71] It is not known what became of the 14 single-sheet charters which remained at Worcester in the 1680s, and which were transcribed then by William Hopkins.[72] The group of 24

---

14 single-sheet charters remaining at Worcester in the 1680s (BL Harley 4660, fol. 1r; ibid., 585–90); and the Somers charters (below).

68 S 89 (BCS 154), S 117 (BCS 234), and S 190 (BCS 416). See also S 1460 (KCD 898), from Worcester or Hereford, and above, n. 62. It should be noted that BL Cotton Augustus ii. 3 (S 89), i.e. the Ismere charter (originally placed by Cotton at the front of the Vespasian Psalter), would appear to have been one of a pair, since a charter answering to much (but not exactly) the same description was seen at Worcester by Young in 1622 and by Dugdale in 1643; that Aug. ii. 9 (S 190) seems to have escaped early from Worcester, to judge from the inclusion of a transcript in CCCC, MS 111; and that Aug. ii. 30 (S 117) was also one of a pair.

69 *Catalogus Librorum Manuscriptorum Bibliothecae Wigorniensis Made in 1622–1623 by Patrick Young, Librarian to James I*, ed. Ivor Atkins and N.R. Ker (Cambridge, 1944), 14. Atkins and Ker state that Hatton's charters were removed from Worcester *before* Dugdale made his list, in 1643; but four or five of them do appear to be included in the list. According to Dugdale (William Dugdale, *Monasticon Anglicanum sive Pandectae coenobiorum*, 1st edn (3 vols, London, 1655–1673), I, 137), Hatton had the *autographum* of S 1429 (BCS 156); and this would presumably account for his provision (ibid., I, 121) of a text with four 'additional' witnesses not found in the copy entered in 'Hemming's Cartulary' (BL Cotton Tiberius A. xiii), even though Tib. A. xiii is the manuscript cited by Dugdale.

70 If one assumes, by analogy with the case of Sir Christopher Hatton, that the charters might have shared the same fate as the books, it may be that the second group of charters passed in the first instance to John Theyer (d. 1673), whose books, catalogued and sold in 1678, included a quantity of Worcester's finest Anglo-Saxon manuscripts, which were among the books bought by King Charles II and now part of the Royal Library in the BL. For Theyer, see *Catalogus*, ed. Atkins and Ker, 17–18, and R.J. Haines, 'John Theyer', *ODNB*, s.v., with further references.

71 S 731 (BCS 1135): *Facsimiles*, ed. Keynes, 40; Julia Barrow, 'The Chronology of Forgery Production at Worcester from c. 1000 to the Early Twelfth Century', *St Wulfstan and his World*, ed. J.S. Barrow and N.P. Brooks (Aldershot, 2005), 105–22, at 118–21.

72 BL Harley 4660, fols. 1–12. These pages represent a most interesting attempt, by Hopkins, to produce a conspectus of available evidence on Worcester charters, comprising: his own list of the 14 single sheets; an extract from Hemming's Cartulary, via Dugdale's *Monasticon*, concerning Bishop Wulfstan's investigation of the Worcester archives; a copy of Dugdale's list of charters at Worcester in 1643; and numbered transcripts of 15 charters on the 14 single sheets. The charters were printed by Hickes, in Hickes and Wanley, *Antiquæ Literaturæ Septentrionalium Libri Duo*, I, 139–41, 142 and 169–76.

charters belonged, c. 1700, to John, Lord Somers;[73] and although they too are now lost, presumed destroyed, all hope of finding them should not be abandoned.[74] At all events, the cathedral did manage to recover *one* of its charters, in 1878; hence, perhaps, its designation, 'Additional MS., in safe'.[75]

Sooner or later, the collections put together by Sir Robert Cotton, Sir Edward Dering, Sir Simonds D'Ewes, Sir Christopher Hatton (Lord Hatton) and Sir Robert Harley (Lord Oxford) found their separate ways into the British Museum, and so into the British Library. In the sale-rooms of London, in the eighteenth century, the more acquisitive antiquaries of succeeding generations were able to indulge their tastes in an open market for antiquities, curiosities and 'ancient charters' of any kind. One surviving collection of Anglo-Saxon charters can be shown to have been the product of such activity;[76] yet this collection could hardly account for all of the charters which circulated on the market in the eighteenth century, and we have to ask what became of the rest.[77]

---

73 The Somers charters were examined and described by Wanley, and were subsequently printed by John Smith; see Hickes and Wanley, *Antiquæ Literaturæ Septentrionalium Libri Duo*, II, 301–303, reprinted in *Hemingi Chartularium*, ed. Hearne, 590–600; and *Historiæ Ecclesiasticæ Gentis Anglorum Libri Quinque, Auctore ... Baeda*, ed. John Smith (Cambridge, 1722), Appendix XXI, 764–82. It is not clear whether Smith printed from the originals, or from transcripts; but even transcripts, whether prepared by or for Wanley, or Smith, would be welcome. For Somers himself, see Stuart Handley, 'John Somers', *ODNB*, s.v., with further references.

74 After the death of Lord Somers, in 1716, Wanley tried hard to get hold of the charters, in their 'very little Oval Deal Box' (*Letters of Wanley*, ed. Heyworth, 350 and 355), and was still trying in the early 1720s (*Diary of Wanley*, ed. Wright and Wright, 25, 29, 38, 152, 430). There is reason to believe that Somers disposed of them before his death and no reason to imagine that they were among the Somers papers destroyed by fire in 1752 (cf. *Catalogus*, ed. Atkins and Ker, 20).

75 S 59 (BCS 203). A full account of the Anglo-Saxon charters at Worcester in the seventeenth century will be published elsewhere.

76 The significant collector at the beginning of the eighteenth century was Peter Le Neve (1661–1729). The major players thereafter included Thomas Martin (d. 1771), James West (d. 1772), Andrew Coltee Ducarel (d. 1785), Gustavus Brander (d. 1787), Robert Austen (d. 1797) and Thomas Astle (d. 1803). It was as a result of his purchases at the Brander sale, in 1790, lot 1174, that Austen completed a collection which remained hidden thereafter until the mid-1870s, when it passed into the hands of W.H. Crawford, of Lakelands, Co. Cork, resurfacing at the Crawford sale in 1891, when it was acquired by the Bodleian Library; see *Crawford Collection*, ed. Napier and Stevenson, pp. v–vii (without reference to Brander). The 'Crawford Charters' are reproduced in *Facsimiles*, ed. Keynes. For James West, in particular, see Nigel Ramsay, 'English Book Collectors and the Salerooms in the Eighteenth Century', *Under the Hammer: Book Auctions Since the Seventeenth Century*, ed. R. Myers, et al. (London, 2001), 89–110. Seven volumes of Astle's incoming correspondence were included in the sale of his literary effects, in 1894, and might prove to be of the greatest interest in this connection, if only they could be located (*Liber Vitae*, ed. Keynes, 76).

77 One wonders how many Anglo-Saxon charters, cartularies containing Anglo-Saxon charters, and transcripts of Anglo-Saxon charters, besides those which we know about, lurked among the manuscripts amassed by Sir Thomas Phillipps (1792–1872). The starting-point is *The Phillipps Manuscripts: 'Catalogus Librorum Manuscriptorum in Bibliotheca D. Thomæ*

The single-sheet charters which came to light in the twentieth century are representative of the various contexts in which more might yet appear. A natural if somewhat complex archival history lies behind the case of a charter of King Eadred for Glastonbury Abbey.[78] The passing of monastic archives into secular hands, after an abbey's dissolution, is represented by the case of the five single-sheet charters from Burton Abbey, in Staffordshire, which reappeared in 1941.[79] The activities of seventeenth-century antiquaries are represented by the tale of the will of Æthelgifu, found in 1939 among the papers of John Selden, although not published until 1968,[80] and also by the tale of the four single-sheet charters known to have belonged in the early seventeenth century to Sir Edward Coke, of Holkham Hall, in Norfolk,[81] one of which is where it should be,[82] leaving three others still to find.[83] Perhaps it is only

---

Phillipps, Bt.' (1968); and thereafter it is a matter of tracking promising items through salerooms. Phillipps MS 19593 contained in its binding a fragment 'relating to Archbishop Aldhelm [i.e. Æthelm (923–6)], King Athelstan, & Worcester, and London Bishoprics, & Glastonbury Abbey', whatever that may have been.

78 S 553 (BCS 887): Lesley Abrams, 'Lucid Intervals: a Rediscovered Anglo-Saxon Royal Diploma from Glastonbury Abbey', *Journal of the Society of Archivists*, 10 (1989), 43–56; *Facsimiles*, ed. Keynes, 32. The charter was transferred from Glastonbury to Wells Cathedral in the thirteenth century; from Wells into the safe-keeping of the Ecclesiastical Commissioners, in London, *c.* 1860; thence for lack of space to the Public Record Office, *c.* 1960; and from the PRO to the Somerset Record Office in 1964.

79 Thomas Landor, of the Manor House, Burton, had acted as agent for the Paget family (Marquesses of Anglesey) in Staffordshire from 1841 to 1864; papers of his are preserved among the Burton estate records in the Paget archive at the Staffordshire Record Office. The charters appear to have passed down the Landor family until 1941, when they were presented by R.H. Landor to the William Salt Library, Stafford. See also *Charters of Burton Abbey*, ed. Sawyer, p. xiv, and *Facsimiles*, ed. Keynes, 4, 7, 12, 17 and 26.

80 For the papers of John Selden, and Sir Matthew Hale, and their discovery at Alderley House, near Wotton-under-Edge, Gloucestershire, and their subsequent history as part of the 'Fairhurst Collection', see Keynes, 'A Charter of King Edward the Elder', 304–305. For the will of Æthelgifu, see Dorothy Whitelock, with N.R. Ker and F.J.R. Rennell, *The Will of Æthelgifu* (Oxford, 1968), and S 1497 (*Charters of St Albans*, ed. Crick, no. 7).

81 Catalogue of Coke's library (Holkham Hall, MS 748B), 'Antiquities and Rarities', in *A Catalogue of the Library of Sir Edward Coke*, ed. W.O. Hassall (New Haven, 1950), 96–8; see also D.P. Mortlock, *Holkham Library: a History and Description* (Roxburghe Club, 2006), 7–32 (Sir Edward Coke).

82 Coke's 'Chartre of St Edward the Kinge to the Abbey of Ramsey' is Holkham Hall, MS 262. It proves to be the single-sheet 'original' of S 1030, dated 1060, and may have a significant bearing on the circumstances in which charters for Ramsey abbey (S 798 [BCS 1310], S 1030 [KCD 809], and others) came into existence. The style is that of the 'Westminster' group of forgeries; cf. the charter of King William I for Ramsey (*Regesta Regum Anglo-Normannorum: the Acta of William I (1066–1087)*, ed. David Bates (Oxford, 1998), 700–706 (no. 220)), also extant as a pretended original (BL, Add. Chart. 74436), with an impression of the so-called 'First Seal' of William I attached, and thus presumably a product of the Westminster forgers. Unfortunately, Edward's charter was found too late for inclusion in *Facsimiles*, ed. Keynes. See also above, n. 31.

83 'A Chartre of Kinge Edgar in the lattine and Saxon tongue anno domini 966. De Dunnington' (*Liber Vitae*, ed. Keynes, 28, n. 120; *Charters of the New Minster*, ed. Miller,

a matter of time before more of the charters seen on the market in the eighteenth century come back to the surface.

The references given above suffice to show that the corpus of charters has increased quite significantly in the past 40 years, and to suggest at the same time that there remains every prospect of its further enlargement, in the same variety of ways.[84] Experience suggests, however, that one is not likely to find something for which one is looking. In general, new material is most likely to come to light by virtue of a collateral discovery made by someone looking for something quite different. The context may be an archive of family or estate papers, whether in a county record office or still in private hands, or perhaps the papers of an antiquary who has not yet received much attention, or which have come to rest in a collection or library overseas. A discovery might be made as a result of the systematic investigation of the scattered papers of one or other of the antiquaries active in the seventeenth and eighteenth centuries, or of intensive work reconstructing the history of a particular monastic archive. It is not that the documents which still await discovery are in any sense 'lost'. They are being carefully looked after by their curators, and waiting patiently to be identified by those who happen to know that their existence has otherwise and hitherto escaped attention.

The case of Burton Abbey, in Staffordshire, merits some further attention, by way of illustration, if only to register the existence of 'better' texts of two Anglo-Saxon charters from the archive, which have been overlooked. The abbey was founded c. 1000 by a king's thegn called Wulfric Spot, and, soon after his death, the foundation was confirmed by charter of King Æthelred the Unready, dated 1004.[85] The abbey was dissolved in 1539 and, about five years later, some part of its muniments passed into the hands of Sir William Paget, latterly Baron Paget of Beaudesert (1505–1563), who had acquired some of the abbey's estates in Staffordshire. The muniments which thus ended up in the archives of the Paget family (Marquesses of Anglesey), of Plas Newydd, comprised several pre-Conquest charters on single sheets, and a much larger quantity of later medieval documentation, including the abbey's main thirteenth-century cartulary.[86] Yet not everything was acquired or retained by the Paget family; for certain items from the Burton archive seem to have found their way into other

---

p. xlii); 'The Chartre of Kinge Eadred in the Lattine and Saxon tongue anno domini 951' (S 554); and 'The Chartre of Kinge Endwlfe anno domini 839'.

84 The tales told by R.M. Wilson, *The Lost Literature of Medieval England*, 2nd edn (London, 1970), 237–8, are always encouraging.

85 S 906 (*Charters of Burton*, ed. Sawyer, no. 28).

86 Three single-sheet Anglo-Saxon charters (S 906 + 1536, 623, and 1863), formerly deposited by the Marquesses of Anglesey in the Burton-on-Trent Museum, are now in the Staffordshire Record Office, Stafford (D603/A/Add/1–3), with the bulk of the muniments of Burton Abbey. A further five single-sheet Anglo-Saxon charters from Burton Abbey, which must once have formed part of the archive, passed in the mid-nineteenth century into the hands of Staffordshire land agent of the Paget family; see above, p. 60 of this chapter. The cartulary is BL Loans MS 30 (Davis, *Medieval Cartularies*, no. 91; *Charters of Burton*, ed. Sawyer, p. xv). Another Burton cartulary from the Paget archive (Davis, *Medieval Cartularies*, no. 92) is now in the Staffordshire Record Office (D603/ADD); see also Vincent, 'Medieval Cartularies', 11.

hands. An important thirteenth-century register containing abbreviated texts of a significant number of Anglo-Saxon charters came into the possession of the Welsh antiquary, Robert Powell Vaughan of Hengwrt (1592–1667), and is now among the Peniarth manuscripts in the National Library of Wales at Aberystwyth.[87] A fifteenth-century register of Abbot Field, which contains a contemporary English version of the will of Wulfric Spot, passed into the hands of the Willoughby family, and remains part of the Middleton collection in the University of Nottingham Library.[88] For his part, the antiquary William Burton (1575–1645), of Fauld (or Falde), near Hanbury, Staffordshire, and of Lindley Hall, Leicestershire, must have been eager and well placed, to acquire some of the Burton charters for himself.[89] He is known to have possessed an original single-sheet charter, dated 951, by which King Eadred granted land at 'Norton' (presumed by him to be Norton juxta Twycross, in Leicestershire) to his thegn Ælfheah; and, for whatever reason, he gave the original to Sir Edward Coke (Lord Coke), of Holkham Hall, evidently retaining a transcript for his own purposes. Burton printed the text of the charter in his *Description of Leicester Shire*, published in 1622;[90] and it is the occurrence of the same charter in the thirteenth-century Burton register (Peniarth 390) that enables one to tell that it came ultimately from the archives of Burton Abbey.[91] From 1622 William Burton occupied the main family seat at Lindley Hall, on Watling Street, south-west of Leicester, and continued to work on the shires of the west midlands; so the question arises whether any more information derived from the pre-Conquest charters of Burton Abbey is to be found among his surviving papers.[92] He died at Fauld in 1645, and was buried in Hanbury. In 1764 Thomas Astle, palaeographer and collector of manuscripts, visited Fauld, 'formerly the seat of Mr Burton, the Leicestershire antiquary' and came away with

---

87 M.D. Evans, 'Robert Vaughan', *ODNB*, s.v., with further references. Vaughan's collection remained at Hangwrt, Merionydd, until bequeathed in 1859 to W.W.E. Wynne, of Peniarth, Merionydd. The manuscripts were sold in 1904 to Sir John Williams, who presented them in 1909 to the newly-founded National Library of Wales at Aberystwyth. The Burton register is NLW, MS Peniarth 390 (Davis, *Medieval Cartularies*, no. 93; *Charters of Burton*, ed. Sawyer, pp. xiv–xv).

88 University of Nottingham Library, MiDc 7 (Davis, *Medieval Cartularies*, no. 94). The contents of the register are described by W.H. Stevenson, in Historical Manuscripts Commission, *Report on the Manuscripts of Lord Middleton* (London, 1911), 247–68, with a transcription of the will of Wulfric Spot at 253–8. In Stevenson's opinion, the version of the will in this register preserved some 'better' readings than the extant OE texts of S 1536.

89 Richard Cust, 'William Burton', *ODNB*, s.v., with further references.

90 William Burton, *The Description of Leicester Shire* (London, 1622), 209–10, with a marginal note, 'The Originall heereof I gave to the right honorable, the Lord Coke, in whose custody now it is'. Unfortunately, the charter cannot be traced at Holkham (above, n. 83).

91 S 554 (*Charters of Burton*, ed. Sawyer, no. 12).

92 On Burton and his papers, see John Nichols, *The History and Antiquities of the County of Leicester* (4 vols in 8, London, 1795–1815), II.ii, 842–5, and HMC, *Papers of British Antiquaries*, 30. For the materials for a new edition of Burton's *Leicestershire*, see Daniel Williams, 'William Burton's 1642 Revised Edition of the "Description of Leicestershire"', *Leicestershire Archaeological and Historical Society Transactions*, 50 (1974–1975), 30–36, drawing attention to Stafford, Staffordshire Record Office, 649/4/1–3.

'great plenty of Chartae Antiquae', which he duly removed to London.[93] Astle does not appear to have acquired any of his Anglo-Saxon charters in this way; but his good fortune at Fauld obviously accounts for the presence of a large quantity of post-Conquest records of Burton Abbey among the Stowe Charters in the British Library.

These facts about the dispersal of the muniments of Burton Abbey in the sixteenth and seventeenth centuries establish the context in which we should approach another strand in the story. In 1596 Michael Griffith, who had been born in 1572 to a Catholic family in London, entered the Jesuit College of St Omer, in Artois, France, and thus embarked on his religious training.[94] After various movements on the continent, he became first rector of the House of Tertians (newly-ordained priests) at Ghent in 1621. A few years later, probably in 1628, Griffith returned to England, and was assigned to the College of the Immaculate Conception, at Nevill Holt, near Market Harborough, in Leicestershire. Amidst his other duties, Griffith occupied himself during the 1630s and 1640s compiling a massive work on the history of the church in Britain. In 1652 he returned to the continent, in order to continue and complete his work, but he fell ill and died at St Omer on 11 August. Evidently his papers were still intact for, 11 years after his death, his major work was published, under his *alias* Michael Alford, as *Fides Regia Britannica sive Annales Ecclesiæ Britannicæ*, 4 vols. (Liège, 1663).[95]

Alford's *Annales* were inspired by and modelled directly upon the *Annales Ecclesiastici* compiled by Cardinal Cesare Baronio (Baronius) (1538–1607), latterly Librarian of the Vatican.[96] The works have the same general appearance, the same annalistic principle of organization and the same range of content (texts of councils, letters, charters, and so on). Father John Keynes, Jesuit provincial of England (1684–1689), wrote of Alford that he had examined all of the libraries in England.[97] Nicholas Harpsfield's *Historia Anglicana Ecclesiastica*, comprising histories of each diocese in England, written while its author was in prison during the 1560s, had been published in 1622;[98] and with help from this work and from several other equally substantial volumes, Alford was able to make effective use of many charters already

---

93 Letter from Astle to Ducarel, 1764, printed by Nichols, *History and Antiquities of the County of Leicester*, IV.2, 668, n. 1.

94 J.T. Rhodes, 'Michael Griffith', *ODNB*, s.v.. The fullest account of him is in Henry Foley, *Records of the English Province of the Society of Jesus* (1875) II, 299–308; see also Geoffrey Holt, *St. Omers and Bruges Colleges, 1593–1773* (1979), 121.

95 Serenus Cressy, *The Church History of Brittany from the Beginning of Christianity to the Norman Conquest* (Rouen, 1668) is essentially an abridged translation of Alford's first three volumes, omitting the texts of the charters, as Cressy himself acknowledged (Preface, §§ 49–53).

96 Philip Caraman, 'An English Baronius', *The Month*, Jan. 1982, 22–4.

97 *Florus Anglo-Bavaricus* (Liège, 1685), reprinted with an introduction by T.A. Birrell (London, 1970), 54.

98 Nicholas Harpsfield, *Historia Anglicana Ecclesiastica* (Douai, 1622). The surviving part of Harpsfield's manuscript (BL Stowe 105) covers the period between the seventh century and the eleventh.

available in print.[99] Yet it is clear that Alford also used manuscript material. He includes texts of several Anglo-Saxon charters from the archives of the New Minster, Winchester, citing in each case the 'Annales' of Hyde Abbey. This is evidently to be identified as the *Liber abbatiae* of Hyde, which came to light in the early 1860s in the library of the Earls of Macclesfield, at Shirburn Castle, Oxfordshire.[100] Alford does not state in whose hands he had seen the manuscript. It has been suggested that he found it, and much else besides, at Shirburn, which belonged in the first half of the seventeenth century to the descendants of Sir Edward Chamberlayne (1480–1543); and the presumption is that Alford had been befriended by this prominent Catholic family.[101] It can be shown, however, that the *Liber abbatiae* belonged in the 1630s to the antiquary Sir Henry Spelman (1562–1641) and did not pass to Shirburn until the mid-eighteenth century;[102] so it would appear that Alford owed his knowledge of the manuscript to his connections with other antiquaries.

Using these sources, Alford was able to incorporate texts of at least sixty Anglo-Saxon charters in his work, drawn ultimately from several religious houses (e.g. Crowland, Glastonbury, Ramsey, St Albans, St Denis, Thorney, Hyde, Worcester). It is interesting to see how he assessed the authenticity of each text; yet the texts themselves are for the most part derived from early printed editions of manuscripts still extant, and thus have no independent value. We should look more closely, however, at the charters of Burton Abbey. His text of King Eadred's charter for Ælfheah, dated 951, would appear to have been taken from William Burton's *Description of Leicester Shire*.[103] Yet Alford's texts of two other charters reveal that he had access to a manuscript or manuscripts now lost. The published texts of the majority of the Burton charters depend on a thirteenth-century cartulary (BL, MS Loans 30) and on a slightly later mid-thirteenth-century register of more varied character (NLW, Peniarth 390).[104] The text of King Eadred's charter for Æthelstan, dated 949, is

---

99   Among other books cited by Alford, we find: Savile's *Rerum Anglicarum Scriptores Post Bedam* (1596); Doublet's *Histoire de l'Abbaye de S. Denys* (1625); Reyner's *Apostolatus Benedictinorum in Anglia* (1626); and Spelman's *Concilia* (1639).

100   *Liber Monasterii de Hyda*, ed. E. Edwards (London, 1866); *Charters of the New Minster*, ed. Miller, pp. xl–xli and xliv. For the library at Shirburn Castle, see *The Library of the Earl of Macclesfield removed from Shirburn Castle*, part 1, Sotheby's auction catalogue, 16 March 2004, 8–21; followed by several more parts. It remains to be seen what else might emerge from Shirburn, by way of papers relating to the formation of the Macclesfield collection. It would appear that Kemble was not aware of Alford's book.

101   Caraman, 'An English Baronius', 24.

102   The manuscript can be identified in Wanley's description of items in John Harding's sale of books and manuscripts from Spelman's library, in December 1709; passed then into the collection of Walter Clavell; and was bought by George Parker (1697–1764), 2nd Earl of Macclesfield, at the Clavell sale in 1742: see *The Liber Vitae of the New Minster and Hyde Abbey, Winchester*, ed. Simon Keynes, Early English Manuscripts in Facsimile 26 (Copenhagen, 1996), 74, nn. 12–13 and 16; see also *Charters of the New Minster*, ed. Miller, p. xliv. The manuscript is now BL Add MS 82931.

103   S 554 (*Charters of Burton*, ed. Sawyer, no. 12): Michael Alford, *Fides Regia Britannica sive Annales Ecclesiæ Britannicæ* (4 vols, Liège, 1663), III, 301.

104   See above, notes 86 and 87. The Burton cartulary is limited to charters which directly concern the abbey; Peniarth 390 was compiled for very different purposes, and contains a

familiar from the latter manuscript.[105] Alford's text is essentially the same, though he provides four additional names at the end of the witness-list.[106] The text of King Æthelred's charter for Æthelsige, dated 987, is also familiar from Peniarth 390.[107] In this case, Alford provides a significantly fuller and in that sense a 'better' text.[108] The charter is closely related to three others issued in the same year, and the fuller text contributes usefully to an understanding of the relationship between them.[109] Alford also shows awareness of King Æthelred's foundation charter for Burton,[110] and provides a Latin translation of the will of Wulfric Spot, said to be from an English manuscript in his possession.[111]

We have to ask ourselves how this material from Burton Abbey had come into Michael Alford's hands. He could have seen the charters in their original single-sheet form, or as entered (with others) in a cartulary of some kind, or as transcripts made by another antiquary. It is not unlikely that he had encountered William Burton (who had Catholic and Jesuit connections), in Leicestershire; but clearly there are various possibilities. The other question is whether Alford had made transcripts for his own purposes; for, if so, it might be as well to keep one's eyes open for any surviving cache of his working papers.[112]

All of the surviving single-sheet charters of the Anglo-Saxon period were preserved throughout the Middle Ages in the archives of religious houses. The great majority have come to rest in the British Library, though significant groups remain in ecclesiastical archives (Canterbury cathedral, Exeter cathedral, Westminster Abbey), and smaller groups remain in the 'secular' archives into which they passed in the aftermath of the Dissolution of the Monasteries, whether still *in situ*, or by now in

---

much wider range of texts.

105 S 545 (*Charters of Burton*, ed. Sawyer, no. 10).

106 Alford, *Fides Regia Britannica*, III, 298–9: '+ Ego Eadmund Dux. + Ego Æthelmund Dux. + Ego Ælfgar Dux. + Ego Wulfric Minister, &c.' He also names the estate as 'Ealun', not 'Eatun'.

107 S 863 (*Charters of Burton*, ed. Sawyer, no. 25).

108 Alford, *Fides Regia Britannica*, III, 408. Alford remarks that the manuscript was defective, which might be taken to imply that he was working from a single sheet.

109 S 863–4 and 866–7: see Keynes, *Diplomas of King Æthelred*, 89–90.

110 Alfred cites Stow in this connection, with apparent reference to Stow's recension (1566) of the Prise-Say register.

111 Alford, *Fides Regia Britannica*, III, 436–7. Certain 'translations' (e.g. 'Alwino' or 'Alcuino', for OE *ælcum*) tend to support his claim; but the relationship between his translation, the version of the will entered in a fifteenth-century Burton register (Davis, *Medieval Cartularies*, no. 94), and the transmitted text of the will itself, is a matter which requires further investigation.

112 Alford's papers were presumably at St Omer, at the time of his death, and perhaps at Liège thereafter, for the printing of his *Fides Regia Britannica*. It is said by Foley (above, n. 94), and others, that Alford had passed some of his time in England in the Jesuit seminary of St Francis Xavier at Combe, near Monmouth, but it is not clear on what basis. In 1679 the seminary was plundered, on the orders of Bishop Croft, of Hereford; the books were removed, and now form part of the Hereford Cathedral Library.

the custody of an appropriate county record office or local museum.[113] Only two original Anglo-Saxon charters remain in what might be regarded as independently 'private' hands. One is the late-tenth-century will of Æthelgifu, from St Albans, which had once belonged to John Selden, and which is now in the Scheide Library, at Princeton.[114] The other is a mid-eleventh-century document from Christ Church, Canterbury, which had once belonged to Sir Edward Dering, and which is now in the collection of Mr Martin Schøyen, of Oslo and London.[115] For historical, linguistic and many other purposes, a seventeenth- or eighteenth-century transcript of a lost single-sheet original, or even of a lost cartulary copy, is no less valuable than the real thing. So, while the appearance of a 'new' single-sheet original would be little short of sensational, the prospect of the identification of 'new' transcripts of otherwise 'lost' charters, or of charters already known from other copies, should be quite enough to keep up the spirits.[116]

---

113 For example, two single-sheet charters from Glastonbury remain at Longleat House; several charters from Abbotsbury Abbey passed into the archives of the Strangways family, of Abbotsbury and Melbury, and are now deposited in the Dorset Record Office; four charters from Hyde Abbey, Winchester, passed into the hands of John Fisher (d. 1591), and from him to Winchester College; S 704, from Buckfast Abbey, passed into the archives of the Petre family, of Devon and of Ingatestone Hall, Essex, and is now deposited in the Essex Record Office.

114 S 1497 (*Charters of St Albans*, ed. Crick, no. 7): Princeton University Library, Scheide Library, MS M140 (*Facsimiles*, ed. Keynes, 15), and above, note 80.

115 S 1220 (*Charters of Christ Church*, ed. Brooks and Kelly, no. 148): Schøyen Collection, MS 600 (*Facsimiles*, ed. Keynes, no. 19).

116 I am grateful to Professor Richard Sharpe for his comments on a draft of this chapter.

Chapter 6

Reculver Minster and its Early Charters

Susan Kelly

In 1802 Mr C.C. Nailor, vicar of the parish of Reculver in Kent, embarked on a project that was to blacken his reputation. His ancient parish church, dramatically situated in the centre of the Roman shore-fort of *Regulbium* on the north Kent coast, was threatened by galloping coastal erosion. Much of the northern part of the fort had tumbled into the sea over the previous two decades, and 1802 saw further crumbling of the cliffs and the collapse of another building, the so-called 'chapel-house' just north-east of the church. The vicar had the further problem that the church was by now remote from most of its parishioners, following the drift of the local population from the ravaged village west of the fort to a new centre around the hamlet of Hillborough, over a mile to the south-west. There was therefore much to be said for Mr Nailor's plan to build a new parish church further inland, in a position more convenient for the congregation and less vulnerable to the elements. But the vicar earned posterity's condemnation by pushing forward a scheme to demolish the old church, finally winning parish agreement for this in 1805. Demolition of the nave and chancel began immediately and soon only low walls and foundations remained of this part of the building. The twin Norman towers of the west end, then crowned with wooden spires, had long functioned as a seamark and were temporarily spared – although their future seemed uncertain as the cliff crept within five yards of the ruins. Salvation arrived in 1809, when the Trinity Board of Navigation purchased the site to preserve the towers and took steps to arrest further erosion. Some of the stone-work from the church was used for the construction of the new church at Hillborough, but other parts of the fabric were more widely scattered: the two columns separating the nave and chancel were sold to a local landowner and set up in his orchard near Canterbury (they have now been re-erected in the crypt of Canterbury cathedral, reunited with a missing capital found on a Reculver farm).[1]

The vandalism of 1805 has paradoxically made it easier to study some aspects of the history of the physical fabric, through investigation of the standing remains and through excavation, which can be supplemented by analysis of early modern descriptions and illustrations: particularly useful is John Leland's account of what he saw when he visited Reculver in around 1540.[2] The earliest phase of the church consisted of a rectangular nave with an apse (semi-circular on the interior, but

---

[1] H.M. Taylor and Joan Taylor, *Anglo-Saxon Architecture* (3 vols, Cambridge, 1965–1978), II, 503–505; George Dowker, 'Reculver Church', *Archaeologia Cantiana*, 12 (1878), 248–68.

[2] *Leland's Itinerary in England and Wales*, ed. Lucy Toulmin Smith (5 vols, London, 1964; original publication 1906–1910), IV, 59–60. The standard archaeological account of the church is C.R. Peers, 'Reculver, its Saxon Church and Cross', *Archaeologia*, 77 (1927),

polygonal on the exterior), built from flint and stone rubble, bonded with Roman brick and tile. Nave and apse were separated by a triple arch supported on two columns, and were flanked by a north and south *porticus* opening from the apse.[3] This four-cell plan resembles that of the abbey-church at St Augustine's in Canterbury, constructed in the early seventh century, where the two *porticus* were intended for burials (the north for the archbishops, the south for the kings of Kent), and there are also parallels with early churches in Kent and elsewhere.[4] It has been generally accepted that this first phase represents that original monastic church, contemporary with the foundation of a minster at Reculver in 669, as recorded in the *Anglo-Saxon Chronicle*. The interior of the apse had a bench running along most of its length, providing seating for the clergy (the missing east end may have had a special seat or throne for the abbot); there is reason to believe that the main altar lay in the east end of the nave and that the apse functioned as a meeting-place for the monks rather than as a chancel, with the flanking *porticus* perhaps used as sacristies.[5] The original plan was later modified by the extension of the outer walls of the two *porticus*, so that the nave was enclosed to the north, west and south by a series of small outer chambers, which were probably used as chapels. The new walls were more impressive, built from blocks of coursed stone, but the general style of construction has been deemed similar to the first phase and the flooring was of the same type: Peers, who excavated the site in the 1920s, considered that this modification dated from no more than a century after 669. This seems to have been the last significant remodelling in the Anglo-Saxon period. Two further phases of construction took place after the Conquest, with the building of twin towers in a remodelled west end towards the end of the twelfth century and the eastward extension of the chancel in the thirteenth; in addition, either then or earlier, the nave walls were pierced in order to turn the flanking external chambers into aisles.

Early modern accounts have preserved some intriguing details of church furnishings. When Leland entered the church he was particularly struck by a free-standing carved stone cross, on his estimate some nine feet high, which stood between the two columns of the triple chancel-arch. Fragments of such a cross have been found at Hillborough and in the ruins at Reculver, and are now preserved in the crypt of Canterbury cathedral, along with the columns.[6] Paint-traces show that

---

241–56, which should be supplemented by Taylor and Taylor, *Anglo-Saxon Architecture*, II, 503–509, and Eric Fernie, *The Architecture of the Anglo-Saxons* (London, 1983), 35–46.

3   For a drawing of the chancel-arch before demolition, see Charles Roache Smith, *Antiquities of Richborough, Reculver and Lymne* (London, 1850), 197.

4   Fernie, *Architecture*, 35–6, 42–3 (with a query about whether the Reculver *porticus* were contemporary with the nave); Bridget Cherry, 'Ecclesiastical Architecture', in *The Archaeology of Anglo-Saxon England*, ed. David M. Wilson (Cambridge, 1976), 151–200 at 163–6.

5   Fernie, *Architecture*, 41–2; H.M. Taylor, 'Reculver Reconsidered', *Archaeological Journal*, 126 (1968), 291–6.

6   For a full evaluation of the cross fragments and columns, see Dominic Tweddle, Martin Biddle and Birthe Kjølbye-Biddle, *Corpus of Anglo-Saxon Sculpture IV: South-East England* (London 1995), 151–62 (cross), 162–3 (columns), and also discussion of the date and stylistic context of the cross in the introduction, 46–61.

the sculpture was once picked out in colours.[7] Debate has raged over the date of the cross, with arguments based both on its position in the church and on its stylistic and iconographical details. Directly in front of the chancel-arch is a stone slab measuring seven feet by three, which appears to be contemporary with the earliest construction. Peers interpreted this as a foundation for the cross, and argued that the latter must then date from *c.* 669. But Taylor makes a very good case for considering that this slab was originally the main altar, and that the cross was set up behind it at a later date; he cites Carolingian parallels for the erection of large crosses behind altars dedicated to the Holy Cross located in such a position, mentioning in particular the evidence for Centula (Saint-Riquier), dedicated in 799, and the St Gall plan of *c.* 820.[8] Moreover, the closest stylistic parallels seem to be with ninth-century sculpture and manuscript illumination.[9] Leland also saw at Reculver 'a very aunciect boke of the Evangelyes *in majusculis literis Romanis* and in the bordes thereof ys a christal stone thus inscribid: CLAUDIA . ATEPICCUS'.[10] A gospel-book written in 'Roman majuscules' is unlikely to have been later than the early ninth century: perhaps it was an Italian import, such as the celebrated sixth-century manuscript now known as the 'Gospels of St Augustine' (CCCC 286), but it could also have been a native product, of the seventh to ninth century, written in uncial or half-uncial, such as the 'Royal Gospels' from St Augustine's (BL Royal 1 E VI). It appears to have had a lavish binding decorated with a Roman cameo.[11] There is no way to tell whether this volume had an ancient association with Reculver minster, or whether it was a later gift to the parish-church. Another feature in the church which drew the attention of early modern commentators was a tomb at the upper end of the south aisle (and thus in the location of the south *porticus* of the original four-cell church). The seventeenth-century antiquarian Weever describes this as being 'of antique form, mounted with two spires', and notes that it was said to have been the burial-place of 'one *Ethelberht*, a Saxon king who had his palace royall here in Reculver'.[12] By the mid-eighteenth century the tomb had disappeared, to be replaced by an inscription and then by a supposedly inaccurate transcription on a wooden tablet. Printed editions of the latter give an early modern doggerel verse, identifying the entombed king as the Æthelberht who received Augustine in 597 (and who was of course buried at St Augustine's in Canterbury).[13] The identity of the tomb's occupant is discussed below.

---

7   C.R. Dodwell, *Anglo-Saxon Art: a New Perspective* (Manchester, 1982), 121.
8   Taylor, 'Reculver Reconsidered'.
9   See Tweddle, Biddle and Kjølbye-Biddle, *Corpus IV*, 46–61. A recent argument for a seventh-century date appears in Ruth Kozodoy, 'The Reculver Cross', *Archaeologia*, 108 (1986), 67–94. The case made there is undermined by petrological evidence: B.C. Worssam and Tim Tatton-Brown, 'The Stone of the Reculver Columns and the Reculver Cross', in *Stone: Quarrying and Building in England A.D. 43–1525*, ed. David Parsons (Chichester, 1990), 51–69.
10 *Leland's Itinerary*, IV, 59–60.
11 For Anglo-Saxon book-bindings, see Dodwell, *Anglo-Saxon Art*, 201–203.
12 John Weever, *Ancient Funerall Monuments* (London, 1631), 260–61.
13 John Duncombe, 'History of Reculver', in *Bibliotheca Topographica Britannica*, ed. John Nicholas (10 vols, London, 1780–90), I, 65–79 at 71–2, and see also 125.

The seventh-century minster-church was built on an east-west alignment in the centre of the fort.[14] The Roman levels have produced significant information, but there is nothing comparable for the subsidiary buildings of the Anglo-Saxon minster, which may have been located in the lost northern sector. Leland remarks that 'the hole precinct of the monastery appereth by the old walle, and the vicarage was maide of the ruines of the monastery'.[15] The minster may have included several nearly coeval churches, apart from the one that survived to become the parish church; this was a regular feature of early minsters, seen for example at St Augustine's and at Malmesbury.[16] Leland seems to refer to one such at Reculver: 'Ther is a neglect chapel out of the chyrch yard wher sum say was a paroch chirch or the abbay was suppressed and given to the bisshop of Canterbury' [i.e. in the tenth century]. This was the so-called 'chapel-house', located in the north-east corner of the fort, which was being used as a cottage when it collapsed in 1802. An eighteenth-century correspondent remarked that 'many Roman bricks are worked into the masonry of the walls, and in the south wall is an arch composed entirely of them'.[17] Another ancient building was a cottage 40 yards WNW of the church, demolished in 1781, said by the same writer to have been 'part of some monastic erection', which appears from an early engraving to have had a Saxon doorway and the proportions of a pre-Conquest church.[18] It has been remarked that the earliest churches built in re-used Roman forts were relatively more likely to be sited in a corner than in the centre of the space.[19]

While much of the discussion of Anglo-Saxon Reculver has focussed on the physical fabric and on the cross, there is also an appreciable quantity of documentary material with which to reconstruct the history of the pre-Conquest minster, its cultural achievements and its internal economy. In particular, a series of diplomas preserved in the cathedral archive at Canterbury has an immediate bearing on developments at Reculver. There are four charters from the seventh and eighth centuries directly in favour of the abbot and community, which illuminate the history of the house during its initial phase as an independent minster closely associated with the kings of Kent (S 8, 31, 1612, 38).[20] Cathedral records trace the minster's fate after the Kentish kingdom was absorbed first into the Mercian empire and then conquered by the West Saxon kings (S 1264, 1436). After the Viking ravages of the ninth century Reculver

---

14 John Blair, *The Church in Anglo-Saxon Society* (Oxford, 2005), 197, fig. 23.

15 *Leland's Itinerary*, IV, 59–60.

16 Blair, *Church*, 199–202; John Blair, 'Anglo-Saxon Minsters: a Topographical Review', in *Pastoral Care Before the Parish*, ed. John Blair and Richard Sharpe (Woodbridge, 1992), 226–66 at 239.

17 Nichols, *Bibliotheca Topographica*, 170.

18 Ibid., and see the engraving opposite 165, which shows both 'chapel-house' and cottage, with a detail of the latter (fig. 6). See also Thomas Hill's map of 1685 (reproduced ibid., opposite 193), and the useful plan in Taylor and Taylor, *Anglo-Saxon Architecture*, 505.

19 Blair, *Church*, 188–9, 196–7; Blair, 'Topographical Review', 235–40.

20 References to charters are from S; interim second edition available on a web-site http://www.trin.cam.ac.uk/kemble/. New editions of all the diplomas discussed here will appear in *Charters of Christ Church, Canterbury*, ed. Nicholas Brooks and Susan Kelly (forthcoming).

emerged as a possession of the West Saxon kings of the newly united English kingdom: in 946 the minster and its lands were formally transferred to Archbishop Oda, as recorded in a controversial diploma, ostensibly written by Dunstan himself (S 546). Finally, an exceptionally odd document from 1020 x 1038 concerns a lease of Reculver land (S 1390). Understanding of the dating and context of these diplomas has greatly improved in recent years, and the present chapter represents an attempt to integrate this new evidence with the existing information about the minster and its setting, following the path blazed by Nicholas Brooks in his extraordinary studies of the ecclesiastical history of Canterbury and Rochester.

The origin of Reculver minster is noted in the Anglo-Saxon Chronicle under the year 669: 'In this year King Ecgberht gave Reculver to the mass-priest Bassa to build a minster'. The chronicler (or his source) clearly considered this to be a significant event. Ecgberht of Kent (664–673) was the great-grandson of King Æthelberht, and related to many royal saints (his aunt was Æthelthryth of Ely); he was also associated with the foundation of the double house at Minster-in-Thanet and of the monastery at Chertsey in Surrey.[21] Ecgberht's reign began in the year of the great plague, which coincided with (and almost certainly caused) the death on the same day of both his father King Eorcenberht and of Archbishop Deusdedit, the first native-born archbishop of Canterbury. The fledgling English church was hard-hit, and so there was an interval before a priest named Wigheard was selected and send to Rome to be consecrated as Deusdedit's successor; it would appear that Wigheard was a member of the Canterbury community and that he was Ecgberht's choice. But the archbishop-elect and his companions died soon after their arrival in Rome and Pope Vitalian made the momentous selection of Theodore of Tarsus as his successor. Consecrated in March 668, Archbishop Theodore did not arrive in England until May 669; his African companion Hadrian was further delayed and it was not until 670 or 671 that he could be installed as the abbot of the Canterbury monastery of SS Peter and Paul (later St Augustine's), which had been vacant since 667.[22]

The foundation of Reculver thus took place against the background of the arrival of a new archbishop, a papal nominee with no English connections, and the allocation of the principal Kentish monastery to the care of another foreigner. King Ecgberht may not have been happy with this turn of events. According to Bede, the king is said to have made the original selection of Wigheard on the basis that an English archbishop would be far more effective in communicating Christian teachings to his people 'since they would receive them at the hands of someone of their own kin and blood and hear them not through an interpreter but in their own native tongue'. Perhaps it is no coincidence that in the year of Theodore's arrival King Ecgberht was involved with the establishment of a house of male religious in a strategic location outside Canterbury.[23] No information has survived about the mass-priest Bassa who

---

21 On Minster-in-Thanet, see D.M. Rollason, *The Mildrith Legend: a Study in Early Medieval Hagiography in England* (Leicester, 1982); for Chertsey, see S 1165.

22 *HE*, 328–32 (Book IV, ch. 1); *Charters of St Augustine's Abbey, Canterbury*, ed. S.E. Kelly (Oxford, 1995), 207.

23 Bede, *Historia Abbatum*, chapter 3: *Venerabilis Baedae Opera Historica*, ed. Charles Plummer (Oxford, 1896), 366–7; tr. J.F. Webb and D.H. Farmer, *The Age of Bede*

was the first founder of Reculver minster, but his name indicates that he was an Englishman.[24] He would have been a senior clergyman: a 'mass-priest' was a priest, a cleric who had attained the highest of the seven appointed orders and was thus qualified to celebrate the mass. It is impossible to reconstruct the circumstances of the foundation of 669 and it may be that Theodore played an active part in events, but we might speculate that King Ecgberht was interested in setting up a centre with a stronger English element at Reculver, distinct from the Canterbury church that was destined to be dominated by Theodore, Hadrian and their non-native followers. It may be significant that the next archbishop after the death of Theodore in 690 was Berhtwald, abbot of Reculver by 679 and perhaps Bassa's immediate successor.

The establishment of early minsters within former Roman forts was a fairly common practice both in mid-Saxon England and on the Continent.[25] The perimeter walls of the fort provided a ready-made monastic *vallum* and the ruinous internal buildings could potentially supply construction material. Reculver was linked by road to Canterbury, some nine miles to the south, but was also in a prime position for sea transport. The Roman fort had been built in the third century at the northern mouth of the significant waterway known as the Wantsum Channel, which divided Thanet from mainland Kent and gave access to the Great Stour river and to Canterbury.[26] The Wantsum (now silted-up marshland) provided a safe route for ships moving between the Thames estuary and the Continent, far superior to the alternative route around the cliffs of Thanet's North Foreland.[27] Reculver probably had its own harbour facilities. It is conjectured that there was a small inlet south of the fort, but more intriguing is the implication of a tenth-century boundary-clause that the now-eroded coast to the north of Reculver may once have included a sandstone-island with its own 'mini-Wantsum', a creek separating it from the mainland with one outfall on the sea-coast and the other debouching into the Wantsum proper.[28] This could have provided a sheltered channel for beaching or berthing ships, north of the fort on its hill-top site. Some aspect of this topography may account for the place-name *Raculf/Regulbium*, derived from an Old British word for 'beak, bill' and with the underlying meaning of 'promontory'.[29]

(Harmondsworth, 1983), 187–8. It has recently been suggested that Ecgberht may at this time have been under the influence of Bishop Wilfrid, himself an important monastic founder (Blair, *Church*, 95).

24   See the Northumbrian thegn Bass (*HE*, 204 (Book II, ch. 20)), and the place-names Baslow, Derbys., Bassingbourn, Cambs., etc. (Eilert Ekwall, *The Concise Oxford Dictionary of English Place-Names*, 4th edn (Oxford, 1960), 30).

25   Blair, 'Topographical Review', 235–9; Richard Morris, *Churches in the Landscape* (London, 1989), 119–20.

26   See Andrew Pearson, *The Roman Shore Forts: Coastal Defences of Southern Britain* (Stroud, 2002), 24–5, 11–13, 141–2.

27   David Hill, *An Atlas of Anglo-Saxon England* (Oxford, 1981), 14.

28   S 546 (discussed further below); Harold Gough, 'Eadred's Charter of A.D. 949 and the Extent of the Monastic Estate of Reculver, Kent', in *St Dunstan: His Life, Times and Cult*, ed. Nigel Ramsay, Margaret Sparks and Tim Tatton-Brown (Woodbridge, 1992), 89–102 at 93–4 (with map 98–9). For the southern inlet, see Pearson, *Roman Shore Forts*, 112.

29   Ekwall, *Dictionary of English Place-Names*, 383.

The Roman garrison was withdrawn and some buildings deliberately demolished c. 360, but there may have been periods of reoccupation up to the late fourth century. The most probable location for early Saxon settlement is the area to the north of the fort, closer to the medieval coastline (perhaps associated with the hypothetical sea-creek between the sea and the Wantsum). Over the centuries coins, glass-ware and metalwork have been found along the shore, probably having fallen from the eroding cliffs.[30] The quantity of seventh- and eighth-century coins picked up from Reculver and its vicinity is paralleled only at *Hamwic*: finds include gold *thrymsas* and some 50 sceattas, with contemporary Merovingian coins and a small group of Northumbrian issues.[31] This concentration is not easily explicable as representing debris from eroded graves.[32] Almost certainly there is some connection with Reculver's position on a major trading route (the finds included an imported pot), and we might speculate that there was at some stage a royal toll-station in the area, comparable to Sarre (discussed below), or even a significant coastal trading settlement. Early modern historians from the sixteenth to eighteenth centuries mention a tradition that King Æthelberht retired to a palace at Reculver, after resigning Canterbury to Augustine and his followers.[33] There is no valid medieval source for this belief, and it seems possible that it evolved from speculation about the identity of the royal personage buried in the south aisle. In general Anglo-Saxon kings seem to have shown little interest in establishing themselves in old Roman forts.[34]

While there is no early evidence for the existence of a royal vill at Reculver, it does seem probable that the fort was the central place of an estate of unspecified size which was handed over to Bassa and his followers as the endowment for the new minster. In the tenth century the territory associated with Reculver minster consisted of 26 sulungs (ploughlands), with a central block of 21 sulungs roughly equivalent to the area of the parishes of Reculver, Hoath and Herne.[35] In the Anglo-Saxon period a very significant part of this central Reculver territory would have fallen within the area of the Forest of Blean, which then extended over a huge area north of Canterbury to the coast.[36] The minster would have had a mixed economy, with the strip of land between Reculver and Hoath suitable for arable cultivation, marshland on the Wantsum fringes used for summer grazing of sheep and cattle, and the forested regions to the west and south-west providing timber and fuel,

---

30 See Audrey Meaney, *A Gazetteer of Early Anglo-Saxon Burial-Sites* (London, 1964), 133.

31 S.E. Rigold and D.M. Metcalf, 'A Revised Checklist of English Finds of Sceattas', in *Sceattas in England and on the Continent*, ed. David Hill and D.M. Metcalf, British Archaeological Reports, British Series, 128 (Oxford, 1984), 245–68 at 258–60.

32 P. Drewett, D. Rudling and M. Gardner, *The South-East to A.D. 1000* (London, 1988), 299.

33 For example, William Lambarde, *A Perambulation of Kent* (London, 1576), 207; Weever, *Funerall Monuments*, 260–61; Smith, *Antiquities*, 192–3; Dowker, 'Reculver Church', 249–50, 267.

34 Blair, 'Topographical Review', 239–40.

35 S 546; Gough, 'Eadred's Charter'.

36 Alan Everitt, *Continuity and Colonization: the Evolution of Kentish Settlement* (Leicester, 1986), 29–30.

and pasture for pigs and other livestock. The production of salt in coastal pans is likely to have been important: the Domesday manor at Reculver boasted five salthouses. The sea and the Wantsum would have provided fish (there was a Domesday fishery) and the minster may have made an early investment in a water-mill, as did St Augustine's (S 25): the tenth-century Reculver bounds point to the existence of a mill on the Hogwell Sewer, probably in the area of Brook Farm (TR 220380).[37] Over the course of its history, the minster would have acquired detached estates elsewhere in Kent, which would have contributed to the community's economy in other ways. But the evidence of the surviving charters highlights another factor that may have represented a significant source of income for Reculver. The minster was located in a prime position on an international trading route, and there is good evidence that the community was exploiting this advantage by the eighth century if not before.

The first Reculver diploma is celebrated as the earliest surviving original diploma from Anglo-Saxon England (S 8). It is in the name of Ecgberht's brother and successor Hlothhere (673–685) and is datable to May 679. The grant was made to Abbot Berhtwald and his minster, and the ceremony of conveyance took place at Reculver itself, described as [*in*] *civitate Reculf*. (It seems probable that this usage reflects Reculver's Roman origins, rather than the existence in the area of any population centre that could be described as a 'city'; Bede refers to Reculver simply as a *monasterium*.)[38] The text of the diploma mentions the consent of Archbishop Theodore and the king's nephew Eadric, but the witness-list suggests that only the king and his principal nobles were present at the conveyance ceremony, which perhaps took place during a royal visit to the minster. Hlothhere's primary donation was of land on Thanet called *Westanae*, but on the day of the ceremony the king added a second property on the mainland, in (the district of) Sturry. The name *Westanae* is etymologically difficult, but can be understood to refer to an estate in the western part of Thanet. When Reculver minster was granted to Canterbury cathedral in 949 (S 546), its territory included a separate area of four sulungs (ploughlands) on Thanet, which may represent the estate conveyed in 679 (or a remaining portion of it). This four-sulung property has previously been placed at St Nicholas-at-Wade, but recent analysis of neighbouring charter-boundaries shows conclusively that the Reculver estate was at Sarre.[39] This has important implications. Sarre was a highly strategic place, overlooking the confluence of the Wantsum and the Great Stour, directly linked to Canterbury via a Roman road and a ferry or ford from Upstreet. In the early 760s it was the site of a toll-station, where the agents of the Kentish kings collected dues on trading ships using the Wantsum route (S 29), but its importance goes back much earlier; a cemetery at Sarre of sixth- to seventh-century date had

---

37 Gough, 'Eadred's Charter', 94–5.

38 James Campbell, *Essays in Anglo-Saxon History* (London, 1986), 106; Blair, *Church*, 86. There is an Old English form of this name in S 38, a cartulary memorandum (*Raculfcestre*).

39 The evidence is set out in *Charters of Christ Church*, ed. Brooks and Kelly. S 497 (A.D. 944) covers Monkton parsh, and refers to 'the Reculver people's boundary' in the vicinity of Sarre; S 512 (A.D. 943) is a landbook for St Nicholas-at-Wade, which must then have been distinct from the Reculver estate.

a very high proportion of male burials with weapons, perhaps those of warriors protecting the port.[40] The grant of Sarre to Reculver must be regarded as a sign of enormous royal favour to the minster, barely a decade old. We can only speculate how the monastic ownership of the site could have co-existed with the existence of a royal toll-station and guardpost there. Reculver's own ships were probably exempt (see below), and it may be that the minster received a share of the royal tolls levied at Sarre.

The diploma of 679 is an extraordinary document, written on nearly transparent parchment in spiky Kentish uncials. Most commentators accept that the whole diploma was the work of a single scribe, who first wrote the details of the principal and supplementary grants, then (probably after an interval) the names of the witnesses. The implication is that the text was copied out before the conveyance ceremony and the subscriptions added afterwards, which is a strong indication of contemporaneity and originality. Indeed the genesis of the document must have been even more complicated, since the repetitive formulation of the text would imply the existence of an original draft that mentioned only the primary grant. We can only speculate about the circumstances in which the earliest English diplomas were produced, and there is still debate about when the production of written records was first undertaken.[41] The 679 diploma is the earliest surviving original, and the earliest copies which are judged to be authentic or to have an authentic basis date from the same decade. It has seemed natural to draw a connection between the arrival of Archbishop Theodore in 669 and the (apparent) sudden appearance of written records in the 670s, and to see charter-production as another area where the archbishop revolutionised the practices of the English church. But there are problems with such a scenario, not least that already in the 670s and 680s there are already distinct diplomatic traditions in the southern English kingdoms (nothing survives from the north and midlands), which seems inconsistent with the idea of a single genesis from Canterbury c. 670. It makes better sense to see a more gradual evolution of the English charter, probably drawing upon a range of models and influences from Merovingian France and the Celtic world, as well as Italy. The lack of any extant texts from before c. 670 is a poser, but could be explained by the use of (less durable) papyrus for earlier records; it may be significant that S 8 has the long, thin proportions of a papyrus document, perhaps indicating the use of a model in that medium.

The probability is that the 679 diploma was written by a Reculver scribe, on the basis of a draft by another party, perhaps Abbot Berhtwald himself. The Latin text is peppered with appalling errors of syntax and eccentric spelling and the formulation is awkward and repetitive. The scribe compounded the problems when copying the draft, for he clearly paid more attention to the individual letter forms than to the

---

40 Sonia Chadwick Hawkes, 'Anglo-Saxon Kent c. 425–725', in *The Archaeology of Kent to A.D. 1500*, ed. P. Leach (London, 1982), 64–78 at 76.

41 See Pierre Chaplais, 'Who Introduced Charters into England? The Case for Augustine', *Journal of the Society of Archivists*, 3 (1969), 526–42; Susan Kelly, 'Early Anglo-Saxon Society and the Written Word', in *The Uses of Literacy in Early Medieval Europe*, ed. Rosamond McKitterick (Cambridge, 1990), 36–62; Patrick Wormald, *Bede and the Conversion of England: the Charter Evidence*, Jarrow Lecture 1984 (Jarrow, 1985).

sense; there are several serious mistakes at line-ends, and some indication that he did not fully understand what he was copying. It is hard to believe that such a diploma could be the product of a draftsman or scribe associated with the supremely learned Canterbury school established by Theodore and Hadrian, still less attributable to Theodore himself or a close associate, and so the likelihood is that the 679 diploma was the work of a Reculver scribe. The archiepiscopal archives are deficient until 798 and so we cannot be entirely confident about the earlier history of charter-production in Kent, but there is a series of telling differences in the formulation of the diplomas surviving from the Kentish minsters (notably St Augustine's, Minster-in-Thanet, Lyminge and Reculver) which seems to indicate that each house had some share in drawing up its own diplomas.[42] S 8 can be regarded as a beneficiary production, and thus as an indication of the lowish scholarly standards of Reculver in the 670s. Bede's notice of Berhtwald's appointment to Canterbury has the careful comment that 'he was a man imbued with knowledge of the scriptures, and very well instructed in ecclesiastical and monastic learning, but he could be in no way compared with his predecessor'; this contrasts with Bede's subsequent remark about Tobias, bishop of Rochester, said to be most learned in Latin, Greek and English. Berhtwald was clearly no scholar.[43]

There is no direct evidence of any further royal benefactions to Reculver during the period of Berhtwald's abbacy, but an oblique reference in a St Augustine's diploma is informative. In 689 the Canterbury community was given a sulung of land on which iron was mined, formerly attached to the royal vill at Lyminge and located to the north of land belonging to the priest and abbot Berhtwald (S 12). It is just possible that the iron-bearing land was in the vicinity of Lyminge itself, but far more likely that it was a detached appurtenance in the area of the High Weald, which had long been the centre of an important iron industry; here the seams were near the surface and could be extracted from open-cast pits, after which the iron would have been partly processed on the site before being transported to Canterbury to be worked into iron implements.[44] We can probably conclude that Abbot Berhtwald's land was also a source of ore. This may have been granted to him as a personal possession, but the conveyance could also have been intended to benefit Reculver, providing it with a source of iron for its own needs and perhaps also for sale or barter.

The donor of the St Augustine's diploma was Oswine, one of the *reges dubii vel externi* who ruled in Kent, sometimes in association with one another, in the troubled years between the death of Eadric in 686 and the emergence of his brother Wihtred as sole ruler in 692 x 694.[45] These uncertain conditions probably account for the long interval between the death of Archbishop Theodore in September 690 and the appointment of Berhtwald of Reculver as his successor in July 692. There may have been a disputed election, perhaps because the powerful Mercian king was pushing his own candidate or perhaps due to disagreement between the various

---

42 *Charters of St Augustine's*, ed. Kelly, pp. lxxiii–lxxxv.

43 *HE*, 474 (Book V, ch. 8).

44 Henry Cleere and David Crossley, *The Iron Industry of the Weald*, 2nd edn by Jeremy Hodgkinson (Cardiff, 1995), 12; *Charters of St Augustine's*, ed. Kelly, 35–6.

45 For the regnal sequence, see *Charters of St Augustine's*, ed. Kelly, appendix 3.

rulers of Kent, some of whom appear to have owed allegiance to the Mercian and East Saxon kings.[46] The choice of a Kentish abbot coincides with the resurgence of Kentish independence in the person of Wihtred, a representative of the ancient Kentish dynasty. At the time of Berhtwald's election Wihtred was ruling jointly with Swæfheard, who was related to the East Saxon royal dynasty, but he had established himself as sole king by July 694. Both king and archbishop remained in power for a long period (Wihtred died in 725 and Berhtwald in 731) and they seem to have enjoyed a good relationship. Wihtred's lawcode, promulgated in 695 in Berhtwald's presence, is largely concerned with issues of ecclesiastical interest, such as the regulation of marriage and wandering clergy, observation of the sabbath and church fasts, and prevention of pagan sacrifice.[47] The first declaration is that the Church is to be free of taxation, and this provision is underlined in the privilege which Wihtred granted to the churches and minsters of Kent in April 699 (S 20). Here he grants immunity from all liability to public tribute, commanding in return that the minsters show him the same respect and obedience that they showed to his royal predecessors. Reculver would have shared in these arrangements.[48] There is no information about the community's situation in Wihtred's reign, but it seems likely that Reculver would have benefited from Berhtwald's continuing support and patronage during this time, as well as from the stable and prosperous state of the kingdom under Wihtred's care.

Wihtred died in 725 and was succeeded by his two sons, Æthelberht and Eadberht. The sequence of Kentish kings in the eighth century has been much distorted by later medieval misreading of the historical evidence, which made these men sequential rulers and confused their successors (who included another Eadberht). Such misconceptions led to unfortunate emendation of the dates and other details of early charters in the archives of the main Kentish churches: the evidence is particularly clear at St Augustine's, but there are also signs of contamination at Christ Church (which preserved the Reculver charters) and Rochester.[49] It has now been established that Æthelberht (II) was king in East Kent and that his brother Eadberht (I) held a position junior to him as king of West Kent. Æthelberht survived until 762, after which he was succeeded as king of East Kent by Eadberht (II), perhaps his son or grandson, who was active c. 762 x 764.[50] Eadberht (I) died much earlier, in 748, and was succeeded by his son Eardwulf, who ruled West Kent for some or all of the period 748–762. Both branches of the family were patrons of Reculver, on the evidence of two surviving charters. The earlier is S 31, an original diploma in the name of Eardwulf of West Kent, which grants to Abbot Heahberht an estate near Rochester, in the vicinity of Higham Upshire, which is said to have been adjacent to the property which his minster had previously received from Eardwulf's father

---

46 Nicholas Brooks, *The Early History of the Church of Canterbury: Christ Church from 597 to 1066* (Leicester, 1984), 77–8.

47 *Die Gesetze der Angelsachsen*, ed. Felix Liebermann (3 vols, Halle, 1903–1916), I, 12–14.

48 For S 20, see *Charters of St Augustine's*, ed. Kelly, no. 10. Note that S 22, which grants control over Reculver and other Kentish minsters to the archbishops, is a ninth-century forgery: see Brooks, *Church of Canterbury*, 191–7.

49 *Charters of St Augustine's*, ed. Kelly, pp. xcvi–cv, 195–203.

50 Ibid., 199–201.

Eadberht (I).[51] The charter has no dating clause, but belongs to the period c. 748 x 762, probably later within that span. The sheet has a tall, narrow format (comparable to that of S 8) and is written in a calligraphic, cursive minuscule; the draftmanship is much better than that of the earlier diploma. From the formulation it is not possible to tell whether S 31 was drafted and written at Reculver; some details may suggest that the draftsman was associated with the Rochester scriptorium, and while this is not conclusive it would be consistent with evidence for the growing involvement of episcopal scriptoria in the production of land-charters during the eighth century.

Slightly later than S 31 is S 1612, a memorandum in the Christ Church cartularies which is based on a lost diploma of Eadberht II. It is ascribed to the year 747, but that conflicts with the internal reference to Archbishop Bregowine (761–764); now that the regnal sequence has been sorted out, the grant can be assigned to the period 762 x 764. Here King Eadberht grants to the church of Reculver and Abbot Deneheah (exemption from) the toll and tribute due on one ship at Fordwich, the port on the Great Stour which served Canterbury. The privilege was clearly associated with a particular ship owned by Reculver, and was to pass to a new vessel if the original was damaged or lost. King Eadberht granted a similar privilege to the abbess and community of Minster-in-Thanet in 763 x 764 (S 29), which involved three ships, two of which were to be exempt at Sarre, while the third (recently built at the minster) was to be exempt from toll at both Fordwich and Sarre. The Minster-in-Thanet community had earlier received toll-privileges from King Æthelbald of Mercia, relating to London and other Mercian ports (S 86–7, 91; with a confirmation by King Offa. S 143), as had the bishops of Rochester, Worcester and London (S 88, 98, 103a, 103b).[52] These ecclesiastically-owned trading ships would have attended the markets to sell the surplus of the churches' estates and the products of their workshops, and to acquire luxuries and necessities such as wine, furs, oil and wax; they may even have been involved in more commercial trading (as suggested by the reference to royal rights of pre-emption in S 29). In addition, these ships would have had a role in transporting passengers: pilgrims, clergy on their way to councils and on visits to other churches, secular travellers such as envoys and exiles. Although only one late toll-privilege to Reculver has been preserved (as opposed to five from Minster-in-Thanet), it seems probable that the minster, with its favourable position on a major trading route, was significant player from an early date; it may well have had a fleet of ships and its own boatyard, as did Minster-in-Thanet. Comparison of the grants in S 1612 and 29 is thought-provoking: the Reculver privilege makes no reference to the toll-station at Sarre, probably because the community's ships were automatically exempt there.

Eadberht II faded from view c. 763 x 764, as Kent entered another period of instability with a rapid turnover of rulers. There is some possibility that he was buried at Reculver. Thomas Elmham, a fifteenth-century historian at St Augustine's,

---

51 A later Christ Church scribe altered Eadberht's name to Ecberht, but the original reading can be distinguished.

52 See Susan Kelly, 'Eighth-Century Trading Privileges from Anglo-Saxon England', *EME*, 1 (1992), 3–28; *Charters of St Augustine's*, ed. Kelly, pp. lxxxv–xc and nos. 49–51, 53; *Charters of St Paul's, London*, ed. Susan Kelly (Oxford, 2004), nos. 7–8.

has a notice to the effect that a King Eadberht (thought by Elmham to have been the son of Wihtred) had died in 761 and had been interred at Reculver rather than in the normal dynastic burial-place in St Augustine's.[53] Elmham has no explanation for this disruption of tradition and points out that it was contrary to the professed wishes of the king: a charter of Eadberht (II) in favour of the Canterbury house has an express reference to his intention to rest there (S 28). It must be conceded that Elmham's information about this period is often skewed by the emended dates in the St Augustine's muniments, which means that the date 761 is almost certainly an inference based on his understanding that Eadberht was the immediate predecessor of Æthelberht (II), who died in 762. Yet there must be some source for this statement about the Reculver burial, which was contrary to St Augustine's interests and not a detail that Elmham would have invented. Eadberht I had been a patron of Reculver, but as king of West Kent he is relatively unlikely to have been buried there. A much better context can be suggested for Eadberht II, who may have been the last direct descendent of the old Kentish dynasty to rule: the political turmoil at his death may have ruled out burial at Canterbury, so that a place had to be found for him in the monastery founded by his ancestor Ecgberht and patronised by himself and members of his immediate family. He could well be the king buried in the south aisle of the church at Reculver, in a position corresponding to the south *porticus* (at St Augustine's kings were buried in the south *porticus*); an inscription or other record identifying him as King Eadberht (grand-)son of King Æthelberht may have given rise to the later belief that it was the earlier King Æthelberht himself that was buried here.[54]

Details of the last known grant to the independent minster at Reculver are recorded in another memorandum in the Christ Church cartularies, which represents a summary of a lost charter in the name of a King Ealhmund concerning a donation of land at Sheldwich near Faversham to Abbot Hwætred and his *familia* (S 38). The cartulary gives the date 784, but this may not be reliable. It would appear that Ealhmund was one of the often obscure kings who ruled in Kent between the death of Eadberht II in 763/4 and the imposition of direct Mercian rule in Kent, which had taken place by 785. For part of this period a King Ecgberht, who began as a ruler of West Kent c. 765, was dominant in both halves of the kingdom, possibly after ejecting his Mercian overlords in the aftermath of a victory at the Battle of Otford in 776. Ealhmund may have been a colleague or a successor (possibly his brother). He was almost certainly of West Saxon origin, for he was the father of the Ecgberht who

---

53 *Historia Monasterii Sancti Augustini Cantuariensis by Thomas of Elmham*, ed. Charles Hardwick, Rolls Series, 8 (London, 1858), 321, 324.

54 An alternative identification would be with 'King' Eadberht Praen, who ruled in Kent during the secession from Mercian rule in 796–8. Apparently a former priest (perhaps a representative of the native dynasty who had been forced into orders), he was mutilated on his defeat in 798 and perhaps imprisoned in the Mercian royal minster at Winchcombe, Gloucestershire, until his release in 811 (*Anglo-Saxon Chronicle*, s.a. 796, 798, in *EHD*, I, 181–2; William of Malmesbury, *Gesta Pontificum Anglorum*, ed. Rodney Thomson and Michael Winterbottom (2 vols, Oxford, 2007), I, 448, cap. 156). See below for links between Reculver and Winchcombe.

came to rule Wessex in 802 and who laid the fortunes of the West Saxon dynasty.[55] The Sheldwich property was probably a dairy-farm or cattle-pasture.[56]

There is no direct evidence at all for the fate of the minster when King Offa assumed direct rule of Kent in or before 785. As a former royal house, perhaps very wealthy, Reculver could have been seized by the Mercian conqueror (who certainly assumed control of other minsters in annexed kingdoms). But lordship over Reculver had passed to the archbishops in or before 811, for in a diploma of that year Archbishop Wulfred refers obliquely to an estate called *Dunwaling land* in the Eastry district 'which I had earlier detached from Reculver church' (*quod a Reacolvensae ecclesiae prius transmotaveram*: S 1264). The place-name means 'Dunwalh's land', and it is possible that it had been donated by the *Dunwalhus pincerna* who held office in the court of Æthelberht II in 741 (S 24); the estate may have been another acquisition from the mid-eighth century, when Reculver was receiving benefactions from Æthelberht's brother, nephew and son/grandson.[57] From the early ninth century onwards, the minster is referred to in the sources as essentially a piece of property. In the first instance it figured, along with Minster-in-Thanet, in a monumental showdown between Archbishop Wulfred and King Coenwulf of Mercia, who seems to have taken control of Minster-in-Thanet and Reculver at some point before 817. Possession of these two houses would have left the Mercian ruler dominant over the commercially strategic Wantsum Channel. The dispute is known only from a partisan and confusing document in the archbishop's name (S 1436). It would appear that Wulfred regained control over Reculver after a humiliating submission to the king in 821, although his campaign to secure Minster-in-Thanet from Coenwulf's heir, his daughter Cwoenthryth, dragged on for several more years. Wulfred's treatment of Reculver can be deduced from a document of 826, in which he supervised a transaction involving Minster-in-Thanet estates without reference to the community there (S 1267). More upheavals may have occurred when King Ecgberht of Wessex conquered Kent in 826/7. He does not seem to have had a good relationship with Archbishop Wulfred, and there may have been a new dispute about control of formerly independent or royal minsters; an agreement reached between Archbishop Ceolnoth and Ecgberht's successor, Æthelwulf, in 839 provided that the minsters should recognise the archbishop and bishops as spiritual lords and the kings as temporal lords.[58]

It seems probable that it was against this complicated background that the Reculver cross was carved from an old Roman column and erected behind the altar before the chancel arch. A date in the early ninth century is certainly implied by the Carolingian parallels and the stylistic evidence (see above). There was a strong

---

[55] *Charters of St Augustine's*, ed. Kelly, 201–203; F.M. Stenton, *Anglo-Saxon England*, 3rd edn (Oxford, 1971), 207, 209–10; Brooks, *Church of Canterbury*, 113.

[56] Everitt, *Continuity*, 168, 170.

[57] A Dunwald (possibly for Dunwalh), thegn of King Æthelberht, made a grant to St Augustine's in 762 before taking his lord's money-bequest to Rome (S 1182; *Charters of St Augustine's*, ed. Kelly, no. 12). See also Alex Burghart and Andrew Wareham, this volume, at n. 36.

[58] S 1438; Brooks, *Church of Canterbury*, 197–201; *Charters of Malmesbury Abbey*, ed. S.E. Kelly (Oxford, 2005), 7.

Mercian tradition of stone sculpture in the eighth century (in Wessex this craft did not develop until the ninth), so it is tempting to speculate that the cross was set up while Reculver was under the control of the Mercian kings.[59] The minster at Winchcombe in Gloucestershire, closely associated with King Coenwulf and his family, and perhaps rebuilt by him in 811, may have had an altar dedicated to the Holy Cross: this is the implication of a note in the Winchcombe annals and of a rhapsodic passage in the supposed foundation-charter of 811 (S 167), spurious in its received form but incorporating material from an early charter.[60] Winchcombe was the repository of Coenwulf's family deeds (see S 1436), and may have been regarded as the head of his proprietary minsters, among which Reculver would seem to have been counted for some years before 821.[61] The erection of a massive cross in the Kentish minster perhaps reflected Winchcombe influence.

It is relatively unlikely that such a major artistic endeavour would have been undertaken later in the ninth century, when Reculver would have been under severe pressure. Viking raids had begun on the Kentish coasts before 800 (see S 134) and intensified from 835 onwards, and it is improbable that a religious community could have maintained a continuous existence through the following decades on such an exposed coastal site. The brethren may have been given a refuge within Canterbury, as were the abbess and community at Lyminge as early as 804 (S 160). All our evidence suggests that by the tenth century Reculver was no longer an important church in Kent, and that control over the minster-site and its territory had devolved to the West Saxon kings. The next relevant document is an astonishing diploma that records King Eadred's grant of the *monasterium Raculfense* to Archbishop Oda and the Canterbury community in 949 (S 546). Ostensibly this is an autograph of Dunstan, abbot of Glastonbury (later archbishop and saint), written with his 'own fingers'. A cause for reasonable doubt: but there may be good reasons to believe the claim.[62] The earlier of the two surviving single sheets cannot be significantly later than the mid tenth century, and there seems no reason to doubt that the diploma reflects a genuine royal donation of this period. The implication is that Reculver and its endowment were under royal control, as seems to have been the case with many other monastic centres after the travails of the ninth century: another significant example was Ely, granted to Archbishop Oda in 957 (S 646). The circumstances of the royal takeover of former minsters are debatable, and it is likely that a number of mechanisms were in operation, including voluntary submission to a king or powerful lord in order to gain protection; a difficult reading in a Kentish will of 871 x 899 suggests that some

---

59 Rosemary Cramp, 'Schools of Mercian Sculpture', in *Mercian Studies*, ed. Ann Dornier (Leicester, 1977), 191–233.

60 BL Cotton Tiberius E iv, fol. 13v: 'DCCCXI: Hoc anno dedicata est ecclesia Wincelecumbe in honore sancte trinitatis sancteque virginis Marie et sancte crucis et omnum sanctorum'; S 167: '... vexillum sancte crucis in quo passus est Iesus Christus ... contra tumultum pravorum tutatrix atque defensatrix ... sancte crucis tutela ...'

61 For Coenwulf and Winchcombe, see Wilhelm Levison, *England and the Continent in the Eighth Century* (Oxford, 1946), 249–59; Steven Bassett, 'A Probable Mercian Royal Mausoleum at Winchcombe, Gloucestershire', *Antiquaries' Journal*, 65 (1985), 82–100.

62 Nicholas Brooks, 'The Career of St Dunstan', in *Dunstan*, ed. Ramsay, Sparks and Tatton-Brown, 1–23 at 17–18; also Brooks, *Church of Canterbury*, 232–6.

communities might dissolve themselves.[63] In S 546 the *monasterium Raculfense* is treated as a landed estate, consisting of a central territory corresponding to the later parishes of Reculver, Hoath and Herne, with an outlier at Sarre in Thanet and a tiny property in the Weald, at Chilmington near Ashford, probably a recent gift to the church. The minster's eighth-century acquisitions at Higham Upshire and Sheldwich had been hived off (perhaps detached by the asset-stripping Archbishop Wulfred, as had been *Dunwaling land* in Eastry). There is no way to discover whether any communal life lingered on in the minster-church and subsidiary buildings. By the time of the Conquest, Reculver was no more than a parish church, with no baptismal function and its lands absorbed into the archiepiscopal endowment, and we might assume that it had lost its status as a significant minster in the course of the ninth and earlier tenth century.[64]

And yet, there is an extraordinary coda which suggests that there was a resurgence of communal life at Reculver, at least for a period in the earlier eleventh century. S 1390 records a lease of a small area of land belonging to St Mary's minster, Reculver, by Archbishop Æthelnoth to two of his thegns. No calendar date is provided, but it must belong to the period 1020 x 1038.[65] The script of the surviving single sheet seems rather later, perhaps even twelfth-century, but the document does not have the hallmarks of a later forgery. There are some astonishing details. The document was drawn up using Continental formulas, and there is a notarial subscription by a priest with the Continental Germanic name Haimeric. The lease is to be held with the consent of the *decanus* of St Mary's, called Givehard, who subscribes along with two *monachi* by the names of Fresnot(us) and Tancrad (the other witnesses are all laymen, styled *milites*, and with English names). The implication of this text is that a small group of churchmen of Continental origin (possibly Flemings) was associated with Reculver at this time: the dean, with two monks and perhaps also the notarial scribe (unless he was attached to Christ Church). We might speculate that the old minster there was provided as a refuge for a body of foreign clerics, just as King Eadmund had given Bath minster to a company of fugitives from Saint-Bertin in Flanders a century before.[66] The circumstances, and their subsequent fate, are likely to remain a mystery.

---

63 S 1508; see translation in *EHD*, I, 538 n. 3. For the background: Robin Fleming, 'Monastic Lands and England's Defence in the Viking Age', *EHR*, 100 (1985), 247–65; David Dumville, *Wessex and England from Alfred to Edgar* (Woodbridge, 1992), 29–54; Blair, *Church*, chapter 6.

64 Brooks, *Church of Canterbury*, 203–204.

65 Blair, *Church*, 361, with edition and translation, 513–14.

66 *EHD*, I, 346–7.

Chapter 7

Stour in Ismere

Margaret Gelling

The single-sheet charter numbered 154 in Birch's *Cartularium Saxonicum* and 89 in Sawyer's *Anglo-Saxon Charters* is generally accepted as being an 'original' of about 736, the date of the grant which it records. It is a famous document and has been subjected to a great deal of scrutiny.[1] There are, however, still a few suggestions which may be offered about it and, since the purpose of the grant was to provide land for a small monastic foundation, the subject is doubly suited to a Festschrift for Professor Brooks, for many of his outstanding contributions to pre-Conquest history have been in the fields of charter studies and the Anglo-Saxon church. The matters which deserve further consideration are the precise location of the land granted and the significance of the transaction for the history of settlement in the north-west part of the area which became Worcestershire.

The charter records a grant of ten hides by King Æthelbald of Mercia 'to my venerable companion Cyneberht for the construction of a monastery'. The land is said to be 'in the province to which was applied by men of old the name of *Husmerae*, next to the River Stour'. There is a typical eighth-century boundary clause, in Latin, which can be translated 'and the aforementioned estate extends in circumference on either side of the above-named river, having to the north the wood called Kinver and to the west another wood whose name is Morfe'. On the reverse of the parchment is noted an addition to the grant. This endorsement can be translated 'there is, moreover, an estate in the above-mentioned wood which is called *Brochyl*. This I, Æthelbald, king of the South English, have granted, conferring it on my faithful ealdorman and companion Cyneberht, with the above-mentioned estate into ecclesiastical right'.

The monastic foundation provided for by this charter is of a kind typical of the eighth century, in which successive members of the founder's family would hold the abbacy and the property would be in the possession of the founder and his heirs. The subsequent history of Cyneberht's foundation is set out by Patrick Sims-Williams.[2] It was given to Worcester by Cyneberht's son, Ceolfrith, and was held by Worcester, despite an attempt at seizure by King Offa, until 816, when Bishop Deneberht ceded it to King Coenwulf in return for privileges for other estates.[3] In the grant of Ceolfrith to Worcester (S 1411) the estate is described as land *in provincia*

---

1   For bibliography on S 89 see *The Electronic Sawyer*, http://www.trin.cam.ac.uk/chartwww/eSawyer.99/S%2082-103.html: to the list of facsimiles of BL Cotton Aug. ii 3 there cited, add the small-scale one in John Blair, *The Church in Anglo-Saxon Society* (Oxford, 2005), 103; for some commentary on the minster established by the grant, see ibid., 102–105, 116.

2   Patrick Sims-Williams, *Religion and Literature in Western England 600–800* (Cambridge, 1990), 148–9.

3   Ceolfrith's grant is S 1411; Coenwulf's agreement with Deneberht is S 180.

Usmerorum quod nominatur æt Sture. In the document which records the settlement of King Offa's claim to this and other estates (S 1257) the Worcestershire place is listed after another estate called *æt Sture* which was by the Warwickshire Stour: here the Worcestershire Stour is 'a place of like name, *æt Sture in Usmerum*'. Stour in Ismere seems a suitable name for use by the modern historian, but there is a probability that the place was known simply as Stour and this could indicate that it was one of the more important land-units situated along the river.

The name of the province in which Cyneberht's monastery lay – *Husmerae* 736, *provincia Usmerorum* in Ceolfrith's undated grant, *Usmerum* 781 – is generally believed to have survived in Ismere House, which is in the neighbouring parish of Churchill and Blakedown, just over the north boundary of Kidderminster and a mile to the east of the Stour. The place-name survey of Worcestershire, however, gives no intermediate references between those in charters and the modern name.[4] The house-name appears on the first edition Ordnance Survey one inch map of 1831, so it has some antiquity, but without medieval documentation the possibility of antiquarianism cannot be ruled out. Various attempts have been made to locate the pond or lake (Old English *mere*) from which the province was apparently named. The latest of the Old English occurrences of the name is in the boundaries of a charter dated 964 (S 726) for Cookley which describe the northern half of the parish of Wolverley and Cookley which adjoins Kidderminster and Churchill. This survey starts at a point called *usmere*, which judging from identifiable features in the rest of the bounds appears to be a small pond near Ismere House at grid reference SO 863798.[5] It is difficult to envisage this pond as a feature from which a province would be named. A further complication is the occurrence of a boundary mark called *usan mere* in the bounds of an estate south of Birmingham, some 12 miles east of Kidderminster,[6] where, again, there may be small ponds, but there is no water feature of major significance. There are some pools on a tributary which joins the Stour at Kidderminster and the modern name Broadwaters appears on the 1832 Ordnance Survey map as that of two forges on this stream. It has been suggested that this was the site of Cyneberht's monastery,[7] but here again, assuming that the pools are not largely artificial, the feature is not a major one. A *mere* which gave name to a province might be expected to be like the glacial lakes of the Shropshire/Cheshire borders, such as Ellesmere and Hanmer, not a duck-pond-sized feature; and *pōl*, not *mere*, would be expected for pools on a stream. In two of the Stour in Ismere records the name is that of a group of people, *Usmerorum* and *Usmerum*, and the possibility might perhaps be considered of an obscure 'tribal' name, like some of those in the Tribal Hidage. This would not, however, explain the use of the name for boundary points. These problems are unsolved and I am aware that the observations in this paragraph are inconsistent with

---

4 Allen Mawer and F.M. Stenton, with F.T.S. Houghton, *The Place-Names of Worcestershire*, English Place-Name Society, 4 (Cambridge, 1927), 278.

5 Della Hooke, *Worcestershire Anglo-Saxon Charter Boundaries* (Bury St Edmunds, 1990), 171.

6 Ibid., 59–61, S 64.

7 Lilian J. Redstone, 'Kidderminster', in *The Victoria History of the County of Worcester*, III, ed. J.W. Willis-Bund (London, 1913), 158–79, at 159.

things I have written previously, and also that my aspersions on the claims of Ismere House to preserve the name *Usmere* do not entirely accord with my use of Stour in Ismere as a convenient name for the monastery.[8]

The most helpful locational statement in Æthelbald's charter is the one which places the estate athwart the River Stour. The statement that it is bounded on the north by the wood called Kinver and on the west by the wood called Morfe is less helpful, though it does indicate the relevant stretch of the river. Three later land-units in the area adjacent to these forests are bisected by the River Stour: these are the parishes of Kinver, Wolverley with Cookley, and Kidderminster. It is not easy to accommodate any of these to the statement that the two woods are respectively north and west of Stour in Ismere. After the Norman Conquest they became royal forests with precisely defined boundaries, but the position of Morfe Forest as defined in thirteenth-century sources does not suit the 736 boundary clause.[9]

The area is at the junction of Shropshire, Staffordshire and Worcestershire. In the thirteenth century the royal forests of Staffordshire were Kinver and Cannock. Morfe was one of the forests of Shropshire, though it lay partly in Staffordshire, and three farms – Morfe Hall, Morfe House and Morfeheath – which preserve the name are in Staffordshire, north-east of Enville. In 1086 there was in Staffordshire a waste estate of five hides called *Morfe*. On the map of mid-thirteenth-century royal forests drawn by Margaret Bazeley,[10] Morfe is shown as lying between and contiguous with the Staffordshire forest of Kinver and the Shropshire forest of Shirlet, the latter being west of the River Severn. Morfe is accorded a very small area on this map, about a sixth of the area of Kinver. Since it apparently extended to the Severn, eight miles west of the Stour, the Morfe farms and probably the Domesday estate would be in its eastern part. The area of Morfe Forest would have to extend considerably further south in the eighth century for it to be accurately described as bounding the west side of any of the land-units which lie athwart the Stour.

The name Kidderminster obviously suggests a connection with Cyneberht's monastery, since, when this name came into use, there must have been either a monastery or an important church there. Kidderminster derives from Old English *Cydelanmynster*, which means 'minster belonging to a man called Cydela'. It would have been more satisfactory from the historian's point of view if it had been *Cyneberhtesmynster* or *Ceolfrithesmynster*. The brief history of the family monastery does not include an abbot named *Cydela*, but he could have been a member of the same family, as the use of personal names beginning with the same letter was commonly practised by Anglo-Saxon families. He could perhaps be fitted into the story as an older brother of Ceolfrith, in charge of the monastery for a brief period after Cyneberht's death. The case for identifying Stour in Ismere with Kidderminster is

---

8   Margaret Gelling, 'The place-name volumes for Worcestershire and Warwickshire: a new look', in *Field and Forest: a Historical Geography*, ed. T.R. Slater and P.R. Jarvis (Norwich, 1982), 59–78 at 69; Margaret Gelling, *Signposts to the Past*, 2nd edn (Chichester, 1988), 92.

9   For sources on thirteenth-century royal forests, see Margaret Ley Bazeley, 'The extent of the English Forest in the thirteenth century', *TRHS*, 4th ser., 4 (1921), 140–72 at 166–72.

10 Bazeley, 'The extent', facing 141.

far from watertight, but the existence of a 'minster' and its association with an owner whose name began with *C-* can be held to support the claim. The two names, *Stur* and *Cydelanmynster*, could have coexisted for some time, the *mynster* name being in local use while the obsolescent earlier name continued in official documents.

The grant recorded on the reverse of the parchment of the 736 charter notes that an estate in the wood of Morfe named *Brochyl* has been added to the grant. This place has not been identified. There are three surviving instances of Brockhill ('badger hill') in north Worcestershire, in Beoley, Shelsley Beauchamp and Tardebigge, and in the eighteenth century there was another in Kingswinford,[11] but none of these could have been in Morfe wood. With five occurrences the name is likely to have been a compound appellative. It may be a local alternative to *brochol* ('badger hole'), which is fairly common elsewhere and occurs once in Worcestershire, in Alvechurch (where, however, in spite of having thirteenth-century spellings *Brochole*, it has the modern form Brockhill).[12] If *broc(c)hyll* does refer to a badger set, the name stresses the mound rather than the cavity. However that may be, it is a pity that it has not survived as a later name in the Morfe area. The Latin word used in the endorsement is *agrum*, which implies cultivated land and probably indicates a settlement.

The final matter to be considered is the bearing of this document on the history of settlement in the area concerned. Sir Frank Stenton probably had this charter in mind when he wrote 'To the west ... there stretched forests which bore British names, such as Morfe and Kinver, and even in the eighth century had not yet been divided out among English settlers'.[13] To the modern historian, however, accustomed to looking for continuity of settlement from pre-English times and to considering the woodland of post-Roman Britain as a precious economic resource rather than a barrier to movement, the two grants of *Stur* and *Brochyl* tell a different story.

Some indication of the nature of Anglo-Saxon land-units is given by the hidage. That of Stour in Ismere rose from ten in King Æthelbald's charter to 14 in Ceolfrith's grant to Worcester and in the agreement reached at the Synod of Brentford in 781. The extra four hides represent the *Brochyl* addition and those assessments of ten and four hides indicate that both units were of far from negligible size and value. It is not likely that either estate was carved from the forest by pioneer Anglo-Saxon settlers. There are charters of 866 (S 212) and 964 (S 726) which deal with two estates, Wolverley and Cookley, in the parish which adjoins Kidderminster on the north. The 866 Wolverley charter contains a list of payments which the grantee made to King Burgred and another list of the rights which the grantee was to enjoy in the common wood of Wolverley. Wulferd gives the king money, animals and a quantity of corn and threshed barley. His rights in the woodland are specified as pasturage for 70 pigs, five wainloads of good brushwood, one oak annually, other timber for building

---

11 The Kingswinford name was published by Deborah Ford, 'A note on a "grant by Aethelbald, King of Mercia, to Ealdorman Cyneberht, of land at Stour in Ismere, Worcs." (no. 154 in Birch)', *Journal of the English Place-Name Society*, 12 (1979–80), 66–9, but her suggestion that this was the *Brochyl* of the charter had to be disallowed as Kingswinford is too far east to be connected with Morfe.

12 Mawer and Stenton, Place-Names of Worcestershire, 333.

13 F.M. Stenton, *Anglo-Saxon England*, 3rd edn (Oxford, 1971), 40.

and sufficient firewood for his needs. Wolverley is rated at five hides. The picture conveyed by this charter is of a unit where arable and pastoral farming coexist and carefully allocated use is made of woodland resources. The picture belongs to a later date than that of the *Stur* and *Brochyl* grants, but it can reasonably be projected back to that date, and perhaps beyond, to a time before the area became part of Mercia. The Mercians are more likely to have been infiltrators than pioneers.

Chapter 8

Was there an Agricultural Revolution in Anglo-Saxon England?[1]

Alex Burghart and Andrew Wareham

One of the most notable features of Nicholas' work has been his discussion of the organisation of the Anglo-Saxon state, drawing upon administrative records in order to illuminate the development of military obligations, the construction of bridges and, most notably, the establishment of a network of fortified boroughs, many of which became England's county towns.[2] These processes can be linked to a wider series of economic changes in the late Anglo-Saxon period, ranging from the invigorating consequences of foreign trade to the establishment of national legislation on weights and measures.[3] Another key strand has been an interest in levels of literacy in the ninth century expressed through a detailed examination of the charters of Christ Church, Canterbury. Nicholas demonstrated that very few Canterbury scribes were able to draft charters in Latin and, when they did, they invariably demonstrated a limited knowledge of grammar and orthography.[4] Vernacular speech and pronunciation, moreover, influenced Latin misspellings in the Canterbury documents,[5] in the same way as anyone's knowledge of a first language affects the types of errors and inappropriate idiomatic expressions which he or she uses in a second language. In short, 'the pontificate of Æthelred (870–889) marked the nadir of illiteracy in the Canterbury community'.[6] Yet, as Nicholas observed, the one document from the 870s and 880s which was of a slightly better quality, namely the will of Ealdorman Ælfred, was written in the vernacular.[7] Thus, the relationship between the vernacular and Latin in the Canterbury scriptorium during the late ninth century was complex and evolving, and it may be erroneous to assume that a decline in Latin was matched by proportionate shortcomings in the uses of the vernacular.

---

    1   Andrew Wareham is based at the School of Arts, Roehampton University London and Alex Burghart at the Department of History, King's College London. The authors are grateful to James Campbell, Jinty Nelson and Chris Thornton for comments.
    2   N.P. Brooks, *Communities and Warfare 700–1400* (London, 2000).
    3   S.R.H. Jones, 'Transaction Costs, Institutional Change, and the Emergence of a Market Economy in Later Anglo-Saxon England', *The Economic History Review*, 46 (1993), 658–78, at 658; Nicholas Mayhew, 'Modelling Medieval Monetisation', in *A Commercialising Economy: England 1086 to c.1300*, ed. R.H. Britnell and B.M.S. Campbell (Manchester, 1995), 55–76, at 59, 70.
    4   N.P. Brooks, *The Early History of Canterbury: Christ Church from 597 to 1066*, Studies in the Early History of Britain (Leicester, 1984), 164–74.
    5   Ibid., 170.
    6   Ibid., 173. Dates of office inserted by the present writers.
    7   Ibid.; see S 1508.

The purpose of this chapter is to draw together these two strands, with two questions arising. First, what was the relationship between Latin and the vernacular in relation to estate management and, second, how far can the evidence for a transformation in the management of rural wealth through leasehold arrangements be connected to an economic spurt in late Anglo-Saxon England?

Agricultural innovations in Anglo-Saxon England

In contributing to a volume celebrating Nicholas Brooks it is appropriate to turn to a sister article addressing similar issues: Brigitte Kasten in her contribution to the *Festschrift* for Dieter Hägermann suggested that monastic leasehold texts served to uphold property rights and acted as a guarantee against the mismanagement of estates.[8] Such conclusions are familiar to medieval historians, but Kasten moves into new territory when she notes that amelioration clauses in Carolingian *precaria* documents improved the value of the land for both the lessor and the lessee and served as agro-political instruments for the benefit of all levels of society.[9] Her work accords with the studies of Rosenwein on the integrative roles played by great abbeys and their friends in zones beset by political fragmentation and economic dislocation.[10] Kasten's arguments can, moreover, be used as a template for understanding economic improvement in other societies and periods, such as England during the middle and late Anglo-Saxon periods.

A second way of looking at these issues is to consider S.R.H. Jones' concept of emergency conversion, whereby a cataclysmic event forces communities and individuals to release treasure and bullion in order to purchase necessities and to pay for new defences.[11] Jones' argument is that the Scandinavian invasions of the late ninth century not only resulted in English bullion being taken to Denmark, Francia and further afield, but also meant that a significant proportion stayed with the great army (*micel here*) within England. In short, money lost to churches and kings was gained for the economy, as a whole, and led to the establishment of a market system. Whether or not one accepts Jones' arguments in full,[12] her approach provides an invaluable insight. If silver and gold were liquidated from their royal and ecclesiastical holdings, then land might also have been affected by such processes.

---

8   Brigitte Kasten, 'Agrarische Innovationen durch Prekarien', in *Tätigkeitsfelder und Erfahrungshorizonte des ländlichen Menschen in der frühmittelalterlichen Grundherrschaft (bis ca. 1000)*, ed. eadem (Stuttgart, 2006), 139–54.

9   Ibid., 142.

10   B.H. Rosenwein, *To Be the Neighbor of Saint Peter: The Social Meaning of Cluny's Property 909–1049* (Ithaca and New York, 1989).

11   Jones, 'Transaction Costs, Institutional Change', *passim*. For the wider context, see N.P. Brooks, 'England in the Ninth Century: The Crucible of Defeat', *Communities and Warfare*, 48–68.

12   For discussion of markets, see R.H. Britnell, *The Commercialisation of English Society, 1000–1500* (Cambridge, 1993), 19; James Campbell, 'Was it Infancy in England? Some Questions of Comparison', in *idem, The Anglo-Saxon State* (London, 2000), 179–99, at 195.

Together Kasten's and Jones' arguments suggest that unsettled political conditions during the ninth century may have led to a freeing up in property relationships so as to give a new lease of life to leasehold as an instrument of economic improvement.

Yet before looking at the leasehold evidence and its relationships with estate management, it is helpful to consider the wider context of rises in agricultural productivity in pre-modern societies. Economic historians suggest four means by which agricultural output can be expanded:[13]

1. an expansion in the geographical area;
2. increases in inputs;
3. local specialization; and
4. technological innovation.

New perspectives on agricultural revolutions have focused attention upon the fourth factor of change, namely technological innovations.[14] These not only include direct investments, such as new crops, livestock and implements, but also more intangible innovations, such as changes in the quality of inputs, improvements in knowledge and new forms of organisation. Most notably, in relation to the Middle Ages, there has been an extensive discussion of the establishment of the system of open fields grouped around nucleated settlements between the ninth and twelfth centuries.[15] In short, agricultural productivity was galvanised by new forms of tenure, coupled with new estate-management skills, which were in turn dependent upon the supply and quality of agricultural advice.[16] Although some of the concepts set out in agricultural advice books and manuscripts were poor or exaggerated, there were also many good ideas,[17] including the application of skills which required no further investment, such as yoking oxen by the neck (rather than by the horns) and limiting the number of horses used to pull ploughs.[18] Consideration of the early modern English evidence is suggestive. Between c.1680 and c.1710 between 0.3 and 0.9 agricultural periodicals were published per year, but during the eighteenth century, with the exception of the 1750s and 1760s, the figure stood at between 1.1 and 1.7, before the number rose to double digit figures during the early nineteenth century.[19] These treatises almost certainly reached beyond circles of authors. From the late fifteenth century between

---

13 Mark Overton and B.M.S. Campbell, 'Productivity Change in European Agricultural Development', in *Land, Labour and Livestock: Historical Studies in European Agricultural Productivity*, ed. B.M.S. Campbell and Mark Overton (Manchester, 1991), 1–50, at 4–7.

14 Useful observations are set out in ibid., 17, 22–3.

15 Carenza Lewis, Patrick Mitchell-Fox and Christopher Dyer, *Village, Hamlet and Field: Changing Medieval Settlements in Central England* (Macclesfield, 2001); Tom Williamson, *Shaping Medieval Landscapes: Settlement, Society, Environment* (Macclesfield, 2003).

16 Overton and Campbell, 'Productivity Change', 26.

17 Ibid., 26.

18 Richard J. Sullivan, 'Measurement of English Farming Technological Change, 1523–1900', *Explorations in Economic History*, 21 (1984), 270–89. The classic English medieval text is *Walter of Henley and Other Treatises on Estate Management and Accounting*, ed. Dorothea Oschinsky (Oxford, 1971).

19 Sullivan, 'Measurement of English Farming', 276.

a fifth and three-fifths of husbandmen and yeomen were literate in England, and it may be that the prodigious rises in agricultural output between the late sixteenth and nineteenth centuries were linked to a literate familiarity with texts concerned with the technologies of farm management.[20]

Early modern advances in knowledge skills may not apply to the conditions that explain rises in agricultural output in earlier periods, yet the fact that such issues have been so greatly neglected in relation to early medieval England encourages a preliminary discussion. These issues need to be placed alongside the emergence of the common fields, water mills and other investments in the infrastructure as factors which may have contributed to the production of substantial agricultural surpluses in England before the Norman Conquest.[21] The textual context of the ways in which vernacular literacy may have improved agricultural productivity in late Anglo-Saxon England is discussed in a later part of this article. First, however, there follows a discussion of the political context and its relationship with the regulation of ecclesiastical leasehold.

Leases, literacy and land management

It is thanks to Nicholas that the 816 Synod of Chelsea no longer languishes in obscurity. Before *The Early History of the Church at Canterbury* it had received scarcely any attention at all, having been classified by Hefele and Leclercq under the heading 'Councils of little importance'.[22] Nicholas drew attention to Chelsea because of its radical attempts to extend episcopal power, most notably by granting bishops the power to select abbots and abbesses within their own dioceses. Another concern of the council was the retention of ecclesiastical land:

> That it be not lawful for bishops, nor abbots, nor abbesses ... to diminish the estates of their churches, nor to grant away the inheritance of them, for any longer than for one man's life (and this with the consent and licence of the family), that it may again be restored to the church. And notwithstanding [the demise] let the original grants, with the other written evidences, be preserved, lest they endeavour afterwards to raise scrupulous contradictions; for it is very dangerous for those who are appointed to be guardians and defensors of convents, to give or take away what is granted to others for the health of their souls to God, and the rest of the holy ones, as their proper inheritance, unless a just cause require it, as relief against famine, or against the depredations of the army, or for obtaining liberty. Otherwise let [the estate] be kept entirely undiminished, lest [the monks] run the risk of perishing by poverty. Let every one rather be content with his own; and give that to those who are, or who are not akin to then, according to their merits.[23]

---

20 Ibid., 278–83.

21 For the general context, see Rosamond Faith, *The English Peasantry and the Growth of Lordship* (Leicester, 1997).

22 C.J. Hefele and Henri Leclercq, *Histoire des Conciles*, IV (i) (Paris, 1911), 8–9.

23 *Councils and Ecclesiastical Documents relating to Great Britain and Ireland*, ed. A.W. Haddan and William Stubbs (3 vols, Oxford, 1869–71), III, 579–86, at 582. Translation from John Johnson, *A Collection of the Laws and Canons of the Church of England* (2 vols, Oxford, 1850–1851), I, 300–308, at 303–304.

From before Chelsea, there are ten charters recording leases, and of these, four are for more than one life.[24] Only one of these is from an archive other than Worcester and it seems likely that the practice of issuing leases was actually much more widespread and sufficiently popular to require the council to limit their use. That more early leases do not survive is perhaps unsurprising; leasing documents by their nature are of temporary use and become redundant on the completion of the lease. In short, despite the paucity of documentation, leasing may have been common in the late eighth and early ninth centuries and this may have had a profound effect on the Anglo-Saxon economy.

The most obvious group of pre-tenth-century leases is that compiled in the second half of the ninth century, when churches used them to acquire loyalty and money. In 849 Bishop Ealhhun of Worcester made over a total of 20 hides to King Beorhtwulf of Mercia (840–852) for an unprecedentedly protracted five lives *pro nostra defensione*, some of which the king then sublet to one of his *ministri*.[25] The monks of Worcester probably felt the need of defence; the previous year a Danish army had been defeated at the mouth of the River Parret in Somerset by the West Saxon ealdormen Eanwulf and Osric.[26] In 855, as the *pagani* were among the Wrekin dwellers,[27] Ealhhun leased 11 hides to Ealdorman Æthelwulf and his wife on the condition that they held themselves 'reconciled and allied to the city of Worcester as well during life as afterwards'.[28] West Mercia was probably being harassed throughout these years and the coalition of West Saxon and Mercian forces sent into Wales in 853 may have been intent on preventing the rulers of the Welsh kingdoms from coalescing with Viking forces.[29] By the 870s bishops were leasing land in return for gold and silver perhaps to pay tribute to the *pagani*, though this is only explicitly stated on one occasion: Bishop Wærferth explained that he had only leased the estate at Nuthurst (Sussex) because of the 'immense tribute of the barbarians, in that same year when the barbarians had stayed at London'.[30] The amount of tribute that the *here* demanded of the Mercians during the ninth century is not recorded, but the *Anglo-Saxon Chronicle* noted that peace was made in 868 at Nottingham,

---

24 S 1254 (718×745), two lives; S 59 (770), three lives; S 1255 (774); S 109 (775/777), three lives; S 62 (777×780); S 1412 (786×796) for Medeshamstede; S 1430 / S 1260 (789 and 803), one life; S 1261 (814?), two lives; S 1262 (798×822), two lives; all from the Worcester archive save S 1412.

25 S 1272 (Worcester); five of these hides were then leased by the king, later that year, to his thegn Ecgberht in return for his obedience and for sixty pounds of gold and silver.

26 *The Anglo-Saxon Chronicle: a Revised Translation*, ed. Dorothy Whitelock, with D.C. Douglas and S.I. Tucker (London, 1961), s.a. 845, *recte* 848.

27 S 206 (Worcester): Gesta est autem huius libertatis donatum . anno dominice incarnationis. dccc . lv o . indictione . iii a . in loco qui vocatur Oswaldesdun . quando fuerunt pagani in Wreocensetun.

28 S 1273 (Worcester), 855: ... *ut seipsos habeant reconciliatos 7 conjunctos tam viventes quam post ad Wegernensem civitatem.*

29 *Anglo-Saxon Chronicle*, A, s.a. 853; A's omission of the 855 Wrekin episode may have been an attempt to conceal the ultimate failure of the joint venture.

30 S 1278 (Worcester) 872.

in 872 at London and in 874 at Repton.[31] Unmentioned payments may lie behind a series of late ninth-century leases: Wærferth granted nine more than those already mentioned;[32] Denewulf of Winchester (879–909) issued six, two of which were for himself;[33] and Archbishop Plegmund (890–923) sold a three-life lease in Canterbury for 385 pence.[34]

Such grants show churches utilising their resources to gain money and favour in the sort of exceptional circumstances that had been foreseen at the synod of Chelsea. But most of these transactions involve either long leases, a lot of money, a considerable amount of land, or a combination of all three, and they may not be entirely representative of an unrecorded norm which dealt in shorter leases and in smaller estates. An early example of a marginally more mundane lease may be preserved in Dunwald's bequest of 762 to SS Peter and Paul, Canterbury (St Augustine's) of a *villa* in the *forum* of Canterbury. Dunwald says that the *villa* was currently held by Hringwine (*nunc Hringwine tenet*), who could have been his tenant.[35] Whatever their arrangement, it is clear that Dunwald could terminate his tenure, either through his own death or by simply granting the land to someone else: Dunwald explained that though he was bequeathing the land he might choose to grant it prior to his death. Hringwine's position, therefore, was not determined by the length of his own life, nor even that of his landlord's, and it may even have been for a fixed number of years.

Tenure for less than a life was probably taking place in some quarters by the eleventh century. One Worcester charter granted a man called Fulder some land for three years on the condition that he returned it along with everything that was on the land when he was given it.[36] The same idea may lie behind a broadly contemporary record from Bury St Edmunds which declares:

> Here is what was found at Egmere after Cole left it, namely 7 oxen and 8 cows and 4 grazing bullocks and 2 inferior horses and 115 sheep, including both full-grown and young ones, and 160 acres sown and 1 flitch of bacon and 1 pig and 24 cheeses.[37]

Cole's lease had evidently expired, either because he had chosen to leave or because he had been driven out. These two cases need not reflect earlier custom in the least, nor should they be expected to shed light on an obscure eighth-century charter, but they reflect the possibility that there were many and varied ways of exploiting landownership that were not necessarily recorded in the same way as other

---

31 *Anglo-Saxon Chronicle*, s.a.

32 S 215 (875) 4 lives; S 1283 (899 x 904) 3 lives; S 1415 (889) 3 lives; S 1416 (892) 4 lives; S 1279 (899) 2 lives; S 1280 (904) 3 lives; S 1281 (904) 3 lives; S 1282 (907) 3 lives.

33 S 1285 (902); S 1287 (879 x 908); S 1444 (900 x 908) to King Edward; S 385 (*c.* 909), lease by Edward to Denewulf and Winchester.

34 S 1288 (CCC) 905 x 923.

35 S 1182 (St Augustine's) 762. See also Susan Kelly, this volume, at n. 57.

36 S 1421 (Worcester) s. xi.

37 Robertson, *Anglo-Saxon Charters*, 197, no. 104: Her onstent gewriten hwæt Eggemere postquam Cole eam dimisit hoc est …

transactions. That they are chance survivals suggests extra layers to landholding not represented in the charters that are the standard fare of Anglo-Saxon estate history.

To a small extent the management of Anglo-Saxon holdings can be inferred from the earliest cases of inventory accounting. A letter from Bishop Denewulf written between 900 and 908 describes how King Edward requested a lease of seventy hides of land at Beddington in Surrey for his lifetime:

> ... there is 70 hides of that land [at Beddington], and it is now completely stocked, and when my lord first let it to me it was quite without stock, and stripped bare by heathen men. And I myself then acquired stock for it which was afterwards available there ... Moreover, my dear lord, the community are now desirous that it be given back to the foundation after your death. Now, of the cattle which has survived this severe winter there are nine full-grown oxen and 114 full-grown pigs and 50 wethers, besides the sheep and the pigs which the herdsmen have a right to have, 20 of which are full grown; and there are 110 full-grown sheep, and seven bondsmen, and 20 flitches; and there was no more corn there than was prepared for the bishop's farm, and there [are] 90 sown acres.[38]

The practical purpose of these details was no doubt to ensure that the king did not strip the land as bare as the heathens had done, yet it is early evidence for the use of inventory procedures in Anglo-Saxon England. It is unlikely that this was the only Winchester estate for which Bishop Denewulf had an accurate assessment or that he was the only bishop who kept one.[39] The pre eleventh-century land documents which survive are almost all solely concerned to establish ownership; it is possible that there were a good many other records in monasteries which related to the upkeep of those lands, their management and worth.

To couple these two ideas of short leases and book-keeping is to raise the prospect of the early management of Anglo-Saxon estates. If leases could be granted for less than a life and records were kept of exactly what was on the land, then landlords were in a sound position to exploit fluctuations in the productivity of land. In the twelfth century, Suger, abbot of St Denis 1122–1151, recognised that leases which allowed regular feedback between holder and owner had the potential to create rises in agricultural output.[40] Landlords encouraged leaseholders to maximise the productivity of the land by setting a maximum viable rent which the holder then sought to outstrip by as much as he could. Suger was aware of how conveniently profitable such a system could be when he encouraged the granting of leases with the caveat that they should be short so as to allow for a regular upward adjustment of rent to account for rising values.[41]

Given the examples of Fulder and Cole, it is possible that these ideas were at work in eleventh-century England. Hypothetically they can be read into the late

---

38 S 1444 (OM, Winchester) 900 × 908; *EHD*, I, no. 101.

39 That this was going on elsewhere appears to be shown by an 866 account of what was on the Bishop of Worcester's land at Seckley when he leased it to King Burgred: S 212 (Worcester) 866.

40 Faith, *The English Peasantry and the Growth of Lordship*, 182.

41 Ibid.; Georges Duby, *The Early Growth of the European Economy: Warriors and Peasants from the Seventh to the Twelfth Century*, tr. H.B. Clarke (London, 1974), 215.

ninth century when both book-keeping and short-term leasing *may* have been taking place in at least some parts of England. Finding them any further back in the past is extremely difficult, but the possibility remains that complex leasing arrangements were under way by the time of Chelsea in 816. An aspirant lay class was evidently anxious to acquire land on as a long a tenure as it could and its anxiety may have been due to a general shortage of land available in perpetuity. Bede famously voiced his fears that too much of the countryside had been acquired by false monastic houses and that there was now not enough to reward the rising stars of the next generation. But Bede's fear that too much property had been permanently taken out of circulation overlooked the ways in which it might be readmitted.[42] It seems highly plausible that during the eighth century monasteries, pseudo-monasteries and perhaps even laymen, in response to demand, started leasing land. How advanced the nature of this leasing was at any point before the eleventh century is extremely difficult to gauge, but it is at least conceivable that short-term leases for profit pre-date, by some considerable stretch, their earliest appearances in the written record. Such leasing conventions, if widespread, would have acted as powerful economic motors, which could have had a profound effect on the productivity of land and thus on the wealth of landholders capable of monitoring their estates. If this was the case, lease management may have been a major factor in the economic development of England.

As close management was only available to those who had access to the written word, it is now worth returning to Nicholas' discussions of literacy in the *Early History of the Church of Canterbury*. The lack of expertise in Latin at Canterbury during the late ninth century gives 'credence to a famous passage of the preface to King Alfred's version of the *Pastoral Care*'.[43] If Alfred's justification for his translation of the *Pastoral Care* is correct, then English literacy was not unusual either in his day or that of his predecessors. Old English documents prior to 871 are not thick on the ground, but those that survive are of the greatest significance. The laws of Æthelberht, Hlothhere and Eadric, Wihtred and Ine were probably all originally written in the vernacular, though their earliest manuscripts are so late as to forbid absolute certainty.[44] Likewise the misnamed 'Tribal' Hidage whose first incarnation was certainly pre-Alfredian.[45] The indications that much else may have been written in English during the early Anglo-Saxon age comes in the papal legates' account of their 786 English councils at which 'the separate chapters were read in a clear voice and lucidly expounded both in Latin and in the vernacular [*theodisce*], in order that all might understand'.[46]

---

42 *EHD*, I, no. 170, 735–45.

43 Brooks, *Early History of the Church of Canterbury*, 164–74, notably 171; see also *Alfred the Great: Asser's Life of King Alfred and Other Contemporary Sources*, ed. Simon Keynes and Michael Lapidge (London, 1983), 126.

44 For further discussion, see Patrick Wormald, *The Making of English Law: King Alfred to the Twelfth Century*, I: *Legislation and its Limits* (Oxford, 2001), 93–106.

45 D.N. Dumville, 'The Tribal Hidage: An Introduction to its Texts and their Histories', *The Origins of Anglo-Saxon Kingdoms*, ed. Steven Bassett (Leicester, 1989), 225–30.

46 BCS 250; the translation is that of *EHD*, I, 839–40, no. 191.

From the mid-ninth century there is evidence for charters being drafted in English. In 844 or 845, a charter by which King Beorhtwulf of Mercia (840–852) donated nine hides in modern-day Buckinghamshire to a nobleman was recorded entirely in English,[47] while a few years later a West Saxon document detailed the characteristics of 45 landscape features in the vernacular.[48] In addition, there survives from the Canterbury archive a group of vernacular documents which record a complex series of annual food renders which were to pass from Abba the reeve and members of his family to the Canterbury community c. 839 × 871,[49] and vernacular documents from East Anglia and Mercia which deal with the management of a swine pasture and the lease of an estate.[50] Although the wide geographical dispersion of these texts argues against a take-off in any particular region for the use of the vernacular to control the management and descent of property, it may point to the increased importance of the vernacular in the first half of the ninth century.

Yet a change in the functionality of Latin and its relationship with English during the late Anglo-Saxon period cannot be taken as being equivalent to demonstrating that the vernacular became an instrument of effective estate management. Nonetheless two post-Alfredian fragments point towards the new importance of the vernacular in the practice of estate management. The Old English *Rectitudines Singularum Personarum*, dating from at least the mid-tenth century, perhaps earlier, is a business-like document, setting out what the manager of an estate could expect to receive from the other people on the property.[51] In the mid-eleventh century this text was brought together with *Gerefa*,[52] which set out the qualifications and duties of a reeve in charge of such an estate. It demonstrates awareness of the need to provide reeves with written instructions so as to sustain the wealth of the land for the benefit of the estate's owners.[53] The origins of *Gerefa* are difficult to establish, but *Rectitudines Singularum Personarum* can be connected to the south-west, perhaps with Bath (Som.) or Glastonbury Abbey (Som.).[54] Both texts, however, share the characteristic of assuming that the estate was under the rule of a single lord and, since their authors recognised that local communities differed, they may have assumed that the texts were to be widely distributed. As Harvey notes, more work is required on these two texts, though they are still sufficient to point to the important role of the vernacular in estate management undertaken by reeves at least from the late tenth century onwards.[55]

---

47 S 204 (CCC) 844 × 845.

48 S 298 (OM, Winchester) 846.

49 S 1195 (CCC) *c*. 850; S 1197 (CCC) 843 × 863; Brooks, *Early History of the Church of Canterbury*, 147.

50 S 1440 (Medeshamstede) 852; S 1437 (Worcester) *c*. 825.

51 The following account is based on P.D.A. Harvey, '*Rectitudines Singularum Personarum* and *Gerefa*', *EHR*, 108 (1993), 1–22.

52 Ibid., 7.

53 Ibid., 8.

54 Ibid., 20–21.

55 Ibid., 22. These issues link up with the themes raised in Richard Britnell, *Pragmatic Literacy, East and West 1200–1300* (Woodbridge, 1997).

Lay literacy, whenever it came to the fore as a powerful economic force, was presumably used, first and foremost, to manage the estates of the great magnates of Anglo-Saxon England. The skills of literacy gave access not only to mechanisms of land management otherwise unavailable, such as closely monitored leasing, but also, perhaps, to written manuals which further extended the efficient administration of estates.

Discussion

Historical discussion of leasehold in an English medieval context has generally been focused upon twelfth-century developments, as raised in the debate conducted between Postan, Lennard and Bridbury.[56] Briefly put, Postan's suggestion was that the rise of leasehold was 'unpropitious for demesne farming ... [which] ... made it difficult to control from afar the management of detached manors'.[57] Although Postan was right to highlight some of the difficulties of control, in some ways leasing allowed closer attention to be paid to the estates in hand and consequently permitted it to be an instrument of economic improvement.

In order to appreciate the wider context of such issues a brief look needs to be taken at the broader transformation of English society between *c.* 900 and the mid- eleventh century, of which rapid urbanisation is a distinctive hallmark.[58] The re-growth of towns required a more substantial surplus from the land as more people became primarily consumers of agricultural wealth rather than producers of it. Such a shift would have been impossible without sizable agricultural surpluses which in turn required the appropriate management of Anglo-Saxon agriculture. The land had to be capable of supplying towns with the food necessary for growth.

Short-term leasing may have been an ancient practice which, during the tenth century, became available to a larger class of landowners as more and more of the laity became literate and applied their skills to the management of their estates. Thus leasehold, supported by book-keeping, perhaps already a potent force in the management of ecclesiastical estates, was extended to the lands of a wealthy secular elite whose own lands then became substantially more productive and helped to encourage urbanisation.

---

56 Michael Postan, 'Glastonbury Estates in the Twelfth Century', *Economic History Review*, 2nd ser., 5 (1952–1953), 358–67; idem, 'Glastonbury Estates in the Twelfth Century: a Reply', ibid., 2nd ser., 9 (1956–1957), 106–18 (reprinted in idem, *Essays in Medieval Agriculture and General Problems of the Medieval Economy* (Cambridge, 1973), 249–77); idem, 'The Glastonbury Estates: a Restatement', ibid., 2nd ser., 28 (1975), 524–7; idem, 'A Note on the Farming Out of Manors', ibid., 2nd ser., 31 (1978), 521–5; Reginald Lennard, 'The Demesnes of Glastonbury Abbey in the Eleventh and Twelfth Centuries', ibid., 2nd ser., 8 (1955–1956), 355–63; idem, 'The Glastonbury Estates: a Rejoinder', ibid., 2nd ser., 28 (1975), 517–23; R.A. Bridbury, 'The Farming Out of Manors', ibid., 2nd ser., 31 (1978), 503–20.

57 Postan, *Essays in Medieval Agriculture*, 276.

58 John Blair, 'Towns', in *Blackwell Encyclopaedia of Anglo-Saxon England*, ed. Michael Lapidge, John Blair, Simon Keynes and Donald Scragg (Oxford, 1999), 451–3.

Another way in which these issues can be considered is to look at English coinage. By the end of Edgar's reign in 975 few parts of England south of the Humber were further than 15 miles from a mint.[59] Prior to his reforms there had been between 25 and 30 working mints in England, a figure which expanded, around 973, to about 50, rising to roughly 70 in the eleventh century. Such an increase implies that there was regional economic demand sufficient to warrant their existence. That coin was being used regularly throughout the southern kingdom suggests that very many people were involved in exchange and that there was much to trade. The creation of new, regulated and centrally monitored mints must have played a significant role in the creation and lubrication of a national economy, but it was systems of land management – such as leasing – which encouraged the generation of the surplus necessary for such a coinage to be of use. The court's ability to harness, ride and drive this boom stands as one of the substantial achievements of medieval statecraft and goes some way to explaining the great wealth of early medieval England. But it was not kings alone who created favourable economic circumstances. Whilst the burh-building in Alfred's reign, the increase in mints in Edward's, their closer management by Æthelstan and the *renovatio monetae* of Edgar's were extraordinary changes which smoothed the route towards more urbanised, specialised and monetised communities in southern and midland England, the success of these programmes required the existence and development of close and careful land management and the widespread production of agricultural surpluses.

In short, this article applies some of the ideas put forward by Kasten and Jones, but shifts attention towards the relationships between leasehold management, vernacular literacy and intensive economic growth.[60] Yet if such issues are to be understood in full it is necessary to follow the lead of the new generation of studies on agricultural revolutions which point to the importance of knowledge and new ways of managing the land, as well as an expansion in land area and increases in inputs, as key means for expanding agricultural output. Such issues lead into analyses of vernacular literacy programmes, *Rectitudines Singularum Personarum* and the records of leasehold arrangements and texts. Leasehold is not generally regarded as an area of study to tease out the full significance of agricultural transformations since it is not normally associated with sustained capital investment and economic growth; nevertheless it may have been played a central role in the transformation of the Anglo-Saxon economy.

---

59 The following account is based on R.H.M. Dolley and D.M. Metcalf, 'The Reform of the English Coinage under Eadgar', in *Anglo-Saxon Coins: Studies Presented to F.M. Stenton on the Occasion of his 80th Birthday, 17 May 1960*, ed. R.H.M. Dolley (London, 1961), 136–68, notably 150–51.

60 Kasten, 'Agrarische Innovationen durch Prekarien', passim; Jones, 'Transaction Costs, Institutional Change', passim.

Chapter 9

'The Annals of Æthelflæd': Annals, History and Politics in Early Tenth-Century England

Pauline Stafford

'The Annals of Æthelflæd' is a name given to a series of entries for the early tenth century, contained in three of the vernacular chronicles which we now know as the 'Anglo-Saxon Chronicles'. They focus on a woman, Æthelflæd, daughter of King Alfred and wife of Æthelred, lord of the Mercians, and on the period of her power in Mercia. The gender of their subject and, to a lesser extent, their geographical concern are remarkable. Their Mercian interest finds echoes elsewhere in tenth-century entries, but has little connection with what now precedes them. This is the longest sustained treatment of a woman anywhere in the Anglo-Saxon Chronicles. These annals are commonly known as the Mercian Register, a term coined by Plummer, who also labelled them the 'Annals of Æthelflæd'.[1] Several years ago, in a volume commissioned by Nicholas Brooks and one which benefited enormously from his help and encouragement, I suggested that these annals should be seen as a continuation of the Alfredian Chronicle, produced at or near the Mercian court in the early tenth century and paralleling those produced in contemporary Wessex.[2] A volume designed to honour the work of Nicholas Brooks is an ideal place to return to that question and explore it in more detail. These entries are, I shall argue, to be understood as history-writing in political context, an understanding which illuminates both the context and the writing. Nicholas's own recent work on myth and politics has been an inspiration here. In the 'Annals of Æthelflæd' his interest in Mercia and its early history meets my own concerns with royal women.

These entries span the years 902 to 924, though they concentrate on 909–919. They are laconic and lack narrative development, but are thematically linked. They begin with the death of Ealhswith – Alfred's widow and Æthelflæd's mother though not so designated here – in 902. They end with the accession of Æthelstan 'chosen king by the Mercians' in 924, and with his marriage of his (unnamed) sister overseas.

---

1 Charles Plummer, *Two of the Saxon Chronicles Parallel* (2 vols, Oxford, 1892–99), I, 92, n. 7. The author gratefully acknowledges the contribution towards work for this chapter of funding from a large AHRC grant for the project 'Gender, Chronicle, Conquest and Nation'.

2 Pauline Stafford, *The East Midlands in the Early Middle Ages* (Leicester, 1985), 67 and repeated in Pauline Stafford, 'Political Women in Mercia. Eighth to Early Twelfth centuries', in *Mercia, an Anglo-Saxon kingdom in Europe*, ed. M.P. Brown and C.A. Farr (London, 2001), 35–49 at 48.

They appear to break off in mid sentence in two chronicles, B and C.[3] D adds that the marriage was to the son of the king of the Old Saxons and has two following entries for 925 and 926 on Æthelstan's relations with the kings of Northumbria and other rulers of Northern and Western Britain.[4] D's 925 entry ends with the record of another woman, another sister of Æthelstan and her marriage to King Sihtric. It is not clear whether D retains a more complete version of these annals, either in its apparent completion of 924, or in its entries for 925 and 926.[5] The group of entries certainly begins with reference to a woman and ends in two if not three of the chronicles which contain them with the marriage of a woman. This is unusual in itself, since women feature rarely in these vernacular chronicles. For example, in the 240 or so entries covering more than 900 years in the now lost Alfredian Chronicle, there are only about 20 references to women.

The consecutive entries are even more remarkable in this respect. They focus on Æthelflæd. In 910, they record her building of the *burh* at *Bremesbyrig*.[6] From 912 until her death in 918 the annals are exclusively concerned with Æthelflæd's activities, especially her military ones: her *burh* building in particular, her retaliatory attack on the Welsh, her taking of fortified places under Danish control, culminating in the oaths and pledges given to her by the people of York in the year of her death. That death was recorded with special emphasis on her rule of the Mercians and its legitimacy: 'the eighth year in which she had held power (*anweald*) with right lordship'. Divine approbation of her activity was made explicit. She acted with God's help: in 913 when, '*Gode forgifendum*', she went 'with all the Mercians' to Tamworth and built the *burh* there, and again with His aid in 917 '*Gode fultmigendum*' and 918 when she besieged Derby and Leicester, which in the latter case she took 'peacefully'. Her first recorded action after her husband's death in 911, the building of the *burh* at *Scergeat*, took place on the eve of the Invention of the Holy Cross. The

---

3   B = *The Anglo-Saxon Chronicle. A Collaborative Edition*, 4: *MS B*, ed. Simon Taylor (Cambridge, 1983); C = *The Anglo-Saxon Chronicle. A Collaborative Edition*, 5: *MS C*, ed. Katherine O'Brien O'Keeffe (Cambridge, 2001). Szarmach suggests it is possible to accept a *lectio difficilior* here and assume that this entry is complete, Paul Szarmach, 'Æthelflæd of Mercia: Mise en Page', in *Words and Works: Studies in Medieval English Language and Literature in Honour of Fred C. Robinson*, ed. Peter S Baker and Nicholas Howe (Toronto, 1998), 105–26, at 108.

4   D = *The Anglo-Saxon Chronicle. A Collaborative Edition*, 6: *MS D*, ed. G.P. Cubbin (Cambridge, 1996).

5   D is a later eleventh-century chronicle. Its compiler(s) had access to Northern material which could explain the extra detail in all these entries. On D's date and sources see Cubbin, pp. lvi–lxxxi with references to earlier work. Simon Walker, 'A context for "Brunanburh"', in *Warriors and Churchmen in the High Middle Ages*, ed. Timothy Reuter (London and Rio Grande, 1992), 21–40, at 28, suggested that the Brunanburh poem, perhaps intended for a tenth-century Chronicle, was written by Cenwald, bishop of Worcester. Cenwald accompanied Æthelstan's sister to Saxony for her marriage. Could he have completed this annal?

6   I follow the dating in C. Not all annals in B are dated. On the dating and chronology of the Mercian Register see F.T. Wainwright, 'The Chronology of the Mercian Register', *EHR*, 60 (1945), 385–92 and '*Cledemutha*', *EHR*, 65 (1950), 203–212.

feast may have had special resonance for a Mercian royal woman.[7] The consecutive entries end in the year after her death, 919, in which Ælfwyn was deprived of all power (*anweald*) among the Mercians (*on Myrcum*) and taken to Wessex three weeks before mid winter.

Ælfwyn was, we assume, Æthelflæd's daughter, though at this point she is called the daughter of 'Æthelred, lord of the Mercians'. This is only the second reference to him in these annals. The first was to his death in 911. His earlier rule as lord of the Mercians merits no mention, though that dates back to the 880s, the decade in which he had married Æthelflæd. Æthelflæd's brother Edward the Elder, king of Wessex and of Mercia from 919, if not from his accession, is also virtually absent. His move into Mercia on Æthelflæd's death in 918 and deprivation of Ælfwyn can be deduced from the 919 entry, but are not explicitly noted here. The single annal between 919 and 924 records his building of the *burh* at *Cledemuth*. Whether by accidental omission or for other reasons, this annal is missing from B. Otherwise the only record of Edward is at his death at Farndon 'in Mercia' in 924, followed by the death very soon after of his son Ælfweard (not here specified as king nor as chosen as king, though at least one regnal list records his brief reign)[8] and the choosing of Æthelstan as king by the Mercians, '*of Myrcum*'.

This conspicuous absence of Edward contrasts sharply with the A chronicle account. Not only does that vernacular chronicle give his activity in detail, it makes clear how much of that activity after 918 if not 912 or 915 was in Mercia. The A chronicle excludes Æthelflæd as systematically as these entries ignore Edward. She occurs only once, at 918, when her death was recorded. There she is not 'Lady of the Mercians', as in the B and C annals, but 'his (Edward's) sister'. Her rule is implied, however, since the annal goes on to note Edward's move into Mercia, to Tamworth where she had died 'and all the people in the land of the Mercians who had been subject to Æthelflæd submitted to him'.

These annals thus have a clear focus on Æthelflæd and her activities as a ruler of Mercia, but *not* on early tenth-century Mercian rulers more generally – her husband or her brother. They concentrate on her military activity, but also on the legitimacy of her rule. The entries present her as a ruler, engaged in the quintessentially kingly and masculine role of a war leader. God's support for her in that role is stressed.

The entries do not, however, begin sharply at the point when she took over from her husband in 911. Consecutive annals begin in 909. Between the death of Ealhswith in 902 and this annal, three years are blank, two contain brief entries on astronomical events, two record the renewal of Chester's defences (907) and the translation of the bones of Oswald from Bardney to Mercia (909). The annals for 902, 907 and 909 may be argued as connected to Æthelflæd and her later activity.[9] Whether or not

---

7 Stafford, 'Political women in Mercia', 39–40 for the significance of St Helena to an earlier Mercian queen. B and C, which contain these entries, also have an entry in 884, not in A, recording the sending of the fragment of the cross to King Alfred by Pope Marinus.

8 The regnal list in the Textus Roffensis has a reign length of four weeks; cf. D, s.a. 924 where he died 16 days after his father.

9 The translation of Oswald may be an 'Æthelflædan' action, and is specifically thus in William of Malmesbury's *GRA*, I, 199 (Book ii, c. 125). A lost charter of Æthelstan, cited in

that connection was made retrospectively is not clear. The deprivation of Ælfwyn in some senses closes the entries, including in narrative tone. But a final annal on the accession of Æthelstan appears to be connected, both by its Mercian emphasis and its 'female' content. The interest of these annals is obvious. Their interpretation, however, is far from easy.

As we now have them, they have been incorporated into three of the vernacular chronicles: B a late tenth-century chronicle (BL Cotton Tiberius A vi),[10] C a mid eleventh-century chronicle (BL Cotton Tiberius B i)[11] and D a later eleventh-century chronicle (BL Cotton Tiberius B iv).[12] B and C derived them from a common exemplar or exemplars of a lost chronicle which ran, like B, to the 970s.[13] I shall call that chronicle B/C. The D version had access either to something like B/C, or, as is now argued, to C or a chronicle very like C.[14] In all these chronicles the annals have been variously combined with other material, producing somewhat different accounts of the tenth century. Since this discussion is primarily concerned with the annals' original form, B, C and B/C are most important. D would be of great significance were the aim to assess later eleventh-century versions of the English past.

These entries should be treated as a group, on the basis of content, but also of the manner of their survival and treatment in later chronicles. In the case of B, C and thus surely of B/C before them, these annals follow the chronicle of Alfred, in other words the vernacular chronicle which ran to 892, plus the West Saxon continuations into the 890s and on to 914, more or less as all these are now found in A. Thus in B, C and B/C the story runs consecutively to 914. It then backtracks to 902, to these annals, and begins again, repeating the death of Ealhswith already copied

---

the early fourteenth century, makes it the foundation of her husband, Æthelred, here confirmed by Æthelstan, calling himself Æthelred's foster son; discussed Carolyn Heighway, 'Gloucester and the New Minster of St Oswald', in *Edward the Elder*, ed. N.J. Higham and D.H. Hill (London, 2001), 102–11 at 103, and cf. Michael Hare, 'The Documentary Evidence to 1086', in *The Golden Minster: the Anglo-Saxon Minster and Later Medieval Priory of St Oswald at Gloucester*, ed. Carolyn Heighway and Richard Bryant (York, 1999), 33–46. Æthelflæd was buried in the church of Gloucester to which Oswald's bones were taken (C and B, s.a. 918). The *burh* building and defence obviously links with her later activity. Ealhswith is her mother. On Gloucester and its churches, see also e.g. Alan Thacker, 'Chester and Gloucester: Early Ecclesiastical Organisation in two Mercian Burhs', *Northern History*, 18 (1982), 199–211.

10 Taylor, *B*, pp. xxiii–xxiv for dating. The genealogical regnal list, now Tiberius A iii fo. 178, with which the MS once ended (later detached – see Taylor, *B*, p. xvii) ends with the unfinished reign of Edward the Martyr, 975–8. Its last entry is for 977, and, in Taylor's view, its script suggests a date – possibly early – in the last quarter of the tenth century.

11 O'Keeffe, *C*, pp. xxvi–xxviii and lxxxix for dating.

12 Cubbin, *D*, pp. xi, lii–lv for dating.

13 *Two Chronicles*, ed. Plummer, II, p. lxxxviii n. 9, P.W. Conner, *The Anglo-Saxon Chronicle. A Collaborative Edition*, 10: *The Abingdon Chronicle AD 956–1066* (Cambridge, 1996), at e.g. p. xxxviii, O'Keeffe, *C*, at e.g. p. lxxviii. For the notion of more than one exemplar behind B and C, see Janet Bately, *The Anglo-Saxon Chronicle, Texts and Textual Relationships* (Reading, 1991), 25.

14 Cubbin, *D*, pp. liii–lv, though here and elsewhere he underestimates the independent elements in D.

from an A-type chronicle.[15] In both B and C, this shift is marked in the manuscript by a run-on of blank year numbers, that is along the line rather than a separate line for each number. A similar run-on follows the entry on Æthelstan. Both B and C then continue with a spasmodic series of mid tenth-century annals which include the famous poems on the battle of Brunanburh and the Relief of the Five Boroughs. There are strong arguments for seeing much if not all of this mid-century material as 'Mercian', though that cannot be pursued here.[16] Again we can presume that this indicates the content and layout of B/C.

This latter lost chronicle, or its exemplar, thus appears to have been a compilation. Its compiler had before him (or her, since a nunnery cannot be ruled out) a chronicle very like A, which ran to 914. S/he also had a text or texts which contained tenth-century material, mostly Mercian, including these annals of the early tenth century. The nature of that lost text or texts has exercised those scholars who have paid any attention to these annals.

A number of tentative reconstructions have been offered. Most have begun from the distinctive content of these annals and from their treatment in the manuscript layout of B and C, and thus surely B/C. B/C's scribe's combination of early tenth-century material was mechanical. S/he simply copied out an A-type chronicle, and then followed it with another set of entries which covered some of the same years. D, by comparison, tried to marry the two accounts into one single narrative, without, it has to be said, complete success.[17] In B/C there was an awkward 'join'. This was marked, and still is marked in B and C, by a run-on of blank annal numbers which link the 914 entry, still very oddly (see below), to the annal from 902 taken from another text. This whole block of entries is then, apparently, separated from the mid-century material by another run-on of blank numbers, which run smoothly from 925 to 933. This layout and content have combined to convince scholars that it was at this point, after 914, that B/C's compiler turned to another text, which contained the Æthelflædan annals and perhaps more. Plummer argued that the new text began before 902 and that we have lost its earlier section; the blank annals are critical to his argument.[18] He was less clear on the nature of this longer text, or of the Æthelflædan material itself. He suggested that the longer text had material common to B/C's other source, hence its omission in the process of compilation; yet that it was a separate text, not already inserted into a Chronicle like B or C. The implication of his arguments is that he felt the Æthelflædan material was in annal form.[19] Szarmach has recently argued strongly that a Latin, possibly poetic *Gesta* of Æthelflæd, lies behind

---

15 *Two Chronicles*, ed. Plummer, I, 92 n. 7.

16 See e.g. Walker, 'A Context for "Brunanburh"', though hovering between Mercian and West Saxon court elements.

17 For example the death of Æthelred in 910 and again in 912 and the Battle of Tettenhall three times, Cubbin, *D*, p. xxxii.

18 *Two Chronicles*, ed. Plummer, II, p. cxviii, n. 3, and cf. p. lxxxviii, n. 9. He argues that a text would not begin with a list of blank numbers – though perhaps an Easter Table might? Earlier annals were omitted because 'they were in substance identical' with what B/C already had.

19 Cf for example. *Two Chronicles*, ed. Plummer, II, p. cxviii and n. 3 with pp. lxii–iii and n. 1 and I, 92 n. 7.

these entries, partly on the grounds of content and sharply differentiated layout, but also on linguistic ones.[20] He does not discuss in detail at what point the Latin poem was turned into vernacular annals.

An original Latin *Gesta* would require a stage of translation of language and form, into Old English and annals. It arguably requires that translation to have been effected before B/C's compiler found this material. B/C's compiler fairly consistently used run-on numbers at the end of a previous entry to indicate blank annals in the source text. The blank years treated in this way within this group of annals, as well as at the beginning, point to a text already in annalistic form as B/C's source here. Nor is this set of annals simply a translated *Gesta* of Æthelflæd. It extends at the beginning and end back to Ealhswith's death and forward to Æthelstan, as well as including a couple of astronomical references. Again this suggests that the Æthelflædan material was part of a longer run of annals. It is conceivable that the compiler of B/C translated a *Gesta*, placed it in a set of annals with other entries, complete with blank years, which s/he then transcribed as run-ons when combining the resulting text with another.

Ockham's razor would cut through all this and produce an argument for B/C's second text as one which was from the beginning in Old English and annal form. That text was once longer at the start, with losses here now represented, at least in part, by the blank annals. That useful tool is not, however, necessarily the most appropriate one to take to the reconstruction of lost texts where so many stages may have been lost. The manuscript layout needs more consideration, as does the content of these annals. And the rather better understood if still problematic early tenth-century annals in the A chronicle should be brought into the argument.

The manuscript layout of B and C and by inference of B/C has been one of the strongest arguments for a separate text used by B/C at this point. It cannot, unfortunately, provide unequivocal guidance as to its nature. This block of entries begins and ends with blank annal numbers, run on along the line, and internally the blank years 903, 906, 908, 922, 923 and, in C alone, 920 are treated similarly, with the blank number on the same line as the end of the previous annal. Run-ons of this type are common in B and C; at times they are the only numbers in B.[21] They are the normal way of treating blank annals in the fully rubricated C, and presumably in B/C. At the beginning, though not the end of this block, they may have a second meaning or function. They arguably indicate the chronological difficulty created by B/C's turning from an A-type text which ran to 914, to a new text with entries before that date. They have been seen to demonstrate the presence of blank annals and/or duplicated material. Plummer's arguments seem to assume that the blank numbers

---

20 Szarmach, 'Æthelflæd of Mercia: Mise en Page', 105–26. Note especially his arguments for Latinate dative absolutes in the vernacular as opposed to the more '"native" prepositional phrases' in the entries for 913 and 917. Janet Bately noted the use of Latinate constructions in the work of Werferth of Worcester: 'Old English Prose before and after the Reign of Alfred', *ASE*, 17 (1988), 93–138, esp. 120–21.

21 B contains few numbers for 'fruitful' annals between 652 and 946, and not consistently after that date. The MS probably never received final rubrication, Taylor, *B*, esp. p. xxxi, xxxvi and l, and for its annal numbering in detail, pp xxxvii–xlix; on C's treatment of annal numbers see O'Keeffe, *C*, pp. xl–xlii.

here were either in the second text, and/or marked duplication between it and the A-type. That is not, however, the only possibility, as Whitelock has pointed out. The blank numbers are not identical in B and C. In C they read 896 to 901, in B 816 to 819, then 900 and 901. Whitelock argued that B here has the closer reading of B/C and B/C's sources. These included an A-type manuscript which had blanks running on as 916, 917 and perhaps beyond. B miscopied these as 816 and 817 and so on, C rationalised them as a run of numbers preceding 902. This would mean that it was the A-type chronicle which was the source of the blank years, leaving fewer grounds to argue for a second text which stretched back before 902. However, it should be noted that recent work has seen C as the product of a very conservative and careful copyist.[22] Although earlier in date, B is not necessarily closer to the original.

If C's enumeration is the closer to B/C, what can that tell us? Does it necessarily indicate that B/C had a second text which had a blank run of annals connecting the Æthelflædan entries to earlier ones which were so like A that they were omitted? Perhaps, though there is no obvious reason why 896 should have marked the point at which such common entries ceased. That date falls within one of the most clearly marked narrative continuations in A, namely the entries for 893–896 inclusive.[23] It is perfectly possible that the compiler here departed from his/her normal practice of using run-ons to indicate blank numbers, instead using them to mark the awkward join. S/he inserted sufficient to fill the space left by the annal for 914 taken from the A-type chronicle, and part of the next line,[24] though the normal practice of C (and arguably B/C) argues against this.

The layout of B and C at first sight offers much. It raises tantalising possibilities, including that of a second text once longer at the beginning. But it can neither prove beyond doubt the existence of such a text, resolve questions about its nature nor help determine whether that text was itself the result of several earlier stages which included at some point a Latin *Gesta*. The content of these entries, however, suggests a different line of enquiry. Most of the entries focus on Æthelflæd, celebrating if not legitimating her rule. The entries in A are similarly centred on Edward. The Æthelflædan entries extend back to 902 and the death of her (Mercian-born) mother, also in A though not at this date, and forward to 924 and Æthelstan's accession, chosen as king *by* though not necessarily solely *of* the Mercians. This looks like a significant break. The consecutive blank years following that should indicate blank years in the sources of B/C. A also has a significant break at around this point, at 920.[25] In both cases the desire to write appears to have ended in the 920s, although

---

22 O'Keeffe, *C,* pp. ciii–cvii and cx, and see her response to Bately's argument at p. lxii.

23 Cecily Clark, 'The Narrative Mode of *The Anglo-Saxon Chronicle* before the Conquest', in *England before the Conquest*, ed. Peter Clemoes and Kathleen Hughes (Cambridge, 1971), 215–35, at 221–4; M.B. Parkes, 'The Palaeography of the Parker Manuscript of the Chronicle, Laws and Sedulius, and Historiography at Winchester in the Late Ninth and Tenth Centuries', *ASE*, 5 (1976), 149–71, at 155.

24 There was space for more numbers on the line in B, fo. 30r and C, fo. 140r. Neither need indicate the layout in B/C and even there such a space might signify miscalculation rather than act as a straightforward guide to the blank numbers in its source.

25 The rest of the page, and thus the rest of the quire, is blank after 920. 924 marks the first entry in Hand 3, on the first folio of a new quire, which is to be dated mid-tenth century,

entries after 919 in the 'Annals of Æthelflæd' are spasmodic and possible losses at the end of 924 creates some room for doubt about the original ending.[26] Other parallels between the 'Annals of Æthelflæd' and the A chronicle are worth pursuing.

A and its evolution have been much debated. It is almost certainly a court chronicle, in the sense argued by Dumville and Wormald, and most likely a Winchester one.[27] Palaeographical study places A's scribes in the reign of Edward the Elder, or just after. It is difficult to be certain whether the first scribal work in it dates earlier than 911, but 911/14 x 930 is the probable date range of scribal activity.[28] The copying of A does not, of course, necessarily represent the dates of the composition of its text. Textually the annals for Edward's reign fall into more or less clearly defined groups. The most distinct are the entries for 915–920.[29] Those from 912 to 914 may represent a group. The annals from 897 to 911 may be the work of a single author or several.[30] The arguments in all cases are on the basis of content and/or stages which this chronicle had reached when it, or copies of it, became known to later chroniclers or compilers. The 897–911 section follows another textual group, the annals for 893–896, seen as the 'first continuation' of Alfred's chronicle. Annalistic writing in the vernacular thus continued in Wessex beyond the 890s into the first decades of the tenth century, latterly if not entirely in the court circle of Edward. This was not necessarily a continuous process, with annals written on a year by year basis. Groups of annals are closely connected and may have been written together and/or by the same author.

There is a strong presumption that, whether singly or as groups, these annals were added to a Chronicle of Alfred, which was continued and updated, albeit spasmodically. The language and form argue for an association from the outset with Alfred's chronicle. Neither annalistic form nor vernacular language should be taken for granted. English was not the obvious language for history-writing in early

---

The Anglo-Saxon Chronicle; a Collaborative Edition, 3: *MS A: a Semi-Diplomatic Edition with Introduction and Indices*, ed. Janet Bately (Cambridge, 1986), 69 s.a. 920 n. 4 and pp. xxxiv–v, David Dumville, *Wessex and England from Alfred to Edgar* (Woodbridge, 1992), 62–66 and 130.

26 The entry on marriage s.a. 924 might be argued to link back to the earlier entries on a woman. But the Æthelflædan material is determinedly not concerned with such familial and arguably 'female' questions. The 924 entry cannot be the first of D's very interesting mid tenth-century series of entries on women, since it is also in B and C, which have very few of these. On balance the argument for seeing these entries as ending in 924 with Æthelstan is strong, but not conclusive.

27 Dumville, *Wessex and England*, 134, contra Parkes, 'The Palaeography', 149–71. Patrick Wormald, *The Making of English Law: King Alfred to the Twelfth Century*, I: *Legislation and its Limits* (Oxford, 1999), 164–72, esp. 171 agrees with Dumville on the difficulty of separating (secular) court from episcopal concerns, but tends to reinstate Parkes' view of Winchester.

28 Dumville, *Wessex and England*, 67–98, esp. 89–96, 127, cf. Bately, *A*, pp. xxi–xxxiv.

29 Janet Bately, 'The Compilation of the Anglo-Saxon Chronicle once more', *Leeds Studies in English*, New Series, 16 (1985), 7–26 at 15; Dumville, *Wessex and England*, 68–9 and M.R. Davidson, 'The (Non)Submission of the Northern Kings in 920', *Edward the Elder*, ed. Higham and Hill, 200–211, esp. 204 for the 'Chronicle of the Triumphs of Edward'.

30 Dumville, *Wessex and England*, 67–9.

England; the Latin of Bede's epitome seems to have remained in use for that activity in the North.[31] Nor were annals an inevitable form. Both were choices of genre and language already made in Alfred's court circle. And A continues the again far from obvious way of treating years without material with a number and blank line, a practice which again the Alfredian chronicler(s) had adopted.[32] The nature of A leaves it beyond much doubt that a chronicle was produced either during the reign of Edward, or less likely soon after. It began with a copy of the Alfredian chronicle and then continued it with annals for Edward's reign, in two or more continuations. One or both of these could have been written after Edward's death, though it is unlikely that both date from then, and both were complete and copied in another manuscript (our A) no later than *c*. 930. Alfred's story was thus appropriated in Edward's court circle; Edward's reign thus became a continuation of his father's story. By the end of the 920s, however, both the composition and the copying of annals had ceased. The years from 924 onwards were added much later.[33] The last continuation took Edward's reign no further than its triumphant representation of the events of 920.

Here, then, are indisputably early tenth-century bouts of annal writing. Their content, themes and probable purpose repay closer scrutiny. It is unclear whether the years 897 to 911 were a single first continuation. But the annals covering events in the years immediately following Alfred's death have a unified theme; the succession to Alfred in 'Angelcynn', more narrowly in Wessex, specifically Edward's succession to his father vis-à-vis the challenge from his cousin, Æthelwold, son of Alfred's older brother, King Æthelred. The entries dated in A to 900, 903 and 904 centre on this. These years also contain *two* references to Edward's mother, Ealhswith: to the death of her brother Athulf and to her own death, recorded at the end of the dramatic events of 902 (A 904) in which Æthelwold died. By comparison, Ealhswith was never referred to in the chronicle of Alfred's reign, which similarly omitted all note of that king's own mother.[34] Together with the unnamed wife of Æthelwold, there are three references to women in four entries which begin A's coverage of Edward's

---

31 See Plummer's perceptive comments on this divide, *Two Chronicles*, II, p. lxxii, n 1. The historical miscellany compiled by Byrhtferth of Ramsey in the late tenth century included a copy of earlier Northern annals, by now if not originally in Latin: Michael Lapidge, 'Byrhtferth of Ramsey and the Early Sections of the *Historia Regum* Attributed to Symeon of Durham', *ASE*, 10 (1981), 97–122 and cf. Peter Hunter Blair, 'Some Observations on the *Historia Regum* Attributed to Symeon of Durham', *Celt and Saxon: Studies in the Early British Border*, ed. Kenneth Jackson and others (Cambridge, 1963), 63–118, including comment on the tenth-century Northern annals found in this twelfth-century Latin compilation.

32 Janet Bately, 'Manuscript Layout and the Anglo-Saxon Chronicle', *Bulletin of the John Rylands University Library of Manchester*, 70 (1988), 21–43 *passim* and at e.g. 42. A is not a simple guide to its predecessors. But other versions of the Alfredian chronicle are witness to this same treatment, see e.g. E.

33 Above, n. 25. There was a deliberate attempt to make it into a continuous story with Edward's chronicle, since the quire containing the Laws, written in the 930s, was displaced at this stage. Conscious choices were made in the growth of the tenth-century chronicle A.

34 Cf. Pauline Stafford 'Succession and Inheritance: a Gendered Perspective on Alfred's Family History', *Alfred the Great, Papers from the Eleventh-Centenary Conferences*, ed. Timothy Reuter (Aldershot, 2003), 251–64 for arguments about women in sources and family politics.

reign. This should, in itself, alert us to the probability that family and its politics were to the fore in the composition of these annals.

Whether as active supporters or, through their own royal blood, as underliners of Edward's royal status, his mother and her family may have been critical to Edward at this point.[35] Their royal blood was Mercian, relevant to any claims Edward had beyond Wessex. Their unusual presence in the chronicle is a warning. The A chronicle's account of these years should not be read as a simple record of events, but as a particular, Edwardian, perspective on them. Æthelwold was a very serious challenger, as James Campbell has recently stressed.[36] He gained initial support in Wessex – witness those who had 'bowed' to him and were with him at Wimborne in 899 – and could claim inheritance from an older ruling son in the direct male line. Strength of support and strength of claim readily combine into a virtuous circle in a succession dispute. Æthelwold's marriage to a woman who had been in a nunnery, thus very probably a royally-born woman, was part of the strengthening of his claim, all this before his move North to gain support from the Scandinavians settled in East Anglia and Northumbria.[37] The A annals bear close reading with a view to this connection. They pointedly de-legitimise Æthelwold, stressing his alliances with the Danes rather than his support within Wessex and probably from 'English' Mercians, judging from the presence of a Mercian claimant among the dead in the final battle of the Holme.[38] What was probably a politically important marriage becomes the abduction of a nameless nun, against the permission of the king and command of the bishop.[39] Æthelwold himself is Edward's 'uncle's son' not 'æðeling' (= claimant to the throne) in A.[40]

---

35 Compare J.L. Nelson, 'Reconstructing a Royal Family: Reflections on Alfred, from Asser Chapter 2', in *People and Places in Northern Europe, 500–1100*, eds. I.N. Wood and Niels Lund (Woodbridge, 1991), 47–66 and Barbara Yorke, 'Edward as Ætheling', in *Edward the Elder*, ed. Higham and Hill, 25–39 for appreciation of this, though with differing interpretations – and for consideration of Edward's own marriage and the likely consecration of his queen at about this point. Cf. Pauline Stafford, *Queen Emma and Queen Edith: Queenship and Women's Power in Eleventh-Century England* (Oxford, 1997), 57, 75, 89–90, 95 and 254.

36 James Campbell, 'What is not known about the Reign of Edward the Elder', in *Edward the Elder*, ed. Higham and Hill, 12–24, at 21–2.

37 The attitude of Mercia and of Æthelflæd and Æthelred must have been crucial in these years, see Stafford 'Powerful women in Mercia', esp. 46.

38 A, s.a. 905, Byrhtsige son of ætheling Beornoth, most likely a Mercian prince, though not specified as such in A. In calling him a son of an ætheling, not an ætheling in his own right, A may again be subtly delegitimising Æthelwold's support. See Stafford, 'Succession and Inheritance: a Gendered Perspective' and 'Powerful Women in Mercia' for a re-reading of relations with 'Mercia' in later ninth-century Wessex.

39 Such a marriage raises questions about the motivation of Alfred's concern to stop women leaving nunneries without his permission – see Laws of Alfred, c. 8: *The Laws of the Earliest English Kings*, ed. and tr. F.L. Attenborough (Cambridge, 1922), 68. 'Reform' needs to be read in a political context, though not as simple and crude political manipulation.

40 A, s.a. 901, B and C, s.a. 901, give him that title. D, s.a. 901 follows B and C.

By contrast the last continuation of Edward's reign, that from 915 to 920, is markedly triumphal in nature,[41] although in this respect it follows on to some extent from the tone of the probably separate section, 912–914. The concern of both these groups is with Edward's military successes north of the Thames, largely in Mercia, and with his building of burhs. 912–914 follows the annal which records the death of Æthelred 'ealdorman in Mercia'. 915–920, if written as a block, belong in the 920s. This latter group includes the only reference in A to Æthelflæd, the record of her death where she is simply 'Edward's sister', followed by Edward's taking of Tamworth and generally of rule in Mercia. The group concludes with the construction of burhs at Nottingham and Bakewell in north-west Derbyshire, and the submission to Edward and choice of him as father and lord by all the rulers of Northern and Western Britain.

In subject matter, these annals obviously follow the geographical progression of Edward's campaigns and his takeover of Mercia, partially in 911, fully in 918/919. They should, however, be read as a text. The entry for 920, for example, is a tendentious West Saxon, or at least southern English interpretation of events.[42] These annals do not merely follow the takeover of Mercia, they respond to it. If they are triumphant celebration, they are also arguably defensive legitimation. This is chronicling from and for a West Saxon court circle celebrating Edward's success, yet defensively so; aware of, if not overtly aimed at, potential Mercian scepticism and arguments which could see his advances on Mercia as less than legitimate.[43] Edward is presented as a successful military ruler, with a special eye to Mercian concerns. By the 920s such chronicling might also have had an eye to questions of succession to his rule, not just in Wessex, but also in Mercia.

The annals of Edward's reign should thus be seen not merely as chronicling for its own sake, but as a series of responses to the political questions of the early tenth century, as they were seen from the West Saxon court. By the second and third decades of that century, those questions would have involved if not centred on rule and succession in Mercia, with a view also to future rule of a combined Wessex-and-Mercia. From the outset the question was of Alfred's inheritance. A chronicle which attached Edward's story to that of his father claimed the inheritance which Alfred's own writing of the past had defined. Such a reading is encouraged by the excellent recent work on history writing which has demonstrated the complex uses of the past in the early middle ages. The writing of history at this period does not simply chronicle the remote or recent past. Through representation of the past and through claims on it, history writing reflects but also justifies the present and thus

---

41 Davidson, 'The (Non)Submission', 204 for the 'Chronicle of the Triumphs of Edward'.

42 Ibid., passim. His exhortation to treat and criticise this section as a text in itself is followed here.

43 Ibid., cf. Walker, 'A Context for "Brunanburh"?' and perceptive discussion of Mercia in tenth- and eleventh-century history by Nicola Cumberledge, 'Reading between the Lines: the Place of Mercia within an Expanding Wessex', *Midland History*, 27 (2002), 1–15.

seeks in some way to influence the future, possibly, though not necessarily, with overt manipulative or propagandist intent.[44]

The political context of this writing requires attention. The years 918–924, viewed against the background of the previous half century, raised a series of political questions. The deaths of the two children of Alfred, Æthelflæd in 918 and Edward in 924, precipitated issues of succession and rule in Mercia and Wessex: separately and individually, as old kingdoms; and combined, as Mercia-and-Wessex. Those issues were predictable and foreseeable. At the end of the ninth century, Alfred had made moves towards a hegemonic control of Mercia from Wessex.[45] Alfred's death in 899 had resulted in a struggle for the succession within Wessex itself. Edward's succession to his father in Wessex was not securely established until 902.[46] His father's inheritance in Mercia was even more problematic. Relations between the West Saxons and the Mercians in the later ninth century had involved military alliance and a series of marriages. Alfred's marriage to Ealhswith had been one and that between Æthelflæd and Æthelred was the last. Alfred's dominance in the 890s over Æthelred, Lord of the Mercians, was as debatable at the time as it still is. Whether as a result of Edward's initial struggle in Wessex, or for other reasons, the dominance of a West Saxon king over rulers of Mercia became even more debatable after 899, though aspirations towards such hegemony remained.[47]

The death of Æthelred in 911 was not marked by an attempt at West Saxon take-over, though Edward did move on London and Oxford – a move which the A chronicle presents in the language of legitimate succession '*feng to*'. Much of Mercia, especially its western sections, remained in the hands of Æthelred's widow, Æthelflæd. Her military activity, in the direction of Leicester and Derby, as well as towards the West and North West, suggests that Mercian elites had lost none of

---

44 See e.g. Rosamond McKitterick, 'Political ideology in Carolingian historiography', in *The Uses of the Past in the Early Middle Ages*, ed. Yitzhak Hen and Matthew Innes (London, 2000), 162–74; Rosamond McKitterick, 'The Illusion of Royal Power in the Carolingian Annals', *EHR*, 115 (2000), 1–20; Rosamond McKitterick, 'Constructing the Past in the early Middle Ages: the case of the Royal Frankish Annals', *TRHS*, 6th ser., 7 (1997), 101–29; Yitzhak Hen, 'The Annals of Metz and the Merovingian Past' in *The Uses of the Past*, ed. Hen and Innes, 175–190. Excellent general comment and some caveats in Innes, 'Introduction', *Uses of the Past*, ed. Hen and Innes, 1–8.

45 Simon Keynes, 'King Alfred and the Mercians', in *Kings, Currency and Alliances: History and Coinage of Sothern England in the Ninth Century* ed. M.A.S. Blackburn and D.N. Dumville (Woodbridge, 1998), 1–45, though my own interpretation would make the alliance much less firm and unproblematic; see 'Powerful Women in Mercia', 44–7 and 'Succession and Inheritance, a Gendered Perspective', 259–61.

46 The family politics of Edward's reign, a king whose succession to his father marks the first vertical succession from father to son in almost half a century would bear more scrutiny. Note, for example, his three marriages, one of which belongs to the critical years of succession dispute 899 x 902, the significance of his mother and her brother, whose deaths are, unusually, noted in A and the attitude of Edward to his own brother – who is a regular witness of Edward's charters. Both Jinty Nelson and Barbara Yorke, see n. 35, have made us aware of the need to scrutinise Edward more closely in this respect, though their perceptive considerations have not progressed much beyond the 890s and earliest years of the reign.

47 Again compare Keynes and Stafford, as n. 45.

their earlier aspirations, to which recovery of areas lost from Mercian control to the Scandinavians should now be added. To read all this as a simple 'partnership' and division of responsibility between Edward and Æthelflæd,[48] is to lose the historic sense of Mercia which these actions also express. In the decades that followed Alfred's death, the role of Edward's sister and Alfred's daughter, Æthelflæd, in the negotiation of the uneasy relationship between these two kingdoms and courts was critical. Her death in 918, just as much if not more than that of her husband in 911, raised questions of succession in Mercia and of the relationship of Wessex and Mercia. Edward moved to take power forcibly and to deprive his niece. His own death in 924, however, reopened exactly the same questions. The events of 924 temporarily resolved them. Æthelstan was chosen as king by the Mercians and then quickly became king of Wessex after his brother's untimely death.[49]

The alliance of Wessex and Mercia in the later ninth century had been military, but also dynastic. The resulting polity of Wessex-cum-Mercia which was fitfully taking shape was itself dynastic, held together by familial ties in marked contrast with later Southern domination over Northumbria. Æthelflæd, a daughter of Alfred and sister of Edward, was uniquely placed to express the ambiguities of that polity, including the Mercian possibilities within it. These possibilities are suppressed in West Saxon readings of the tenth century and in modern historians' acceptance of these in their own picture of the inevitable rise of an England based on this southern kingdom. Recognition of the tension between Wessex and Mercia, alongside their growing unity, is essential to a full understanding of tenth- and eleventh-century English history. Edward's annals are at least in part responses to the early tenth-century phase of these developments. What light does all this throw on the 'Annals of Æthelflæd'?

The parallels between the histories of brother and sister should be underlined. First, those of genre, language and layout. The annalistic form, vernacular language and treatment of blank years in which Edward's court-chronicling continued that of his father find direct counterparts in Æthelflæd's story as B/C had it. At some stage this material took a form heavily influenced, like Edward's, by the chronicle of Æthelflæd's father.[50] This does not in itself prove that this was their original form, though it strengthens other pointers in that direction. The parallels of content,

---

48 As, e.g. F.T. Wainwright, 'Æthelflæd, Lady of the Mercians', in F.T. Wainwright, *Scandinavian England*, ed. H.P.R. Finberg (Chichester, 1975; originally published in *The Anglo-Saxons: Studies in Some Aspects of their History and Culture Presented to Bruce Dickins*, ed. Peter Clemoes (London, 1959), 53–69), 305–24 at 310 and *passim*, or Stafford, *East Midlands*, 112.

49 There is no contemporary evidence for his rearing in Mercia, which I and others have too readily accepted on the basis of William of Malmesbury's 'lost source' – on which see Michael Lapidge, 'Some Latin Poems as Evidence for the Reign of Athelstan', *ASE*, 9 (1981), 61–98. Dumville, *Wessex and England*, 146 was wisely sceptical of Malmesbury's unsupported statement – though cf. the early fourteenth-century evidence citing Æthelstan's fostering by Æthelred, Æthelflæd's husband – above, n. 9.

50 Ironically, the arguments for circulation of the chronicle, by minimising questions of choice, may have obscured how significant Alfred's chronicle was in influencing subsequent historical writing in England.

focus and subject and of the chronological limits of the stories, have already been noted. The Æthelflædan annals, in their concern with burh building and military activity north of the Thames and particularly across the borders of 'English' Mercia, emerge as particularly close to those of Edward after 912 and especially after 915.[51] Edward's annals were demonstrably produced in the first decades of the tenth century, responding to pressing contemporary questions centred on claims to rule. The argument for placing the original 'Annals of Æthelflæd' at that same date is strengthened by comparison. These two sets of annals appear almost as a dialogue, or rather as two responses to very similar political questions and context.

As with Edward's annals, it is difficult to be sure whether production was in Æthelflæd's own lifetime, with a view to her own claim or the claims of a successor, or after her death. The fact that Æthelflæd's story ends with her death might argue that it was retrospective. Edward's chronicle may have been composed in stages. Some of Æthelflæd's story could have been contemporary with her, some or all of it rewritten after her death. It certainly continued to be relevant as long as rule in and of Mercia was an issue, whether in or after the brief rule of her daughter or in the context of some later claim.

Some later claim to what? Should we read the 'Annals of Æthelflæd' as a text of early tenth-century Mercian separatism, a chronicle written in a context in which separate rule of Mercia was being asserted and claimed? Could the Annals of Æthelflæd have followed a lost Mercian chronicle? Or did they, like Edward's annals, continue an Alfredian chronicle, and, like Edward's, claim the paternal inheritance, but now for a Mercian-based descendant of Alfred? Any answer, however tentative, must first return to that tantalising 'longer text'.

If a Mercian chronicle ever existed, it has disappeared virtually without trace. Mercian material follows these entries, which in many ways mark a reorientation of the geographical focus of the vernacular chronicles. But very little precedes them.[52] There was once, however, an account of the 890s which was more Mercian in tone, giving much more prominence to Æthelflæd's husband. The late tenth-century Chronicle of Æthelweard used a chronicle which contained it. Æthelred was here a king and a virtual campaigning equal with the then prince, Edward.[53] Did that account once precede the Annals of Æthelflæd? There is a tantalising break in its narrative precisely at 895, before B/C's first blank annal number, 896. And the reference to Ælfwyn as Æthelred's daughter in 919 might indicate that he was originally more important in the text.

---

51 And the importance of *burh* building as a – deliberate – continuation of the activity of previous Mercian kings is underlined by Steven Bassett, 'Divide and rule? The Military Infrastructure of Eighth- and Ninth-Century Mercia', *Early Medieval Europe*. 15 (2007), 53–85. Here, too, we have parallel activity of brother and sister which had important resonance in relation to a Mercian past.

52 On possibly Mercian annals in the Chronicles, including B and C, pre 892, i.e. those sections deriving from the Alfredian Chronicle, see *EHD*, I, 122 and n. 5. The entries in question were already in the ninth-century West Saxon chronicle and cannot be evidence of a different, Mercian Chronicle preceding the Æthelflædan annals.

53 *The Chronicle of Æthelweard*, ed. Alistair Campbell (Edinburgh, 1962), 49–51.

But there are strong arguments against seeing Æthelweard's Mercian entries as part of a lost chronicle of ninth-century Mercia, or ever associated with the Æthelflædan material. In the source which Æthelweard used, the 890s were apparently already a continuation of the Alfredian chronicle. His source does not appear to have included these annals on Æthelflæd. If Æthelweard had access to an account of Æthelflæd's activities he studiously ignored all but her death.[54] His working methods make all conjecture about his sources hazardous, but this would be a significant editorial omission. His annals of the 890s should arguably be read as yet another tantalising fragment of contemporary history-writing c 900 A.D. They trumpet the successes of a late ninth-century Mercian king, but in tandem with a West Saxon prince and following from a West Saxon, Alfredian past. They appear to be another indication of how far the Alfredian chronicle influenced historical writing at this date. If history reflects politics in some way, they are themselves no simple Mercian separatist statement.

Although a lost chronicle of Mercia cannot be ruled out, it is more likely that the longer text began with Alfred's chronicle, as arguments from genre and language suggested. Æthelflæd's annals, like those of Edward, would have followed those of her father. Such an attachment reflected – to put it no more strongly – a claim on Alfred's past and inheritance. Æthelflæd's annals arguably derive from a context in which such a claim could and would be made – for a Mercian-based or supported but West Saxon-born or connected would-be ruler of Wessex-cum-Mercia. Æthelflæd herself, or Ælfwyn if not Æthelstan after her? Separatism would not necessarily have been the goal of early tenth-century rulers of Mercia, nor of all sections of the Mercian elites who supported them. There was another prize: Mercian-based or at least Mercian-orientated rule of 'Angelcynn'.[55] That was a goal in some senses realised in Æthelstan's reign. Æthelstan was chosen in and by Mercia, though whether as king *of* Mercia or as a candidate for rule of Wessex and Mercia is more debatable. Accident ensured that he quickly came to rule both. Æthelflæd, a West-Saxon born woman but also a ruler of Mercia and descendant of Mercian rulers through her mother, would have been a crucial figure for anyone who wished to achieve such an end, whether during her own lifetime or immediately after her death. A chronicle celebrating her, but continuing that of her father would have expressed such aspirations. The 'Annals of Æthelflæd' like the 'Annals of Edward' fall silent in the 920s. Both had addressed contemporary questions of succession to 'Angelcynn'. Those questions were resolved, at least temporarily, by Æthelstan's accession.

Æthelflæd's story and annals survive in later chronicles, B/C and B, finally in the eleventh-century D. By the date of the B chronicle, and B/C before it, these annals formed part of a history which incorporated Æthelflæd, albeit a little uncomfortably, and Mercia into a wider southern English story. Alfred's chronicle with Edward's continuations led, not quite seamlessly, into a more Mercian-focused history of the mid tenth century. That culminated in the West Saxon genealogical regnal table which had prefaced A, if not Alfred's chronicle itself, now brought up-to-date with

---

54 Ibid., 53, and here very like the E Chronicle.
55 For a related discussion, see Foot, this vol.

kings to the 970s.[56] It may be no accident that B ends in the midst of a disputed succession to a king whose own rule had begun as a bid for the throne launched from Mercia. D offers a tantalising mid eleventh-century, possibly post-1066, view of English history, and one which deliberately combined northern and more southern material. Study of these later chronicles has much to tell us of the various, evolving and shifting notions of the kingdom of 'Angelcynn' over the tenth and eleventh centuries. That is beyond the scope of this paper, though the survival of Æthelflæd and her story as part of them requires note.

This chapter has been concerned only with the early tenth-century stage of that kingdom, and with the chronicles which were produced in it and the significance of the history they told. It has argued that the 'Annals of Æthelflæd' should be placed in that context, and can in turn illuminate it and its politics. What has been suggested here can be no more than plausible reconstruction, moving from the firm ground of surviving chronicles on to more speculative terrain, though guided by recent rethinking of history writing in the early middle ages. However, the potential of such reconstruction for our understanding of the political world of the early tenth century makes the venture worthwhile. The 'Annals of Æthelflæd' and their creation may offer precious insight into the political situation and possibilities of early tenth-century England. They should remind us, if such reminder is necessary, to keep Mercia firmly in view as those possibilities unfolded.

---

56 Above, n. 10. Kenneth Sisam, 'Anglo-Saxon Royal Genealogies', *Proceedings of the British Academy*, 39 (1953), 287–348, at 332–4 questioned whether the genealogical Table was originally produced to be the Preface to Alfred's Chronicle. His argument about its absence from other vernacular Chronicles does not allow for the editing of prefatory material as the Chronicles came to be seen and used in different ways. David Dumville, 'The West Saxon Genealogical Regnal List and the Chronology of Early Wessex', *Peritia*, 4 (1985), 21–66 also argued for its separateness. Such arguments, by emphasising the choice made to include it, suggest the 'dynastic' nature of chronicles which use it as a preface – or culmination. I return to the preface and its date in 'Reading Women in Dynastic and 'National' Chronicles: Eadburh, Cuthburh, Cwenburh and the Anglo-Saxon Chronicles', in *Agire da donna: Modelli e pratiche di rappresentazione (secoli VI–X)*, ed. Cristina La Rocca (Turnhout, 2007), 269–89.

Chapter 10
The First Use of the Second Anglo-Saxon *Ordo*

Janet L. Nelson

In recent decades, the history of the Anglo-Saxon coronation *ordines* has become clearer as part of a general lifting of fog in the Channel.[1] Liturgy's supra-regnal character, and the consequently frequent crossing of liturgical books from Francia to England and vice versa, no longer need to be insisted on as providing the context for ritual developments. So far, so good. Key points have remained debatable, though; and among these is the question of the occasion on which the Second *Ordo* was first used. I argued nearly 20 years ago that that occasion was the inauguration of Edward the Elder at Pentecost 900. There were two main reasons for that view: one was the presence in the consecration prayer of references to two peoples, to paternal glory and to unity, which seemed to me then to fit the political circumstances of 899–900 better than 924–925; the other was the presence of a queen's *ordo* alongside the king's and that accorded with Edward's married situation rather than Æthelstan's unmarried one.[2] Patrick Wormald never was persuaded by what amount to no more than circumstantial arguments. He remained convinced that the inauguration of Æthelstan in 925 was the likeliest occasion for the Second *Ordo*'s first use.[3] He thought the theme of a union of two peoples peculiarly apt for Æthelstan 'in the aftermath of Edward's vigorous suppression of Mercian (semi-)independence'. He pointed out, further, that the provision of a queen's *ordo* to follow the king's 'could just as well be another addition to the base-text ... in which case it could have been revised for the returning Louis IV in 936'. Nicholas Brooks has left the question open: 'it was ... either Archbishop Plegmund or Archbishop Athelm who introduced into English royal ritual the ring, the crown itself, and much liturgical ceremony

---

[1] I use the term 'coronation' *ordo/ordines* simply because it is in general use, although Anglo-Saxon liturgical books usually named the rite a benediction (or benedictions), or consecration. Coronation in the modern sense, meaning the whole inauguration-rite, did not become common usage until the eleventh century and later, see J.L. Nelson, *Politics and Ritual in Early Medieval Europe* (London, 1986), 295, 388 n. 58.

[2] Nelson, 'The Second English *Ordo*', in *Politics and Ritual*, 361–74, at 365–6 (for the original publication see below, n. 8).

[3] See P. Wormald, *The Making of English Law* (Oxford 1999), 447, n. 114. Patrick Wormald and I had a number of conversations about this question: he had been strongly influenced by the still-unpublished work of Michael Wood (but see below, n. 41, for reference to another important paper by Wood on Æthelstan), in addition to the fundamental work of Derek Turner and Christopher Hohler discussed below.

that was perhaps of West Frankish origin'.[4] I hope to confirm that highlighting archiepiscopal initiatives is exactly the best way forward, and I offer the present paper in gratitude to the scholar who has done most to reveal the 'wider horizons' of Canterbury thinking in the tenth century.[5]

Another way of addressing the question of the Second *Ordo*'s first use is to consider the evidence for the First *Ordo*. The beginning of wisdom in understanding earlier medieval rites is the distinction between date of composition and/or first use and date of first extant manuscript. In the case of the First *Ordo*, while internal and comparative evidence combine to show that composition predated 856 and circumstantial evidence points to 838 (or 839) as likely date of first use, the earliest manuscript evidence is some 70 years later. That evidence is contained in the so-called Leofric Missal and Nicholas Orchard's recent new edition of this book puts discussion on a firmer basis than ever before.[6] The core of the book is in fact a sacramentary (hereafter, following Orchard, called *A*), for which the palaeographical evidence indicates *c.* 880–*c.* 920 as the date-frame and which Orchard convincingly argues was produced for Plegmund of Canterbury not earlier than 909.[7] *A*'s text of the First *Ordo* gives a first visual impression of being different from the version that survives in two early eleventh-century manuscripts.[8] Is this a case of the later

---

4   Nicholas Brooks, 'The Cathedral Community at Canterbury, 597–1070', in *The History of Canterbury Cathedral*, ed. Patrick Collinson and Nigel Ramsay (Oxford, 1995), 1–37, reprinted in Nicholas Brooks, *Anglo-Saxon Myths: State and Church 400–1066* (London, 2000), 101–54, with the sentence here quoted at 129.

5   The present paper is particularly indebted to Brooks, 'The Cathedral Community', 128–42 (the sub-section on 924–1016, 'Widening horizons') and above all to Nicholas Brooks, *The Early History of the Church of Canterbury* (Leicester, 1984), 209–53 (chapter 10).

6   *The Leofric Missal*, ed. Nicholas Orchard, HBS, 113–14 (London, 2002), commentary at I, 99–105, with the relevant texts at II, 429–32 (fols. 302v–306r). A facsimile is online at http://www.image.ox.ac.uk/pages/bodleian/Bodl579/main.htm.

7   *Leofric Missal*, ed. Orchard, I, p. 20, considers various possibilities for the identity of the scribe (specifically 'the artist' responsible for the major and minor initials): 'a Frenchman living and working in France; a Frenchman working in England; or an Englishman working in England in an unfamiliar idiom'. Orchard, ibid., I, pp. 16–20, 25–6, discusses sacramentaries produced at St-Amand or elsewhere in north-eastern France (Arras, Cambrai, Noyon, Corbie) in the second half of the ninth century and with comparable decorative, palaeographical or liturgical features to *A*. On all criteria, cross-Channel contacts provide the context for *A*; but Orchard, ibid., I, p. 131, excludes the possibility that *A* was written in northern France. The content locates *A*'s production or destination at Canterbury: Orchard, ibid., I, p. 83: 'Its pontifical [i.e. rites for a bishop's use] is an archbishop's pontifical', and cf. p. 105. A *terminus ante quem non* is supplied by the superscription for the mass of the Four Crowned Martyrs which can only have been written by someone using the Martyrology of Ado of Vienne, produced in 858: ibid., I, pp. 48–50, 56.

8   Thanks to the Henry Bradshaw Society, all three manuscripts of the First *Ordo* can now easily be consulted in print: *A* (formerly cited as 'Leofric') in Orchard's edition of the Leofric Missal (as above, n. 6); that of the Lanalet Pontifical in *The Lanalet Pontifical*, ed. G.H. Doble, HBS, 74 (London, 1937), pp. 59–63 (with only the incipits of the prayers appearing also in *The Benedictional of Archbishop Robert*, ed. H.A. Wilson, HBS, 24 (London, 1903); and the so-called Egbert Pontifical in *Two Anglo-Saxon Pontificals*, ed. H.M.J. Banting, HBS, 104

manuscripts preserving, like fossils in amber, bits of an earlier version, while the earlier manuscript, *A*, presents a revision? When dealing with liturgical books, it is always wise to be prepared for this possibility. But this is not what has happened here. What *A* offers is the same rite with a number of the rubrics, but not the final one, left out.[9] The scribe perhaps began by assuming the officiant would use a separate set of instructions for performance, with the texts of the prayers to be recited on a separate rotula (this was the situation envisaged by Hincmar when describing in a letter to a Lotharingian colleague how episcopal consecration was performed at Rheims) but then, through a change of mind, included the lengthy final rubric in full.[10]

The *terminus post quem* for the production of *A* rests, first and foremost, on the presence in its mass for the dedication of a church of two 'propers' (i.e. purpose-made prayers) for St Andrew, suggesting that the Canterbury scribe included the mass as performed for the dedication of Wells cathedral, according to Orchard, 'in 909'.[11] Orchard further points out that *A* provides plural forms for the episcopal ordination rite, indicating multiple ordinations on a single occasion, and Orchard argues, referring to 'several reliable sources', that the occasion was Plegmund's consecration of seven bishops, including one for the new see of Wells, 'in 909'.[12] Orchard has overlooked, or discounted, Nicholas Brooks' deft and definitive unmasking of the story of Plegmund's consecration of seven bishops on a single day as 'pseudo-history' concocted in the south-west (Exeter?) in the late tenth century.[13] Not even bishops should be multiplied beyond necessity. It remains possible that Plegmund consecrated more than one bishop on some particular occasion, but direct

---

(London, 1989), 109–13. Banting's commentary ibid., xx–xxvi notes but does not really take on board the views of *The Claudius Pontificals*, ed. D.H. Turner, HBS, 97 (London, 1971), pp. xxix–xxxiii, xxxviii–ix, and takes no account of J.L. Nelson, 'The Earliest Surviving Royal *Ordo*: some liturgical and historical aspects', in *Authority and Power: Studies in Medieval Law and Government presented to Walter Ullmann*, ed. Brian Tierney and Peter Linehan (Cambridge, 1980), 29–48, repr. in Nelson, *Politics and Ritual*, 341–60.

9 In rubrics before the final one, the later manuscripts identify the officiants as *omnes pontifices*; but in the final rubric those manuscripts and also *A* coincide in using the word *episcopi*. This difference (and other small variants in the final rubric as given by *A* and the later manuscripts, for which see Nelson, 'The Earliest Surviving Royal *Ordo*', 358) points to the existence of different versions of the rubrics dating from different stages of the *ordo*'s history, and combined in slightly different ways in now-lost exemplars. Perhaps *A*'s scribe and/or Plegmund himself blenched at *pontifices* in this context: see below.

10 Framing the *ordo* in the mass can be called neither an addition, nor a change: it is an alternative way of presenting directions for liturgical performance. *A*'s *ordo* could have been performed in exactly the same way: *Leofric Missal*, ed. Orchard, I, 100.

11 Ibid., 29, 65, 79, 83. The same point was briefly noted already by C.E. Hohler, 'Some Service Books of the Later Saxon Church', in *Tenth-Century Studies: Essays in Commemoration of the Millennium of the Council of Winchester and Regularis Concordia*, ed. David Parsons (London, 1975), 60–83 at 68.

12 *Leofric Missal*, ed. Orchard, I, p. 80, citing *GRA*, I, 205 and also Brooks, *Early History*, 210–213. See further Patrick Conner, *Anglo-Saxon Exeter. A Tenth-Century Cultural History* (Woodbridge, 1993), 215–6.

13 Brooks, *Early History*, 212.

evidence for 909 is non-existent.[14] Orchard's key point about the St Andrew 'propers' stands, however, and the date of Wells' foundation thus remains the *terminus post* for the writing of *A*.[15] What was that date? It is unlikely to have been very long after Plegmund's journey to Rome and back in 908, for that journey, exceptionally difficult and dangerous as it was at this time, and unattempted by any of Plegmund's predecessors since Wulfred in 814–815, can only have been undertaken for pressing reasons which Nicholas Brooks has persuasively argued were a typical blend of self-interest, ecclesiastical concerns and *raison d'état*.[16] Once papal agreement had been obtained for increasing the number of West Saxon sees from two to five, there would have been no reason to delay implementing the decision.[17] I am happy to agree with Simon Keynes that Plegmund's 'wider political interest' did not exclude 'a hidden or reserved agenda' which was to enhance the influence of Alfred's surviving Mercian contingent at Edward's court and in his kingdom.[18] However, I would construe the outcome as less Edward's firm continuation of King Alfred's conciliatory and consensual policy towards Mercia than as a demonstration of the limits imposed on Edward's 'vigorous' regime, at least before 918, by Canterbury horizons – which may be conceived as at once ecclesiastical and Kentish – and also by Mercian horizons. Plegmund's thinking was framed by his own origins and by his career, fostered as it was by Alfred. Plegmund could conceive of changes which divided, hence weakened, the old West Saxon sees of Winchester and Sherborne. Armed with papal authority, but also, necessarily, with Edward's support, he was in a position to implement them. Edward perhaps had good motives, personal and political, for wanting to cut both West Saxon bishoprics down to size.[19] Plegmund had his own reasons as *Cantuar*. These may have included, as Alex Woolf suggests, being 'able to stack the episcopate with his own men, reform-minded bishops';[20]

---

14 See the exemplary study of A.R. Rumble, 'Edward the Elder and the Churches of Winchester and Wessex', in *Edward the Elder*, ed. N.J. Higham and David Hill (Manchester, 2001), 230–47, esp. 242–3.

15 *Leofric Missal*, ed. Orchard, I, 82–3, briefly considers and rejects, in my view rightly, the alternative St Andrew dedication of Rochester.

16 Brooks, *Early History*, 210–211. The years around 900 posed particular difficulties for travellers to Rome, with Saracens ensconced at Fraxinetum (Garde-Freinet) from 891, Magyar raids into northern Italy becoming increasingly frequent, and bandits ubiquitous: see Peregrine Horden and Nicholas Purcell, *The Corrupting Sea. A Study of Mediterranean History* (Oxford, 2000), 135–6; C. Di Cave, *L'arrivo degli Ungheresi in Europa* (Spoleto, 1995), 107–53; Odo, *Vita Geraldi Auriliacensis* I, c. 27; II, cc. 17, 20, 25; PL 133, cols. 658, 680, 681–2, 684 (Gerald, d. 909, encountered bandits on a series of pilgrimages from the Auvergne to Rome).

17 Presumably with this in mind, Simon Keynes, 'Edward, king of the Anglo-Saxons', in *Edward the Elder*, ed. Higham and Hill, 40–66 at 50, dates the division of the West Saxon sees '*c*. 910'.

18 Keynes, 'Edward', 49–50.

19 These reasons are offered by Rumble, 'Edward the Elder and the Churches', 243–4, but only after an alternative proposition: 'Perhaps Plegmund originally suggested [the reorganisation] to the king.'

20 Alex Woolf, 'View from the West: an Irish perspective', in *Edward the Elder*, ed. Higham and Hill, 89–101 at 99.

but reform in practice amounted to a strong institutional and long-term interest in strengthening metropolitan power. Plegmund, in short, was an ecclesiastical big man in Hincmarian mould, who left a deep impression on the church in Edward's Anglo-Saxon kingdom.

An appreciation of Plegmund's churchmanship raises the stakes involved in *A*'s rite for the consecration of a king. Orchard writes that *A* 'could perfectly easily embody the substance of the *ordo* [that is, the First *Ordo*] used by Plegmund at the coronation of Edward the Elder in 900'.[21] This formulation seems to me, now, to understate a case. Though Orchard himself does not exclude the possibility that the Second *Ordo* existed at the time that *A* was written, I think we have to infer otherwise. For, on Orchard's showing, Plegmund commissioned a book that included rites of church dedication and episcopal consecration to which the archbishop had given the imprimatur of his own personal use. This is likely to be true *a fortiori* of the king's consecration, a rite of exceptional importance in anyone's book. Put this the other way round: Plegmund is highly unlikely to have commissioned a new pontifical that included a coronation *ordo* already superseded in use by a new one he himself had recently introduced. Suppose for a moment longer that the Second *Ordo had* been produced late in Alfred's reign, as I argued in 1986. It is hard to imagine where else than at Canterbury, or somewhere with which the archbishop had close contact, anyone would have produced it. In other words, if the production of the Second *Ordo* were to be linked with Alfred's latter years, then it would also have to be linked with Plegmund. That double connexion is precisely what I think the new dating of *A* excludes. At Canterbury *c.* 910, the king's *ordo* considered current was, still, the First *Ordo*. No-one had yet demanded a new one. Orchard warns, rightly, that 'the conception of "new" and "old" in the middle ages was patently not the same as our own', calling in support the use 'sporadically and according to no discernible plan' by Canterbury scribes of earlier forms of episcopal profession: they 'seem to have copied whatever came to hand'. But a form of episcopal profession is not an *ordo*, still less a coronation *ordo*. It seems to me impossible to reconcile the notions of Plegmund as patron of *A* and Plegmund as consecrator of Edward following the Second *Ordo*. Plegmund, a political operator in Hincmar's league, was, unlike Hincmar, no inventor of royal *ordines*.

There are times when a scholar must admit that s/he was wrong. But that cannot be the end of the matter. I bear some share of responsibility for propagating the scenario in which Plegmund featured as first user of the Second *Ordo*, in 900, for Edward, and therefore, given my present conviction that the rite used in 900 was indeed the First *Ordo* as preserved in *A*, I owe it to my colleagues and not least to Nicholas Brooks, to think through the implications of this revisionist thinking. Recall the nature of the *ordo* with which Plegmund and Edward were satisfied in 900, a rite that had, probably, been used for Æthelwulf (838 or 839) and each of his four sons in turn: Æthelbald (855 or 856 or 858), Æthelberht (856 or 858), Æthelred (865), and Alfred (871). If twice made custom, then a West Saxon liturgical custom would have been well-established within that mid-century generation. The First *Ordo* prescribed for *omnes pontifices* together with *principes* to hand the king his sceptre, and for *omnes*

---

21 *Leofric Missal*, ed. Orchard, 105.

pontifices to place on the head of the new king not a crown but a helmet. It ended with a three-fold acclamation of the king by 'the whole people (*omnis populus*) with the bishops (*episcopi*)', and the *principes* kissing the newly-enthroned king.[22] The *Ordo* included prayers, some of them ancient, from the common liturgical stock of Latin Christendom, of course; but the elements just listed are not paralleled in Continental *ordines* and must be presumed English. The older historiography characterised these traits as 'archaic'.[23] Perhaps they are better termed distinctive, and purpose-built: they highlighted the military qualities expected of a king, and, as a corollary, the recurrent preference in the ninth and tenth centuries for fraternal rather than filial succession, which in turn signalled a persisting elective element in West Saxon king-making symptomatic of the strength of aristocratic and regional identities within a composite kingdom. These features should be compared with East rather than West Francia.[24] At the same time, Continental kingdoms in general contrasted with Wessex because of their shared Carolingian legacy.

Every early medieval king-making depended far more on contingent circumstances than would become the case later on. The inauguration of Edward is a notable case in point. What at first sight seems a relatively well-prepared and smooth succession turned out not to be so. Alfred's death precipitated a crisis. The rebellion of Edward's cousin Æthelwold started promptly and went on for perhaps three years, and in the eyes of many Englishmen as well as Scandinavians this ætheling had claims stronger than Edward's own.[25] The delay in staging Edward's consecration, from late October 899 until 8 June 900, may have been a matter of necessity, or at least discretion, rather than choice.[26] Even had a new *ordo* been available (one made earlier, before Alfred's death), the king and the archbishop might well have seen this as a time for appealing to the old rather than adventuring with the new. In fact no new *ordo* was available. Edward's consecration thus followed custom.[27] Firmly

---

22 *Two Anglo-Saxon Pontificals*, ed. Banting, 'Egbert', 110: 'Hic omnes pontifices cum principibus dant ei sceptum in manu', and 112: 'Hic omnes pontifices sumant galeum [sic] et ponant super caput ipsius'. See above, n. 9.

23 For references, see Nelson, 'The Earliest Surviving Royal *Ordo*', 354, 356.

24 Janet L. Nelson, 'Rulers and Government', in *The New Cambridge Medieval History*, III, *c. 900–c. 1024*, ed. Timothy Reuter (Cambridge, 1999), 95–129, at 102–103.

25 Barbara Yorke, 'Edward as Ætheling', in *Edward*, ed. Higham and Hill, 25–39, at 29–31; Richard Hall, 'A Kingdom Too Far: York in the Early Tenth Century', ibid., 188–99, at 189; *The Anglo-Saxon Chronicle: a Collaborative Edition, 3: MS A*, ed. Janet Bately (Cambridge, 1986), 61–2, s.a. 900–904 (for 899–902).

26 For the date, *Chronicon Æthelweardi: the Chronicle of Æthelweard*, ed. A. Campbell (London, 1962), 51 (Pentecost).

27 The suggestion of Simon Keynes, *The Diplomas of Æthelred 'the Unready' 978–1016* (Cambridge, 1980), 270–71, on the say-so of the late twelfth-century author Ralph Diceto, that Edward was consecrated at Kingston was offered tentatively – noting that Ralph could well have projected back from 925 and after. Keynes, 'Edward', 48, turns the suggestion into a categorical assertion, which I hesitate to follow. Brooks, 'The Cathedral Community', 129, n. 62, regards Ralph's testimony here as 'very doubtful'. Kingston was a place with twofold symbolic significance: it was on the Mercian-West Saxon boundary, and it was the nearest place to the point where the Thames became tidal. Patrick Wormald kindly pointed out to me long ago the second of these facts.

enshrined in ecclesiastical record, Æthelwulf's inauguration represented a dynastic and regnal watershed. Plegmund affirmed this, and at the same time exploited its legitimising force, by having the traditional *ordo* incorporated into the pontifical he commissioned on (or not long after) his return from Rome.

Plegmund's own personal crisis of legitimacy from 897 until 908 also needs to be factored into the situation. In January 897, in Rome, which was far beyond Anglo-Saxons' geographical horizon but ever-close to their hearts and minds, Formosus (891–896), the pope who had sent Plegmund the pallium, had been subjected to a famously gruesome *damnatio memoriae* when his corpse was disinterred, 'tried', condemned and flung into the Tiber.[28] For the next few years, papal successions oscillated dizzyingly between pro- and anti-Formosan factions. In the latter camp, Sergius III (904–911) went so far as to require the reconsecration of clergy Formosus had ordained. Whatever else disturbed the last years of Alfred's reign, these alarming events can only have intensified Anglo-Saxon anxiety. Plegmund awaited the opportunity to put his archiepiscopal position beyond challenge – as he did in 908.

The further implication of contextualising *A* within the priorities and constraints of *c*. 900 is that we need to return to the consecration of Æthelstan in 925 as an alternative scenario for the first use of the Second *Ordo*. We are back on ground that was familiar before any alternative was seriously proposed.[29] The Second *Ordo*'s influence on West Frankish, and later French, *ordines* from later in the tenth century onwards is, in turn, best explained, as Derek Turner first suggested, on the hypothesis that in 936, when Louis IV returned from exile at Æthelstan's court to rule the West Frankish kingdom, a version of this *Ordo* 'got across the Channel'.[30] But perhaps the case can be strengthened from the earlier end as well. The Frankish elements in the Second *Ordo*, especially those from the *ordines* of 'Erdmann' and 'Seven Forms' belong a little more comfortably in the 920s rather than the 890s: though neither of those West Frankish *ordines* can be dated very precisely, 'Erdmann' is generally said to have been composed '*c*. 900', but the 'Seven Forms' have been assigned to a slightly later date, sometime in the first half of the tenth century.[31] The presence in

---

28 Liutprand of Cremona, *Antapodosis* I, 30, ed. J. Becker, MGH, Scriptores Rerum Germanicarum (Hanover 1915), 23–4. See further for what follows, Girolamo Arnaldi, 'Appunti sulla crisi dell'autorità pontificia in età post-Carolingia', *Studi Romani* 9 (1961), 492–507; P. Llewellyn, *Rome in the Dark Ages* (London 1971), 292–300.

29 Hohler, 'Some Service Books', 67–70, 78–80; Brooks, *Early History*, 215.

30 *Claudius Pontificals*, ed. Turner, p. xxxiii. See further Hohler, 'Some Service Books', 68; Nelson, 'Second English *Ordo*', 368, and N.J. Abercrombie, *The Life and Work of Edmund Bishop* (London, 1959), 520 (Appendix, 'E.B. on Coronation'), for the quotation from the great liturgical scholar Edmund Bishop.

31 See *Ordines Coronationis Franciae. Texts and Ordines for the Coronation of Frankish and French Kings and Queens in the Middle Ages*, ed. Richard Jackson (2 vols, Philadelphia, 1995–2000), I, Ordo XIII ('Erdmann'), 142–53, and Ordo XIV (Jackson calls this the '*Ordo* of Eleven Forms', but I prefer to retain the older name of 'Seven Forms'), 154–67. Jackson himself, *Ordines*, 28, keeps open the possibility of a *terminus a quo* for the 'Seven Forms' in the last part of the ninth century. See on both these *ordines* and on their wider context the fundamental work of C.A. Bouman, *Sacring and Crowning: The Development of the Latin Ritual for the Anointing of Kings and the Coronation of an Emperor before the Eleventh*

all the Second *Ordo* manuscripts of a queen's *ordo* need not exclude the new king's *Ordo*'s use in 925 (though Æthelstan's unmarried state in 925 was significant),[32] but is perfectly explicable as a result of later supplementation, whether desirable for the sake of completeness, or necessary for subsequent occasions when the *Ordo* was used (though not in 936, for Louis IV did not marry until 939).[33] The structure of the consecration-prayer, and certain variants in its wording, can be explained in terms of the circumstances of Æthelstan's succession, as Wormald felicitously put it, 'on a Mercian ticket'.[34] For Edward's removal of his niece Ælfwynn in 918 left the elder of his two sons Æthelstan, who had been brought up in Mercia, a likely contender for that kingdom, while the death of Ælfweard, the younger brother and designated heir to Wessex, within a month of his father's on 17 July 924, though it strengthened Æthelstan's position within the dynasty, did not guarantee his succession.[35] Not only was his acceptance by the Mercians, which perhaps occurred in the autumn of 924, a quite separate event from his acceptance in Wessex, but Æthelstan was not consecrated until 4 September 925. This time-lag in itself, and the coolness of Æthelstan's subsequent relations with the New Minster Winchester, suggests a period of negotiation long enough for anyone minded to do so to produce a new *ordo* supplied with judicious insertions to reflect Æthelstan's circumstances. It is in this context that the repeated reference in the consecration prayer to the king's being elected to rule two peoples and the added words, *pariter* and *utrique*, appear especially meaningful. The phrase about 'establishing and governing the apex of paternal glory unitedly' belongs here too, but it also evokes the intra-dynastic conflict that delayed Æthelstan's establishment in Wessex as it had Edward's a generation before and whose resolution was to be the key to future stability.[36] There were other significant innovations. The helmet was replaced by the crown, now the royal symbol *par excellence* in Continental kingdoms. Æthelstan's depiction crowned,

---

Century (Groningen, 1957). It is of course possible, as George Garnett has argued in an unpublished paper, that a splicing of 'Erdmann' and the 'Seven Forms' was already made in Francia before being brought to England.

32 Nelson, 'Rulers and Government', 103–104, for the suggestion that a king's non-marriage, here as in other cases, was a negotiated succession strategy resolved on by competing groups within and around a royal dynasty, with an uncle in effect postponing but not excluding younger nephews' claims.

33 I thus accept the gist of Wormald's point, see above, at n. 3. For the obscure history of the queen's consecration in England, the work of Pauline Stafford is fundamental: see especially 'The King's Wife in Wessex, 800–1066', *Past and Present*, 91 (1981), 3–27 and *Queen Emma and Queen Edith* (Oxford, 1997), 60, 162–8.

34 Wormald, *Making*, 447, n. 114.

35 *The Liber Vitae of the New Minster and Hyde Abbey Winchester*, ed. Simon Keynes (Copenhagen, 1996), 19–22, illuminatingly discusses the possibility of intra-dynastic conflict-resolution in 924–925: cf. n. 31 above, and also the comments of Simon Keynes, 'England, c.900–1016', in *The New Cambridge Medieval History*, III, ed. Reuter, 456–84, at 467–8.

36 See *The Liber Vitae of the New Minster*, ed. Keynes, 19–20; Alan Thacker, 'Dynastic Monasteries and family cults', in *Edward the Elder*, ed. Higham and Hill, 248–63, at 254.

on coins and in a celebrated manuscript, may reflect this directly.[37] Ring, sword and rod, were other symbols whose liturgical transmission was incorporated into the Second *Ordo*. Earlier kings had worn rings and had given them as rewards for fidelity. In the Second *Ordo*, investiture with the ring was said to signal acceptance of the responsibilities of an 'establisher of Christianity'. The sword was depicted emphatically as a defensive instrument, 'for mercifully helping widows and orphans and restoring things left desolated'. The rod was given 'so that you may understand how to soothe the righteous and terrify the reprobate, [and] teach the right way to those who stray, and stretch forth a hand to those who have fallen'. All this presented the consensual and conciliatory face of kingship. Last but not least, the inauguration ended with an enthronement and a prayer that the new king:

> hold fast the state which you have held by paternal suggestion ...; remember to show honour to the clergy in due places, so that the mediator between God and men may strengthen you as mediator between clergy and people in the throne of this kingdom.[38]

With these prayers and rites, the English *ordo* was aligned with the *ordines* of post-Carolingian Continental kingdoms. The multiplication of manuscripts, and the production of successive, somewhat revised, versions of the Second *Ordo* entrenched it in Anglo-Saxon episcopal thought and practice.[39] It became one of the sources of the medieval French ordo as well.

Two final questions arise. One is about the infusion of West Frankish liturgical influences that underlies the composition of the new *ordo*. This can be perfectly well credited to the cross-Channel political and cultural contacts dimly discernible in the latter years of Edward, the most important of which was the marriage of Edward's daughter Eadgifu to the West Frankish king Charles the Straightforward in 919 at a moment when Charles's position seemed, for a while, stronger than ever and hence the prospects of political benefits from this alliance were at their most alluring.[40] Michael Wood, in still unpublished work, has made a very strong case for the young Æthelstan's having received in his father's reign a good Christian education in part

---

37 C.E. Blunt, 'The coinage of Athelstan', *British Numismatic Journal*, 42 (1974), 35–160; cf. the ruler-portrait of Æthelstan on the frontispiece to the Life of Cuthbert in Corpus Christi College Cambridge MS 183, fol. iv, a manuscript given by the king to the community of St Cuthbert: see Simon Keynes, 'King Athelstan's books', in *Learning and Literature in Anglo-Saxon England*, ed. Michael Lapidge and Helmut Gneuss (Cambridge, 1985), 143–201, at 173–4.

38 I cite the prayer 'Sta et retine', from the Sacramentary of Ratoldus, ed. *Ordines Coronationis*, ed. Jackson, 190. For further comment, see Nelson, 'The Second English *Ordo*', 361, 365.

39 For these manuscripts, see J.L. Nelson and R.W. Pfaff, 'Pontificals and Benedictionals', in *The Liturgical Books of Anglo-Saxon England*, ed. R.W. Pfaff, Old English Newsletter Subsidia 23 (Kalamazoo MI 1995), 87–98.

40 See J.L. Nelson, 'Eadgifu (*d.* in or after 951)', in *ODNB*, XVII, 526–7. Eadgifu was the mother of Louis IV. For Edward's Breton contacts, see *EHD*, I, 892, no. 228. See further David Dumville, *Liturgy and the Ecclesiastical History of Late Anglo-Saxon England* (Woodbridge, 1992), 113.

via these same Continental contacts, so that he became king with a cultural agenda of his own already in mind.[41]

The other, final, question is about the possible author of the Second *Ordo*. Canterbury, again, is surely the likeliest place to look. In 923, Athelm succeeded Plegmund as archbishop. He had been transferred, uncanonically, from Wells and it is an attractive surmise that he set the precedent of travelling to Rome to receive his pallium in person and square any irregularity with the pope.[42] At Canterbury, they must have recalled Plegmund's bold mission for legitimacy. The Rome journey was as risky in 923 as it had been in 908. Anglo-Saxon circumstances had changed, though. Athelm, unlike Plegmund, was a West Saxon and his appointment to Canterbury signalled a new era: the Mercian option had palled. Athelm's short pontificate (he died on 6 January 926) was long enough to show that he was the first Cantuar since the eighth century not to issue his own archiepiscopal coinage. Plegmund had levelled the episcopate of Wessex; Athelm felt the levelling hand of a king of the English.[43] Athelm had already 'collaborated in ... [Edward's] ambitious royal programmes'. He was ready to do the same for Edward's successor. On 4 September 925, when Æthelstan was consecrated at Kingston, Athelm was there to officiate and he attested the new king's first, symbolically-laden, grant to St Augustine's Canterbury.[44] Though the idea of a 'Wells element' specific to the Second *Ordo*'s 'liturgical parentage' can be discarded,[45] there seems more strength than ever in Brooks' hypothesis of 20 years ago, that Athelm 'composed ... or organized [the Second *Ordo*'s] compilation'.[46]

---

41 Meanwhile, important aspects of Æthelstan's early life are highlighted in Wood, '"Stand strong against the monsters": kingship and learning in the empire of King Æthelstan', in *Lay Intellectuals in the Carolingian World*, ed. Patrick Wormald and J.L. Nelson (Cambridge, 2007), 192–217.

42 Brooks, *Early History*, 216.

43 Brooks, *Early History*, 214.

44 S, revised, S.E. Kelly, *The Electronic Sawyer*, http://www.trin.cam.ac.uk/chartwww, no. 394; see also *The Charters of St Augustine's, Canterbury*, ed. S.E. Kelly, Anglo-Saxon Charters, 4 (Oxford, 1995), 100–103, no. 26, on some evident problems with this charter, but the date, at least, seems acceptable.

45 Hohler, 'Some Service Books', 66, used the St Andrew 'propers' to link the Sacramentary of Ratoldus with England, and with Wells, and hence to suggest a 'limiting date' of 908. By then discussing, 67–8, the Second *Ordo* in Ratoldus and the English pontificals (see above n. 11), and by going on to discuss *A* (the Leofric Missal), 69–70, which he dated to 'around 900' without noting that the St Andrew 'propers' were already there, Hohler opened the way to Brooks' inference, *Early History*, 215, about the 'Wells element'.

46 Brooks, *Early History*, 215.

Chapter 11

Where English Becomes British: Rethinking Contexts for *Brunanburh*

Sarah Foot

It was with characteristic self-effacement that Nicholas Brooks recently joined the currently-fashionable debates about ethnic identity and the ways in which early medieval communities saw themselves (or were perceived) as 'nations', 'peoples' or 'races'.[1] His particular interest has been in the assertion of a notion of English identity, notably in the ways in which this was constructed (by Bede and others) to allow a multi-ethnic British and English population to accept a shared notion of Englishness. Brooks's reticence prevents him from trumpeting the originality of his contributions, but his essays stand apart from others on the same subject. Their especial importance is that they consider this question in terms not just of England but of Britain; the demonstration that Alcuin, for example, used the term 'English' to apply to the whole island of Britain ('he certainly writes as if the English church was the church of Britain and the English bishops were the bishops of Britain'[2]) sheds a quite different light on these issues. This essay reflects further on the importance of thinking as much about the British as the English in the later context of the mid-tenth century.

In some earlier essays on the making of English identity I have located at the court of King Alfred (king of Wessex 871–899) the origins of the idea of an imagined community of the 'English' as opposed to separate Anglo-Saxon peoples: West Saxons, Mercians, East Angles or Northumbrians. There I have suggested that the collection of vernacular annals known as the *Anglo-Saxon Chronicle* played a key role in the promotion of the idea of the *angelcynn* as a people with a shared past and the promise of a shared future.[3] On one occasion, I looked beyond the Alfredian annals of the 880s and 890s to the reign of King Æthelstan (924–939) and the entry for the year 937, which consists entirely of a verse account of a battle

---

1 Nicholas Brooks, *Bede and the English*, Jarrow Lecture, 1999 (Jarrow, 2000); 'Canterbury, Rome and the Construction of English Identity', in *Early Medieval Rome and the Christian West: Essays in Honour of Donald A. Bullough*, ed. Julia M.H. Smith (Leiden, 2000), 221–246; 'The English Origin Myth', in his *Anglo-Saxon Myths: State and Church, 400–1066* (London and Rio Grande, OH, 2000), 78–89; 'English Identity from Bede to the Millennium', *Haskins Society Journal*, 14 (2003), 33–51.
2 Brooks, 'English Identity', 43.
3 Sarah Foot, 'The Making of *Angelcynn*: English Identity before the Norman Conquest', *TRHS*, 6th series, 6 (1996), 25–49, at 27–37; 'Remembering, Forgetting and Inventing: Attitudes to the Past in England after the First Viking Age', *TRHS*, 6th series, 9 (1999), 185–200, at 197–9.

that took place in that year at a place called *Brunanburh*.[4] The poem celebrates the victory of the 'sons of Edward' (Æthelstan and his younger brother Edmund) against a combined force of Dublin Norse led by Anlaf (Olaf Guthfrithsson), Scots under Constantine II and the Strathclyde Welsh led by Owain of Strathclyde. It ends with a rousing conclusion setting this great victory in a wider, historical context; as Tennyson translated it:[5]

> Never had huger
> Slaughter of heroes
> Slain by the sword edge –
> Such as old writers
> Have writ of in histories –
> Hapt in this isle, since
> Up from the East hither
> Saxon and Angle from
> Over the broad billow
> Broke into Britain with
> Haughty war-workers who
> Harried the Welshman, when
> Earls that were lured by the
> Hunger of glory gat
> Hold of the land.

Here was, I argued, that promise of a future destiny fulfilled. Æthelstan's achievement was placed in the widest possible historical context, his victory being greater than that won by any Anglo-Saxon force since the first migration to British shores of Saxons and Angles (the peoples from whom Alfred's *angelcynn* were built).[6] Significantly the victory was won on an occasion on which Angles and Saxons had fought as one – West Saxon and Mercian forces together under a single leader (ll. 20–27) – and the authority of the Chronicle itself was invoked as evidence for the validity of the historical comparison (l. 68). Æthelstan's acquisition (and retention) of power over all the Anglo-Saxons in the island is portrayed as representing the culminating achievement of generations of 'English' kings before him. His reign, encapsulated in this poem, represents a significant step towards the making of the *angelcynn*. Æthelstan was England's first monarch.

Before reflecting further on the force of this interpretation, we should look more closely at the poem itself. It is important to recognise the extent to which this

---

4 Citations of the Old English text of the *Anglo-Saxon Chronicle* (hereafter *ASC*) are taken from the edition of the C manuscript (BL, MS Cotton Tiberius B. i) by Katherine O'Brien O'Keeffe, *The Anglo-Saxon Chronicle: A Collaborative Edition*, 5: *MS C* (Cambridge, 2001); the entry for 937 is at 77–9. Translations follow that made by Dorothy Whitelock, published in *EHD*, I, no. 1.

5 Alfred Tennyson, *Ballads and Other Poems* (London, 1880), 169–78, at 178.

6 Sarah Foot, 'Finding the Meaning of Form: Narrative in Annals and Chronicles', in *Writing Medieval History*, ed. Nancy Partner (London, 2005), 88–108, at 101–102.

poem stands apart from its immediate context in the manuscripts of the *Chronicle*. Generally the *Chronicle* offers a rather sparse account of Æthelstan's reign. Not only are there fewer entries than the yearly accounts that had, by the 920s, become normal practice, but the prose has become much leaner and more laconic, closer in style to the annals of the earlier *Anglo-Saxon Chronicle*.[7] In that context, the insertion of the poem under the year 937 is even more arresting. Many scholars have been rather dismissive of the poetic quality of the text, drawing attention to the fact that it is not only deeply formulaic but positively derivative (as many as 21 of the half lines of the poem may be found elsewhere in the corpus of Old English poetry).[8] In fact, since this was meant to be a formal poem, one might argue that it was by design highly contrived; its author sought deliberately to write in a manner different from everyday speech, more rhetorical and pointed than the workaday prose of a conventional annal. The formal patterns of parallel sequences that characterise the poem are, Ann Johnson has suggested, intentional – signs of the poet's aesthetic skill, rather than his plagiaristic incompetence.[9] One could go further and argue, with Simon Walker, that the poem's conservative structure and language 'constitute a crucial part of its contemporary appeal and serve to remind the poem's audience of the values and traditions now under attack'.[10] These should not be seen as signs of the poet's incompetence.

---

7   For general discussion of style in the *ASC* see Cicely Clark, 'The narrative mode of the Anglo-Saxon Chronicle before the Conquest', in *England Before the Conquest: Studies in Primary Sources Presented to Dorothy Whitelock*, ed. Peter Clemoes and Kathleen Hughes (Cambridge, 1971), 215–35.

8   Alistair Campbell, *The Battle of Brunanburh* (London, 1938), 38–9; compare this dismissive characterisation by R.I. Page, 'A Tale of Two Cities', *Peritia*, 1 (1982), 335–51, at 336: '... only 73 lines of indifferent verse ... as full of clichés as a B.B.C. cricket commentary.' Although this technique of constructing verse on the basis of existing, conventional and formulaic collocations may appear similar to the Latin poetic form cento (the stitching together of lines from pre-existing poems by other poets in order to create new verse), that is clearly a self-consciously literary exercise rather divorced from the somewhat different use of traditional diction that we find here. On cento see *Brill's New Pauly: Encyclopaedia of the Ancient World*, ed. Hubert Cancik and Helmuth Schneider (7 vols, Leiden, 1996–2005), III, cols 115–18. More helpful for understanding the *Brunanburh* poet's technique is his apparent appeal to metonomy; the use of a formula or formula-type expression in order to evoke a typical context, and thereby lend an associative richness to every formula; see John Miles Foley, *Immanent Art* (Bloomington, Indiana, 1991), 29–33, 35–6. Compare also Alain Renoir, *A Key to Old Poems: the Oral-Formulaic Approach to the Interpretation of West-Germanic Verse* (University Park, Pennsylvania, 1988), 119, for discussion of the evoking of themes within Old English verse; once the pattern of the theme is established, Renoir has argued, the audience can thereafter recall it with only a few details and is able itself to 'supply the missing elements'. Recourse to traditional tropes and conventional phrases from the existing poetic canon is one way in which the *Brunanburh* poet reinforces his central themes. I am grateful to Peter Orton and Philip Shaw for advice on this point.

9   Ann Johnson, 'The Rhetoric of *Brunanburh*', *Philological Quarterly*, 47 (1968), 487–493, at 493.

10   Simon Walker, 'A Context for *Brunanburh*', in *Warriors and Churchmen*, ed. Timothy Reuter (London, 1992), 21–39, at 37.

It may clarify the discussion to come if the shape and content of the poem are briefly described:[11]

1–10a The heroes. The first lines identify the poem's heroes – Æthelstan and his younger brother, Edmund – and set them in their genealogical context (as the sons of Edward the Elder and the heirs of the West Saxon dynasty). From the outset the hearer acquires the idea that this family has historically been successful in battle and in defending its lands and peoples.

10b–20a The enemy. Here the poet identifies the enemy as Scots (*Sceotta*) and the 'host from the ships' as men of the North (*guma norþerna*) and depicts them as doomed to die, stressing the extent of the slaughter. The action is placed within the span of a single day.

20b–36b The fighting. A description of the fighting and list of the casualties (five kings, seven of Anlaf's earls and a host of seamen and Scots); on the winning side are the West Saxon horsemen accompanied by the Mercians. Anlaf had come 'over the tossing waters' to fight (*ofer æra gebland*, line 26b); in defeat he fled to his ship to escape, in other words, back to Dublin.

37a–52b The despair of the defeated. These lines emphasise the age of King Constantine of the Scots and his pain at the loss of his son as well as kindred and friends; the poet gloats in the totality of the defeat of men once renowned for their military prowess.

53–59 Departure. The poet parallels the dejected departure of the humiliated remnant of the Norsemen, from *Dingesmere* over the sea to Dublin, with the triumphant return of the English king and prince to Wessex.

60–65a Aftermath. Here the dead are portrayed as carrion to be scavenged by birds and animals.

65b–end Significance. In conclusion, the poet sets the battle in its wider temporal and historical context.

With the five other poems entered into the otherwise prose *Anglo-Saxon Chronicle* during the tenth century, the poem on the *Battle of Brunanburh* shares, Thomas Bredehoft has observed, 'a concern with English nationalism, an explicit focus on the royal succession in the West Saxon line' and a tendency to locate recent events in a more distant past.[12] Compare, for example, the poem that is the annal for

---

11 In dividing up the poem thus I follow Campbell's edition, *The Battle of Brunanburh*.
12 Thomas A. Bredehoft, *Textual Histories: Readings in the Anglo-Saxon Chronicle* (Toronto, 2001), 78.

the year 942, known as the 'Capture of the Five Boroughs'. Edmund, Æthelstan's brother and successor, frames the poem; the first and last lines stress his kingship and his West Saxon royal lineage.[13] As a whole, that poem celebrates two successes: Edmund's restoration of the Mercians to the West Saxon fold (the kingdom had been overrun by the Norseman Olaf immediately after Æthelstan's death in 939);[14] and his capture of the so-called Five Boroughs, lands in the north eastern midlands that had been heavily settled by Danes in the late ninth and early tenth centuries.[15] That act is portrayed as one of liberation, the freeing of anglicised – and thus implicitly Christianised – Danes from the pagan Norsemen (led by Olaf) who had harassed them and held them 'in heathen shackles' until this redemption.[16] This poem's historical perspective is narrower than that of the *Brunanburh* poem, but no less significant. Edmund, *Engla þeoden*, lord of the English, is given hegemony over not just Saxons and Angles (the Mercians) but also over the Danes of the Five Boroughs.[17] An 'English' race, consisting of different ethnic groups all subject to West Saxon leaders of proven military ability and united in their opposition to pagan, outside foes is here being constructed (and defined) through the pages of the Chronicle.

In large measure, the 'Capture of the Five Boroughs' poem offers a celebration of the extension of English identity under West Saxon overlordship. Others have read the *Brunanburh* poem in a similar light and certainly Æthelstan's reputation as the first king of the English has had a long history and was well established soon after the Conquest. At Worcester in the early twelfth century an anonymous hand inserted into a manuscript of John of Worcester's *Chronicon*, beside the pedigrees for the two Northumbrian royal dynasties of Bernicia and Deira, a series of marginal comments about various rulers; the last of these reads: 'the vigorous and glorious king Æthelstan who first ruled alone the kingdom of the English over all England.'[18] However, I have

---

13 *ASC*, s.a. 942, line 2: '*Her Eadmund cing, Engla þeoden,/ mecga mundbora Myrce geode*'; 'In this year, King Edmund, lord of the English, protector of kinsmen, overcame Mercia'; line 13: '*afora Eadweardes, Eadmund cing*': 'the son of Edward, Edmund the king'.

14 *ASC*, s.a. 941, 943 (D); Simeon of Durham, *Historia Regum*, s.a. 939, ed. Thomas Arnold, *Symeonis monachi opera omnia*, Rolls Series, 75 (2 vols, London, 1882–5), II, 2–283, at 125; Smyth, *Scandinavian York and Dublin*, II, 89–106.

15 The Five Boroughs were Derby, Leicester, Lincoln, Nottingham and Stamford. See Allen Mawer, 'The Redemption of the Five Boroughs', *EHR*, 38 (1923), 551–7.

16 *ASC*, s.a. 942, line 10 '*on hæþenra hæfteclommum*'.

17 A charter of Edmund's younger brother, Eadred dated 946 (S 520) reported his own consecration to 'sovereignty of the quadripartite rule' in England on the death of his brother Edmund, who had 'royally guided the government of kingdoms of the Anglo-Saxons and Northumbrians, of the pagans and the Britons' ('... post obitum Eadmundi regis .qui regimina regnorum. Angulsaxna 7 Norþhymbra. Paganorum. Brettonumque septem annorum intervallo regaliter gubernabat ...').

18 Oxford, Corpus Christi College, MS 157, p. 52: 'Strenuus et gloriosus rex Athelstanus solus per totam Angliam primus regnum Anglorum regnauit'; discussed by Cyril Hart, 'The early section of the Worcester Chronicle', *Journal of Medieval History*, 9 (1983), 308, and illustrated ibid., figure 6, 270. One might note, as Julia Barrow has shown, that John of Worcester gave epithets to all those tenth-century kings he thought had been most effective in uniting and bringing glory to the kingdom of the English. His description of Æthelstan as 'strenuus et gloriosus' occurs in *The Chronicle of John of Worcester*, s.a. 925, 934 and 940,

come to question whether I have been right to read the *Brunanburh* poem solely in the context of the creation of an imagined community called the English.

A little historical background may be helpful to those not familiar with the history of early tenth-century England. King of the West Saxons after the death in 924 of his father, Edward the Elder, Æthelstan inherited the combined kingdom of Wessex and Mercia that had been created by his father, his aunt and his grandfather (King Alfred) and was heir also to their newly-coined royal style: *Angulsaxonum rex*, king of the Anglo-Saxons.[19] Yet during his own reign Æthelstan was to lay claim to far greater territorial power than that held by any of his illustrious ancestors, and by the time of the battle commemorated in this poem had overlordship over the whole island of Britain. In 927, on the death of his brother-in-law, the Danish king Sihtric of York, Æthelstan had annexed the kingdom of the Northumbrians. He drove out Sihtric's son Guthfrith, and brought under his rule (John of Worcester says 'overcame in battle and put to flight') all the kings who were in this island ('the kings of all Albion', *reges totius Albionis* in the Worcester Chronicler's words).[20] The kings of the West Welsh and of Gwent, of the Scots and of Bamburgh made peace with Æthelstan and swore him oaths in the place called Eamont, just south of Penrith in Cumbria.[21] The magnitude of this occasion was marked in a contemporary verse epistle, written by a clerk in the king's entourage called Peter and known by its first line, '*Carta dirige gressus*' (Letter, direct your steps).[22] There the poet spoke of those 'whom he now

---

ed. R.R. Darlington and Patrick McGurk, tr. Jennifer Bray and Patrick McGurk (2 vols to date, Oxford, 1995–1998, in progress), II, 368, 388, 394. See Julia Barrow, 'Chester's Earliest Regatta? Edgar's Dee-Rowing Revisited', *EME*, 10 (2001), 81–93 at 90.

19 This is to gloss over the apparent confusion surrounding Æthelstan's inheritance of his father's throne alluded to in the so-called 'Mercian Register', s.a. 924 (an independent collection of annals of Mercian origin for the years 902–24); see Charles Plummer, *Two of the Saxon Chronicles Parallel: With Supplementary Extracts from the Others* (2 vols, Oxford, 1892; reissued 1952), I, pp. lxxii–lxxiii. The Mercian Register is the subject of one of the other papers in this volume – Pauline Stafford, '"The Annals of Æthelflæd": Annals, History and Politics in Early Tenth-Century England'. Æthelstan's accession was discussed at greater length by William of Malmesbury, *GRA*, I, 206–207. For Æthelstan's regnal styles see further below; discussion of the style 'king of the Anglo-Saxons' can be found in Simon Keynes, 'King Alfred and the Mercians', in *Kings, Currency and Alliances*, ed. M.A.S. Blackburn and David N. Dumville (Woodbridge, 1998), 1–45, at 34–9; Keynes, 'The West Saxon Charters of King Æthelwulf and his Sons', *EHR*, 109 (1994), 1109–1149; and Keynes, 'Edward, King of the Anglo-Saxons', in *Edward the Elder, 899–924*, ed. N.J. Higham and D.H. Hill (London, 2001), 40–66, at 51, 54 and 61–2.

20 *ASC*, s.a. 926 (D): '7 Sihtric acwæl, 7 Æþelstan cyning feng to Norðhymbra rice. 7 ealle þa cyngas on þyssum iglande wæron he gewylde', ed. G.P. Cubbin, *The Anglo-Saxon Chronicle: a Collaborative Edition*, 6: *MS D* (Cambridge, 1996), 41; John of Worcester, *Chronicon*, s.a. 926, pp. 386–7.

21 *ASC*, s.a. 927. Compare also *GRA*, I, 212–15.

22 Michael Lapidge, 'Some Latin Poems as Evidence for the Reign of Athelstan', *ASE*, 9 (1981), 61–98, at 89–91, reprinted in his collected papers, *Anglo-Latin Literature 900–1066* (London and Rio Grande, 1993), 49–86, at 71–81. The poem was modelled on one addressed to Charlemagne, which began '*Carta, Christo comite*': *Poetae Latini Aevi Carolini*, ed. Ernst Dümmler, Karl Strecker, Ludwig Traube and Paul von Winterfeld, MGH, Poetae Latini Medii

rules with this Saxon realm now made whole': *cum ista perfecta Saxonia* (lines 9–10).[23] Soon after, Æthelstan forced the kings of the Welsh to meet him at Hereford, submit to his authority and pay an unprecedentedly high tribute to him annually.[24] As one means of ensuring Welsh co-operation, Æthelstan kept their princes at his court, their presence being visible through their attestation of several of his charters, which bear witness to the peregrinations of the royal court around the king's realm.[25] Oaths such as those sworn at Eamont, or by the Welsh at Hereford were, in Æthelstan's eyes, binding. When Constantine of the Scots broke his in 934, the West Saxon king led a punitive expedition by land and sea into Scotland, ravaging as far as Caithness in the Norse kingdom of Orkney according to one source, and forcing the defeated Scottish king into the making of a new peace.[26]

This was the realm that was at stake at Brunanburh in 937. Æthelstan's hegemony over the whole mainland of Britain – the Celtic kingdoms of Cornwall,[27] Wales and Scotland as well as the old Anglo-Saxon kingdom of Northumbria – was threatened by an alliance between Constantine and the Norse king Olaf. A Scots-Norse victory would have re-created the Norse kingdom of York and reinforced the importance

---

Aevi (4 vols in 5, Berlin, 1881–1923), I, 399–400, no. 4. See also W.H. Stevenson, 'A Latin Poem Addressed to King Athelstan', *EHR*, 26 (1911), 482–7, at 484–5.

23 Lapidge chose to translate *Saxonia* as 'England', which is understandable in the context but does not reflect the poet's choice of noun most effectively. If *Petrus* the author was of continental origin, as both Stevenson and Lapidge surmised, that might explain his perception of England as the land of the Saxons, notwithstanding the contemporary coining of that label for the territory of the continental Saxons. Otherwise one might wonder if this term reflected Welsh usage. For discussion of early medieval words for England, the English and the Anglo-Saxons see Susan Reynolds, 'What do we mean by "Anglo-Saxon" and the "Anglo-Saxons"', *Journal of British Studies*, 24 (1985), 395–414 and for the early eleventh-century coining of a noun for England, Patrick Wormald, '*Engla lond*: The Making of An Allegiance', *Journal of Historical Sociology*, 7 (1994), 1–24. For some eighth-century uses of *Saxonia* to denote the land of the English see Foot, 'The Making of *Angelcynn*', 41, n. 69.

24 *GRA*, I, 214–7. Henry Loyn, 'Wales and England in the Tenth Century: the Context of the Æthelstan Charters', *Welsh History Review*, 10 (1980–1981), 283–301; reprinted in his *Society and Peoples: Studies in the History of England and Wales c. 600–1200* (London, 1992), 173–99.

25 Loyn, 'Wales and England', 290–295. The charters witnessed by the Welsh kings (who are there described as *subreguli*) are S 400, 407, 413, 416–7, 418a, 425 and 434–5 (the last two are spurious, but probably based on an authentic charter of 935). For a vivid illustration of Æthelstan's itinerant kingship see David Hill, *An Atlas of Anglo-Saxon England* (Oxford, 1981), 87, fig. 155.

26 *ASC*, s.a. 934; John of Worcester, *Chronicon*, s.a. 934, pp. 388–91. It was the twelfth-century historian Simeon of Durham who reported that the king 'then subdued his enemies, laid waste Scotland as far as Dunnottar and *Wertermorum* with a land force, and ravaged with a naval force as far as Caithness': *Historia regum*, ed. Arnold, II, 124. See Benjamin Hudson, *Kings of Celtic Scotland* (Westport, CT, and London, 1994), 76–8.

27 William of Malmesbury reported that once Æthelstan had subdued the Welsh he proceeded to tackle the Western Britons (Cornish), forced them out of Exeter and fixed the boundary of their territory at the river Tamar: *GRA*, I, 216–217.

of the York-Dublin axis.[28] Not only would this have checked the expanded power of Wessex but also, and perhaps rather more immediately, it would have imperilled the continued security of the midland kingdom of Mercia. Since, as we have already seen, the Dublin Norse overran Mercia immediately after Æthelstan's death and did indeed at the same time re-establish the Norse kingdom of York, these were not unreasonable anxieties.[29] It is not coincidental that the *Brunanburh* poet laid much stress on the presence of Mercian contingents on Æthelstan's side in this battle; that Mercians should identify themselves so closely with West Saxon interests was crucial to the promotion of any notion of a combined realm, whatever word might be used to describe it. Of course if Æthelstan had, as William of Malmesbury alleged, spent much of his youth in Mercia at the court of his and uncle and aunt, Ealdorman Æthelred and his wife, Æthelflæd (daughter of King Alfred) and particularly if he had played some military part in Mercian campaigns to capture the Danelaw and later represented his father's interests in Mercia after his aunt's death in 918, his capacity to attract the loyalty of Mercian forces could have been considerable.[30] Just how close the field of battle was to Mercian territory, and thus how immediate its threat might have felt to the midland Angles, remains disputed, but it may help to explore the place-name evidence in a little detail.

Although there are numerous theories about where the battlefield might have lain, there is still no consensus among historians as to the location of *Brunanburh*. From the Old English poem it is clear that the battle took place neither in Wessex nor in the lands of Constantine of the Scots, for both kings travelled to the battlefield from some distance. One may further reasonably assume that the site was either near to the coast or not far from a river that flowed out to open sea, since the enemy forces were close enough to their landing point to be able to escape to their ships and sail away, albeit having to ride hard, with the English in pursuit, in order to get there.[31] That the battle took place in northern Britain also seems likely. John of Worcester asserted that the Norse landed at the mouth of the River Humber,[32] but no other source reports this and it seems implausible that a fleet setting sail from Dublin would have taken the difficult route round the north of Britain in order to attack from the east. Essentially, there are two possible routes into this question. One is to explore place-name evidence looking for places that sound like, or were once spelt like *Brunanburh*; the other is to look at the accounts of the battle in the *Brunanburh* poem and also – more dubiously – in the narrative of the battle of Vínheiðr in *Egils*

---

28 For the wider significance of the Dublin-York axis see Alfred P. Smyth, *Scandinavian York and Dublin: the History and Archaeology of Two Related Viking Kingdoms* (2 vols, Dublin, 1975–1979); on the battle of *Brunanburh* itself see II, 31–61 and for discussion of the Scots' role in this Norse-Scottish alliance see also Smyth, *Warlords and Holy Men* (Edinburgh, 1984), 203–205.

29 Smyth, *Scandinavian York and Dublin*, II, 43–5, 89–100.

30 *GRA*, I, 210. There are problems with William's account of Æthelstan's youth, see Lapidge, 'Some Latin Poems', 62–71; a contrary view is argued by Michael Wood, *In Search of England: Journeys into the English Past* (London, 1999; paperback edition, 2000), 149–68.

31 *Battle of Brunanburh*, lines 32b–36.

32 John of Worcester, *Chronicon*, 392–3, s.a. 937.

Saga[33] and to see whether the comments each makes about the topography of the battle-field matches any of the place-name evidence. The second of these strategies may perhaps be dealt with first. Others have commented on the folly of relying unduly on the testimony of a thirteenth-century saga for precise information about the topography of ground fought over in 937. Ian McDougall has shown the most forcibly how ludicrous it is to pay much attention to the statements about the lie of the land in *Egils Saga*. As he has argued, the detail is all provided within an account of the various ruses Æthelstan deployed to try to gain time to muster an army to face the invading Norse; the saga gave an account of the layout of the land not in order to identify the site, but to show how Æthelstan deceived the enemy as to the number of his tents and the size of his army. This was a stock stratagem and described accordingly.[34]

One of the difficulties is that the battlefield is given several different names in the various medieval sources that describe it, on the basis of which a number of putative identifications of the site of the battlefield can be made.[35] Of the forty or so suggestions made previously – ranging geographically from Leland's suggestion that it might have been at Axminster in Devon, to Camden's alternative view that this was *Brumeford* in Northumberland[36] – three are worth closer attention: Brinsworth, South Yorkshire, Burnswark, Dumfriesshire and Bromborough in Cheshire, on the Mersey estuary.[37] Brinsworth has a certain attraction for an author writing formerly in Sheffield, but the case is far from compelling. Its most persuasive advocate has

---

33 Gwyn Jones, *Egil's Saga: Translated from the Old Icelandic with Introduction and Notes* (New York, 1960), 122–6 (ch. 52).

34 Ian McDougall, 'Discretion and Deceit: a Re-Examination of a Military Stratagem in *Egils Saga*', in *The Middle Ages in the North-West*, ed. Tom Scott and Pat Starkey (Oxford, 1995), 109–42. Also Campbell, *The Battle of Brunanburh*, 68–80. Campbell argued (69–70) that although 'there can be no doubt that the description of the battle on the Vinheithr is based on a tradition of a battle in which Æthelstan fought desperately and victoriously against an invading army composed at least partly of Scots and commanded by a chief named Olafr ... The details as given in the saga are so often demonstrably incorrect that there seems no reason to attach any weight to them when they cannot be controlled.'

35 The different readings were listed and discussed by Campbell, *The Battle*, 60–65 and have recently been re-examined by Paul Cavill in a paper which argues for the importance of taking account of the landscape as well as the philological evidence: 'The Battle of *Brunanburh*' (forthcoming). I am grateful to Dr Cavill for making a draft of his paper available to me before publication.

36 Leland argued for Axminster on the basis that the church there had the tombs of 'many noble Danes slain in King Æthelstanes time at a batel on Brunesdoun thereby; and the scepultres likewise of sum Saxon lordes slain on the same field': *The Itinerary of John Leland in or about the Years 1535–1543*, ed. L. Toulmin Smith (5 vols, London, 1906–1910), I, 243. William Camden, *Britannia; sive florentissimorum regnorum Angliae Scotiae, Hiberniae, et insularum adjacentium ex intima antiquitate chorographica descriptio*, 6th edn (London, 1607), 671; cf. *Britannia: or a Chorographical Description of Great Britain and Ireland, together with the Adjacent Islands*, ed. Edmund Gibson (London, 1753), 1097, where the identification with *Brumeford* is described as *dubitante*. See further Campbell, *The Battle*, 58–9.

37 For surveys of the various identifications see John Henry Cockburn, *The Battle of Brunanburh and its Period elucidated by Place-Names* (London and Sheffield, 1931), 35–70;

been Michael Wood, who wrote an evocative account of his school-boy ventures into South Yorkshire from Manchester Grammar School, in which he mused on the view from White Hill, that seemed to him evoke topography of the battlefield as described in *Egils Saga*.[38] While one could support the notion that the battle was fought in the Don valley (especially if one wanted to place some credence on John of Worcester's statement that Olaf landed at the Humber), the place-name evidence here is insurmountable. It is impossible to make Brinsworth (first attested as *Brinesford* in Domesday Book) into *Brunanburh*.[39] If the Norse had landed not on the Humber but on the western side of Britain, the Solway Firth would be an alternative area to search for a battle-site. Burnswark, near Ecclefechan in Dumfriesshire, had some early advocates and its case has recently been reasserted.[40] Onomastically, this identification must rest on Gaimar's description of the place as *Bruneswerc*,[41] although one might conceivably think it assisted by Simeon of Durham's description of the battle having been '*Etbrunnanwerc uel Brunnanbyrig*'.[42] Although topographically the site may indeed be promising, this alone is not sufficient to confirm the identification.[43]

On both onomastic and strategic grounds, the case for Bromborough in Cheshire is the most compelling.[44] That Bromborough was previously known as *Brunanburh* is a strong factor in its favour and there is no need for special pleading to understand the name to mean 'the stronghold of a man called *Bruna*'.[45] Extensive Scandinavian

---

McDougall, 'Discretion and Deceit'; and Paul Hill, *The Age of Æthelstan: Britain's Forgotten History* (Stroud, 2004), 140–53.

38 Wood first made this case in a paper entitled 'Brunanburh revisited', *Saga Book of the Viking Society*, 20.3 (1980), 200–17; the fuller account is in his *In Search of England*, 203–21. The case for Brinsworth was first made by Cockburn, *The Battle* and was supported by A.H. Byrne, *More Battlefields of England* (London, 1952), 44–60. Byrne rejected the place-name evidence in favour of what he called 'Inherent Military Probability'.

39 Cavill, 'The Battle'; see also McDougall, 'Discretion and Deceit', 122–3.

40 Thomas Hodgkin was the first to argue its claims in *The Athenaeum* (15 August 1885), 239; his views were supported by George Neilson, 'Brunanburh and Burnswork', *Scottish Historical Review*, 7 (1909), 37–9; W.S. Angus, 'The Battlefield of Brunanburh', *Antiquity*, 11 (1937), 283–93; most recently, Kevin Halloran, 'Brunanburh Reconsidered', *History Today*, 56.6 (June 2006), 2–3.

41 *L'Estoire des Engleis*, line 3517, ed. Alexander Bell, Anglo-Norman Texts, 14–16 (Oxford, 1960), 112. This is the reading of only one manuscript; others read *Brunewerce* and *Brunewerche*.

42 Simeon of Durham, *Historia ecclesiae Dunhelmensis*, in *Symeonis Monachi Opera*, ed Arnold, I, 76 (Book II, ch. 18).

43 Halloran, 'Brunanburh Reconsidered', 2–3.

44 A case for Bromborough was first argued by Edmund Gibson in his edition of the Anglo-Saxon Chronicle: *Chronicon Saxonicum, seu annales rerum in Anglia præcipue gestarum* (Oxford, 1692), appendix, separately paginated: 'Regulae ad investigandas Nominum Locorum Origines', 4, s.v. *brun*.

45 John Dodgson, 'The Background of Brunanburh', *Saga Book of the Viking Society*, 14 (1956–1957), 303–316; reprinted in *Wirral and its Viking Heritage*, ed. Paul Cavill, Stephen E. Harding and Judith Jesch (Nottingham, 2000), 60–69, at 60. See also John Dodgson, *Place-Names of Cheshire*, IV (Cambridge, 1972), 237–40. An eighteenth-century map of Cheshire illustrated on the cover of *Wirral and its Viking Heritage* marks the place as *Brunburgh*: 'The

settlement in the Wirral from the late ninth century onwards, together with the significance of the Mersey estuary for ships sailing to England from Ireland, makes this, in military terms, a likely place for an invading fleet to land.[46] This identification addresses the fact that the battle was seemingly preceded by Scandinavian attacks in Mercia and further accounts for the prominence given to Mercian participation in the battle, without requiring one to look, as Smyth has done, for a location in southern Mercia that requires both Scots and Norse forces to have penetrated deep into Æthelstan's territory.[47] Additional support for locating the battle at Bromborough lies in its proximity to a place called Thingwall; Paul Cavill and others have argued recently that the 'ding' of *Dingesmere* in the poem (line 54), where the defeated Norsemen retreated to their ships before sailing back to Dublin in humiliated defeat, refers to the þing of Thingwall (meaning 'the place where an assembly meets'). They suggest that *Dinges mere* may best be understood as the wetland or marshland by the assembly-meeting-point.[48] If the identification with Bromborough were correct, then this would locate the battle at the boundary between the Norse Wirral and Anglo-Saxon controlled Mercia, strategically a highly significant location.[49] This would reinforce the presumption made earlier that this battle was as critical to the Mercians as it was to the West Saxons in the English army.

When Æthelstan and his brother, the king and the ætheling, had won and five young kings lay dead on the field of battle, together with seven of Olaf's earls and a countless host of seamen and Scots, just what had this joint West Saxon/Mercian force achieved? The poet gloated over the ignominy of the hasty flight of the Norse leader, yet in many ways the defeat was more crushing for Constantine, king of the Scots. Constantine's son was dead and his credibility among his own people seriously weakened by so crushing a defeat, a point noted by the later tenth-century chronicler, Æthelweard, who observed that after this battle the Scots had here been forced to

---

County Palatine of Chester. By H. Moll Geographer' (1724). See also Alan Thacker, 'Anglo-Saxon Cheshire', in *A History of the County of Chester*, ed. B.E. Harris, A.T. Thacker and C.P. Lewis, Victoria History of the Counties of England (4 vols in 5 parts to date, Oxford, 1979–2005, in progress), I, 237–92, at 260; N.J. Higham, 'The Context of *Brunanburh*', in *Names, Places and People*, ed. A.R. Rumble and A.D. Mills (Stamford, 1997), 144–56.

46 F.T. Wainwright, 'Ingimund's Invasion', *EHR*, 63 (1948), 145–67; reprinted in *Wirral and its Viking Heritage*, ed. Cavill, Harding and Jesch, 43–59; Judith Jesch, 'Scandinavian Wirral', ibid., 1–10.

47 Smyth's argument that *Brunanburh* lay in the area of the forest *Bruneswald* and so should be sought near Leighton Bromswold in Huntingdonshire or Newton Bromswold in Northamptonshire rests in part on his acceptance of John of Worcester's assertion that Olaf landed on the Humber and also on extrapolation from the progress of the Norse leader's campaign in Mercia after Æthelstan's death. But the onomastic evidence is not convincing: Cavill, 'The Battle'.

48 Paul Cavill, Stephen Harding and Judith Jesch, 'Revisiting *Dingesmere*', *Journal of the English Place-Name Society*, 36 (2003–2004), 25–38, at 36.

49 See also A.H. Smith, 'The Site of the Battle of Brunanburh', in *London Mediaeval Studies*, I, ed. R.W. Chambers, F. Norman and A.H. Smith (London, 1937), 56–9, and Richard Coates, 'A Further Snippet of Evidence for Brunanburh = Bromborough', *Notes and Queries*, 45.3 (1998), 288–9.

bow their necks.[50] It was probably not long after that Constantine abdicated and retired to St Andrews.[51] Certainly this was an engagement of sufficient significance elsewhere in Britain for it to be reported in non-English sources including the Pictish Chronicle, the *Annales Cambriae* and the Annals of Clonmacnoise.[52] To the annalist of Ulster, this was a 'great victory' that Æthelstan enjoyed, a 'great, lamentable and horrible battle' that was cruelly fought between the Saxons and the Norsemen in which several thousand Norsemen died as well as a large number of Saxons, but from which the Norse king, Amlaíb, escaped with a few followers.[53] Others would thus seem to have shared the view of the *Brunanburh* poet that this was a battle of some significance, but the Chronicle poem goes farther than any of these other accounts. To the poet's mind this had been the greatest battle in Anglo-Saxon memory. But in what sphere should we locate Æthelstan's confirmed hegemony? Is this really an argument about England and the English?

In support of my previous view that the *Brunanburh* poem reinforced a sense of English nationhood, I looked at the royal styles adopted by Æthelstan. At the start of his reign he had used in his charters the title 'king of the Anglo-Saxons', continuing the style first adopted by his grandfather Alfred and used also by his father, Edward the Elder.[54] This title fairly reflected his and his predecessors' authority over a combined West Saxon and Mercian polity, but it was scarcely adequate after 927 and Æthelstan's acquisition of Northumbria. Those military and political achievements were reflected in the adoption of much more grandiose regnal styles after 927; a number of charters from 928 onwards termed him *rex Anglorum*,[55] a style that

---

50 *The Chronicle of Æthelweard*, ed. Alistair Campbell (London, 1962), 54.

51 Hudson has argued that Constantine was no more than a client king for his last years and suggested that he retired *c.* 943: *Kings of Celtic Scotland*, 81–2.

52 The Pictish Chronicle (a tenth-century compilation) reported the battle within an account of the reign of Constantine III: Et bellum Duinbrunde in xxxiiii. ejus anno ubi cecidit filius Constantini': *Chronicles of the Picts, Chronicles of the Scots*, ed. William F. Skene (Edinburgh, 1867), 9. The Welsh *Annales Cambriae* mentioned a '*Bellum Brune*' *c.* 938: *Annales Cambriae*, ed. John Williams ap Ithel, Rolls Series, 20 (London, 1860), 17. The Annals of Clonmacnoise survive only in a seventeenth-century English translation; they reported a battle between the Danes of Dublin and the Danes of England against the Saxons on the plains of *othlynn* where there was a great slaughter (numbered improbably in thousands), among whom was Constantine's son, Cellach; see Campbell, *The Battle*, 159; Smyth, *Scandinavian York and Dublin*, II, 38–40.

53 *The Annals of Ulster (to AD. 1131), Part I, Text and Translation*, ed. Seán Mac Airt and Gearóid Mac Niocaill (Dublin, 1983), 384–5.

54 The style '*Angul Saxonum rex*' is found in S 396–7; compare also S 394 (*rex Saxonum et Anglorum*); see Keynes, Charters of the West Saxon Kings', 1147–9; Edward king of Anglo-Saxons', 44–5. Among the inscriptions in Coburg Landesbibliothek, MS 1 is one describing Æthelstan as '*rex Angulsaxonum et Mercianorum*': Simon Keynes, 'King Æthelstan's Books', in *Learning and Literature in Anglo-Saxon England*, ed. Michael Lapidge and Helmut Gneuss (Cambridge, 1985), 143–201, at 189–93.

55 Æthelstan used the style *rex Anglorum*, 'king of the English' in S 399–400, 403, 412–13, and 416. See Harald Kleinschmidt, 'Die Titulaturen englischer Könige im 10. und 11. Jahrhundert', in *Intitulatio III: Lateinische Herrschertitel und Herrschertitulaturen vom 7. bis zum 13. Jahrhundert*, ed. Herwig Wolfram and Anton Scharer (Vienna, Cologne and

made him, self-evidently, king over a people whom in Latin we might term the *gens Anglorum* (as Bede had done, following the example of Pope Gregory), a people whom in English Alfred termed the *Angelcynn*.[56] In Æthelstan's reign, one might reasonably argue were the seeds of an English monarchy. But is this the best reading of Æthelstan's view of his own authority? And is the English angle that most promoted by the *Brunanburh* poem? I no longer think so.

It was re-reading Simon Walker's sole foray into pre-Conquest history, an essay in the *Festschrift* for Karl Leyser tentatively called 'A context for Brunanburh?' that caused me to rethink this question. For Walker – coming to the text, it must be remembered, from the perspective of the later middle ages – the *Brunanburh* poem resonated not with 'Englishness' but with claims to a lordship over all of Britain. He, too, began with the last nine lines, but he heard in them most loudly the references to the island of Britain and the defeat of the British (*weallas*). These lines, he argued, give:

> an important indication of the poem's immediate purpose, for, by comparing Athelstan's triumph at *Brunanburh* to the earliest Anglo-Saxon victories over the Britons, its closing lines clearly seek to rank him among the small band of kings, accorded the title *bretwalda*, who held the rule over all the kingdoms of the southern English. The implicit comparison is, indeed with Northumbrian kings such as Edwin, Oswald and Oswiu who 'had still greater power and ruled over all the inhabitants of Britain, English and Britons alike.'[57]

Although the whole vexed question of the *bretwalda* cannot detain us here, the point is a sufficiently important one to merit a couple of comments. The passage from Bede that Simon Walker was here quoting is the paragraph in book II, ch. 5 of his *Ecclesiastical History* which follows his obituary notice for Æthelberht, king of Kent, who died in 616. Æthelberht was, as Bede observed, the first king among the English to receive the Christian faith, but he was the third to hold *imperium* (by which I understand Bede to mean wide power over several peoples); the other kings holding similar power listed by Bede were, in order: Ælle, a fifth-century king of the South Saxons, Ceawlin of Wessex, Æthelberht of Kent, Rædwald of East Anglia and the three Northumbrians just named, Edwin, Oswald and Oswiu. Bede did not attempt to confer any Latin title on these kings; he merely described the breadth of the power they wielded.[58] Yet the compilers of the *Anglo-Saxon Chronicle* in the ninth century used this passage to a rather different end. Explaining the conquests of an earlier West Saxon king (Ecgberht, Alfred's grandfather) and his acquisition of power over all the lands south of the Humber, the chronicler depicted him as heir to

---

Graz, 1988), 75–129, at 107–108; and David N. Dumville, *Wessex and England from Alfred to Edgar* (Woodbridge, 1992), 169–70.

56 Foot, 'The Making of *angelcynn*', 38–41; Brooks, *Bede and the English*, 6–8 and 13–14.

57 Walker, 'A Context', 2, quoting *HE*, 148–51 (Book II, ch. 5).

58 Patrick Wormald, 'Bede, the *Bretwaldas* and the Origins of the *gens Anglorum*', in *Ideal and Reality in Frankish and Anglo-Saxon Society*, ed. Patrick Wormald, with Donald Bullough and Roger Collins (Oxford, 1983), 99–129; Stephen Fanning, 'Bede, Imperium and the Bretwaldas', *Speculum*, 66 (1991), 1–26; Simon Keynes, 'Rædwald the Bretwalda', in *Voyage to the Other World: the Legacy of Sutton Hoo*, ed. Calvin B. Kendall and Peter S. Wells (Minneapolis, MN, 1992), 103–23.

these early, powerful kings conferring on him (and on them) the title of *bretwalda/ brytenwalda*. Both the correct orthography for this noun and its meaning are disputed, but this term may have been intended to imply that the chronicler sought to claim for Ecgberht the inheritance of some entitlement to be seen as ruler of Britain. While he did not hold this extended realm for very long, it is not entirely fanciful to see Ecgberht's power as similar to that of the Southumbrian kings named by Bede who exercised *imperium* south of the Humber. Æthelstan's claim to be seen in such a light was, however, considerably stronger; like Edwin, he ruled over English and Britons alike.[59]

Can we see any signs that Æthelstan was thought of as a ninth *bretwalda*, or at least as heir to the *imperium* formerly exercised by the *bretwaldas*? In the poem 'Carta dirige gressus', written after the submission of Constantine and the other kings at Eamont in 927, not only was the achieving of the political unity among the Anglo-Saxons celebrated in that phrase *ista perfecta Saxonia* (line 10), but there is also a direct reference to Britain. Æthelstan arms the army of the Saxons throughout all Britain: Ille, Sictric defuncto/armat tum in prelio/Saxonum exercitum/per totam Bryttanium'.[60] As Michael Lapidge observed, the fact that Constantine and the other northern leaders acknowledged the supremacy of Æthelstan on this occasion made him, in effect, king of all Britain.[61] Let us return to the question of the styles by which Æthelstan liked to be known as king. I have already suggested that in the aftermath of his acquisition of Northumbria in 927 there was a re-evaluation of the terms in which the king was addressed, a reconsideration that we can with some confidence locate within the royal court, following Simon Keynes's close demonstration of the significance of a royal chancery in the production of many of Æthelstan's charters.[62] In the early 930s we can see a further shift in gear, up from *rex Anglorum*, king of the English, to some distinctly grandiose, quasi-imperial language adopted better to reflect the nature of Æthelstan's new realm.[63] One title used frequently is that found in the famous Amounderness charter, issued while the king was on his way north in 934: 'ego Æðelstanus rex Anglorum, per omnipotentis dextram quae Christus est, totius Brittanniae regni solio sublimatus'; 'I Æthelstan, king of the English, elevated by the right hand of the Almighty, which is Christ, to the throne of the

---

59 Dumville, *Wessex*, 153–4, 169–71; Michael Wood, 'The Making of King Æthelstan's Empire: an English Charlemagne?', in *Ideal and Reality*, ed. Wormald, 250–72, at 250–52, 271–2.

60 The first line of this fourth stanza presents a number of difficulties. Stevenson elected here to print 'Ille Sictric defunctum', following the version of the text in BL, Cotton MS Nero A. ii, fos. 10v–11v: 'A Latin Poem', 486. Lapidge, however, preferred the reading of Durham, Cathedral Library, MS A. II. 17, pt 1, fo. 31v, taking 'Sictric defuncto' as an ablative absolute phrase and the nominative 'Ille' thus referring to Æthelstan: 'Some Latin Poems', 77–8.

61 Lapidge, 'Some Latin Poems', 91.

62 Simon Keynes, *The Diplomas of King Æthelred 'the Unready' 978–1016: a Study in their Use as Historical Evidence* (Cambridge, 1980), 39–44.

63 Eric John noted that Æthelstan was the first king to grant bookland throughout England: *Orbis Britanniae and Other Studies* (Leicester, 1966), 46.

whole kingdom of Britain'.[64] Another frequently found style uses the Greek imperial title *basileus*: 'nodante dei gratia basileos Anglorum et eque totius Brittannie orbis curagulus' ('by grace of God king of the English and equally guardian of the whole country of Britain').[65] Some, but by no means all of his charters he also attests with the subscription *rex totius Britanniae*,[66] which is the legend customarily found on his coins from *c.* 927 onwards.[67] There is even one, highly problematical, document dated 934 and supposedly issued 16 December in that year at Frome in Somerset to the *familia* of Holy Trinity, Winchester, where the Latin epithet 'rex et rector totius huius britannie insule largiente domino et omnibus eius sanctis' is rendered in Old English as Ic ÆÞELSTAN Ongolsaxna cyning 7 brytænwalda eallæs ðyses Iglandæs þurh Godæs sælene and ealra his halegra'.[68]

We may accept that there was an ideology about Britain and rulership over the whole island of Britain current at the court of Æthelstan.[69] More strikingly, that notion finds currency elsewhere, in non-English texts. The Welsh prophecy poem *Armes Prydein*, probably composed around 930 (namely after Æthelstan's subjugation of the Welsh kings) called him the 'Great King' and saw his conquests as completing the theft of land from the British begun by Hengest and Horsa. A later Welsh history of kings also stressed Æthelstan's significance; speaking of the Saxons it reported, 'and thus after casting off the lordship of the Britons from them they thereupon ruled all England with Edelstan as their prince who first of the English wore the Crown of the Island of Britain'.[70] Geoffrey of Monmouth ended his *Historia regum* with reference to Adelstan, the king under whom the Saxons had thrown off the dominion of the British; to him perhaps, as Michael Wood has argued, the battle of *Brunanburh* represented a turning point in the matter of England and the matter of Britain, a key moment for the British.[71] In the thirteenth-century Icelandic *Egils saga* there

---

64 S 407 (AD 930 for 934); see also S 412, 413, 416, 417, 418, 419, 421, 422, 425, 426, 434, 435, 436. Compare also the slightly dubious charters where he is called *rex et rector*, or *gubernator et rector*, a title which may reflect styles current at Æthelstan's court: S 427, 411, 450.

65 S 429–31, 438, 446.

66 S 431, 437, 445–6.

67 C.E. Blunt, 'The Coinage of Athelstan, 924–939: a Survey', *British Numismatic Journal*, 42 (1974), 36–160, at 56. Marion M. Archibald and C.E. Blunt, *Sylloge of Coins of the British Isles 34, British Museum Anglo-Saxon Coins V, Athelstan to the Reform of Edgar 924 – c. 973* (London, 1986), pp. xix–xx.

68 S 427. It is just possible that a genuine text underlies this bilingual charter, but it cannot be authentic in the form in which it survives.

69 For the mythologies associated with the political and ecclesiastical aspiration towards a united Britain in the middle ages see R.R. Davies, *The First English Empire: Power and Identities in the British Isles 1093–1343* (Oxford, 2000), 31–53.

70 *The Text of the Bruts, from the Red Book of Hergest*, ed. John Rhys and J.G. Evans (Oxford, 1890), 255; quoted *Armes Prydein: the Prophecy of Britain from the Book of Taliesin*, ed. Ifor Williams and Rachel Bromwich (Dublin, 1982), p. xviii.

71 *The Historia regum Britannie of Geoffrey of Monmouth*, 1: Bern, Bürgerbibliothek, *MS. 568*, §207, ed. Neil Wright (Cambridge, 1984), 147; for a translation, see Geoffrey of Monmouth, *The History of the Kings of Britain*, tr. Lewis Thorpe (Harmondsworth, 1966), 284; see Michael Wood, *In Search of England*, 151.

is a lengthy account of a supposed meeting between Egil Skallgrimsson and King Æthelstan following the battle of Vínheiðr (a victory of the English king Æthelstan over a combined force of Norse and Scots that is probably to be equated with the battle of *Brunanburh*). Egil composed a drapa for the king in which he compared him with a king Ælle (to whom he assumes Æthelstan to have been related) while stressing that he, so kin-famed, achieved more.[72] The Ælle of the drapa has conventionally been identified with the usurping Northumbrian king of that name who died in the Danish siege of York of 867, an identification that has always seemed implausible, not least because it is so insulting.[73] It might rather be to Ælle of Deira or Ælle of the South Saxons. The latter suggestion appealed to Simon Walker because that Ælle was, as noted above, the first of the seven *imperium*-holding kings in Bede's *History*, and this allusion would thus reinforce the British interpretation of the significance of the battle.[74] The British theme was raised also by the late tenth-century Latin chronicler Æthelweard. He called Æthelstan a very mighty king, *rex robustissimus*, and reported that *Brunanburh* was still in his own time called the 'Great Battle' in popular parlance. After Æthelstan had driven the barbarian forces from the shores of the ocean and the Scots and Picts had submitted, 'the fields of Britain (*Britannidis arva*) were consolidated into one, there was peace everywhere and abundance of all things, and since then no fleet has remained here, having advanced against these shores, except under treaty with the English'.[75]

The problem of studying the reign of Æthelstan is made particularly acute by reason of the paucity of contemporary sources; we have already discussed how little narrative there is provided in the *Chronicle*, and although Michael Wood would like us to believe there was once a tenth-century life of the king, no contemporary biography now survives comparable to that we have for Alfred.[76] Such material as we do have tends to lead us to focus on *'rex pius adelstan'*.[77] Much of the recent scholarly work on this reign has focused on the king's religious activities, his interest in the continental monastic reform movement, his collection of manuscripts, the scholars present at his court and interest in the relics of the dead.[78] Putting the *Brunanburh* poem at the centre of a reconsideration of his reign offers a quite different emphasis. It is not solely that we have the military commander here, for he

---

72 *Egil's saga*, ch. 55, poem 21, transl. Jones, 134.
73 Jones, *Egil's Saga*, 247.
74 Walker, 'A Context', 23.
75 *Chronicle of Æthelweard*, ed. Campbell, 54.
76 Michael Wood, 'The Lost "Wars of King Æthelstan"' (forthcoming).
77 Walker, 'A Context', 38–9. 'Rex pius Æðelstan' is the first half line of a poem entered uniquely in London, BL, Cotton MS, Tiberius A ii, fo. 15r, in a Caroline minuscule written by a continental hand. This late ninth- or early tenth-century Gospel book, probably from Lobbes, was acquired by Æthelstan and given by him to Christ Church Canterbury, according to the prose dedication on fo. 15r that describes the king as *'Anglorum basyleos et curagulus totius Bryttaniae'*. See Keynes, 'King Æthelstan's Books', 147–53 and, on the poem, Lapidge, 'Some Latin Poems', 93–7.
78 J. Armitage Robinson, *The Times of Saint Dunstan: the Ford Lectures Delivered in the University of Oxford in the Michaelmas Term, 1922* (Oxford, 1923), 51–80; Keynes 'King Æthelstan's Books'.

is commemorated elsewhere, too. Peter, author of *Carta dirige gressus*, had depicted the king arming the army of the English for battle throughout Britain; the author of *Rex pius Æðelstan* stressed that God had set Æthelstan as king over the English 'plainly so that this king himself, mighty in war, might be able to conquer other fierce kings, treading down their proud necks.'[79] Ælfric, monk of Cerne and later abbot of Eynsham, drawing attention to English kings 'victorious because of God', included in his list Æthelstan 'who fought against Anlaf and slaughtered his army and put him to flight, and afterwards with his people dwelt in peace'.[80] The *Brunanburh* poet causes us to see Æthelstan through different eyes. Simon Walker argued that the authorship of the poem might plausibly be located not at the royal court in Wessex but rather in the scriptorium at Worcester, and he tentatively suggested that Cenwald, bishop of Worcester 929–958, might have been responsible. Cenwald had been a clerk in Æthelstan's household, went with him on the northern campaign in 927 and accompanied two of the king's sisters to the Ottonian court in 929.[81] He was later remembered at Worcester as a close associate of this king's and that community had access to other traditions about the battle of *Brunanburh* as is shown in the version of events given by John of Worcester.[82] Walker's argument in favour of Cenwald's possible influence over the composition of the poem is a convincing one and it is strengthened by the relationship between the pre-occupations of the poem and those of the author (Cenwald or another member of the cathedral community at Worcester during his time) of a group of so-called alliterative charters from the reigns of Æthelstan's successors, Edmund and Eadred.[83] More difficult is Walker's tentative suggestion that the poem was written during the reign of Æthelstan's younger brother Edmund. It is conceivable that we should read the poem in the style of mirrors for princes and see its celebration of Æthelstan's achievement as a muted call to Edmund to restore his elder brother's realm, yet this is not a wholly convincing argument. The poem does indeed stress the legitimate inheritance of the West Saxon royal line and makes much of both Æthelstan and his brother Edmund as the sons of Edward, but Walker's presumption that the repeated mention of Edmund in some way diminishes or detracts from his brother's achievement can be challenged. Rather one might read this as serving to counteract the unpleasant rumours obviously circulating during the king's reign that he was not royal by birth:[84] here were two legitimately-born members of this distinguished line fighting and winning together. Similarly, one can read differently the fact that the *Brunanburh* poet has remarkably little to say about the Almighty. Apart from the kenning for the sun – *Godes condel beorht* – in line 15,

---

79 *Rex pius Æðelstan*, lines 5–6; Lapidge, 'Some Latin Poems', 95–6.

80 *The Old English Version of the Heptateuch: Ælfric's Treatise on the Old and New Testament and his Preface to Genesis*, ed. S.J. Crawford (London, 1922), 416–17.

81 E.E. Barker, 'Two Lost Documents of King Æthelstan', *ASE*, 6 (1977), 139–43; Keynes, 'King Æthelstan's Books', 198–201.

82 Walker, 'A Context', 28–31.

83 Ibid., 29–30.

84 The legend reported both by Hrotsvitha of Gandersheim and later by William of Malmesbury in his *Gesta regum*, that Æthelstan's mother had been a concubine: *Gesta Ottonis*, lines 81–1, *Hrotsvithae Opera*, ed. Paul von Winterfeld, MGH, Scriptores Rerum Germanicarum in usum scholarum, 34 (Berlin 1902), 207; *GRA*, I, 206.

divine intervention is not mentioned; unlike Louis III on the battlefield at Saucourt in 881 (celebrated in the *Ludwigslied*),[85] Æthelstan won because of his own valour and 'the accumulated and inherited *virtus* of his kindred'. Edmund's actions, however, in his own praise poem are compared with the redeeming work of Christ as he freed the Danes from the bondage of captivity under the Norsemen.[86] The poem on the battle of *Brunanburh* fits most obviously into the rhetorical *milieu* of Æthelstan's court, a circle where Cenwald had begun his career and with which he retained contact after his promotion to the see of Worcester.[87]

The scribe who listed the relics that Æthelstan gave to the church at Exeter reminded his audience that Æthelstan 'ruled England singly, which before him many kings had shared between them'.[88] Yet, according to the *Brunanburh* poet, he went on to do more than that. With all the Celtic rulers of the mainland of Britain acknowledging his lordship, Æthelstan was not just king of the English: he was truly *rex totius Britanniae* and he and those around him used imperial language and imagery to reinforce that notion of an empire of Britain.[89] Æthelstan was the most powerful ruler in Britain since the Romans, as Æthelweard acknowledged when he said that in his time 'the fields of Britain were consolidated into one'.[90] Led by the arguments of both Simon Walker and Nicholas Brooks, I have therefore changed my mind about *Brunanburh*: this is a poem not only about the English people but about the realm of Britain.[91]

---

85 *Ludwigslied*, tr. J. Knight Bostock, *A Handbook on Old High German Literature* (Oxford, 1955), 2nd edn, rev. K.C. King and D.R. McLintock (Oxford, 1976), 239–41.

86 Walker, 'A Context', 38.

87 *Contra* Donald Scragg, 'A Reading of *Brunanburh*', in *Unlocking the Wordhord*, ed. Mark C. Amodio and Katherine O'Brien O'Keefe (Toronto, 1998), 109–22.

88 Oxford, Bodleian Library MS Auct. D.2.16 (*S.C.* 2719), fo. 8r; see Patrick W. Conner, *Anglo-Saxon Exeter: a Tenth-Century Cultural History* (Woodbridge, 1993), 25–6, 171–87.

89 Wood, 'The Making of Æthelstan's Empire'.

90 Æthelweard, *Chronicon*, 54; quoted above.

91 An earlier version of this chapter was read to the medieval discussion group at Sheffield and I am grateful to those present for their comments and suggestions and also to Julia Barrow, Paul Cavill, Philip Shaw and Peter Orton for help over specific points of detail.

Chapter 12

Archbishop Dunstan: A Prophet in Politics?

Catherine Cubitt

In his biographical sketch of St Dunstan, Nicholas Brooks acutely describes the saint as a 'holy man of distinction' and comments on the disruptive nature of Dunstan's presence at the court of King Edmund. This epithet reminds the reader of the uncompromising nature of Dunstan's spirituality and the power in earthly affairs he was to derive from his relationship with the divine.[1] The influence of Dunstan, like that of his later contemporaries, Æthelwold and Oswald, is now recognised as a major factor in the policies of the late tenth-century Anglo-Saxon kings.[2] For example, it appears that Dunstan was a crucial supporter of the young king, Edward, in the succession dispute on the death of King Edgar, while Æthelwold favoured the claims of Æthelred, son of the consecrated queen.[3] In these and other matters, the political authority of these men was rooted in their episcopal office, with its responsibility for royal counsel and its ministry of consecration. According to a story recorded in the late eleventh century, Dunstan withstood courtly discontent at the designation of Edward as king: 'But when, at the time of [Edward's] consecration, some of the leading men of the nation had wished to oppose [it], St Dunstan persevered single-mindedly in his election, and, taking hold of the banner of the holy cross which was customarily carried before him, he fixed it upright in the middle, and with the remaining pious bishops consecrated him king'.[4]

---

1 Nicholas Brooks, 'The Career of St Dunstan', in *St Dunstan, His Life, Times and Cult*, ed. Nigel Ramsay, Margaret Sparks and Tim Tatton-Brown (Woodbridge, 1992), 1–23, at 11.

2 Pauline Stafford, 'The Reign of Æthelred II, a Study in the Limitations on Royal Policy and Action', in *Ethelred the Unready*, ed. David Hill, British Archaeological Reports, British Series, 59 (Oxford, 1978), 15–46; Barbara Yorke, 'Æthelwold and the Politics of the Tenth Century', in *Bishop Æthelwold: his Career and Influence*, ed. Barbara Yorke (Woodbridge, 1988), 65–88.

3 Nicholas Brooks, *The Early History of the Church of Canterbury* (Leicester, 1984), 249–50.

4 *Edward King and Martyr*, ed. Christine Fell, Leeds Texts and Monographs, New Series (Leeds, 1971), 2: 'Sed dum consecrationis eius tempore nonnulli patriae optimates resistere uoluissent, sanctus Dunstanus in electione eius unanimiter perseuerans, uexillum crucis sanctae, quod ex consuetudine prae se ferebatur, arreptum in medio statuit, eumque cum reliquis religiosis episcopis in regem consecrauit …'. See too Osbern's *Vita sancti Dunstani*, in *Memorials of St Dunstan, Archbishop of Canterbury*, ed. William Stubbs, Rolls Series, 63 (London, 1874), 69–128, at 114. Fell notes the close parallels between these two texts (and also the *Vita* by Eadmer, *Memorials of St Dunstan*, ed. Stubbs, 162–222). She suggests that a common source may lie behind these three accounts. In this connection it is worth

In seeking to uncover the political aspects of religious authority, it is easy to overlook the spiritual in the political. The saintly charisma of bishops like Dunstan and his tenth-century colleagues was inseparable from the authority of office; their ability as shrewd politicians was not undermined by their reputation as men of God.[5] This chapter will examine one aspect of Dunstan's career, his reputation as a prophet and it will consider this in relation to the power of cursing and excommunication.

Dunstan's power of prophecy seems to have been acknowledged within his own lifetime, and certainly not long after his death. A fulsome verse letter to him as archbishop (959–988), includes, among the many epithets bestowed upon him, 'praesagus', 'foretelling'.[6] In his *Life of St Æthelwold,* Wulfstan of Winchester described Dunstan in these words, 'he was like a pillar that cannot be moved, outstanding in learning and action, beautiful as an angel, strong in alms and prophecy'. Later in the *vita*, Dunstan appears as a visionary whose dream of the tree of monastic cowls foretells Æthelwold's leadership of the monastic movement. Wulfstan, a proficient and able hagiographer, was writing perhaps for Æthelwold's translation in 996, but certainly before *c.* 1000.[7] Dunstan was less well-served by his biographer than his friend and fellow monk-bishop, Æthelwold, had been. This author, B., writing between 995 and 1005, produced a deeply interesting but somewhat eccentric biography, which is much fuller on Dunstan's early years than on those of his episcopal ministry. Lapidge has memorably characterised B.'s depiction of his subject as a 'frantic and possessed zealot ... excessively prone to visions' and as a 'difficult and tormented figure'.[8] B. certainly portrays Dunstan as a visionary: indeed, one might say that his claim to sanctity rested upon this, since

---

mentioning Thomson's comments concerning a now-lost early eleventh-century Old English *vita* of Dunstan which was apparently used by Osbern: see below at n. 21.

5   For a perceptive analysis of this aspect of Bishop Wulfstan II's career, see Ann Williams, 'The Cunning of the Dove: Wulfstan and the Politics of Accommodation', in *St Wulfstan and his World*, ed. J.S. Barrow and N.P. Brooks (Aldershot, 2005), 23–38. See also David Rollason, 'The Concept of Sanctity in the Early Lives of St Dunstan', in *St Dunstan*, ed. Ramsay, Sparks and Tatton-Brown, 261–71.

6   'Epistola ad Dunstanum Archiepiscopum', in *Memorials of St Dunstan*, ed. Stubbs, 371. The author addresses Dunstan as 'brother' which suggests that it was written by a fellow bishop.

7   'quasi columna inmobilis, doctrina et actione praecipuus, angelico uultu decorus, elemosinis et prophetia praepollens': *Vita Æthelwoldi*, 24–7, 56–7, cc. 14, 38 (translation from this volume). For the dating of the biography, see ibid., p. xvi. On the image of the column in Benedictine Reform texts, see Robert Deshman, 'The Imagery of the Living Ecclesia and the English Monastic Reform', in *Sources of Anglo-Saxon Culture*, ed. P.E. Szarmach and V.D. Oggins (Kalamazoo, 1986), 261–82. For an excellent account of the cult of Dunstan, see Alan Thacker, 'Cults at Canterbury: Relics and Reform under Dunstan and his Successors', in *St Dunstan*, ed. Ramsay, Sparks and Tatton-Brown, 221–45. And see too Nigel Ramsay and Margaret Sparks, 'The Cult of St Dunstan at Christ Church, Canterbury', ibid., 311–23.

8   *Sancti Dunstani Vita Auctore B.*, in *Memorials*, ed. Stubbs, 3–52; for comment, see Michael Lapidge, 'Dunstan', in *ODNB*, s.v.; Michael Lapidge, 'B. and the Vita S. Dunstani', in *St Dunstan*, ed. Ramsay, Sparks and Tatton-Brown, 247–259, at 247–8.

visions far outweigh any other miracles in B's *Vita*, representing roughly two thirds of miraculous events described.[9]

B.'s collection of visions include spiritual conflicts indicative of his interior life, such as appearances by the devil in the guise of a beast, as well as glimpses of heavenly creatures, like the dove who visited his dying friend Æthelflæd at Glastonbury, or the holy virgins singing at St Augustine's, Canterbury.[10] Episodes like these, while they appear to us today as more symptomatic of derangement than sanctity, may have confirmed to Dunstan's contemporaries that he was a man of a profound spirituality, filled with the Holy Spirit and in touch with a higher world. B. introduces a sequence of visions with these words: '... however long he, shrouded in a fleshly robe, lived here below, whether he remained wakeful in his mind or whether he rested detained by sleep, he always remained in the higher places, as the Apostle Paul says: "For our abode is in the heavens"'.[11]

His visions included foreknowledge of events to come. His very first miracle, as a child, was a nocturnal dream of his own rebuilding of the monastery of Glastonbury. As an adult, he foresaw the death of a boy at Glastonbury and those of two kings, Eadred and Edmund. Dunstan is not only able to see the demon responsible for Edmund's assassination, but also interprets the dream of his lay travelling companion to show how it forewarns of the death of the king and the degeneration of the kingdom afterwards, as its leaders abandon the way of truth.[12] Moreover, B. comments on the prophetic nature of Dunstan's visions and laments that they went unheeded:

> For behold, how soon the predictions of the blessed man concerning the king became clear. Indeed, they were manifest from the earliest times, not excepting the times of King Eadwig, if king he can rightly be called who ruled neither himself nor others well. For indeed, the blessed father Dunstan was moved by the spirit of God, as the Apostle says; therefore, like a son of God, he had deserved these mysteries and other things like them; so much so indeed that quite a few people declared that he brought forth utterly vacuous verbal absurdities, while he was preaching in prophetic speech and by the inspiration of the Holy Spirit, things which we saw afterwards performed with the clearest signs.[13]

---

9 *Memorials of St Dunstan*, ed. Stubbs, 7, 15–16, 19, 26–8, 30–31, 35, 40–49, cc, 3, 9, 11, 16–17, 20, 23, 29, 30, 34, 36.

10 *Memorials of St Dunstan*, ed. Stubbs, 18–19, 48–8, cc. 11, 36.

11 *Memorials of St Dunstan*, ed. Stubbs, 40, c. 29: 'quod quamvis hic carneo septus velamine deguisset in imis, mente tamen sive vigilaret, sive somno detentus quiesceret, semper manebat in superis, ut Paul ait apostolus: "Nostra autem conversatio in coelis est"'.

12 *Memorials of St Dunstan*, ed. Stubbs, 31, c. 20 (Eadred), 44–6, cc. 31–3 (Edmund), 47, c. 34 (the boy).

13 *Memorials of St Dunstan*, ed. Stubbs, 44–6, cc. 31–3; quotation from 46, c. 33: Ecce enim quam mature de rege beati viri claruere præsagia. De principibus autem non nisi Eadwigi regis temporibus, si rex jure queat appellari qui nec sese nec alios quosque bene rexerat, patuere. Quoniam quidem beatus pater Dunstanus spiritu Dei, ut ait apostolus, agebatur, idcirco hæc et his similia quasi filius Dei promuererat mysteria; in tantum quoque ut plerique eum assererent vanissima verborum deliramenta proferre, dum ore prophetico Sanctique Spiritus inbutione perplura prædiceret, quæ postea signis evidentissimis conspeximus facta'.

B. here identifies Dunstan as a man inspired by the Holy Spirit and suggests that Dunstan's prophecies about Edmund's successor Eadwig concerned the right governance of the kingdom, visionary advice which was not followed. In B.'s account, Dunstan was not only a visionary, but also a prophet whose foresight into the future had an implicitly political dimension. It is worth noting that when Edmund restores Dunstan to favour and makes him abbot of Glastonbury, prompted by his narrow escape from death, the King realises that 'that he had been almost destined to imminent death for the punishment of so great a man'.[14] B. explicitly therefore links royal policy to the fear of the holy man.

B. was writing for Archbishop Ælfric, not on commission but in a failed attempt to gain patronage. While his *Vita* may have been unsuccessful as a form of career advancement, it was certainly received positively at Canterbury, since it served as the basis for the liturgical lections put together by Adelard of Ghent for Archbishop Ælfheah, and it should probably be identified with the *Life* of St Dunstan which the abbot of St Augustine's, Wulfric, sent to Abbo of Fleury for versification.[15]

Adelard's series of liturgical lections on the *Life* of Dunstan places an even more pronounced emphasis on the saint's visionary and prophetic powers, and strengthens their political dimension. While Adelard uses B.'s *Vita* as his chief source, he was not averse to improving on it to suit the taste of his audience, modifying Dunstan's family connections by linking him to Archbishop Athelm of Canterbury, for example. Nicholas Brooks has cogently argued that this and other changes represent inventions on the part of Adelard.[16] Adelard, in excerpting B.'s *Vita*, omitted much, including details about his life at Glastonbury and the royal court. But he retained Dunstan's visions and augmented these so that they form a more predominant part of his account of the saint. Nine visions seen by Dunstan are recounted, with only four other miracles performed by him. In addition to these, he includes three other new prophetic or visionary episodes on the part of others, for example equipping Dunstan with the standard hagiographical motif of maternal premonition of his future greatness.

The connection between Dunstan's spiritual powers and contemporary politics is made more explicit. For example, when Dunstan vanquishes demons, they leave him for the royal court and there foment evil-doing amongst Eadwig's concubine and the courtiers. Adelard adds a prophecy by Dunstan of the peace which Edgar will bring to the church at the birth of the future king. Finally, at the death of Dunstan, Adelard describes how the dead saint was welcomed by each rank of the elect, by the patriarchs, prophets, apostles, martyrs and virgins and he briefly indicates the saint's own credentials for membership of these saintly elites. The passage describing his enrolment amongst the prophets is the longest of these and deserves quoting in full:

---

14 *Memorials of St Dunstan*, ed. Stubbs, 24, c. 14: 'se esse pro tanti viri vindicta finitimae morti ferme deputatum'.

15 *Memorials of St Dunstan*, ed. Stubbs, 409, no. 33; Wulfric was abbot of St Augustine's *c.* 985 x 1006. Adelard may also have had access to the lost *Old English Life*.

16 Brooks, 'Career of St Dunstan', 3–4.

Prophets, I say, because he foresaw in his spirit, among the many things which he foretold, the attack of the barbarians which we also suffer, and he prophesied that it would come after his own future death; from them may God, the deliverer of all, free his people by the pious intercessions of his great seer.[17]

This is the first account of Dunstan's prophecy of the Viking invasions of Æthelred's reign.[18] These two additions had clear contemporary resonances, highlighting the great and peaceable reign of Edgar, guided by his archbishop in contrast to the devastating Viking raids of Æthelred's reign, foretold by the same. Is there implicit criticism here of Æthelred's reign? Another of Adelard's additions described how St Andrew commanded Dunstan to elevate Ælfheah (the dedicatee of the lections) to his first see of Winchester. Dunstan is able easily to win Æthelred's agreement because 'The king, however, recognised well that Dunstan was a very solid cube of faith and truth and knew that to go against his invincible authority was dangerous ...'.[19]

These accounts of Dunstan show that within 30 years of his death he was regarded as a saint whose sanctity was characterised by his special access to the supernatural, manifest in his visions and foresight. These visions were manifestations of spiritual conflict with demons and privileged access to saintly company, but they were not limited to the interior religious life. Dunstan had foreknowledge of the deaths of Edmund, Eadred and perhaps also of Æthelstan. B's account indicates that Dunstan's prophecies concerned the bad kingship of Eadwig. By the early eleventh century, a prophecy concerning the Viking attacks was attributed to the saint which offered salvation in the form of his intercession. In their comments on Dunstan's relations with Kings Edmund and Æthelred, both B. and Adelard depict Dunstan as a living holy man of fearsome powers.

Dunstan's reputation as a prophet who foresaw the ill-consequences of royal and national sin received elaboration at the hands of his post-Conquest biographers and of other historians. The first to offer a new, updated version of his life was Osbern, an English monk who had been at Christ Church, Canterbury since childhood. Osbern was not only a champion of Anglo-Saxon saints, but personally devoted to Dunstan, experiencing two miracles performed posthumously by the archbishop and visiting his cell at Glastonbury.[20] In the late 1080s or early 1090s, he produced a new *vita* for Dunstan and added a set of *miracula*, making good the glaring lacuna concerning

---

17 Adelard of Ghent, *Vita sancti Dunstani*, in *Memorials of St Dunstan*, ed. Stubbs, 67: Prophetae, dico, quia inter plura quae praedixit barbarorum quoque quam patimur impugnationem in spiritu praevidit, et post excessum suum venturam prophetavit, a quibus populum suum liberet omnium liberator Deus, tanti vatis Sui piis intercessionibus.

18 Simon Keynes, 'The Declining Reputation of King Æthelred the Unready', in *Ethelred the Unready*, ed. Hill, 227–53, at 237.

19 *Memorials of St Dunstan*, ed. Stubbs, 62: 'Rex autem Dunstanum fidei et veritatis cubum pernoscens solidissimum, ejusque invincibili auctoritati contraire sciens periculum ...'

20 J.C. Rubenstein, 'Osbern', in *ODNB*, s.v.; J.C. Rubenstein, 'The Life and Writings of Osbern of Canterbury', in *Canterbury and the Norman Conquest, Churches, Saints and Scholars, 1066–1109*, ed. Richard Eales and Richard Sharpe (London, 1995), 27–40 and M.L. Colker, 'A Hagiographic Polemic', *Mediaeval Studies*, 39 (1977), 60–108, esp. 68–96.

Dunstan's posthumous miracles. Osbern states that he was drawing upon ancient sources; Rodney Thomson has argued that both he and William of Malmesbury had access to a now lost Old English *Life* of the saint, which was dedicated, like B.'s *Life*, to Archbishop Ælfric.[21]

The 70 or so years separating his account from Adelard's had seen not only Æthelred's death and the accession of Cnut and his sons, but also the Norman Conquest, which was viewed by some contemporaries as a divine punishment for sin. Osbern's account is therefore more doom-laden than those of B. or Adelard and he incorporates a number of prophecies of the disasters of Æthelred's reign. For example, his coronation is made the occasion for a speech by the archbishop prophesying the miserable fate awaiting Æthelred's line and his kingdom because he attained the throne through his mother's assassination of his brother.[22] On his deathbed, Dunstan is again made to forewarn the English of their future subjection to other peoples.[23] On another occasion, Dunstan utters an ominous warning concerning the consequences of Æthelred's attack on the see of Rochester.

This story can be found in another early post-Conquest source, Sulcard of Westminster. His account and that of Osbern diverge in their details. According to Osbern, Dunstan tried to protect the see by buying off the king who, however, took the cash but allowed his men to rampage freely. This occasioned Dunstan's contemptuous response:

> Since you have preferred money to God, silver to the Apostle, your greed to my will, the evil things which the Lord has spoken of will quickly come upon you, evil things such as have never been from when the people of the Anglo-Saxons began to reign until this time. Nevertheless, these things will not happen while I am alive, because this is what the Lord has said.[24]

---

21 William of Malmesbury, *Saints' Lives: Lives of SS. Wulfstan, Dunstan, Patrick, Benignus and Indract*, ed. and tr. Michael Winterbottom and R.M. Thomson (Oxford, 2002), pp. xviii–xx; Osbern, *Vita sancti Dunstani*, in *Memorials of St Dunstan*, ed. Stubbs, 70, reports the loss of many records in the fire at Canterbury, but 'Sed ab his, inquiunt, aliqua in patrium id est in Anglicum sermonem translata supersunt, ex quibus id quod petimus elicere, et in Latinam denuo poteris linguam Deo suffragante transferre'. See also William of Malmesbury, *Saints' Lives*, p. xviii, for his possible use of an Old English Life.

22 *Memorials of St Dunstan*, ed. Stubbs, 114–15, c. 37: 'Quoniam aspirasti ad regnum per mortem fratris tui, quem occidit ignominiosa mater tua, non deficiet gladius de domo tua saeviens in te omnibus diebus vitae tuae, interficiens de semine tuo, quousque regnum tuum transferatur in regnum alienum cujus ritum et linguam gens cui praesides non novit. Nec expiabitur nisi longa vindicta peccatum tuum et peccatum matris tuae et peccatum virorum illorum qui interfuere consilio illius nequam'.

23 *Memorials of St Dunstan*, ed. Stubbs, 124–5, c. 43: 'Predico etiam vobis Anglorum gentem dira ac diuturna mala ab exteris gentibus esse passuram, sed in fine dierum miserationem Dei super eam stillaturam, vobis autem commodum erit horum verborum reminisci, ut sive haec ad peccatorum emendationem, seu ad perficiendam virtutem contigerint, animas vestras divinae semper dispositioni subjiciatis, ne sicut mali filii diligatis blandientem, erudientem, quod a vobis remotum sit, contempnatis …'.

24 *Memorials of St Dunstan*, ed. Stubbs, 117, c. 39: 'Quoniam praetulisti pecuniam Deo, argentum apostolo, meae voluntati tuam cupiditatem, velociter venient super te mala quae

Here the misfortunes which afflict England after the death of Dunstan are linked to Æthelred's greed and arrogance. Osbern does not clarify what disasters were predicted, but, in Adelard's lections, the troubles which happen after Dunstan's death are the Viking raids. Osbern is followed in his account, as in other aspects of his *Vita*, by William of Malmesbury.[25]

Sulcard of Westminster was writing for his abbot, Vitalis (*c.* 1076 x *c.* 1080); his account therefore is at least contemporary with Osbern's and may be a little earlier. While little is known of the biographical facts of Sulcard's life, he has been linked to Rochester on the basis of the inclusion of this episode (which in itself is irrelevant to the history of Westminster Abbey). It is also possible that traditions concerning Dunstan were circulating at Westminster since he had refounded the abbey. Sulcard's version of the Rochester episode is, therefore, of interest not only as an early witness but also because it is the most circumstantial and plausible. Sulcard states that the grievance between the king and bishop went back to Æthelred's transfer of a 'mansio' into the hands of a thegn, in response to his request. The bishop, in ignorance of the king's high-handed action, evicted the thegn and this led to Æthelred's devastation of Rochester and its lands. The king also threatened the bishop himself. Dunstan told that Æthelred that he had not acted justly in giving the lands of St Andrew to the thegn and that he had not acted 'regaliter' in his attack on the see. But Æthelred did not respond and so:

> As a result, when he saw that he would make no progress, he was aroused with this prophetic prediction against the king: 'Because you have not shown reverence to the Apostle Andrew', he said, 'and you have not feared to set on fire his church and the kingdom which God gave to you, there will not be lacking to you the burning of fire and the shedding of blood for as long as you shall live'.[26]

Sulcard explicitly links this prophecy with the Viking raids that afflicted England after Dunstan's death.

Simon Keynes has shown how many aspects of this account agree with more contemporary witnesses to Æthelred's reign. His ravaging of Rochester is recorded in the Anglo-Saxon Chronicle, s.a. 986 (in C, D, and E): 'In this year the king laid waste the diocese of Rochester. In this year the great murrain first occurred in England.'[27]

---

locutus est Dominus, mala qualia non fuerunt ex quo gens Anglorum regnare coepit usque ad tempus illud. Attamen vivente me ista non erunt, quoniam et hoc locutus est Dominus'.

25 William of Malmesbury, *Saints' Lives*, 274: Dunstan's words relate to Æthelred's greed: 'Quoniam pretulisti argentum Deo, pecuniam apostolo, cupiditatem michi, uelociter uenient super te mala quae locutus est Dominus. Sed haec me uiuente non fient, quia et hoc locutus est Dominus'.

26 B.W. Scholz, 'Sulcard of Westminster: "prologus de construccione Westmonasterii"', *Traditio*, 20 (1964), 59–91, at 89–90: 'Vnde vbi se nichil videt proficere, hoc aduersus regem vaticinio accenditur prophecie: "Quia reuerenciam", inquid, "non exhibuisti sancto apostolo Andree, eiusque ecclesiam regnumque tibi a deo datum non reveritus es succendere, quoad vixeris non deerit tibi combustion ignis et effusio sanguinis"'. See Simon Keynes, *The Diplomas of King Æthelred the 'Unready' 978–1016* (Cambridge, 1980), 178–9.

27 *Two of the Saxon Chronicles Parallel*, ed. Charles Plummer and John Earle (Oxford, 1892), 125, s. a. 986: 'Her se cyning fordyde þet biscop rice æt Hrofeceastre. And her com

This annal belongs to the section of the Chronicle from 983 to 1016, written up retrospectively, between 1016 and 1023, by one author perhaps in London. Clark and Keynes have shown that Chronicler was a gifted and opinionated contemporary commentator whose account is deeply coloured by hindsight.[28] He may, according to Keynes, have been reworking material already in existence; the annals from 983 to 990 belong to the older laconic style of Chronicle reportage, while, after 991, the style becomes more discursive and subjective. The 986 annal in its entirety cannot be exactly contemporary, since it refers to the 'first' arrival of the murrain in England. But it does represent an early eleventh-century view (not long after Adelard's lections).[29] I would suggest that the juxtaposition of Æthelred's attack on the see and the arrival of the cattle plague is not an artless conjunction but signals an implicitly causal relationship: divine punishment for the king's wrong-doing.

Sulcard's account fits neatly with the contemporary charter record: witness lists suggest that Bishop Ælfstan of Rochester ceased to attend the royal court from 985 until 988. Further, two Rochester charters record Æthelred's transfer of Rochester property to a layman (in 987) and his subsequent remorseful restoration of it in 995 and 998.[30] In these charters, Æthelred expresses his penitence for the wrongdoing suffered by Rochester and describes how the grace of God has prompted him to recognise the injuries he inflicted on St Andrew through the devil's urging. He expresses the hope that his belief that his sincere repentance and the restoration of the property will regain his favour with the saint:

> Believing that I have found grace in the sight of the Apostle who showed himself most mild among his people, and who prayed for those who crucified him, I might truly assent with my whole heart to the restoration of the aforesaid estate to the church of the blessed Apostle.[31]

This contemporary record indicates that some viewed the king's attack on the see as an offence to its holy patron so great that it might imperil the ultimate salvation of the royal soul.

In this connection it is interesting to note Dunstan's devotion to the apostle Andrew. In B.'s *vita*, Andrew merits mention only as a marginal figure, when he

---

ærest se myccla yrf cwalm on Angel cyn' (translation from *EHD*, 233).

28 Keynes, 'Declining Reputation of King Æthelred the Unready', in *Ethelred the Unready*, ed. Hill, 227–53, at 229–35; Cecily Clark, 'The Narrative Mode of *The Anglo-Saxon Chronicle* before the Conquest', in *England before the Conquest*, ed. Peter Clemoes and Kathleen Hughes (Cambridge, 1971), 215–35, esp. 224–30.

29 Keynes, 'Declining reputation', 230 and see 233–4 and 246, n. 29 for the incorporation of earlier material, especially the annals for 983–990.

30 Keynes, *Diplomas*, 178–80.

31 *Charters of Rochester*, ed. Alistair Campbell, Anglo-Saxon Charters 1 (London, 1973), 43, no. 32 (S 893): 'credens me et gratiam inuenire in conspectu apostoli. qui in populo suo mitissimus apparuit. Et pro crucifigentibus se exorauit. Et ut toto corde prefatum rus ad ecclesiam eiusdem beati apostoli me restituere ueraciter approbarem …' Elsewhere in the charter, Æthelred is made to say: 'iccirco domini compunctus gratia quicquid tunc instigante maligno contra sanctum dei apostolum me inique egisse recogito …'. See too S 885, no. 31 in Campbell's edition.

appears in a vision as one with Saints Peter and Paul, chastising the saint for his refusal of a see. Of the trio, he alone is made to speak and to administer a beating to Dunstan.[32] In the later lections of Adelard, he is a more prominent figure, for example, comforting the saint in exile in Ghent.[33] Adelard also has a rather more elaborate version of this dream which is interpreted as presaging Dunstan's elevation to the archbishopric of Canterbury. The roles of Peter and Paul are explained by his election to London and Worcester. But the role of Andrew has to be explained in the following fashion: 'But the sword offered by St Andrew of Rochester bears a semblance of the priestly fillet of Rochester: although he was not enthroned in the see, yet he made it his own by care and solicitude'.[34] Do these enigmatic words hint at Dunstan's intervention to rescue the see from Æthelred's fury?

These divergent stories about the consequences of Æthelred's ravaging of Rochester are indicative of the legends circulating in the eleventh and twelfth centuries concerning Æthelred. Later lives of Dunstan were written by Eadmer of Canterbury and by William of Malmesbury, largely following Osbern's account. William piles on the ignominy with relish, telling how the infant Æthelred defiled his own baptismal font to Dunstan's consternation, a sure sign of his future failure as a king. William adds a story which must derive from Glastonbury tradition since it is unrecorded elsewhere and the historian has close links with this house, composing his *vita* for its monks.[35] A wealthy layman, Ælfwold, thinking himself to be fatally ill, sought admission as a monk to the community and made appropriate donations of landed property. However, once he recovered his health in the salubrious environment of the monastery, the rigours of its life became repulsive to him. He left the monastery, and pressed the monks and abbot for the return of his estates. When this failed, he bribed King Æthelred who allowed him to seize the land with violence. The monks appealed to Dunstan, their patron, who uttered these words: 'Look for vengeance to the Mother of the Lord. As for him, let foxes eat him'. Needless to say, in due course, Ælfwold fell ill, sought and gained permission to be buried at Glastonbury. But when his body was being carried to the house, it fell off its bier and was consumed by foxes.

While the details of this story cannot be as securely verified as those concerning the Rochester episode, it does have contemporary resonances. The practice of laymen seeking to end their days in a monastery or arranging their burial there is well attested. One of the greatest of all Anglo-Saxon magnates, Æthelstan Half-King, retired to Glastonbury in 956/7, and his son, Æthelwine, was buried at Ramsey, to which he

---

32 *Memorials of St Dunstan*, ed. Stubbs, 30–31, c. 20.

33 *Memorials of St Dunstan*, ed. Stubbs, 60, *Lectio* vi, perhaps a version of B.'s lengthy vision at the same point, ibid., 34–5, c. 23.

34 *Memorials of St Dunstan*, ed. Stubbs, 56–7, 60–61 (*Lectiones*, iiii, vii), with quotation from 61: 'At gladius a Sancto Andrea oblatus Rofecistris infulae speciem tenet, in qua etsi non sedit, cura tamen et sollicitudine suam fecit …'.

35 Keynes, *Diplomas*, 180–181, and D.H. Farmer, 'Two biographies by William of Malmesbury', in *Latin Biography*, ed. T.A. Dorey (London, 1967), 157–76. William of Malmesbury, *Saints' Lives*, 280–83: 'A Domini matre ultionem exigite; illum comedant uulpes' (at 280).

had been a generous patron.[36] Two prominent ealdormen at the court of Æthelred, Ordulf and Æthelmaer, are thought to have retired to monasteries, the former to Tavistock and the latter temporarily to Abingdon.[37] Æthelred's support of Ælfwold's seizures is of a piece with an early phase of his reign when he seems to have pursued a policy enabling lay appropriations such as those experienced by Rochester at the same period. While William's Ælfwold cannot be identified, it is a common Anglo-Saxon name and one borne by a number of minor nobles in Wessex at that time.[38] Moreover, we know that Glastonbury retaliated against such incursions by resorting to ecclesiastical authority. William also preserves a papal letter dating to 982 x 998 which threatens a *dux*, Ælfric, with excommunication if he does not cease his attacks on Glastonbury property.[39]

William frames his account of this incident with some intriguing comments, anxiously disclaiming any possibility that his hero here might be cursing the wretched Ælfwold. He prefaces the chapter with the statement 'even words he uttered by chance and not of set purpose did not lack fulfilment' and he pointedly says immediately after Dunstan's ominous utterance, 'I do not believe that he said this with any intention of cursing, but rather that it slipped out by chance or in a moment of prophetic inspiration'.[40] William's concern presumably reflects ecclesiastical disapproval of cursing. Secular cursing is explicitly condemned by Ælfric (following St Augustine) and in Lantfred's Translation and Miracles of St Swithun.[41] However, prophecy and cursing are closely related phenomena: the Bible is full of curses which offended against the command of Christ to love one's enemies and bless those who curse.[42] These were interpreted in patristic and early medieval thought as 'prophecy

---

36 Cyril Hart, 'Athelstan "Half-King" and his Family', *ASE*, 2 (1973), 115–44 at 128, 135, also printed in his *The Danelaw* (London, 1992), 569–604; Ann Williams, '*Princeps Merciorum gentis*: the Family, Career and Connections of Ælfhere, Ealdorman of Mercia, 956–83', *ASE*, 10 (1982), 143–72; Byrhtferth's *Vita Sancti Oswaldi*, in *Historians of the Church of York*, ed. James Raine, Rolls Series, 71 (3 vols, London, 1879–94), I, 474–5.

37 Keynes, *Diplomas*, 209.

38 See the *Prosopography of Anglo-Saxon England* site at http://www.pase.ac.uk, s.v. Ælfwald.

39 *Councils and Synods with Other Documents relating to the English Church*, I, ed. Dorothy Whitelock, Martin Brett and C.N.L. Brooke (2 vols, Oxford, 1981), I, 173–4. Later in the period, the monks of Ely excommunicated Asgeir the Staller, one of the wealthiest landowners in England and a member of Edward the Confessor's household, for the theft of Ely's estate at High Easter: see note 70 below.

40 William of Malmesbury, *Saints' Lives*, 280–81: 'etiam uerba quae casu non studio effunderet effectu non carerent' and 'Quod illum non crediderim dixisse maledicentis animo, sed uel pro casu lapsum uel uaticinio impulsum.'

41 Lantfred of Winchester, *Translatio et Miracula S. Swithuni*, in *The Cult of St Swithun*, ed. and tr. Michael Lapidge (Oxford, 2003), 252–323, at 324–27. *Ælfric's Catholic Homilies. The Second Series: Text*, ed. Malcolm Godden, Early English Text Society, Second Series, 5 (Oxford, 1979), 14–18 (II, 2, lines 79–217), and see Godden's helpful commentary in his *Ælfric's Catholic Homilies. The Second Series: Introduction, Commentary, and Glossary*, Early English Text Society, Second Series, 18 (Oxford, 2000), 358–62.

42 Luke 6, 27–8, and see the discussion of Lester K. Little, *Benedictine Maledictions: Liturgical Cursing in Romanesque France* (Ithaca and London, 1993), 88–108.

in the guise of imprecation'.[43] Sulcard's report of Dunstan's words on the ravaging of Rochester could be interpreted as such. In Osbern's *vita*, when Dunstan makes his baleful speech at Æthelred's coronation, his words are those of warning: disasters will follow unless those responsible for the death of Edward repent. It is notable how many of Dunstan's prophecies forecast doom.

Other eleventh-century bishops were less inhibited about their power to curse. A later successor of Dunstan at Worcester, Ealdred, archbishop of York (1060–1069), is said to have reacted to abuses of secular authority in this way three times. The most famous example is that recorded by William of Malmesbury in his *Deeds of the Bishops*, when the Norman sheriff of Worcester encroached with his castle-building upon the monastery's cemetery. Ealdred responded in imprecatory verse: 'If you are called Urse, may you have God's curse ..., that of myself and all consecrated bishops, if you do not take away your castle. You can be sure that your descendants will not for long have an inheritance on the ground belonging to St Mary', a prediction that came true. William also recounts how Ealdred cursed William the Conqueror for his excessive taxation of the English, and how he died before the king's messengers were able to reach him to tell him of the king's change of heart.[44] A similar story of Ealdred's relations with the Conqueror is told in the *Chronicle of the Archbishops of York*, a twelfth-century northern chronicle.[45] When the sheriff of York appropriated the archbishop's food renders, Ealdred travelled to London to petition the king. Processing in great state from St Paul's to Westminster Abbey, he responded to the king's attempted greeting by a public rebuke, reminding him of how he had consecrated him king. But now for the blessing he had bestowed, he would be forced to impose a curse because the king, through his agent, had broken his coronation oaths and become a persecutor of the church. At these words, William threw himself at the archbishop's feet and asked what had earned so terrible a complaint. Ealdred's awesome tactics obtained the desired result and the misappropriations were made good.[46]

These two, closely similar stories probably represent genuine traditions concerning Ealdred. His successor at Worcester, the holy bishop, Wulfstan II, was also a man of God who resorted to dramatic action when necessary. His biography reports two incidents of maledictory pronouncements. William of Malmesbury also reports how Wulfstan defended his see against forces rebelling against William Rufus, by hurling

---

43 John Chrysostom, *Expositiones in psalmos*, no. 108, quoted in Little, *Benedictine Maledictions*, 95.

44 William of Malmesbury, *Gesta Pontificum Anglorum*, ed. and tr. Michael Winterbottom and R.M. Thomson (Oxford, 2007), forthcoming; the translation used here is from William of Malmesbury, *The Deeds of the Bishops of England*, tr. David Preest (Woodbridge, 2002), 168–9.

45 *Historians of the Church of York*, ed. Raine, II, 345–54. This appears to be a mini-hagiography or biography devoted to Ealdred and could be of earlier origin than the Chronicle's compilation. My thanks to Dr Christopher Norton for alerting me to this and the following passage and to the material here. I am also indebted to Prof. David Bates for discussion of Ealdred and William.

46 *Historians of the Church of York*, ed. Raine, II, 351–2.

'the thunderbolt of his curse against the traitors who had not remained loyal to their lord' and inflicted great terror amongst the attacking soldiers.[47]

These later examples of episcopal cursing may represent a retrospective attribution to tenth- and eleventh-century bishops of maledictory propensities more typical of the twelfth century.[48] On the other hand, these stories appear to emanate from diverse sources, William, Coleman (Wulfstan's chaplain) and the anonymous northern author of the York Chronicle (perhaps even drawing on an earlier text). They may derive from authentic material. Ealdred's rhythmical vernacular curse, quoted in Old English by William, can be compared to other curses in Old English rhyme preserved in manumission records where the statement of the purchase of freedom is followed by the words: 'criste hine ablende þe þis gewrit awende'. These are preserved in an early eleventh-century manuscript of Old English Gospels from Bath, CCCC 140, and can be dated to c. 1061 by their reference to Abbot Ælfwig.[49]

While there is scant evidence to indicate that earlier Anglo-Saxon bishops were wont to utter full-blooded curses but there is some evidence to suggest that they, like Dunstan, were given to fearsome negative prophecies. Dunstan's relative, Bishop Ælfheah Calvus of Winchester (934/5–951) was instrumental in fostering Dunstan's early career, both at court and in urging his monastic vocation upon him.[50] He shares many characteristics with Dunstan, as a courtier (of Æthelstan's), monk and saint and he can be seen as an influential precursor of monastic reform. The evidence for acknowledged sanctity can be found in his inclusion in the *Resting Places of Saints* and in eleventh-century Winchester calendars and a litany.[51] Wulfstan of Winchester reported that his tomb was adjacent to the high altar in the Old Minster and, in his *Life of Æthelwold*, describes him as 'strong in the spirit of prophecy'. He goes on to describe how Ælfheah consecrated Æthelwold and Dunstan priest on the same day, alongside another cleric named Æthelstan. Ælfheah predicted the glorious futures of

---

47 William of Malmesbury, *Gesta Pontificum*, ed. Winterbottom and Thomson, forthcoming; translation from William of Malmesbury, *The Deeds of the Bishops of England*, tr. Preest, 193.

48 See, for example, the excommunications performed by Hugh of Lincoln and Thomas Becket discussed in R.H. Helmholz, 'Excommunication and the Angevin Leap Forward', *Haskins Society Journal*, 7 (1995), 133–49, at 137–8, 139–40.

49 *The Old English Version of the Gospels*, ed. R.M. Liuzza, Early English Text Society, 304 and 314 (2 vols, Oxford, 1994–2000), I, pp. xxv–xxix; see also Rolf H. Bremmer Jr, 'An Old English Rhyming Curse', *Notes and Queries*, 40.4 (1993), 434–5.

50 For Ælfheah, see David Dumville, *Wessex and England from Alfred to Edgar* (Woodbridge, 1992), 164–5; Joseph Armitage Robinson, *The Times of St Dunstan* (Oxford, 1913), 82–3; Guy Lanoë, 'Approche de quelques évêques moines en Angleterre au Xe siècle', *Cahiers de civilisation médiévale*, 19 (1976), 135–50. His burial at Old Minster, Winchester, is listed in the *Resting Places of Saints*; Wulfstan of Winchester reported that his tomb was adjacent to the high altar. The miraculous delivery of him and Dunstan from falling masonry is recorded in B.'s *Vita sancti Dunstani*, in *Memorials of St Dunstan*, ed. Stubbs, 14–15, c. 8. For the *Resting Places*, see Felix Liebermann, *Die Heiligen Englands: Angelsächsischen und lateinischen* (Hanover, 1889), 15. See also Wulfstan, *Epistola specialis ad Ælfegum episcopum*, in *The Cult of St Swithun*, ed. Lapidge, 394–5.

51 Liebermann, *Die Heiligen Englands*, 15. The calendar entries and Wulfstan of Winchester reference are noted by Lapidge, *Vita Æthelwoldi*, 12, n. 1.

the first two, listing the sees which they would hold. But for Æthelstan, he foretold that he would abandon his vocation and die miserably after a life of dissolution.[52] William of Malmesbury repeats this story and adds one more of his own. Ælfheah was exhorting the people on Ash Wednesday to devote themselves in the Lenten discipline of abstinence from sex and alcohol when some bright spark amongst his audience made a joke of the impossibility of doing both. Ælfheah responded by mournfully noting that this man did not know what the next day would bring. When the next day dawned, the man was found dead, strangled in bed.[53] The reliability of this tradition is reinforced by its proximity to a story about the bishop told by Ælfric in his Lives of Saints which records how a lay member of his episcopal entourage insisted on drinking alcohol in Lent and was killed by a boar. One wonders if Ælfric has omitted some dire words of warning uttered by the Bishop.[54]

Like a number of Dunstan's prophecies, Ælfheah's recorded miracles include a minatory element: the saint's words presage ill. The ninth and tenth centuries saw the rise of a cursing culture amongst Benedictine monks which has been charted by Lester Little. Little draws attention to the liturgical cursing performed by monasteries, usually attempting to regain stolen property. These included ritual curses and the performance of special liturgical services, *clamores*, which besought the help of the saints in restoring justice and in threatening malefactors with earthly and heavenly punishment. These included prayers and often lengthy lists of terrifying curses. Another text, a ninth-century forgery from the abbey of Saint-Wandrille, claimed that the curse to be used against those who attacked the monastery had specifically been given to it by the seventh-century pope, Martin I. In the tenth century, Fleury produced a similar text, purporting to be a letter from Pope Leo (probably Leo VII, 936–939), demanding that the bishops support the abbot of Fleury in defending the community's properties and including an excommunication formula with many curses. Little observes that evidence for monastic cursing is concentrated in the area between the Charente and the Rhine.[55]

It was to these regions that the English Benedictine reformers travelled for inspiration at precisely this time. Dunstan was in exile from 956 to 958 at St Peter's, Ghent, which had close links with Saint-Wandrille.[56] Æthelwold's pupil, Osgar, and

---

52 *Vita Æthelwoldi*, 12–13, c. 8; *Epistola specialis ad Ælfegum episcopum*, in *Cult of St Swithun*, ed. Lapidge, 394–5.

53 William of Malmesbury, *Gesta Pontificum*, ed. Winterbottom and Thomson, forthcoming (Book II, ch. 75).

54 *Ælfric's Lives of the Saints*, ed. and tr. Walter W. Skeat, Early English Text Society, Original Series 76 and 82, 94 and 114 (2 vols, London, 1881–1900), I, 266–7. Bishop Ælfheah refuses to bless the man's cup, a suggestive detail which hints that the story may once have contained the parallelism between blessing and cursing which is common. I have wrongly identified the bishop in my 'Bishops, Priests and Penance in Late Saxon England', *EME*, 14 (2006), 41–63, at 51, n. 46.

55 Little, *Benedictine Maledictions*, esp. 38–9, 44–51, 107–108, 146–9.

56 Brooks, 'Career', 16–18; Veronica Ortenberg, *The English Church and the Continent in the Tenth and Eleventh Centuries. Cultural, Spiritual and Artistic Exchanges* (Oxford, 1992), 221. The abbey of St-Wandrille (Fontenelle) was recolonised by monks from Ghent shortly after Dunstan returned to England: Eckhard Freise, 'Fontenelle, St-Wandrille de', in

Oswald himself and his follower, Germanus, spent time at Fleury, whose customs are reflected in the *Regularis Concordia*.[57] The influence of this Frankish cursing culture may be reflected in two documents from New Minster, Winchester. The first is the famous foundation charter of New Minster, Winchester, which may have been drafted by Æthelwold himself. This charter contains three spiritual sanctions. The first two are anathemata: one threatens the former canons of the house with damnation and hellfire if they plot against the monks, while the second anathematises anyone attempting to expel the monks from New Minster or another reformed community with the curse of Cain, warning of future misery and damnation. These two are labelled anathemata in the text, while the third is headed 'De maledictione minuentium', being paired with a 'benedictio' on those who increase the monastery's property. Anyone attacking New Minster's property will be cursed with misfortune in the present life, damnation in the next and incur the enmity St Mary and all the saints.[58]

The defences of New Minster extended beyond anticipatory anathemata and curses. A tenth-century glossed psalter, BL Royal 2 B V, linked to Bishop Æthelwold, includes a Marian office inserted in the eleventh century with a prayer against an enemy of the house.[59] As its editor points out, the purpose of the office is to beseech God and the saints to intervene on behalf of the community against its predators. It was intended therefore to act as a sort of *clamor* against the community's enemies. It should be associated with New Minster, Winchester, but the provenance of this part of the manuscript has been confused. The book therefore merits a little further attention.

The psalter itself is copied in a Phase III Anglo-Saxon square minuscule, dated to the mid-tenth century. The Old English gloss and marginalia in the manuscript

---

Lexikon des Mittelalters, ed. Robert Auty and others (9 vols, Munich, 1977–98), IV, cols 624–6 at 625.

57 Donald Bullough, 'St Oswald: monk, bishop and archbishop', in *St Oswald of Worcester: Life and Influence*, ed. Nicholas Brooks and Catherine Cubitt (London, 1996), 1–22, at 6–7, 19–20; John Nightingale, 'Oswald, Fleury, and continental reform', in *St Oswald of Worcester*, ed. Brooks and Cubitt, 23–45, at 22, 30–31.

58 'DE MALEDICTIONE MINUENTIUM: Minuentem. perpetua possideat miseria. In Domini manens persecutione. eius genitricis sanctorumque omnium incurrat offensam. Presentis uite aduersitas illi semper eueniat. Nulla ei bonitatis accidat prosperitas . Omnia eius peculiar inimici uastantes diripiant. In futuro autem eterni miserrimum cum ędis in sinistra positum damnent cruciatus. si non satisfactione emendauerit congrua. quod in Domini usurpans detraxit censura': text from Alexander Rumble, *Property and Piety in Early Medieval Winchester* (Oxford, 2002), 90–91; S 745. Note also S 956, *Charters of New Minster, Winchester*, ed. Sean Miller, Anglo-Saxon Charters, 9 (Oxford, 2001), no. 33, a restoration of land to New Minster made by King Cnut in 1019. This refers to the powerful miracle-working saints, Grimbald and Iudoc, on the day of the grant. Cnut had been tricked into granting the land to a 'young man' and when he was apprised of the deceit, he restored the land to New Minster and cursed the false charters which he had made for the young man. Was the power miracle-working of the two local saints related to the restoration of land?

59 *Facsimiles of the Horae de Beata Maria Virgine: from English MSS of the Eleventh Century*, ed. E.S. Dewick, HBS, 21 (London, 1902).

are copied in the same hand as the text.[60] Seven leaves were added with the Marian office and a preceding prayer which calls for the Virgin, and Saints Eadburg and Machutus to assist the brothers of a church dedicated to Mary regain stolen property. Gretsch has argued strongly for an association between the psalter and its gloss and Æthelwold himself. Dumville would like to eliminate Winchester as its scriptorium on palaeographical grounds, arguing Phase III square minuscule was practised at Winchester (as elsewhere) only in the period 939/40 x 959, the time when he thinks the psalter was copied. However, he considers Glastonbury or Abingdon possible places of origin for the manuscript and either of these would still allow a link with Æthelwold.[61]

The textual evidence of the psalter gloss suggests that the manuscript was at Winchester in the eleventh century, since it served as the model for four other glossed psalters which have been associated with Winchester. The Marian office in the manuscript was printed by Dewick, who dated its addition to between 1066 and 1087, attributing it to Nunnaminster because of the appeals to St Eadburg in the prayer, whom he regarded as the patron of that house. His Nunnaminster hypothesis received support in the form of the Domesday account of the appropriation of the manor of Itchen Abbas from Winchester by Hugh Fitz Baldric, an incident which he believed was the prompt for the Marian office.[62]

However, Ker dated the hand of the Marian office 'early in s. xi',[63] too early therefore for Dewick's association with the depredations of Hugh FitzBaldric at Nunnaminster. Moreover, while Eadburg may have been honoured at Nunnaminster, her conjunction with Machutus in the prayers points firmly to New Minster, Winchester. Machutus (also known as Machlonus) was culted at New Minster, Winchester, and his feast on 15 November is regarded by Dumville as one of the defining Winchester commemorations.[64] It is found under the name Machlonus

---

60 N.R. Ker, *Catalogue of Manuscripts containing Anglo-Saxon* (Oxford, 1957), 318–20. D.N. Dumville, *English Caroline Script and Monastic History: Studies in Benedictinism A.D. 950–1030* (Woodbridge, 1993), 14, n. 33; 'English Square Minuscule Script: the Mid-Century Phases', *ASE*, 23 (1994), 133–64, at 149–50; and 'On the Dating of Some Late Anglo-Saxon Square Liturgical Manuscripts', *Transactions of the Cambridge Bibliographical Society* 10 (1991), 40–57, at 48.

61 Arguments summarised in Mechthild Gretsch, *The Intellectual Foundations of the English Benedictine Reform* (Cambridge, 1999), 264–6; Dumville, *English Caroline Script*, 14, n. 33; Dumville, 'English Square Minuscule script', 149–50; and Dumville, 'On the Dating of Some Late Anglo-Saxon Square Liturgical Manuscripts', 48.

62 Dewick, *Facsimiles*, pp. xi–xii. Dewick's dating has been followed by Mary Clayton, *The Cult of the Virgin Mary in Anglo-Saxon England* (Cambridge, 1990), 70–77, and others (*Vita Æthelwoldi*, p. lxix, n. 116), but Dumville, 'English Square Minuscule Script', 149–50, has also dated the inclusion of the office to *c*. 1000, while apparently following Dewick in tentatively assigning the office to Nunnaminster, Winchester. I.B. Milfull, *The Hymns of the Anglo-Saxon Church: a Study and Edition of the Durham Hymnal* (Cambridge, 1996), 61–2, affirms the Winchester origin and suggests probably New Minster.

63 Ker, *Catalogue of Manuscripts*, 320.

64 Dumville, *Liturgy and the Ecclesiastical History of Late Anglo-Saxon England: Four Studies* (Woodbridge, 1992), 58; likewise Milfull, *Hymns*, 61.

in four New Minster calendars or related texts dating from the eleventh century, including the Ælfwine prayerbook.[65]

Further, Dewick's hypothesis was shaky for other reasons: he himself pointed out that phrases in the opening prayer indicate a male community, not a female one:

'Lord of all things, Lord, we beseech you, who love all justice, that you may avenge the injury to your servants. Be present in our trouble, and gladden us with your comfort and be present through the merits and intercession of your glorious mother Mary, ever virgin, in whose court we serve your majesty ... that you might have mercy on us, for we are placed in difficulty ... You also, St Mary, ever virgin, be present in our difficulty and pluck our possession from the hand of our enemy'.[66]

The consistency of male forms in this opening prayer is notable: it appears to be the prayer of a male community in a house dedicated to the Virgin.[67] Given the associations of the original psalter with Æthelwold, New Minster Winchester is a very plausible option for its early eleventh-century home.

The evidence for Marian offices in England also strengthens a Winchester provenance for this part of the manuscript.[68] Bishop Æthelwold is said to have composed an office in honour of the Virgin which Lapidge has associated with the private office in BL Cotton MS Titus D xxvi and xxvii, the private prayer book of Ælfwine, abbot of New Minster (1031–1057). This manuscript was copied at New Minster in the third decade of the eleventh century.[69] The office in Royal 2 B V is not a private office, but a full office for communal recitation, probably composed, as Dewick suggested, for the particular task of regaining stolen property.

The simplest interpretation of Royal 2 B V is that the psalter and its gloss were copied at Glastonbury, Abingdon or Old Minster, Winchester, for Æthelwold. The manuscript came into the acquisition of New Minster at some point and there the Marian office was copied into it, as the result of some theft of its property. The Royal Psalter has been viewed as a scholarly rather than a devotional book, but

---

65 These findings are from Rebecca Rushforth, *An Atlas of Saints in Anglo-Saxon Calendars* (Cambridge, 2002), based on BL, Cotton Titus D xxvii, Cambridge, Trinity College, R 15 32, BL, Cotton Vitellius E xviii and BL, Arundel 60. These manuscripts also all contain the feast of St Eadburg on 15 June, and two (Vitellius E xviii and Arundel 60) have an additional feast for the saint on 18 July. Four other calendars or related texts also include feasts for both saints: Salisbury, Cathedral Library, MS 150, Bodl., Ms Douce 296, CCCC, MS 422 and BL, Cotton Vitellius A xviii. CCCC 422, the Red Book of Darley, was influenced by Winchester usages; other manuscripts are located in south-west England and at Crowland.

66 Dewick, *Facsimiles*, cols 1–2: 'Dominator omnium, domine, quesumus, qui omnem diligis iustitiam, et iniuriam seruorum tuorum uindicas, adesto nobis in presenti tribulatione. et tua letifica consolatione. et presta per merita et intercessionem gloriosę genetricis tuę semper uirginis marię in cuius atrio magestati tue famulamur ... ut nobis miserearis, quia in angustia positi sumus ... Tu quoque, sancta Maria semper uirgo, adesto angustie nostre et erue de manu inimici nostri possessionem ...'

67 'Tue semper uirginis Marie in cuius atrio magestati tue famulamur'.

68 Discussed by Clayton, *Cult of the Virgin Mary*, 65–81.

69 *Vita Æthelwoldi*, pp. lxix–lxxv.

its association with the community's saintly founder may have given it a special charisma. The Marian office with its curse may have been copied into it to partake of some of the book's spiritual power.

The evidence of the Marian office in the Royal psalter suggests, therefore, that by the early eleventh century English Benedictine monks had begun to practise liturgical cursing, just as their continental contemporaries had. Such ceremonies may shed further light on William's story about Dunstan's curse on the depredator of Glastonbury: his response to the monks, telling them to look to Mary for vengeance, a possible reference to a monastic *clamor* to their patroness. Later in the period, the monks of Ely excommunicated Asgeir the Staller, one of the wealthiest landowners in England and a member of Edward the Confessor's household, for the theft of their estate at High Easter. According to the *Liber Eliensis*, Asgeir was forced to come to terms with the monastery through a combination of royal coercion and public disgrace.[70]

It is worth considering another possible influence on the maledictory tendency in tenth and eleventh-century England. The Irish canonical collection entitled the *Collectio Canonum Hibernensis* includes a separate section, *De maledictionibus*, which assembles various biblical and patristic passages on the subject. As Wiley has shown, these implicitly hedge the practice around with conditions. Cursing must be in the form of a prayer, a plea to God for divine justice to separate from the church those who have refused all correction. *Maledictiones* must be pronounced only in the form of a prophecy and not with the wrong intention.[71] The *Collectio* was known in later Anglo-Saxon England: it was used as a source for canon law by Archbishops Oda and Wulfstan, and perhaps by the homilist, Ælfric.[72] Several manuscripts of this text are known to have travelled to England by the early eleventh century, and two have connections with Christ Church, Canterbury.[73] The canons in the *Collectio* concerning cursing may have been known to Dunstan and his contemporaries.

---

70 *Liber Eliensis*, ed. E.O. Blake, Camden Society, 3rd series, 92 (London, 1962), 165–6 (Book II, c. 96), translated by Janet Fairweather, *Liber Eliensis: a History of the Isle of Ely from the Seventh Century to the Twelfth* (Woodbridge, 2005), 196–8. On Asgeir, see Ann Williams, 'Asgar the Staller', in *ODNB*, s.v.; Andrew Wareham, *Lords and Communities in Early Medieval East Anglia* (Woodbridge, 2005), 116–17; P.A. Clarke, *The English Nobility under Edward the Confessor* (Oxford, 1994); Simon Keynes, 'Ely Abbey 672–1109', in *A History of Ely Cathedral*, ed. Peter Meadows and Nigel Ramsay (Woodbridge, 2003), 3–58, at 38–9.

71 Dan M. Wiley, 'The Maledictory Psalms', *Peritia*, 15 (2001), 261–79, at 273–6; *Die irische Kanonenssammlung*, ed. Hermann Wasserschleben, 2nd edn (Leipzig, 1885), 227–9 and see LXI, 1: '... Redde retributionem superbis, sed haec non optantis animo, sed prophetantis dicuntur.'

72 See the material assembled in Shannon Ambrose, 'The *Collectio Canonum Hibernensis* and the Literature of the Anglo-Saxon Benedictine Reform', *Viator*, 36 (2005), 107–18.

73 On the transmission of the Collectio, see now Roy Flechner, 'A Study and Edition of the Collectio Canonum Hibernensis', Oxford D. Phil, 2006. I am indebted to Dr Flechner for discussing this with me. Three manuscripts of the text can be located at Worcester by the early eleventh century, including Bodl. MS Hatton 42, which was glossed by Archbishop Wulfstan (the Homilist): Patrick Wormald, 'Archbishop Wulfstan and the Holiness of Society', in

The *Collectio* distinguishes between cursing and excommunication, dealing with them in separate books. A malediction may be used against anyone, pagan or Christian, and has punitive intent; excommunication serves as a means of correction for the faithful and may be issued with varying degrees of severity.[74] The two are, however, closely related. Helmholz has argued that the twelfth century saw an increasingly legal approach to excommunication, requiring due process, and he distinguishes an earlier approach that allowed for more ad hoc excommunicating, more akin to cursing. Unlike his predecessor, Oda, Dunstan is not known to have issued any canons, nor, like Archbishop Wulfstan, to have pursued an interest in canon law. However, Adelard illustrates Dunstan's constancy in performing his episcopal duty of the correction of wrongdoing, by saying that he had refused to obey a papal letter allowing a lay couple to maintain their wrongful union and presumably cancelling the archbishop's excommunication.[75] Nicholas Brooks has raised the possibility that Archbishop Oda's separation of King Eadwig from his wife, Ælfgifu, in 958 was the result of a more stringent interpretation of the canons governing the prohibited degrees of marriage.[76] The story of Dunstan's intervention at Oda's behest at Eadwig's coronation to stop the king's unseemly behaviour with Ælfgifu seems to be a distorted memory of clerical disapproval of the match, and suggests Dunstan was sympathetic to Oda's view. Moreover, it is likely, as Brooks has pointed out, that Dunstan's support for the succession of Edward the Martyr may have resulted from a view that Edward's mother, Æthelflæd the White, was the lawful wife of Edgar.[77] It is possible that marriage was increasingly subject to canonical scrutiny in tenth-century England, and that it was a matter of concern to both Oda and Dunstan. Here it is worth noting the possible association of Bodl., MS Bodley 718, a volume of canon law and penitential texts, with Dunstan. This manuscript was copied by the same scribe as BN, MS latin 943, a pontifical linked directly to the archbishop. It is a particularly handsome, well laid-out and finely illuminated manuscript, not a utilitarian working copy, and looks as though it was

---

his *Legal Culture in the Early Medieval West* (London, 1999), 225–5, at 238–9. According to T.A.M. Bishop it was supplemented by a quire copied by a scribe of Christ Church, Canterbury, around the year 1000: 'Notes on Cambridge Manuscripts, Part VII: the Early Minuscule of Christ Church, Canterbury', *Transactions of the Cambridge Bibliographical Society*, 3 (1959–63), 413–23. Note that the idea that the Hatton manuscript once belonged to Dunstan is very weak: see B.C. Barker-Benfield, 'Not St Dunstan's book?', *Notes and Queries*, 40 (1993), 431–3. Another manuscript of the *Hibernensis*, BL, Cotton Otho E xiii, has also been associated with Christ Church, Canterbury, see D.N. Dumville, 'Wulfric cild', *Notes and Queries*, 40 (1993), 5–9.

74 See the useful comments by Wiley, 'Maledictory Psalms', 276–7.

75 *Memorials of St Dunstan*, ed. Stubbs, 67 (*Lectio* XII): 'quidam illustrium pro illicito matrimonio saepius ab eo redargutus, sed non correctus, gladio tandem evangelico est a Christo divisus'.

76 Brooks, *Early History*, 224–5.

77 Brooks, *Early History*, 249–50; see also Yorke, 'Æthelwold', 84–5 and Pauline Stafford, 'The Reign of Æthelred II', in *Ethelred the Unready*, ed. Hill, 15–46, at 23.

intended to impress and designed for a high status owner.[78] An interest in canon law on Dunstan's part would not be out of keeping with his continental connection: his friend, Abbo of Fleury, put together a canon law collection.[79]

In later canon law, an anathema was a particularly grievous form of excommunication, threatening the evil-doer with eternal damnation. In the tenth century, the legal distinctions between types of excommunication may have been less clear cut.[80] Anathemas were a routine part of Anglo-Saxon diplomatic and the only form of sanction which pre-Conquest charters contained. It is difficult to assess the status of such curses: numerous legal disputes survive shedding light on the villainous disregard of Anglo-Saxon charters and appropriation of the property they safeguarded. However, it may be unwise to dismiss these diplomatic sanctions as pure form. Firstly, there is some evidence to suggest that in the case of solemn ecclesiastical charters, they may have been enacted as part of a solemn ritual. Byrhtferth's Life of St Ecgwine gives a fictitious account of the creation of an eighth-century privilege for the monastery at Evesham, but here Byrhtferth may be drawing upon his contemporary experience of diplomatic procedures. Bishop Ecgwine brought back from Rome a papal privilege which was read out at a great royal assembly. The king then ordered a privilege to be drawn up by the archbishop of Canterbury and this was placed by him on the altar of the church at Evesham during its mass of consecration. The archbishop and the congregation accompanied this deposition with prayers of protecting the community and its possession and with a terrible anathema.[81]

The threats of earthly misfortune and eternal damnation contained in such documents may not always have been easily shrugged off. In 993, Æthelred the Unready assembled a major council at Pentecost in Winchester to discuss the consequences of his sale of the abbacy of Abingdon in violation of privileges issued

---

78 Cubitt, 'Bishops, Priests and Penance', 58–9. For the palaeography, see Richard Gameson, 'The Origin of the Exeter Book of Old English Poetry', *ASE*, 25 (1996), 135–85, 162–3. Note too that London, Lambeth Palace Library, MS 149, which is corrected by the same scribe, contains a copy of Augustine's *De adulterinis coniugiis*.

79 On Abbo, see Pierre Riché, *Abbon de Fleury: Un moine savant et combatif (vers 950–1004)* (Turnhout, 2004), 165–70.

80 On this see Catherine Cubitt, 'Bishops and Councils in Late Saxon England: the Intersection of Secular and Ecclesiastical Law', in *Recht und Gericht in Kirche und Welt um 900*, ed. Wilfried Hartmann (Munich, 2007), 159–67.

81 Byrhtferth's *Vita sancti Ecgwini*, in *Vita (sic) quorundam Anglo-Saxonum: Original Lives of Anglo-Saxons and Others who Lived before the Conquest*, ed. J.A. Giles (London, 1854), 379–81. Sarah Hamilton has pointed out to me a contemporary continental parallel to Byrhtferth's account described in Susan Boynton, *Shaping a Monastic Identity: Liturgy and History at the Imperial Abbey of Farfa, 1000–1125* (Ithaca, NY, 2006), 13: in 1060 two altars at the monastery of Farfa were rededicated and the monastery obtained confirmation of the abbey's possessions and privileges from Pope Nicholas II. The Pope sent three legates to Farfa to proclaim the anathema at mass on the feast of the Exaltation of the Cross in the presence of many notable members of the laity and religious.

by his father Edgar and his uncle, Eadwig.[82] The charter, which Keynes sees as a product of the royal writing office, states that the disasters which had afflicted England after the death of Bishop Æthelwold in 984 had prompted Æthelred to reflect on his own conduct and to repent of the ill-advised actions of his youth. He then specifies his violation of the Abingdon privileges which were obtained by Æthelwold and equipped with lengthy curses in their sanctions.[83] Æthelred is made to declare in the charter that he has convened the council: 'Therefore, meditating with a watchful heart these things with myself and as much desiring to be freed quickly from so terrifying an anathema.'[84] As a result of taking their counsel, Æthelred restores the privilege of free abbatial elections and then rejects the money he had obtained for the abbacy, anathematising it.

These events, as Keynes has shown, are the turning point of Æthelred's reign when he rejected his policy of favouring lay appropriations of ecclesiastical property. Almost every subsequent year of his reign witnesses a restitution of a church property or a donation to a religious house. These include restorations of property alienated from the see of Winchester in the years between 984 and 993 and the explicitly pietistic grants to St Andrew's Rochester (discussed above), when Æthelred's remorse for his earlier sanctioning of property thefts is lengthily described.[85] It is clear that the Council of 993 represented a significant penitential gesture on the part of Æthelred and one which reverberated down later years. The timing of this council to coincide with the feast of Pentecost, which commemorates the descent of the Spirit, the divine agent of compunction and remorse, is significant.[86]

The charters issued after 993 include requests for the prayers of the church and of the saints which are commonly found in Anglo-Saxon charters, but sometimes these appear with apparently extra emphasis, for example, in the Rochester example quoted above, where Æthelred's desire to regain the favour of St Andrew, who had interceded for those crucified with Christ, is spelt out. A charter of 997 for Old Minster, Winchester documents a similar restoration. Æthelred once more acknowledges his youthful culpability in allowing the misappropriation and now, with the greater maturity of adulthood, returns the property, 'I recognised that I unjustly held this, and fearing the heavenly judgment, that I had incurred the anger of the Apostle, I

---

82 S 876, edited and discussed by Susan Kelly in her *Charters of Abingdon Abbey*, Anglo-Saxon Charters, 7–8 (2 vols, Oxford, 2000–1), I, pp. lxxxiv–cxv and II, 477–83, no. 124.

83 On the significance of this charter and the events which it records, see Keynes, *Diplomas*, 176–208; Pauline Stafford, 'Political Ideas in Late Tenth-Century England', in *Law, Laity and Solidarities*, ed. Pauline Stafford, J.L. Nelson and Jane Martindale (Manchester, 2001), 68–82; Cubitt, 'Bishops and Councils in Late Saxon England', 162–7; Catherine Cubitt, 'Politics of Remorse', in *Anglo-Saxon England and the Continent*, ed. Hans Sauer and Joanna Story, forthcoming.

84 *Charters of Abingdon Abbey*, ed. Kelly, II, 478: 'haec igitur mecum uigilanti pectore uoluens et citius a tanto tamque exhorrendo anathemate liberari cupiens'.

85 Keynes, *Diplomas*, 178–81; S 885 and 893 for Rochester and S 891 for Old Minster, Winchester. See the quotation from S 893 quoted above.

86 On the timing of the council, see Cubitt, 'Politics of Remorse', and Catherine Cubitt, 'Property and Piety: Politics and Ideology in the Benedictine Reform', in *Commemorative Volume for Patrick Wormald*, ed. Stephen Baxter (forthcoming).

establish now the renewal of the charter'. The property restored had been granted to Old Minster by his predecessors, including Kings Eadred and Edgar.[87] This, like the Rochester charter, suggests that Æthelred's appropriation of ecclesiastical property had incurred the wrath of the patron saints of the see.[88] In another charter for Abingdon Abbey, Æthelred describes how the bequests of his father Edgar had been overturned after his death and directed to Æthelred himself, then an ætheling. These were lands which apparently had traditionally been allocated to the king's sons. However, years later, possibly in 999, Æthelred felt moved to compensate the community for their loss:

> Now, however, because it seems to me very grievous to incur and bear the curse of my father, by retaining this offering which he made to God for the redemption of his soul, and because the grace of God has deigned to bring me to an age of understanding ... I therefore determine both to honour the aforesaid holy monastery with a suitable gift ... first for the love of Almighty God and of his blessed Mother, that she may deign to be a faithful intercessor for me to our Lord God; then for the love of my father's soul and for the eternal redemption of my own soul, and also for the sake of my children ...[89]

In this charter, Æthelred is made to express the fear of his father's curse, probably that accompanying his bequests, because of the alienation of the property.

Ælfric of Eynsham, writing probably in the mid 990s, made a direct connection between the ravages of famine, disease and Viking attacks in his homily on the prayer of Moses:

> Well may we think how well it fared with us when this island was dwelling in peace, and the monastic orders were held in honour, and the laity was ready against their foes, so that our report spread widely throughout the earth. How was it then afterward when men rejected monastic life and held God's services in contempt but that pestilence and hunger came to us, and afterward the heathen army had us in reproach?[90]

As Keynes points out, these lines are an extremely suggestive commentary on monastic patronage at this date.[91]

---

87 S 891, J.M. Kemble, *Codex Diplomaticus Aevi Saxononici* (6 vols, London, 1839–1848), no. 698: 'cognoui me hanc iniuste possidere, et supernum metuens examen, furoremque apostolicum incurrere, huius nunc scedulae renouatione constituo'.

88 S 891, Kemble, *Codex*, no. 698.

89 S 937, *Charters of Abingdon*, ed. Kelly, I, 503–7, no. 129; translation from *EHD*, 582–3, no. 123.

90 *Ælfric's Lives of Saints*, ed. and tr. Skeat, I, 294–5: Wel we magon geðencan hu wel hit ferde mid us, þaða þis igland wæs wunigende on sibbe, and munuclif wæron mid wurðscipe gehealdene, and ða woruldmenn wæron wære wið heora fynd, swa þæt ure word sprang wide geond þas eorðan. Hu wæs hit ða siððan ða þa man towearp munuclif, and Godes biggengas to bysmore hæfde, buton þæt us com to cwealm and hunger, and siððan hæðen here us hæfde to bysmre?

91 Simon Keynes, 'Wulfsige, Monk of Glastonbury, Abbot of Westminster (*c* 990–993), and Bishop of Sherborne (*c* 993–1002)', in *St Wulfsige and Sherborne*, ed. Katherine Barker, D.A. Hinton and Alan Hunt (Oxford, 2005), 53–97, at 66–7.

Conclusion

Hagiography concerning Dunstan from shortly after his death saw him as a major prophet whose foresight, like that of his Old Testament predecessors, could predict the unhappy consequences of royal and national sin. His reputation as a holy man seems to have been terrifying, as the stories concerning King Edmund's remorse at Cheddar and Æthelred's obedience over the election of the bishop of Winchester imply. His visionary powers did not detract from his authority in the spiritual and secular worlds: on the contrary, they were an important component of it. It would be unwise to draw too firm a line between powers as a holy man and his activities in other areas, like liturgical and monastic reform. His reforming zeal and abilities were of one piece with his spiritual powers. His interest in canon law and consanguinity was part of a continuum with the power to excommunicate and to curse.

These reflections do shed light upon the politics of Æthelred's reign. Later authors, like William of Malmesbury, took great delight in dire prognostications about this unfortunate king, gleefully recording stories like that concerning the defilement of his baptismal font, which look like later and malicious confections. However, the contemporary diplomatic record clearly indicates anxieties that the anti-clerical policies of the early part of the reign had offended God and resulted in the punishment of the Viking raids. These fears do not seem to have been dispelled by King Æthelred's new piety and his restorations of church property. Rather the charters indicate continuing and perhaps intensifying fears that insufficient property had been restored and fears of continuing curses. St Dunstan was, as Nicholas Brooks so aptly described him, 'a holy man of distinction', a religious figure of immense stature in the uncertain politics of the tenth and eleventh centuries when prelates and kings alike needed to be both politically canny and spiritually wise.

Chapter 13

A Mass for St Birinus in an Anglo-Saxon Missal from the Scandinavian Mission-Field

Alicia Corrêa

One of the more intriguing legacies of the English Christian missions in Scandinavia is the survival of fragments of late Anglo-Saxon service-books in the bindings of sixteenth- and seventeenth-century volumes of administrative records. Presumably, the confiscation of ecclesiastical property at the Reformation in Scandinavia (1530–1536/7) placed books such as these in secular hands.[1] Since they no longer had a liturgical function, a more practical use was made of the parchment as reinforcement strips in the bindings of post-Reformation registers and civil accounts.[2] To date, fragments have been identified representing over 20 Anglo-Saxon service-books, which are datable on palaeographical grounds from *c*. 890 to the Conquest. These have been catalogued by Helmut Gneuss.[3] The corpus is by no means complete; as more Reformation books are rebound for conservation purposes, the Anglo-Saxon finds continue to increase.[4]

---

1   C.H. Christensen, 'Scandinavian Libraries in the Late Middle Ages', in *The Medieval Library*, ed. J.W. Thompson, repr. with supplement by B.B. Boyer (New York, 1957), 477–508, esp. 487–97 and 502–6. For general information on this period, see T.B. Willson, *History of the Church and State in Norway from the Tenth to the Sixteenth Century* (London, 1903), 295–357.

2   Cf. Lilli Gjerløw, *Adoratio crucis* (Oslo, 1961), 29–32 (discussing fragments from Oslo, Rijksarkivet, Mi. 1); Lilli Gjerløw, 'Fragments of a Lectionary in Anglo-Saxon Script Found in Oslo', *Nordisk Tidskrift för Bok- och Biblioteksväsen*, 44 (1957), 109–22; Lilli Gjerløw, 'Fragment of a Twelfth-Century Croyland Calendar Found in Norway', *Nordisk Tidskrift för Bok- och Biblioteksväsen*, 45 (1958), 99–106; T. Schmid, 'Om Sankt Swithunusmässan i Sverige', *Nordisk Tidskrift för Bok- och Biblioteksväsen*, 31 (1944), 25–34.

3   Helmut Gneuss, *Handlist of Anglo-Saxon Manuscripts: a List of Manuscripts and Manuscript Fragments Written or Owned in England up to 1100* (Tempe, Arizona, 2001), 134–5, 143–5; see also Helmut Gneuss, 'A Preliminary List of Manuscripts Written or Owned in England up to 1100', *ASE*, 9 (1981), 1–60, and Helmut Gneuss, 'Addenda and Corrigenda to the Handlist of Anglo-Saxon Manuscripts', *ASE*, 32 (2003), 293–305.

4   Jan Brunius (archivist, Swedish National Archives), is in the process of compiling a catalogue (*Medeltida Böcker i Fragment*) of the large collection of fragments (some 30,000 leaves in total, from various medieval liturgical, scientific and law manuscripts) in the Swedish National Archives, Stockholm.

A few of these fragments have already been published and some of those with Anglo-Saxon features have received particular attention.[5] It should not be surprising that these service-books contain liturgical features characteristic of Anglo-Saxon England. An Anglo-Saxon priest or bishop would have embarked on his work in Scandinavia equipped with the essential tools of the trade, that is, those service-books most necessary for use by a cleric (either secular or monastic).[6] As a member of the Anglo-Saxon church familiar with that liturgy, this person would have had at least two options open to him: the importation of service-books which had been copied in England, or the copying of English service-books in Scandinavia. In either case, the books which serviced the young Scandinavian churches have left an important legacy, albeit as remnants in the bindings of early modern books. One set of these fragments so far identified contains a mass for St Birinus, an unmistakably Anglo-Saxon feature: I wish to draw attention to this particular set and its implications for Anglo-Saxon church history and the Scandinavian missions.[7]

The fragments in question, originally Oslo, Riksarkivet, Lat. fragm. 206 + 209, nos. 1–4 + 239, nos. 6–7, have recently been renumbered as Lat. fragm. 209, nos. 1–6 + 239, nos. 6–7.[8] The currently accepted date and place of origin of these fragments (early eleventh-century Winchester) should be reviewed in the light of the following discussion.

Eight folios have been so far identified which contain liturgical *formulae* belonging to an Anglo-Saxon missal. That is to say, the texts represent prayers, biblical lessons and chants (with musical notation) for use by the celebrant (priest or bishop) at the mass. These fragments have all been extracted from seventeenth-century books from Nedenes, Norway. The dates of the 'host' books, along with their

---

5 Schmid, 'Om Sankt Swithunusmässan i Sverige', 28–31, publishes the mass for St Swithhun surviving from an eleventh-century Anglo-Saxon missal (Stockholm, Kammararkivet, Mi. 1), which is thought to have been in use in Skara, Sweden, because most of the fragments come from bindings of Skara books; see Gjerløw, *Adoratio crucis*, 13–28 and 31–41 for the extra-liturgical prayers for the veneration of the Holy Cross on Good Friday which have survived within the fragments of an eleventh-century missal (Oslo, Rijksarkivet, Mi. 1), once in use, apparently, in the diocese of Oslo. The Good Friday prayers have preserved the important modifications stipulated in *Regularis Concordia*, written 964 x 975. These same fragments also preserve a copy of the famous *Exultet* prayer for the Easter vigil (see Gjerløw, *Adoratio crucis*, 41–3), with an important variant reading that seems to have circulated in this form only in Anglo-Saxon England and, indeed, in only one other Anglo-Saxon service book, the so-called *Missal of Robert of Jumièges*, ed. H.A. Wilson, HBS, 11 (London, 1896), 90–92 (see n. 15 below for bibliography on this manuscript). For this *Exultet* see E. Moeller, *Corpus praefationum*, 2 vols in 5, Corpus Christianorum, Series Latina, 161 and 161 A-D (Turnhout, 1980–1981), I, no. 522.

6 Service-books used by clerics are listed by Helmut Gneuss, 'Liturgical books in Anglo-Saxon England and their Old English terminology', in *Learning and Literature in Anglo-Saxon England*, ed. Michael Lapidge and Helmut Gneuss (Cambridge, 1985), 91–141.

7 I am grateful to Helmut Gneuss for drawing my attention to this fragment, listed as no. 871.5 in Gneuss, *Handlist*, 134, with the entry 'Oslo, Riksarkivet, Lat. fragm. 206, 209, 1–4 and 239, 6–7. Missal (f): s. xi in., Winchester'.

8 I am grateful to the librarian and staff of the Rijksarkivet in Oslo for providing me with a set of excellent photographs of these fragments.

fragmentary Anglo-Saxon *liturgica* which they contain, are listed here. The opening word(s) of each side is noted in round brackets; supplied readings are noted in square brackets.

? Nedenes 1643
    Lat. fragm. 239–6r (audierunt): [*Natale S. Andreae*]
Nedenes 1643
    Lat. fragm. 209–5r (michi): continuation of [*Natale S. Andreae*]
? Nedenes 1643
    Lat. fragm. 239–6v (Omnipotens): [*Depositio S. Birini*]
Nedenes 1643
    Lat. fragm. 209–5v (Andree): [*Octauus*] *S. Andreae.* [*Natale*] *S. Lucie*
Nedenes 1642
    Lat. fragm. 209–1r (et eius): [*unius confessoris*], *plurimorum confessorum*
        Lat. fragm. 209–2r (exorare): continuation of *plurimorum confessorum, missa in natale un*[*ius uir*]*ginum* [*sic*]
        Lat. fragm. 209–1v (specie): continuation of *un*[*ius uir*]*gin*<*is*>
        Lat. fragm. 209–2v (laborius): continuation of *un*[*ius uir*]*gin*<*is*>
Nedenes 1643
    Lat. fragm. 209–6r (tue): [*missa pro monachis*], *miss*[*a sacerdotis propria*]
    Lat. fragm. 209–6v (-UNIO-): [*missa sacerdotis*], [*missa sa*]*cerdotis propria*
Nedenes 1643
    Lat. fragm. 209–3r (Da quesumus): [*missa sacerdotis*]
        Lat. fragm. 209–4r (perpetuam): continuation of [*missa sacerdotis*], *alia m*[*issa*] *sacer*[*dotis pro se canere debet*]
Nedenes 1648
    Lat. fragm. 239–7r (mihi): continuation of *alia m*[*issa*] *sacerd*[*otis pro se canere debet*]
Nedenes 1643
    Lat. fragm. 209–3v (non habet): continuation of *alia m*[*issa*] *sacerd*[*otis pro se canere debet*]
    Lat. fragm. 209–4v (-entibus): continuation of *alia m*[*issa*] *sacerd*[*otis pro se canere debet*], *mis*[*sa pr*]*o salute uiuorum uel mortuorum*
Nedenes 1648
    Lat. fragm. 239–7v (eorum): continuation of *missa pro salute uiuorum uel mortuorum*

The strips come in thin rectangular shapes, *c.* 57 x 112 mm and 58 x 119 mm (vertical orientation), or 110 x 56 mm and 115 x 57 mm (horizontal orientation): one fragment is a thicker, less symmetrical rectangle, *c.* 140/130 x 99 mm (horizontal orientation). Ruling is clearly visible, but the letter-forms do not sit easily on the ruled line; the bases of the letters often dip above or below that line. The ruled lines are some 8–9 mm apart.

There are two sizes of letters: that for prayers and lessons is normally 3 mm tall with ascenders and descenders each extending another 3 mm; that for chants is normally half-size. Since the letter-size of the chants is only some 1.5 mm in height, the musical notation has ample room in the ruled space of each line. The physical formation of the neumes is by no means crowded and is, on the whole, elegantly executed. Of the two sections which provide neumes (that is, for the masses of St Andrew and of St Lucy and for the masses of the *Commune sanctorum*), at least two scribes have been responsible for writing the notation. One scribe has written notation pertaining only to the incipits to the chants of the *Commune sanctorum*, and a second scribe has written elaborate notation to the full chants for the feast of Andrew and Lucy. The formation of the neumes for the latter is 'Anglo-Saxon' in at least one respect: that is, the upper stroke of each ascender finishes in a pronounced, and elongated, hook, the angle of the descending stroke being perfectly parallel with the ascending element.[9] The work of both music-scribes is consistent with a date in the later eleventh century.

The fragments illustrate a range of scripts: as display scripts rustic capitals are employed for rubrics to individual prayers, and mixed minuscule and majuscule for rubrics to each feast. These are generally quite poorly executed. The text-script is reasonably consistent throughout the fragments. It is Anglo-Caroline minuscule of a sort associated with the closing years of the Anglo-Saxon period, one of the late forms of Style IV.[10] It is clear that the variety found here – showing spiky-topped **e**, sweeping-headed **f** and **s**, heavy-wedged ascenders which in some cases are beginning to split into forks, very tall **s** + **t** ligatures, and occasionally use of trailing-headed tall **a** (see, especially, Lat. fragm. 209–1) – is unlikely to belong to a date earlier that the third quarter of the eleventh century. A particularly striking characteristic of the script is the preference for round, single-compartment **a**. A comparandum for this script may be found in BL Cotton Tiberius A iii, of Canterbury origin, in the work of the later scribes.[11]

As I noted above, the fragments are from a missal. Missals are divided, as a general rule, into several sections. Three of these are represented in our fragment.

1. Four masses are associated with the sanctoral calendar, that is, feasts connected with the calendar of saints' days: these are St Andrew (30 November), Deposition of St Birinus (3 December), Octave of St Andrew (7 December), and St Lucy (13 December).
2. Three masses are associated with the *Commune sanctorum*, that is, that section carrying masses where the *category* of saint is distinguished (martyr, confessor, virgin) but not the *name* of the saint. This section provides material for the celebration of local saints (according to her/ his category), for whom

---

9 I am grateful to Dr Susan Rankin for advice on the notation. She comments further that there is little indication that either scribe was making an attempt to portray the musical pitch for each chant. It is significant that there are two types of musical notation, one brief the other elongated: this means that the scribe of the *text* of the prayers, chants and readings, for the Andrew and Lucy masses, was aware of the length of horizontal space required for the musical notation and that she/he spaced out the letters accordingly.

10 D.N. Dumville, *English Caroline Script and Monastic History: Studies in Benedictinism, A.D. 950–1030* (Woodbridge, 1993), 111–40.

11 On this manuscript, see N.R. Ker, *Catalogue of Manuscripts Containing Anglo-Saxon* (Oxford, 1957; rev. imp., 1990), 240–48 (no. 186); see also n. 66 below.

specific prayers, chants, or readings were not included in the sanctoral. The *Commune sanctorum* feasts which have survived in our fragment are for the 'Common of one confessor', 'Common of many confessors' and 'Common of one virgin'.

3. Several masses are extant for votive commemorations, that is, services for a time of special need, or at a special event; these include one mass for a monk, at least three (possibly as many as five) masses for a priest, and one mass for the living and for the dead.

Aside from the obvious interest of the mass for St Birinus, which I shall discuss in a moment, the sequence of feasts celebrated here is instructive. Liturgical *formulae* for the feasts of St Andrew (30 November), nos. 1–3,[12] and St Birinus (3 December), nos. 4–5, occur on the recto and verso, respectively, of one fragment (Lat. fragm. 239, no. 6). It is therefore unlikely that another feast could have come between them. Indeed, by chance, the lower portion of that same folio has survived in Lat. fragm. 209, no. 5. On the recto is the continuation of the feast of St Andrew for 30 November; on account of the high status commonly awarded to this feast, all the proper chants and lessons are included, making it a lengthy entry. On the verso occur two entries: (a) the remains of the prayers (no chants or lessons are included here) for St Andrew's octave feast (that is, the eighth day after the main feast, therefore 7 December), nos. 6–8, followed immediately by (b) the rubric, first chants and collects for the feast of St Lucy (13 December), no. 9.

There is accordingly little doubt that the sequence of feasts at this point in the sanctoral was intended to be as follows: Andrew (30 November), Birinus (3 December), octave of Andrew (7 December), Lucy (13 December). This is unusual. For a start, the sequence octave of St Andrew – St Lucy omits St Damasus (11 December), one of the important feasts added in the eighth century to Frankish sacramentaries. Additions such as these were incorporated into the 'mixed Gregorian' sacramentaries of the tenth century and this sacramentary tradition enjoyed a wide circulation as the source of liturgical books from late Anglo-Saxon England.[13] Secondly, if, as seems to be the case, the feast of St Andrew immediately preceded that of Birinus, then this sequence omits the feast of SS. Crisanthus and Daria (1 December), another addition belonging to the eighth-century Frankish reforms.[14] In Anglo-Saxon England, with one exception, service-books had the fuller sanctoral, that is, one which included the feasts of SS. Crisanthus and Daria and of St Damasus. Only the so-called 'Missal of Robert of Jumièges', datable to the first 15 years of the eleventh century, origin unknown but variously attributed to Canterbury (Christ

---

12 See Appendix I, to which the numbers of the prayers refer.
13 On the families of sacramentary, see nn. 32–5 below.
14 The 'Old Gelasian Sacramentary' is the oldest surviving example of the 'Roman Sacramentary' (in Vatican, Reg. lat. 316): *Liber sacramentorum romanae aecclesiae ordinis anni circuli*, ed. L.C. Mohlberg and others (Rome, 1960). Here, however (edition, nos. 1073–5), the feast of SS. Crisanthus and Daria occurs *before* that of St Andrew.

Church), Ely, or Peterborough, preserves this same 'attenuated' sequence.[15] The textual correspondence in other respects between the 'Robert Missal' and our Oslo fragment is, however, not exact, as will become clear later.[16] Nonetheless, as far as the sanctoral is concerned, the Oslo missal seems to have followed an exemplar of the 'Gregorian' sacramentary, or one of its derivatives, rather than its Frankish counterpart.[17]

One other oddity concerning the range of feasts preserved in these fragments (considering now all three sections), is the number of special prayers for the priest himself, nos. 20–27. These masses form part of the votive masses, the first and last of which are for monks and for the salvation of the living and the dead, respectively. The prayers for the priest are in the first person singular, and, in many cases, reference is made directly to the sacraments, the consecration of which is the sole responsibility of the priest. In performing a mass such as this, the presbyter intended to prepare himself, on a penitential and sacrificial level, for his ultimate duty as the 'steward of the mysteries of God' for the Christian people.[18] Most of the 'larger' Anglo-Saxon service-books preserve two or three masses of this kind.[19] It is difficult to determine the number of masses represented in the Oslo fragment; a comparison with the liturgical sources for these prayers indicates that no fewer than *five* masses are represented here.[20] The implications of this will be discussed further below.[21]

---

15 *Missal of Robert of Jumièges*, ed. Wilson. For discussion of the script, contents and history of the manuscript (Rouen, BM, Y.6 [274]), with further bibliographical information, see D.N. Dumville, 'On the Dating of Some Late Anglo-Saxon Liturgical Manuscripts', *Transactions of the Cambridge Bibliographical Society*, 10 (1991), 40–57, at 52; see also D.N. Dumville, *Liturgy and the Ecclesiastical History of Late Anglo-Saxon England* (Woodbridge, 1992), 87. The litany has been discussed and edited by Lapidge, *Anglo-Saxon Litanies*, 82 and 270–72 (no. xl).

16 See text below at note 69.

17 On families of sacramentary, see notes 32–5 below.

18 See the discussion, with further references, by I.H. Dalmais, 'The Ministerial Exercise of the Priesthood of Christ' in *The Church at Prayer: an Introduction to the Liturgy*, ed. A.G. Martimort and others, tr. M.J. O'Connell (4 vols, London, 1986–8), I, 249–51.

19 See, for instance, the two *missae sacerdotis propriae* in the *Missal of Robert of Jumièges*, ed. Wilson, 251–3. Other examples may be found in the late ninth-century and Continental part ('part A') of the 'Leofric Missal': *The Leofric Missal*, ed. F.E. Warren (Oxford, 1883), 180–82, and in the late tenth-century sacramentary from Ramsey or Winchcombe: *The Winchcombe Sacramentary: Orléans, Bibliothèque municipale, 127 [105]*, ed. Anselme Davril, HBS, 109 (1995); on this last, see n. 37 below.

20 According to the 'Gregorian' tradition, two masses are represented here, GrTc 2163 and GrTc 2183 (see the abbreviation-table to Appendix I, and the discussion of liturgical families in nn. 32–5 below). In certain witnesses of the 'Eighth-Century Gelasians', however, in particular the 'Angoulême Sacramentary' (*Liber Sacramentorum Engolismensis: Ms. BN, lat. 816, le sacramentaire d'Angoulême*, ed. Patrick Saint-Roch, Corpus Christianorum, Series Latina, 159C (Turnhout, 1987), nos. 2302, 2306), these two prayers form the collect and postcommunion of the same mass. This mass, however, is a votive *pro temptatione carnis*, the rubric of which does not correspond with the extant rubric in the Oslo fragment: *Miss[a sa]cerdotis propria*.

21 See below, p. 183.

The layout of the missal is very clear; there is no indication that the organisation of the various elements was completed in a haphazard manner. These elements occur in the order in which they are recited in the service. The surviving section (as preserved on Lat. fragm 209, no. 1) of the mass of many confessors in the *Commune sanctorum* provides a good example of this arrangement. The mass-set (nos. 11–13) is clearly identified with the rubric 'Plurimorum confessorum'.[22] The opening antiphon ('Timete Dominum') and collect ('Deus qui nos sanctorum ... gaudere') are distinguished by an enlarged initial (that of the collect larger than that of the antiphon) written in different-coloured ink (probably red). The liturgical *formulae* for the lessons, including the chants which are associated with each lesson, are identified by the appropriate rubric followed by the incipit: *lec*[*tio*] 'Lingua sapientia', *gr*[*adualis*] 'Exultabunt sancti', *all*[*eluia*] 'Mirabilis Deus', *lec*[*tio*] 'Designavit Dominus' (Luke 10, 1–7), and *of*[*fertorium*] 'Mirabilis Deus'. The next two proper prayers of the mass-set, the secret ('Suscipe Domine et munera ... adiuuemur') and preface ('Et magestatem [*sic*][23] tuam ... [auxilium]'), each begin on a new line. Each prayer is introduced by a rubric and has the added attraction of having the initial letter enlarged so that, like the initial letter of the collect, it encompasses two full lines of ruled space; it is written in a different colour of ink.

In general format, this layout varies little from that displayed in the 'Missal of the New Minster, Winchester', written there in the second half of the eleventh century.[24] Service-books such as these fragments and the New Minster book may be classified as representatives of the 'comprehensive type' of missal which was being produced in Anglo-Saxon England from the second half of the tenth century onwards.[25] In addition, it is important to note that neumes are written for every chant-text which is copied in these Oslo fragments, whether for its incipit or for the full chant-text. Also, not every mass is provided with musical chants and readings. As in the 'New Minster Missal', only the feasts which are most important from a liturgical point of view are provided with chants and lessons proper to the occasion. In our Oslo fragment, these are the mass for Andrew on 30 November (but *not* his octave), the mass for Lucy (13 December) and all of the extant masses from the *Commune Sanctorum*.[26] The assumption to be made is that these masses were occasions of very special importance. By contrast, the mass (3 December) for Birinus and that for Andrew's octave (7 December) and all of the votive masses are provided with the mass-set of prayers, but not the chants and Biblical readings, which were proper to that occasion. Presumably, the chants and readings were taken from elsewhere, either from the

---

22 The rubric may have begun with the word 'missa' but the right portion of the folio has been trimmed away. In any case, abbreviated rubrics for masses belonging to the same series are not uncommon.

23 Note that *magestatem* is an example of Anglo-Latin spelling.

24 *The Missal of the New Minster, Winchester*, ed. D.H. Turner, HBS, 93 (London, 1962). On this book (Le Havre, BM, 330), see *Vita Æthelwoldi*, p. cxxiii.

25 Gneuss, 'Liturgical Books', 100–101 and 'List', fragments, nos. 143, 212, 454, 524, 572, 649, 789, 871, 872, 875, 936, with eight supplementary items among which the present missal fragment is included.

26 But note that while the full readings are apparently supplied for the feast of St Andrew on 30 November, only the incipits for the readings are supplied in the *Commune sanctorum*.

Sunday mass, or as regards a particular saint, from the appropriate section of the *Commune Sanctorum*. We should not interpret this as evidence that feasts, such as that for Birinus, were *un*important; however, within the broader perspective of the divine hierarchy, they held second place behind, for example, the feasts for the apostles of Christ and the Virgin Mary. In the 'New Minster Missal', for instance, feasts for the New Minster saints Grimbald (8 July) and Iudoc (13 December, with translation on 9 January) have this limited provision, that is, proper prayers without proper chants or lessons.[27] These two characteristics – the occurrence of neumes and the combination of masses with, and without, chants and lessons – may be interpreted simply as part of the way in which these service-books were organised at that time.

Some discussion should now be made about the texts of the liturgical *formulae* in these fragments. As far as the lectionary is concerned, the lessons extant in the Oslo fragments, which occur for Andrew (30 November) and for many confessors, correspond with those in the 'New Minster Missal'.[28] The Oslo fragments also provide an Epistle-lesson for the common of a virgin but, since the New Minster book does not provide chants (except for one *alleluia*) or lessons for its three masses for the common of a virgin, no connection may be made.[29]

The correspondence of the chant-texts is far less regular than one would expect. The chants for Andrew (30 November) and Lucy (13 December) are the same in each book.[30] By contrast, the chants provided for the 'Common of many confessors' in the Oslo fragment do not match those in the 'New Minster Missal'. With the exception of the *alleluia*, the extant sung tests (*antiphona, gradualis, offertorium, communio*) derive from a different tradition.[31]

The fragmentary prayers from this Oslo missal are probably the most instructive of the three types of texts (lessons, chants and prayers) under discussion here. The prayers from the mass preserve several characteristics which give a classic

---

27 Mass for these feasts may be found in *Missal of the New Minster*, ed. Turner, 122, 192–3 and 56–7, respectively.

28 The correspondence is as follows: for the feast of St Andrew, the Oslo missal offers Rom. 10, 10–18 for the Epistle reading and Matt. 4, 18–22 for the Gospel reading, both of which may be found in *Missal of the New Minster*, ed. Turner, 187. For many confessors, the Oslo missal offers 'Lingua sapientium' for the Epistle reading, and Luke 10, 1–7 for the Gospel reading, both of which may be found in the *Missal of the New Minster*, ed. Turner, 203.

29 The three masses in question are two for a virgin and one for a virgin who is not a martyr: *Missal of the New Minster*, ed. Turner, 204–5. Only the Epistle reading for the Common of one virgin is now extant in the Oslo missal; the reading is 'Simile regnum'. The extant chants for this Common are as follows: gradual: 'Specie tua'; alleluia: 'Diff'- (fragment is cut off at this point); offertory: 'Filie regum'.

30 No variant readings occur other than the omission of the word *Simoni* from the communion-chant of the mass for Andrew; this is supplied above the line (complete with chants), perhaps by the scribe who wrote the musical notation (cf. Lat. fragm. 209, no. 5). For the mass of Andrew, the extant chants (that is, the gradual, alleluia, offertory and communion-chants) are identical to those offered in *Missal of the New Minster*, ed. Turner, 187–8. For the mass for Lucy, only the antiphon has survived; this is identical to that in *Missal of the New Minster*, ed. Turner, 191.

31 For the chants of the Common of many confessors in the Oslo missal, see text above at note 22.

demonstration of what one would expect to find in an Anglo-Saxon sacramentary of the eleventh century. Most prayers derive from the so-called 'mixed Gregorian' sacramentary of the tenth century: that is, a sacramentary tradition which combined elements from the basic *Hadrianum*,[32] the 'Supplemented Gregorian',[33] the 'Eighth-Century Gelasian'[34] and various new compositions by the Carolingian reformers of the ninth century, the last of which has great relevance to the prayers preserved in our Oslo missal.[35]

I have been able to locate a source or analogue for 27 of the 28 fragmentary prayers extant in the remnants of this missal.[36] The collect (no. 21) for the third mass for a priest in the lower portion of Lat. fragm. 209–6 (-UNIO-) is illegible and its original text can no longer be identified. Certain Gregorian *Hadrianum* prayers can be found in the mass-sets for the feast-days of Andrew (30 November), nos. 1–3, and Lucy, no. 9. Such prayers are found in most Anglo-Saxon service-books.

Prayers for the 'Common of many confessors', nos. 11–14, for the 'Common of one virgin', nos. 15–17, and for the votive mass for the living and the dead, no. 28, derive from the 'Supplemented Gregorian'. Most of these prayers are commonly found in Anglo-Saxon service-books; however, the longer version of the preface in the mass for a virgin has no analogue known from Anglo-Saxon England.[37] In this respect, our Oslo fragment may be said to have preserved a more undiluted

---

32 The sacramentary sent by Pope Hadrian to Charlemagne in the late 780s (the 'Gregorian *Hadrianum*' = GrH).

33 GrH with a first stage of additional material added by Carolingian reformers, the 'Supplement' = GrSp; on this development see Jean Deshusses, *Le sacramentaire grégorien: Ses principales formes d'après les plus anciens manuscrits*, 3 vols, Spicilegium Friburgense 16, 24, 28 (Fribourg, 1971–82), I.

34 For an example of the so-called 'Eighth-Century Frankish Gelasians' see the 'Gellone Sacramentary' (GeG): *Liber sacramentorum Gellonensis*, ed. Antoine Dumas and Jean Deshusses, Corpus Christianorum, Series Latina, 159, 159A (Turnhout, 1981).

35 In the ninth century, the combination of 'Gregorian' with 'Gelasian' received much additional material at the hands of Carolingian reformers: on this last stage in the evolution of the 'mixed-Gregorian' (= GrTc), see Deshusses, *Le sacramentaire grégorien*, II–III; see also text below at n. 39. In general on the textual evolution of the 'mixed Gregorians' see Cyrille Vogel, *Medieval Liturgy: an Introduction to the Sources*, rev. and tr. W.G. Storey and R.K. Rasmussen (Washington D.C., 1986), 102–5, 132–3, and Moeller, *Corpus Praefationum*, I, lxvii–lxxii.

36 For a complete list of the prayers extant in this fragment, with collation against a limited number of sources and analogues in other Anglo-Saxon service-books, see Appendix I.

37 On the textual tradition of this preface, see Moeller, *Corpus Praefationum*, no. 776, though the *apparatus criticus* to this entry is in error when it includes the Missal of New Minster (*Missal of the New Minster*, ed. Turner, 204) among the witnesses, since this work preserves only the first half of the preface. Other examples of liturgical books from Anglo-Saxon England which are almost exclusively influenced by Continental 'Gregorians' are the 'Durham Collectar' (*The Durham Collectar*, ed. Alicia Corrêa, HBS, 107 (London, 1992)); the tenth-century (?) fragmentary sacramentary, preserved in London, Society of Antiquaries, MS 154*, probably from Brittany, and imported into England in the tenth century; and the 'Winchcombe Sacramentary' (*The Winchcombe Sacramentary*, ed. Davril; on the non-English aspects of this collection, see Alicia Corrêa, 'The Liturgical Manuscripts of Oswald's Houses',

relationship with the 'Supplemented Gregorian'. The collect for the 'Common of one confessor' (no. 10) and the mass-set (nos. 6–8) for, and indeed the observance of, the octave of St Andrew on 7 December, are characteristics of the 'Eighth-century Gelasian'. The mass-set for the octave of St Andrew occurs regularly in the Anglo-Saxon books; the collect for a confessor does so less often, but an analogue may be found in the collectar compiled for Bishop Wulfstan II of Worcester (1062–1095).[38]

The textual history of the prayers associated with the votive masses for monks (nos. 18–19) and priests (nos. 20–27) is more peculiar. There is nothing unusual about the Continental sources of these prayers. Of the ten extant prayers belonging to these votive masses, all derive from the 'mixed Gregorian' tradition. To be more precise, four of them derive from one particular stage in the textual development of that sacramentary, that is, from the various prayers which Carolingian reformers added to the combined 'Gregorian' and 'Frankish Gelasian' repertory which I noted above.[39] Indeed, at least one mass-set represented in our Oslo missal (nos. 23–4) is likely, on grounds of stylistics and manuscript transmission, to have been composed by Alcuin.[40] What is surprising is that these particular prayers in the Oslo missal are rarely encountered in Anglo-Saxon service-books. I have been able to find analogues for only three of the ten prayers. For example, in the votive mass for monks (nos. 17–18), the secret and postcommunion preserved in the Oslo missal derive from the mass-set available in a limited number of Continental 'mixed Gregorians'.[41] Although other Anglo-Saxon mass-books, such as the 'Robert Missal' and the 'Leofric Missal' also show a familiarity with this mass-set, the correspondence is not exact. Both 'Leofric' and 'Robert' provide a secret different from that witnessed in this particular 'mixed Gregorian' mass and in the Oslo missal.[42] Similarly, both 'Leofric' and 'Robert' share nearly identical mass-sets for the priest; the first and third masses in 'Leofric' largely agree with the two in 'Robert'.[43] By contrast, the

---

in *St Oswald of Worcester: Life and Influence*, ed. Nicholas Brooks and Catherine Cubitt (London, 1996), 285–324, at 298).

38 *The Portiforium of St Wulstan*, ed. Anselm Hughes, HBS, 89, 90 (2 vols, London, 1958–1960), I, 157 (no. 2072).

39 See n. 35 above.

40 See the collation tables at end of this paper: I am referring to prayers nos. 2101 and 2103 of Deshusses, *Le sacramentaire grégorien*, II.

41 Deshusses has traced these prayers to a limited number of 'mixed Gregorian' manuscripts: Düsseldorf, Landes- und Stadtbibliothek, D1; BN, lat. 2291 and lat. 12050.

42 The secret commonly used in Anglo-Saxon books is 'Munera quesumus Domine quae pro nostra ... tribue provenire salutem' (GrTc 3202). See, for example, 'part A' of the 'Leofric Missal' (*Leofric Missal*, ed. Warren, 186), and *Missal of Robert of Jumièges*, ed. Wilson, 250, for *in monasterio monachorum*. It is somewhat surprising that 'part A of the 'Leofric Missal' does not preserve the 'Continental' version of this mass given that this part of the manuscript appears to have been written at Saint-Vaast, Arras, in the late ninth century (Dumville, *Liturgy*, 39–45; Dumville, *English Caroline Script*, 94–6).

43 The prayers for the masses for the priest in the 'Leofric' and 'Robert' missals derive largely from the 'Supplemented Gregorian'. For the first masses in the 'Leofric Missal' (*Leofric Missal*, ed. Warren, 180–1), see GrSP 1280–1284; for the second (*Leofric Missal*, ed. Warren, 181), see GrSp 1285–1288; for the third (*Leofric Missal*, ed. Warren, 181–2), see GrTc 2078–2080, 2088.

eight prayers for the priest in the Oslo missal sit uncomfortably among these English witnesses. While both 'Leofric' and 'Robert' and the Oslo fragments derive their respective prayers from the same general tradition – that of the 'mixed Gregorian' – their compilers have gone about this operation in different ways; that is, each had access to different groups of prayers in that tradition.[44]

In one sense, however, the exemplar of the Oslo missal has not depended entirely on Continental models. In addition to the repertory of prayers deriving from the 'mixed Gregorian', the Oslo missal has a mass of which only the collect and secret have survived (nos. 4–5), for the deposition of St Birinus, first bishop of Wessex (with his see at Dorchester-on-Thames), 634/5–649/50. Birinus was sent by Pope Honorius I to Anglo-Saxon England as a missionary.[45] Before he set off for England, he was consecrated bishop by Asterius, archbishop of Milan. Birinus arrived in Wessex, c. 634, and baptized Cynegils, king of the West Saxons (d. ? 642), in 635 at Dorchester.[46] He was appointed bishop of Wessex, with his see at Dorchester, by Cynegils acting in concert with his overlord, Oswald, king of Bernicia (634–642); Birinus is said to have made numerous conversions.[47] He died in 649/50 and was buried at Dorchester on 3 December. According to Bede, Hædde, bishop of Winchester (676–?705), had Birinus' body translated to Winchester, an event commemorated on 4 September.[48] Æthelwold, bishop of Winchester, placed the relics in a new shrine in the newly constructed Old Minster, c. 980, and King Cnut is alleged by a post-Conquest Winchester annalist to have donated a *feretrum*, or portable reliquary, for the relics of Birinus in 1035.[49]

At first glance, this hagiographical evidence suggests that the cult of Birinus was firmly based at Winchester. By inference, one could claim, as has been done, that our fragment was copied at Winchester.[50] However, if we look more closely at the collect

---

44 The 'Winchcombe Sacramentary' provides yet another version of 'mixed Gregorian' prayers for the *propria missa sacerdotis* (it offers two masses); its prayers do not correspond with the 'Robert Missal', the 'Leofric Missal', or the Oslo missal. See *The Winchcombe Sacramentary*, ed. Davril, nos. 1877–1880 and 1881–1883; these correspond with GrTc 2852, 2853, 2859, 2854 and GrTc 3003–3005, respectively.

45 *HE*, 232 (iii, 7); *Venerabilis Baedae opera historica*, ed. Charles Plummer (2 vols, Oxford, 1896), I, 139–40. See also William of Malmesbury, *De Gestis Pontificum Anglorum*, ed. N.E.S.A. Hamilton, Rolls Series, 52 (London, 1870), 157–8, 164, and, for further information on the cult of Birinus, see Bollandists, *Bibliotheca Hagiographica Latina* (2 vols, Brussels, 1899–1901), with supplement by Henryk Fros (1986), nos. 1360–1364 and *Three Eleventh-Century Anglo-Latin Saints' Lives: Vita S. Birini, Vita et Miracula S. Kenelmi and Vita S. Rumwoldi*, ed. Rosalind Love (Oxford, 1996), pp. xlix–l, lx–lxxiv.

46 *The Anglo-Saxon Chronicle: a Revised Translation*, ed. Dorothy Whitelock with D.C. Douglas and S.I. Tucker (London, 1961), s.a. 634, 635, and cf. Birinus' baptism of Cuthred, son of Cynegils, s.a. 639.

47 *HE*, 230, n. 1 and 232.

48 *HE*, 232 and cf. *Anglo-Saxon Chronicle*, s.a. 650 (Birinus is here described as a Roman).

49 *Three Eleventh-Century Anglo-Latin Saints' Lives*, ed. Love, p. lxi; T.A. Heslop, 'The production of *de luxe* manuscripts and the patronage of King Cnut and Queen Emma', *ASE*, 19 (1990), 151–95 at 157 and 186–7.

50 Another 'Winchester' saint occurring in an Anglo-Saxon fragment surviving in Scandinavia is Swithun, a mass for whom has survived in Stockholm, Kammararkivet, Mi. 1.

and secret for Birinus preserved in this fragment and at the commemorations made to Birinus in other Anglo-Saxon service-books, it becomes obvious that the connection between this missal and Winchester cannot be substantiated on this evidence alone.

It is necessary, first, to examine the appearances of Birinus in the Anglo-Saxon liturgy. Within Anglo-Saxon service-books, Birinus is found in five liturgical contexts: calendars, litanies, prayers for mass and office, blessings and as special invocations in liturgical prayers. Within the liturgical year, Birinus was commemorated twice: his deposition on 3 December and his translation from Dorchester to Winchester on 4 September. Thus Birinus occurs twice in most Anglo-Saxon calendars.[51] The occurrence of both feasts together in 14 calendars out of 20 indicates the popularity of his cult as an entry in calendars, but does not imply that the feasts were necessarily commemorated in any given community. Evidence from calendars must be combined with Birinus' appearance in other liturgical contexts, for example litanies, that is, lists of saints' names invoked at various services. His name occurs in a total of 15 litanies (from 14 different manuscripts);[52] six of these manuscripts also contain calendars which I have noted above as having an entry (or entries) for Birinus.[53] The combination of both a calendar *and* a litany-entry for Birinus presents stronger evidence that his cult was in fact commemorated at the community which used the liturgical book in question. The communities represented by these manuscripts are Winchester, both Old and New Minsters, Crowland (Lincs), and Bury St Edmunds (Suffolk).

Perhaps the most dependable indicator that a cult of a given saint was observed in any community comes from the prayers and blessings which were said at the mass and office on the feast-day of the saint. Seven Anglo-Saxon service-books preserve prayers or a blessing for the feast(s) of Birinus.[54] None of these seems to derive from the Continental corpus of prayers. Since these prayers and blessings are used *for* an

---

Unfortunately this single piece of evidence has persuaded the editor of this mass to place the fragment at Winchester (Schmid, 'Om Sankt Swithhunusmässen', 25–34), despite the fact that the feasts of Swithun are well represented in several non-Winchester service books.

51 See Francis Wormald, *English Kalendars before A.D. 1100*, HBS, 72 (London, 1934). Only in Bodl., Digby 63 (*S.C.* 1664) (Northumbria), BL, Cotton Vitellius A xviii (? Christ Church, Canterbury) and Bodl., Douce 296 (*S.C.* 21870), does he appear only once, for his deposition on 3 December.

52 Note that in CCCC, 422, his name occurs in two separate litanies: *Anglo-Saxon Litanies*, ed. Lapidge, 66 and 125–31 (no. VIII).

53 The manuscripts which have Birinus both in the calendar (twice) and in a litany are: CCCC, 391 (*saec.* xii1, *rescriptus*) and 422; BL, Arundel 60 and Cotton Titus D xxvii; Bodl., Douce 296 (only *one* entry in calendar, for his deposition); and Vatican, Reg. lat. 12.

54 A possible eighth witness may be New York, Pierpont Morgan Library MS 926, fos 74r–76r, copied over the second half of the eleventh century at St Albans, in which survives the musical portions of a rhymed office, possibly secular, for St Birinus (edited by K.D. Hartzell, 'A St Albans Miscellany in New York', *Mittellateinisches Jahrbuch*, 10 (1975), 20–61, at 58–9, with discussion 38–42). See also my discussion, in n. 66, of the invocation to Birinus in the vesper-office preserved in BL, Cotton Tiberius A iii, a liturgical miscellany. For the earliest *vita* (which is admittedly post-Conquest), see *Three Eleventh-Century Anglo-Latin Saints' Lives*, ed. Love, 1–47, with discussion pp. xlix–lxxxviii; David Townsend, 'An Eleventh-Century Life of Birinus of Wessex', *Analecta Bollandiana*, 107 (1989), 129–59.

Anglo-Saxon saint and, since they occur, as far as I am aware, only in Anglo-Saxon books, there is good reason to argue that these liturgical *formulae* were specially composed for the Anglo-Saxon liturgy in honour of Birinus.[55] Three of these service-books are sacramentaries, one is a collectar and three are benedictionals.[56] Of these, only the 'Missal of the New Minster' (Winchester New Minster, *saec.* xi²), the 'Vitellius Sacramentary' (? Canterbury Christ Church, *saec.* xi³/⁴) and the 'Portiforium of St Wulfstan' (Worcester, but based on a Winchester exemplar, *saec.* xi²) offer prayers for both the feasts (4 September and 3 December) of Birinus.[57] This suggests that the cult was particularly important at those centres.

There is evidence to suggest, not surprisingly, that the two communities at Winchester held Birinus in special reverence. Unlike the 'Vitellius Sacramentary', the 'Missal of the New Minster' offers a *prefatio* for both feasts. Since prefaces are longer and more elaborate than the other three proper prayers in a mass-set, it was customary for composers of prefaces to dwell in greater detail on the miracles associated with the saint. Accordingly, prefaces are regarded as important compositions which were undertaken in honour of special occasions.[58] Secondly, the 'Wulfstan Portiforium' offers no fewer than three collects for his deposition and another two for his translation. Normally, a feast of lesser importance was given only a single entry in this particular type of book. Further, although it is customary for a collectar to extract its prayers from the mass, I cannot find analogues for two of the three collects for the deposition in any other mass-book, Anglo-Saxon or otherwise.[59] Finally, in the lengthy series of 'private prayers' for individual saints, the 'Wulfstan

---

55 On Anglo-Latin liturgical compositions in general, see esp. Andrew Prescott, 'The Text of the Benedictional of St Æthelwold', in *Bishop Æthelwold: his Career and Influence*, ed. Barbara Yorke (Woodbridge, 1988), 119–47; *Vita Æthelwoldi*, pp. lxvii–lxxvii; Alicia Corrêa, 'A Mass for St Patrick in an Anglo-Saxon Sacramentary', in *Saint Patrick, A.D. 493–1993*, ed. D.N. Dumville (Woodbridge, 1993), 245–51 and Alicia Corrêa, 'St Austraberta of Pavilly in the Anglo-Saxon liturgy', *Analecta Bollandiana*, 115 (1997), 77–112 .

56 The sacramentaries are 'The Missal of the New Minster' (Le Havre, BM, 330); 'The Missal of Robert of Jumièges' (Rouen, BM, Y.6 [274]); and the 'Vitellius Sacramentary' (BL, Cotton Vitellius A xviii). The collectar is the 'Wulfstan Portiforium' (CCCC, 391). The benedictionals are the 'Canterbury Benedictional' (BL, Harley 2892); BN, lat. 987; and the so-called 'Samson Pontifical' (CCCC, 146). See Appendix II for liturgical *formulae* associated with Birinus in these Anglo-Saxon service-books.

57 *Missal of the New Minster*, ed. Turner; *Portiforium of Saint Wulstan*, ed. Hughes; for discussion and bibliographical references, see Lapidge, *Anglo-Saxon Litanies*, 65 (no. VI), where the litany is edited on pp. 115–19; for discussion of the collectar see *The Durham Collectar*, ed. Corrêa, 126–8. On the origins of Vitellius A xviii, see Corrêa, 'A Mass for St Patrick'. The manuscript has not received a full edition; only the masses for Anglo-Saxon saints have been printed by Warren, *The Leofric Missal*, 303–7.

58 On prefaces, see also my discussion in 'A mass for St Patrick', 247–8. See especially Moeller, *Corpus Praefationum*, I, viii–xxxiv, esp. viii–x and xix–xxii; and A.G. Martimort, 'The Prayer of the Celebrant', in *The Church at Prayer*, ed. Martimort, I, 156–61.

59 On the typical manner in which collectars were compiled by extracting prayers from the mass-set, see *The Durham Collectar*, ed. Corrêa, esp. 20–21. For a list of all prayers and blessings associated with Birinus, see appendix II below. That two of the three prayers for the deposition find no analogues suggests either that the compiler of the 'Wulfstan Portiforium'

Portiforium' has a collective prayer for SS. Birinus, Swithhun and Æthelwold who were 'patroni et protectores' of Winchester.[60] This evidence suggests that a higher-than-average level of devotion existed at Winchester, a conclusion which is to be expected for a centre where the saint's relics lay.

Nonetheless, the prayers for St Birinus appear to have been transported fairly readily to other areas in Anglo-Saxon England.[61] The 'Wulfstan Portiforium', though derived from a Winchester exemplar, was compiled at Worcester. The so-called 'Missal of Robert of Jumièges', which I mentioned above as being associated with a community in south-eastern England, also preserves a mass for the deposition of St Birinus on 3 December.[62] Its mass includes a preface, which indicates a high level of devotion. In fact, one could be forgiven for assuming that this mass-set derived from the Winchester cultus; for the collect, secret and preface in the 'Robert' book correspond with those in the New Minster book. But the postcommunions are not identical; in this, 'Robert' agrees with the 'Vitellius Sacramentary'. As I mentioned above, the 'Vitellius Sacramentary', while not including a preface, does provide a collect, secret and postcommunion for both the deposition and translation feasts of St Birinus.[63] Thus, both the 'Robert Missal' and the 'Vitellius Sacramentary' provide evidence that there was at least one centre in eleventh-century Southumbrian England where the cult of St Birinus was awarded special significance.

Evidence provided by Anglo-Saxon benedictionals indicates that the transmission of the cult of Birinus to other centres outside Winchester was indeed very effective. A benedictional carries a particular type of elaborate and (liturgically) very important prayer, called a blessing, which the bishop was to recite at mass. These blessings were called 'proper', that is, the text changed according to the feast celebrated on that day.[64] Two blessings for the deposition of St Birinus survive in Anglo-

---

knew of another mass, now lost, or that these office-collects were newly composed for the occasion.

60 *The Portiforium of Saint Wulstan*, ed. Hughes, II, 15.

61 See the observation by Edmund Bishop in F.A Gasquet and Edmund Bishop, *The Bosworth Psalter* (London, 1908), 59–68.

62 *The Missal of Robert of Jumièges*, ed. Wilson, 229–30. See note 15 above.

63 At this point I am not sure where that leaves us in measuring the devotion towards Birinus in the 'Vitellius Sacramentary'. Since this service-book is very rigorous in omitting all prefaces unless they are associated with feasts of the very highest grade, I should be inclined not to put too much emphasis on the fact that no preface is provided for Birinus. The fact that both of his feasts are commemorated suggests that the 'Vitellius' book awards the same degree of importance to Birinus as does, for example, the New Minster book. On the prefaces in the 'Vitellius Sacramentary' see Corrêa, 'A Mass for St Patrick', 248, esp. n. 7.

64 On benedictionals and blessings, see Dumville, *Liturgy*, 66–95; Gneuss, 'Liturgical books', 133; Pierre Jounel, 'Blessings and Popular Religion', in *Church at Prayer*, ed. Martimort, III, 263–80; *Corpus Benedictionum Pontificalium*, ed. E. Moeller, Corpus Christianorum, Series Latina, 162, 162A–C (2 vols in 4, Turnhout, 1971–9), IV, pp. viii, xvii–xx, xxii–xxxviii; Andrew Prescott, 'The Structure of English pre-Conquest Benedictionals', *British Library Journal*, 13 (1987), 118–58, and esp. Andrew Prescott, 'The Text of the Benedictional of St Æthelwold'; *The Claudius Pontificals*, ed. D.H. Turner, HBS, 97 (London, 1971), pp. xi–xx; G.G. Willis, *Further Essays in Early Roman Liturgy*, Alcuin Club Collections, 50 (London, 1968), 86–7.

Saxon benedictionals. They occur in three manuscripts, each of which preserves textual evidence indicating that they derive from Christ Church, Canterbury: Paris, Bibliothèque Nationale, lat. 987 (part 2) (*saec.* xi^2), fo. 107r/v, and Cambridge, Corpus Christi College, 146 (*saec.* xi^{in}), pp. 274–5, both offer the same blessing; the so-called 'Canterbury Benedictional', London, British Library, Harley 2892 (*saec.* xi^2) offers a different text.[65] Clearly, more than one tradition was available at Christ Church; whether one of these derived from Winchester is beside the point. The fact is that, by the second half of the eleventh century, the feast of St Birinus on 3 December was given a very high status at Christ Church, Canterbury.[66]

The extant prayers in the Oslo missal (nos. 4–5) do not offer new material which can contribute to the discussion above. Both collect and secret correspond to that found in the 'New Minster Missal' and the 'Robert Missal'.[67] The Oslo missal carries some erroneous readings in the collect: instead of the correct phrase 'beati Birini confessoris tui atque pastoris nostri', the Oslo fragment offers '[be]ati Birini confessoris tui adque *pastores* n[ostri]'.[68] Instead of *ouile* (sheepfold) in the phrase 'in hoc sacratissimum ouile', the Oslo fragment offers *oliue* (?olive). Finally, the Oslo fragment provides two variant readings: instead of the phrase 'ut cum eodem pastore nostro', the Oslo fragment reads 'ut eodem pastore nostro interueniente';

---

65 Both of these blessings have been edited by Moeller, *Corpus Benedictionum Pontificalium*, II, no. 1058 (for the blessing in Harley 2892), and II, no. 1500 (for the blessing in BN, lat. 987 and CCCC 146). For the blessing in Harley 2892, see also the edition by R.M. Woolley, *The Canterbury Benedictional*, HBS, 51 (London, 1917), 118 (note that the Birinus blessing used in lat. 987 and CCCC 146 also occurs in Harley 2892 for the feast of St Augustine, archbishop (*The Canterbury Benedictional*, ed. Woolley, 95–6). For discussion of the text, see Prescott, 'The Structure', 132–3 and Corrêa, 'St Austraberta'. On BN, lat. 987 (part 2), which was compiled for Christ Church, Canterbury, from Winchester material at some time in the second half of the eleventh century, see Prescott, 'The Text', esp. 133–5, Corrêa, 'St Austraberta' and Dumville, *Liturgy*, 84–5. CCCC 146, the so-called 'Samson Pontifical', carries an *ordo* for the ordination of an archbishop; this ritual could therefore have been used only by an archbishop. Palaeographical evidence would place this book at Christ Church: see esp. Dumville, *Liturgy*, 72–3.

66 One other piece of evidence for the cult of Birinus at Christ Church may be found in BL, Cotton Tiberius A iii (Christ Church, Canterbury, *saec.* xi^{med}). This manuscript, a liturgical miscellany, carries a votive vesper-office for All Saints. Among the saints invoked in this office are Birinus, Cuthbert, Swithhun, Iudoc, and Æthelthryth (see my Appendix II, no. xvii). The liturgical implications of this have been discussed by Michael Lapidge, in *Vita Æthelwoldi*, pp. lxxv–lxxvii. For an edition of the litany of this manuscript, and for further bibliographical information, see Lapidge, *Anglo-Saxon Litanies*, 71 and 174–7 (no. XVIII); see also Dumville, *Liturgy*, 137. The fact that this obviously Winchester-derived office was copied at Christ Church, Canterbury, indicates that these saints formed part of the 'classic' sanctoral commemorated at the main ecclesiastical centres in Anglo-Saxon England.

67 The secret is also found in the 'Vitellius Sacramentary'; see Appendix I.

68 Professor Andy Orchard has suggested that the scribe may have been misled by the reading *adque* (instead of *atque*, 'and'), whose beginning the scribe probably mistook for the preposition *ad* (meaning 'at'); the latter requires an accusative, hence *pastores*, and the scribe may have taken *–is* as a common spelling fault for *–es*. I am grateful to Professor Orchard for his remarks on the Latinity of these prayers.

for the secret, the Oslo missal offers an inferior reading, *oblata*, instead of the more common form *oblatio*. I give here an edition and translation of the collect and secret. The readings in square brackets I have supplied from the 'Missal of the New Minster' and the 'Robert Missal'.

> Omnipotens sempiterne Deus qui nos pia deuotion[e be]ati Birini confessoris tui adque (*sic*) pastores n[ostri in hoc sa]cratissimum oliue (*sic*) congregasti concede quesumus [ut eo]dem pastore nostro interueniente ad celes[tis ui]te gaudia peruenire mereamur. Per.
> Secr[eta]
> [S]it tibi Domine nostre deuotionis oblata accepta[bilis, ut beato Birino confessore tuo intercedente utrumque et tuae placeat maiestati et nostre proficiat saluti. Per.]

> Almighty everlasting God, who has assembled us in this most sacred sheepfold (*ouile*) on behalf of the pious devotion of your confessor and our pastor (*pastoris*), blessed Birinus, grant, we beseech you, that we may be worthy to attain the rewards of eternal life with the same, our pastor. {OMITS interveniente}
> Secret
> May this sacrifice of our devotion be acceptable to you, Lord, so that, with your confessor, blessed Birinus, interceding, it may be both pleasing to your majesty and beneficial to our salvation.

Any conjectures concerning the preface (if any) and postcommunion which must once have completed this mass-set in the Oslo missal would be difficult to make. Clearly, several mass-sets for Birinus were in circulation in Anglo-Saxon England. The surviving service-books give testimony that at least four different combinations of prayers for the mass-set were used for the feast of Birinus on 3 December.[69] The mass-set in the Oslo fragment may have been drawn from any one of the four known combinations, or it may have provided yet one further variation. One conclusion to be drawn, nonetheless, is that liturgical devotion to Birinus had a wide diffusion in Anglo-Saxon England. Therefore, attributing this fragment to Winchester purely on account of the fact that it preserves a mass for St Birinus is unreliable.

In sum, there is no certain indication that this fragment was compiled at Winchester. The mass for Birinus survives in several other Anglo-Saxon manuscripts, some of which do not hail from that centre. Evidence from calendars, litanies and benedictionals indicates that his cult was highly regarded in several other communities in Anglo-Saxon England, and in particular at Christ Church, Canterbury. Aside from the mass for Birinus, no other 'Anglo-Saxon' element has been preserved in this fragment. The masses for Andrew and Lucy and for the *Commune sanctorum*, are all standard features of medieval service-books. The more unusual aspects of this fragmentary missal, from a textual point of view, are those 'Gregorian' characteristics which are not present in most of the other Anglo-Saxon service-books. These are the 'Gregorian' sequence of sanctoral feasts, similar only to the 'Missal of Robert of Jumièges', the preface for the Common of a virgin, which derives directly from the

---

[69] The important witnesses are the 'Wulfstan Portiforium', the 'Vitellius Sacramentary', the 'Missal of Robert of Jumièges' and the 'Missal of the New Minster, Winchester'. For the prayers which each of them ascribe to the feast of 3 December, see Appendix II.

'Supplemented Gregorian', and the votive prayers for a priest, all of which derive, directly or indirectly, from the 'mixed Gregorian' of the tenth century.

The multiple 'special' masses for the priest require some explanation. These masses were to be said for the priest's spiritual benefit. Textually, the sources for these prayers are closely related to the 'mixed Gregorians'. Although most Anglo-Saxon service-books relied heavily on this sacramentary tradition, none carries this particular collection concerning the special needs of the priest, nor, apparently, such a profusion of these masses. Was this a result of compiling a missal for missionary needs? In eleventh-century Scandinavia, the missionary priest may have travelled constantly and perhaps lacked that 'community' of clerical assistants who would ordinarily have been supporting him during liturgical services. It is arguable that priests 'operated' before parishes had been delineated and that bishops had no sees as we understand the word in relation to late Anglo-Saxon England.[70] In the end, although the evidence is slight, it is possible to argue that this missal had been specially compiled for an Anglo-Saxon missionary working abroad. Had more Anglo-Saxon service-books survived, it may be that these special masses for the priest would have enjoyed a wider circulation in Anglo-Saxon England. At any rate, the Oslo fragments do give us one more illustration that the liturgical heritage peculiar to late Anglo-Saxon England was being transported to Scandinavia[71] and that these liturgical exports have much to tell us about the Anglo-Saxon Church and its liturgy.[72]

---

70 For literature on missionary priests and bishops, see Lesley Abrams, 'The Anglo-Saxons and the Christianisation of Scandinavia', *ASE*, 24 (1995), 213–49; F. Birkeli, 'The Earliest Missionary Activities from England to Norway', *Nottingham Medieval Studies*, 15 (1971), 27–37; K. Helle, 'The Organisation of the Twelfth-Century Church in Norway', in *St Magnus Cathedral and Orkney's Twelfth-Century Renaissance*, ed. Barbara Crawford (Aberdeen, 1988), 46–55; Christopher Hohler, 'The Cathedral of St Swithun at Stavanger in the Twelfth Century', *Journal of the British Archaeological Association*, 3rd series, 27 (1964), 92–119, at 94–5; C.J.A. Oppermann, *The English Missionaries in Sweden and Finland* (London, 1937); *The Christianization of Scandinavia*, ed. Birgit Sawyer, Peter Sawyer and Ian Wood (Alingsås, 1987), esp. 68–87; Peter Sawyer, 'Dioceses and Parishes in Twelfth-Century Scandinavia', in *St Magnus Cathedral*, ed. Crawford, 36–45.

71 I wish to thank Professors Michael Lapidge and David Dumville for reading this article in typescript and for offering me the benefit of their critical judgement.

72 For a different set of liturgical prayers for Birinus, see the late eleventh-century material in Oxford, Bodleian Library, Digby 39, fo. 56r–v (*Leofric Missal*, ed. Warren, 307). For musical notation from an office for Birinus, see Hartzell, 'A St Albans miscellany', noted here in Appendix II, no. xviii.

Appendix I

Sources/ analogues for the prayers in the Oslo missal fragment. The folios are specified by the first word in parentheses. The following abbreviations are used for the sources/ analogues.

BCant	'Canterbury Benedictional', as pd by Woolley
GeA	'Angoulême Sacramentary', as pd by Saint-Roch, *Liber sacramentorum Engolismensis*
GeG	'Gellone Sacramentary', as pd by Dumas and Deshusses, *Libersacramentorum Gellonensis*
GeV	'Old Gelasian', as pd by Mohlberg, *Liber sacramentorum romanaeaecclesiae ordinis anni circuli*
GrH	Gregorian (*Hadrianum*), as pd in vol. i of Deshusses, *Le sacramentaire grégorien*
GrSp	Gregorian (Supplemented), as pd in vol. i of Deshusses, *Le sacramentaire grégorien*
GrTc	Gregorian (comparative texts), as pd in vols. ii and iii of Deshusses, *Le sacramentaire grégorien*
LMa	'Leofric Missal', as pd by Warren
MNM	'Missal of the New Minster, Winchester', as pd by Turner
MRob	*Missal of Robert of Jumièges*, as pd by Wilson
Vit. A xviii	'Vitellius Sacramentary' (London, British Library, Cotton Vitellius A xviii)
Wf	'Wulfstan Portiforium', as pd by Hughes

Prayer Number	*Folio Number*	*Type of Prayer*	*Sources/Analogue (limited selection)*
[Natale S. Andreae]			
1	239–6r (audierunt)	secreta	GrH 771; MNM 187; MRob 229
2	209–5r (michi)	prefatio	GrH 772; MNM 187
3	209–5r (michi)	post communionem	GrH 773; MNM 188; MRob 229
[Deposito S. Birini]			
4	239–6v (Omnipotens)	collecta	MNM 189; MRob 229
5	239–6v (Omnipotens)	secreta	MNM 189; MRob 230; Vit. A xviii, fo. 146r–v
[Octavus] S. Andreae			
6	209–5v (Andree)	collecta	GeV 1085; GeG 1705; MNM 190; MRob 230

Prayer Number	Folio Number	Type of Prayer	Sources/Analogue (limited selection)
7	209–5v (Andree)	secreta	GeV 1086; GeG 1706; MNM 190; MRob 230
8	209–5v (Andree)	post communionem	GeV 1087; GeG 1707; MNM 190; MRob 230
[Natale] S. Lucie			
9	209–5v (Andree)	collecta	GrH 784; MNM 191; MRob 230
[Unius confessoris]			
10	209–1r (et eius)	collecta	GeG 1781; GrTc 3316; Wf 2072
Plurimorum confessorum			
11	209–1r (et eius)	collecta	GrSp 1236; MNM 203; MRob 237
12	209–1v (et eius)	secreta	GrSp 1237; MNM 203; MRob 237
13	209–1v (et eius) + 209–2r (exorare)	prefatio	GrSp 1716; MNM 203; MRob 237
14	209–2r (exorare)	post communionem	GrSp 1238; MNM 204; MRob 237
Un[ius uir]gin\<is\>			
15	209–2r (exorare)	collecta	GrSp 1239; MNM 204
16	209–1v (specie)	secreta	GrSP 1241; MNM 204
17	209–1v (specie) + 209–2v (laborius)	prefatio	GrSp 1717; GrTc 3390; (cf. MNM 204, 1st half only)
[Pro monachis]			
18	209–6r (tue)	secreta	GrTc 2261
19	209–6r (tue)	post communionem	GrTc 2264; GrSp 1312; MRob 250; LMa 186
Miss[a sa]cerdotis propria			
20	209–6r (tue)	collecta	GeA 2302; GrTc 2163
[Missa sacerdotis]			
21	209–6v (-UNIO-)	post communionem	GeA 2306; GrTc 2183
[missa sa]cerdotis propria			
22	209–6v (-UNIO-)	collecta	??

Prayer Number	Folio Number	Type of Prayer	Sources/Analogue (limited selection)
[Missa sacerdotis]			
23	209–3r (Da quesumus)	secreta	GrTc 2101 (Missa Alcuini)
24	209–3r (Da quesumus) + 209–4r (perpetuam)	post communionem	GrTc 2103 (Missa Alcuini)
Alia m[issa] sacer[dotis pro se canere debet]			
25	209–4r (perpetuam) + 239–7r (mihi)	collecta	GeG 1867; GrTc 2078; MRob 252; LMa 181
26	239–7r (mihi) + 209–3v (non habet)	secreta	GeG 1870; GrTc 2084
27	209–3v (non habet) + 209–4v (-entibus)	post communionem	Cf. GrTc 2082; cf. MRob 252
Mis[sa pr]o salute uiuorum vel mortuorum			
28	239–7v (eorum)	collecta	GrSp 1448; MRob 311; LMa 192

Appendix II

Prayers and blessings for St Birinus in Anglo-Saxon service-books.[67]

Deposition (3 December)

(i) **collecta**   'Deus qui nos per beatum confessorem tuum atque pontificem Byrinum ad cognitionem ... sentiamus suffragia.'
(Manuscripts: Vit. A. xviii, fo. 146r.

(ii) **collecta**   Omnipotens sempiterne Deus qui nos pia deuotione beati Byrini confessoris ... peruenire mereamur.'
Manuscripts: MNM 189; Oslo, Riksarkivet, no. 4 (as numbered above); MRob 229

(iii) **secreta**   Sit tibi Domine nostre deuotionis oblatio acceptabilis .. maiestati et nostre proficiat saluti.'
Manuscripts: MNM 189; MRob 230; Vit. A.xviii, fo 146r/v; Oslo, Riksarkivet, no. 5 (as numbered above).

(iv)	**prefatio**	Qui beatum Birinum confessorem tuum nobis doctorem donare dignatus es ... super nos predicamus gratiam abundanter effulsam.' Manuscripts: MNM 189; MRob 230. Ref: Moeller, *Corpus Praefationum* V, no. 838.
(v)	**post communionem**	'Concede quaesumus omnipotens Deus ut beati Byrini confessoris tui nos ubique .. tui nominis peruenire donasti.' Manuscripts: MNM 189; Wf 1983.
(vi)	**post communionem**	'Mysteriis refecti Domine Deus quesumus ut beati Byrini... obtulimus maiestati.' Manuscripts: MRob 230; Vit. A.xviii, fo 146v.
(vii)	**alia oratio**	'Deus qui in diuersis populis preclaros uerae fidei constituisti doctores ... et futura beatitudinis gloriam consequantus.' Manuscripts: Wf 1982.
(viii)	**alia oratio**	Deus qui preconem uerbi tui Birinum pontificalis gloriae honore sublimasti ... fonte salutis purgauit renascendo.' Manuscripts: Wf 1984.
(ix)	**benedictio**	(a) 'Deus qui per euangeli[c]um beati pontificis Byrini ministerium ... deuotionem. (b) Et qui plurimorum pro salute laboriosam suscepit ... per interentionem. (c) Qui etiam post mortem miraculis meruit luculenter ... obtineat suffragis.' Manuscripts: BCant 118. Ref: Moeller, *Corpus Benedictionum Pontificalium* II, no. 1058.
(x)	**benedictio**	(a) 'Multiplicet in uobis Dominus suam benedictionem ... agnitionem. (b) Eius ubique uos ab omni malo protegat ... peccatorum remissio. (c) Quo per tanti suffragatoris interuentum ... uenerabile sacramentum.' Manuscripts: CCCC 146, pp. 274–5; (BCant 95–6, for Archbishop Augustine); Paris, BN, lat. 987, fo. 107r/v (and fo. 92r), for Archbishop Augustine). Ref: Moeller, *Corpus Benedictionum Pontificalium* II, no. 1500.

Translatio (4 September)

(xi) **collecta**	'Deus qui nos veneranda festivitatis ... salutis eterne.' Manuscripts: MNM 155; Vit. A xviii, fo. 118r; Wf 1913.
(xii) **secreta:**	Munera qui tue deferimus maiestati ... redemptione gaudere.' Manuscripts: MNM 155; Vit. A xviii, fo. 118v.
(xiii) **prefatio**	'Cuius uiuifice incarnationis assumpta ... coronam percepit.' Manuscripts: MNM 155 Ref: Moeller, *Corpus Praefationum*, IV, no. 205.
(xiv) **post communionem**	'Haec nos Domine communio salutaris ab omni ... nobis adquirat.' Manuscripts: MNM 156; Vit. A xviii, fo. 118v.
(xv) **post communionem**	'Deus qui beatum Byrinum confessorem tuum atque pontificem presenti ... adiuuari mereamur in celis.' Manuscripts: MNM 156; Wf 1914.

Liturgical invocations

(xvi) **psalter oratio**	'O presules semper in Christo summo honore colendi, Birine et Swithune et sancte Athelwolde, cum omnibus sanctis ... merear adiungi mansionibus in aeternum'. Manuscripts: Wf p. 15 of Hughes's edition.
(xvii) **de omnibus sanctis ad vesperam**	'Beate Birine, predicator egregie, succurre nobis tua sancta intercessione.' Manuscripts: London, British Library, Cotton Tiberius A iii, fo. 5r–v. Commentary: Lapidge, *Vita Æthelwoldi* pp. lxxv–lxxvii.

Musical portions of the Office

(xviii)	Rhymed office (possibly secular; containing responsories for matins, antiphons for lauds, vespers, and the lesser hours). Manuscripts: New York, Pierpont Morgan Library, 926, fos 74r–76r. Commentary: Hartzell, 'A St. Albans Miscellany', pp. 38–42, with edition on pp. 58–9.

Chapter 14

The Saint Clement Dedications at Clementhorpe and Pontefract Castle: Anglo-Scandinavian or Norman?

Barbara E. Crawford

There were two churches dedicated to St Clement in Yorkshire, one at Clementhorpe, York, on the River Ouse, and the other a chapel in the Castle of Pontefract. These were apparently the most northerly St Clement churches in England and their existence raises some interesting, if unanswerable, questions about their origin and function, for neither of them was a typical medieval parish church. A discussion of their history and location touches on ethnic, cultural, economic, topographic and toponymic issues, all of which are relevant to the overall study of the cult of St Clement in England.[1] The main aim of this overall study is to look at the known circumstances of all those surviving churches – and the not inconsiderable number of churches which have not survived – in an attempt to try and make an assessment of possible circumstances which could have underlain the choice of Clement for patron saint of each particular church.[2]

The distribution of churches dedicated to St Clement in the British Isles is very uneven, and rather peculiar. There are about fifty known medieval foundations in England, four in Scotland, none in Wales and only one in Ireland (in Dublin). Of the English examples thirty were east of the River Thames, in the Danelaw, with two in London, some scattered examples around the coast of south-east England and a cluster in the far south-west. Immediately south and west of the Thames the number of dedications is very few indeed (see Fig. 14.1). The preponderance can therefore be seen to be in the Danelaw with an additional link to ports around some other coastal parts of England. However this 'Danelaw' link is only applicable to the southern part of the area settled by Danes in the ninth century. North of the Humber there is a marked absence of any Clement churches, except for the two to be discussed here, which are of course in the southern part of Northumbria, although Pontefract actually lies south of the river system which flows into the Humber estuary. This

---

 1   This is part of a long-running study of the cult of St Clement in England, Scotland, Norway and Denmark, see n. 90 below.

 2   In this study I have been fortunate to benefit from the gallant efforts of many friends and acquaintances who have helped me to track down the sites of obscure and vanished churches dedicated to Clement. Nicholas was among these and I offer this contribution in recognition of his response to my request for help in relation to St Clement's, West Bromwich (neither obscure nor vanished) and St Clement's, Rochester, which formerly stood at the south-eastern end of the bridge over the River Medway.

Figure 14.1 Map of medieval churches dedicated to St Clement in England

overall absence may have something to do with the non-urbanised nature of Anglo-Saxon and Norman Northumbria, in which York and Pontefract were almost the only urban conglomerations.

Clementhorpe and Pontefract castle are therefore two northern outliers of the main area of distribution of churches dedicated to St Clement. We might perhaps expect them not to be typical examples of the genre, which is in fact the case. What are the typical examples like? It is the link with urban centres which is most striking, for virtually all the pre-Conquest boroughs in East Anglia had a Clement church (except Thetford), as did three of the Five Boroughs (Lincoln, Leicester and Stamford). Other established urban centres further south and west, such as Oxford, Winchester, Worcester and Exeter also had one, as well as some of the south-east and south coast ports, already mentioned, like Rochester, Hastings, Sandwich and Old Romney. In nearly all the urban locations the Clement church is closely linked with the sea and waterway and very often it is located at the end of the bridge or river crossing (Oxford, Cambridge, Huntingdon, Norwich, Rochester and Worcester). These factors have been noted by previous historians[3] and the strong assumption has been that they must be associated with the Danish communities who were involved in trading and who adopted Clement as their patron saint in circumstances where their lives were in danger from the sea on which they spent a good deal of their time. St Clement was well-known as a protective saint for seafarers.

This strong association with the sea and with the Danish trading community therefore stamps the urban churches, although the question of when exactly the churches were founded is not easy to answer. The general assumption has been that the examples in towns and ports are of tenth- or eleventh-century date. The rural ones highlight other situations where a fear of drowning is very relevant. Of the seven examples in Lincolnshire four are on a coast which has been subject to very great change and in situations where there was serious erosion. In fact two of the churches (Sutton and Skegness) were both washed away in the later middle ages. They appear to have been (and Grainthorpe certainly was) built on mounds of ash and sand left behind by extensive salt production. These were unstable and their populations must have lived in fear of inundation.[4]

In both Lincolnshire and Norfolk the popularity of the cult in the surrounding localities probably reflects spin-off from the urban centres and the impetus to choose Clement could have been underlain by commercial factors, especially fishing. It is noteworthy that the church of Fiskerton, a few miles down river from Lincoln, at a crossing place of the River Witham, a location which had been immensely significant as a cult place since the Bronze Age,[5] was dedicated to Clement. Leofgifu of London gifted it to Peterborough Abbey, leading to a dispute between the abbey and Queen

---

3   Jeremy Haslam, ed. *Anglo-Saxon Towns in Southern England* (Chichester, 1984); Jeremy Haslam, *Early Medieval Towns in Britain, c. 700 to 1140* (Princes Risborough, 1985); Tim Tatton-Brown, 'The Anglo-Saxon Towns of Kent', in *Anglo-Saxon Settlements*, ed. Della Hooke (1988); Brian S. Ayers, *The English Heritage Book of Norwich* (London, 1994); Nigel Baker and Richard Holt, *Urban Growth and the Medieval Church: Gloucester and Worcester* (Aldershot, 2004), 207–10.

4   Richard Morris, *Churches in the Landscape* (London, 1989), 346.

5   Naomi Field and Mike Parker Pearson, *Fiskerton: an Iron Age Timber Causeway with Iron Age and Roman Votive Offerings: the 1981 Excavation* (Oxford, 2003); David Stocker and Paul Everson, 'The Straight and Narrow Way: Fenland Causeways and the Conversion of the Landscape in the Witham Valley, Lincolnshire' in *The Cross goes North: Processes of Conversion in Northern Europe, AD 300–1300*, ed. Martin Carver (York and Woodbridge, 2003), 271–88; David Stocker, 'The Washingborough to Fiskerton Causeway' in *The Monasteries of the Witham Valley* (forthcoming).

Edith,[6] and this evidence shows that the manor was valuable, probably because of the produce of fishing. One of the few Clement churches south of the Thames was at Fisherton, near Salisbury, and duplication of the 'fisher' place-name with another church dedicated to Clement can hardly be coincidental. This moreover is in a part of the country where Danish influence is most unlikely to be relevant to the choice of saint, and alerts us to the likely knowledge of Clement's protective powers for those who fished, and who had to cross dangerous fords, among the Anglo-Saxon population.

Certainly there is evidence to show that Clement was well-known and revered in Anglo-Saxon England: his feast (23 November) appears in all but one of the 27 calendars.[7] He occurs in litanies[8] and is regularly commemorated in liturgical books and in martyrologies.[9] His relics could be found at Bath, Canterbury, Glastonbury, Hyde Abbey (Winchester), Lincoln, St Alban's, Salisbury, Waltham, Windsor Royal Chapel and York, although they counted for only a few among many relics of other saints at most of these major churches and some may be post-1100.[10] His passion and miracles were recounted by Abbot Ælfric in his homily for 23 November.[11] An important piece of evidence for him being revered as a saint with properties to help those in danger of drowning is in the Anglo-Saxon metrical calendar, where there is reference to the feast of the man who drowned on the sea-floor 'for which reason formerly lots of men often call on Clement in their need' (*besenctum on sægrund sigefæstne wer, on brime haran, þe iu beorna fela Clementes oft clypiað to þearfe*).[12]

All this connection with the sea and danger of drowning is a reflex of the traditional story of Clement's martyrdom. His well-known reputation as the 'seafarer's saint' arises from the circumstances of his martyrdom by drowning, in the Sea of Azov, during the Trajanic persecutions in the late first century AD. Clement was probably third successor to St Peter, and wrote an authoritative Letter to the Corinthians *c.* 96 AD.[13] There is little more that can be historically attested about him, although traditions about his supposed martyrdom were circulating in the fifth century. A

---

6 Peter Sawyer, *Anglo-Saxon Lincolnshire*, A History of Lincolnshire, 3 (Lincoln, 1998), 241.

7 Rebecca Rushforth, *An Atlas of Saints in Anglo-Saxon Calendars* (Cambridge, 2002).

8 *Anglo-Saxon Litanies of the Saints,* ed. Michael Lapidge, HBS, 106 (London, 1991), 248–52.

9 Michael Lapidge, 'The saintly life in Anglo-Saxon England' in *The Cambridge Companion to Old English Literature*, ed. Malcolm Godden and Michael Lapidge (Cambridge, 1991), 243–263.

10 I.G. Thomas, *The Cult of Saints' Relics in Medieval England*, unpublished Ph.D thesis, University of London (1974).

11 Joyce Hill, 'Ælfric's Homily for the Feast of St Clement', in *Ælfric's Lives of Canonised Popes*, ed. Donald Scragg, Old English Newsletter Subsidia, 30 (Kalamazoo, MI, 2001), 99–110.

12 Elliott Van Kirk Dobbie, *The Anglo-Saxon Minor Poems*, The Anglo-Saxon Poetic Records, 6 (London, 1942), 49–55.

13 *The Oxford Dictionary of Saints*, ed. David Hugh Farmer, 4th edn (Oxford, 1997), 105–106; Frances Arnold-Forster, *Studies in Church Dedications, or England's Patron Saints* (3 vols, London, 1899), I, 275–82.

great deal of apocryphal 'Clementine literature' (the *Acta*) concocted an elaborate story of his banishment to the Crimea where he was so successful in converting the prisoners in the marble quarries, and among the local community, that the Roman authorities got rid of him by throwing him into the sea with an anchor round his neck – the anchor thus becoming his special attribute.[14] This gave him a particular association with those in danger of drowning, and he was also successful in praying for a well of spring water to fertilise the barren land, so that he is found quite often associated with wells.[15] Miracles followed his burial in a stone shrine on a rocky islet surrounded by water which receded once a year for his adherents to visit. The most famous miracle concerned a child who had been cut off by the returning waters and was presumed drowned but was found by his mother the next year safe and sound. These are important legends for understanding the association of Clement churches with places subject to flooding and near fords, as is very evident in eastern England.

This martyr-pope was potentially a powerful saint of the early church but, for the cult to take off, relics were needed. Such relics were miraculously discovered by Cyril and Methodius, the apostles of the Slavs, who, during their missions among the Khazars in the Crimea, found some scattered bones and an anchor on a mound in the Sea of Azov.[16] They took these relics to Rome in 867 where they were interred amid great rejoicing in the church of San Clemente.

This was a most important development for the spread of the cult in both east and west, and probably led to a great expansion of churches dedicated to Clement. As far as northern Europe is concerned, the evidence of church dedications shows that Clement became popular in certain areas, as around the middle Rhine for instance, but not in others. For present purposes it is the pattern of churches in the North Sea world which is of significance, for after conversion the Danes in particular found in him a congenial protector for them in their maritime activities. The evidence of the location of Clement churches in Denmark, particularly in early urban centres, has been understood to show that many of these churches can with certainty be related to the eleventh century and some of these to the first half of that century, probably from the reign of Cnut. They were in places which were of political importance and in several instances appeared to relate to royal estates and residences in the towns.[17] This evidence has been taken to suggest that Clement's later fame as a protective saint for seafarers cannot have been the whole explanation for his adoption at this early date, and that other factors have to be considered, prime among them being a 'power-political significance', and part of a 'conscious act to maintain, with the help of the patron saint, a demand for political power'.[18] How exactly the cult came

---

14 Dietrich Hofmann, *Die Legende von Sankt Klemens in den skandinavischen Ländern im Mittelalter*, Beiträge zur Skandinavistik, 13 (Frankfurt am Main, 1997), 12.

15 Ibid., 170.

16 Ibid., 144–5.

17 Barbara Crawford, 'The Cult of Clement in Denmark', *Historie*, Jysk Selskab for Historie (2006, part 2), 235–82 at 238–40, 272–3.

18 Erik Cinthio, 'The Churches of St Clemens in Scandinavia', *Archaeologia Lundensia*, 3 (1968), 103–116, at p.113.

to Denmark in these early days of church establishment is not known, although it could have been from the south, from Germany, or more probably from the west, from England.[19] In Norway, where there is evidence for the establishment of some early Clement churches in the towns by the kings, interest in the saint could also have come from the east, via royal connections with Kiev, which was a centre for the cult in the Russo-Byzantine church. Olaf Haraldsson (the Saint) might also have been influenced by the cult of Clement when he was baptised in Rouen; here there was a church dedicated to Clement near the ducal mooring-place, at the gateway to the ducal palace, in the early eleventh century.[20]

It will be clear from this that there were many sea-borne influences and cross-currents in this late Viking period, which could explain the spread of the cult among the newly-converted Danes and Norwegians, as also the popularity of Clement in the Danish-settled parts of England. Exactly which way these currents flowed across the North Sea and who the main promoters of the cult were is not easy to define, but is not the concern of this particular study. Nor must we forget that the cult of this early papal martyr was well-known among the Anglo-Saxons, so there was an existing stratum of popularity which newly-converted Danes could build on when they were looking for suitable protectors to whom they wished to dedicate their own ecclesiastical foundations. It is not easy to be certain exactly which of these ethnic and cultural elements is most relevant to the study of individual foundations. With all these caveats in mind we can now turn to the two churches known to have been dedicated to St Clement in Yorkshire.

Clementhorpe

Clementhorpe is a suburb of York, in the extra-mural settlement which lay south-west of the city and on the west bank of the River Ouse (Fig. 14.2). This was part of an extensive trading zone which may have been laid out in the Anglo-Scandinavian period by the archbishops.[21] This whole area was probably one of the shires in which the archbishop had the 'third part' mentioned in Domesday Book.[22] The shire concerned included Monkgate, Layerthorpe, Walmgate, Fishergate and Clementhorpe, which 'constituted a large shipping and marketing area straggling… along the Ouse and

---

19 Hofmann, *Die Legende*, 172–3, 187.

20 B.E. Crawford, 'The Churches dedicated to St Clement in Norway. A Discussion of their Origin and Function', *Collegium Medievale*, 17 (2004), 100–31. It is striking that there were no dedications to St Clement in Sweden proper, only round about Lund (which at this date was a Danish royal centre) and on the island of Gotland (where the Danish kings also had interests).

21 David Palliser, 'York's West Bank: Medieval Suburb or Urban Nucleus?' in *Archaeological Papers from York presented to M.W. Barley*, ed. P.V. Addyman and V.E. Black (York, 1984), 101–108 at 105.

22 A.G. Dickens, 'The "Shire" and Privileges of the Archbishop in Eleventh-Century York', *Yorkshire Archaeological Journal*, 38 (1953), 131–47.

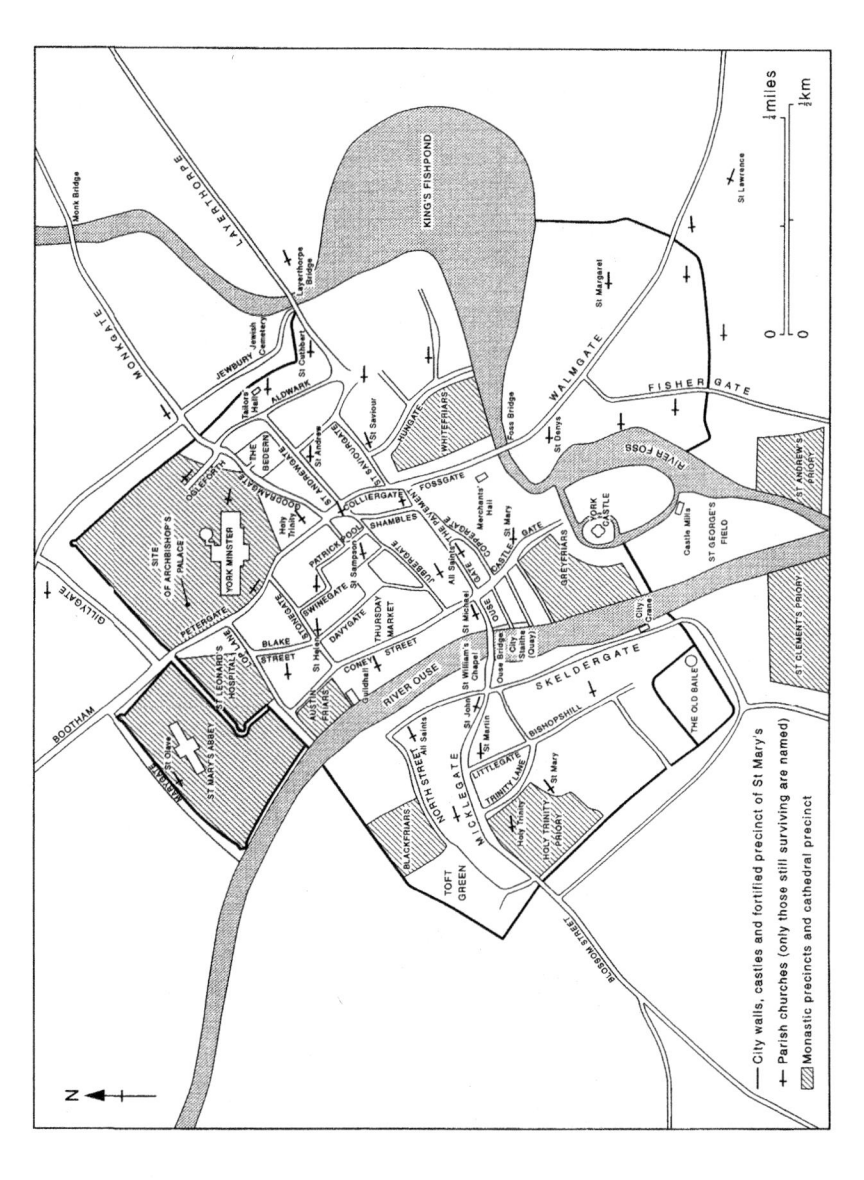

Figure 14.2 Plan of collegiate and monastic precincts in medieval York, with the site of St Clement's priory on the west bank of the River Ouse

the Foss, an area characteristic of the Anglo-Danish world of commerce'.[23] It may be that this originated in a royal grant and that the regular street-plan of Bishophill reflects a formal lay-out by the archbishops,[24] although Clementhorpe was outside the wall and further downriver. The name Clementhorpe is first documented 1070 x 1080 in the record of the archbishop's rights in York where 'alle Clemethorpe' is included[25] and there can be little doubt that these possessions date from the late Anglo-Scandinavian period. The archbishop's overlordship of Clementhorpe and the economic basis for it is well demonstrated in a slightly later inquisition (1106) which confirmed that 'all the toll in Clementesthorpe from all the ships which touch there shall be the archbishop's and below C. as far as the archbishop's land stretches; and the whole custom of fish shall be the archbishop's from both sides of the water'.[26] The significance of maritime access and resources linked to fishing at Clementhorpe is here clearly stated, which resonates with the Clement churches in Fiskerton, downriver from Lincoln and Fisherton, close to Salisbury, already mentioned. Later in the middle ages all the York shipwrights who were taxed lived in the parishes of Clementhorpe and St Mary the Old.[27]

The very name 'Clementhorpe' is of some interest and one can presuppose that it was given because of the dedication of the local church, although evidence for the dedication to Clement comes after the founding of the nunnery by Archbishop Thurstan between *c*. 1125 and 1133.[28] There are two factors to be noted about the name Clementhorpe; it is virtually unique to have this saint's name incorporated into an English place-name,[29] and it is unusual to have the name of a saint used as the first element of a 'thorpe' place-name, although there are many instances of personal names as a first element. There are of course many 'thorpe' place names in the north of England, usually denoting secondary settlements around areas of dense Scandinavian settlement,[30] and Clementhorpe was not the only satellite holding in the archbishop's liberty to be given a 'thorpe' name. One can perhaps surmise that when the name Clementhorpe was given it was the church's dedication which was the most symbolic element about the riverside settlement and the settlement's main

---

23 A.G. Dickens, 'York before the Norman Conquest' in *The Victoria History of Yorkshire: the City of York*, ed. P.M. Tillott (London and Oxford, 1961), 2–24 at 20.

24 Palliser, 'York's West Bank', 105.

25 David Palliser, *Domesday York*, Borthwick papers, 78 (York, 1990), 25 and 7.

26 R.B. Dobson and Sara Donaghey, *The History of Clementhorpe Nunnery*, The Archaeology of York: Historical Sources for York Archaeology after AD 1100, 2/1 (London, 1984), 8.

27 Palliser, 'York's West Bank', 105–106, and quoting J.H. Harvey, *York* (London and Sydney, 1975), 115–6 and 120 that 'the maritime quarter of York was still in the archbishop's fee ... in and near Clementhorpe'. Note that the seal of the later nunnery appears to show St Clement holding a ship (Dobson and Donaghey, *Clementhorpe Nunnery*, plate III).

28 Dobson and Donaghey, *Clementhorpe Nunnery*, 9.

29 The place called St Clements in Cornwall is named after the church dedication, but the parish also had an older alternative name – Moresk.

30 Gillian Fellows Jensen, *Scandinavian Settlement Names in Yorkshire* (Copenhagen, 1972), 153, where it is said that the element remained in use as a place-name forming element into the eleventh century, and indeed post-1066.

significance was its association with the saint. This may point towards a specially-established community of fishermen-traders who chose – or had chosen for them – the name of Clement as their patron and protector in the maritime dangers which they faced as a result of their occupation. As Dobson and Donaghey say 'it seems hard to resist the conclusion that his appearance in that place-name was due to the Scandinavian settlers of York and its vicinity at some indeterminable date in the tenth or eleventh century',[31] but it might also be said that it was due to the particular occupation of a sector of the Scandinavian population. Clearly the name would only have been given after the Danish community was converted, and the date of that event is in itself an open question, although a recent assessment believes that it happened 'relatively quickly' after the Danish conquest of York in 866/7.[32] But where did the initiative come from that inspired them to choose Clement? Might he not have been suggested as a suitable patron by one of the archbishops if they were responsible for sponsoring a planned settlement on the west bank? They may well have encouraged traders to settle downstream around the mooring and unloading place where Clementhorpe developed, and at the same time might have seen to the pastoral requirements of the trading community. It has recently been argued that the archbishops were the real commercial and political leaders in York during the reigns of the Danish and Irish-Norse kings.[33] They were also closely involved with many of the churches in the west bank quarter, several of which are known to have had Saxon predecessors.[34]

The strategic significance of the archbishops' district is evident from the building of castles in the area after the Norman Conquest. The Old Baile 'was planted across the heart of the archbishop's Bishophill-Clementhorpe commercial district'.[35] Somewhere hereabouts lay the earliest Guildhall, mentioned as *les gildegard* in the *c.* 1080 list of archiepiscopal rights. The prominence of the area in the city's commercial history faded in the thirteenth and fourteenth centuries, and, as Palliser says, 'it is to archaeological rather than documentary evidence that we must look for further information on the great days of the west bank'.[36] Any doubts about the existence of a church at Clementhorpe before the foundation of the nunnery there by Archbishop Thurstan in the early twelfth century should be dispelled by the archaeological discovery of 'a massive structure of pre-Conquest date' aligned east-west on the site.[37] It must have been a public building, most probably a church, and, if so, clearly one that had been founded by someone or a group of people with

---

31 Dobson and Donaghey, *Clementhorpe Nunnery*, 7.

32 David Rollason, *Northumbria, 500–1100. Creation and Destruction of a Kingdom* (Cambridge, 2003), 237. See discussion of the 'rapidity' of conversion in the Danelaw by Lesley Abrams, 'The Conversion of the Danelaw' in *Vikings and the Danelaw*, ed. James Graham-Campbell, Richard Hall, Judith Jesch and David Parsons (Oxford, 2001), 31–44.

33 Rollason, *Northumbria*, 228–9.

34 Palliser, 'York's West Bank', 104.

35 Ibid., 106.

36 Ibid., 107.

37 D.A. Brinklow, 'Archaeological Investigations', in Dobson and Donaghey, *Clementhorpe Nunnery*, p. 5. This is seen as 'evidence to suggest, if not to prove, the existence of a church on the site before the Conquest': Barbara Wilson and Frances Mee, *The Medieval*

wealth. Coins of mid-ninth and mid-eleventh century date are said to prove that it dated from the Anglo-Scandinavian period.[38]

This study of the putative origins of the church dedicated to St Clement in York therefore throws into relief the very great problems in knowing whether such churches can really be seen as evidence of a Danish initiative in the Anglo-Scandinavian period. The historical evidence for the existence of the church dates from the foundation of a Norman nunnery, but the place-names and archaeology give strong hints of a building of pre-Conquest date. The wider context of the Anglo-Scandinavian period indicates that this saint would have been chosen by or for the mercantile community whose members must frequently have been in danger of drowning. The Anglo-Saxon predecessors of the Norman archbishops, in whose lordship the church lay, and who initiated the monastic development of Clementhorpe in the twelfth century, may have been significant in the creation of Clementhorpe as a commercial enterprise in the tenth or early eleventh century. The choice of the saint to whom the church was dedicated, and after whom the settlement was called, may have been part of that creation.

Pontefract Castle

Archbishop Thurstan, who founded the Benedictine priory of nuns at Clementhorpe, was also involved in the confirming of endowments of the chapel dedicated to St Clement in the castle of Pontefract by Ilbert II de Lacy c. 1135.[39] However the confirmation document (as known from Dodsworth's copy) quite clearly states that the original foundation was by Ilbert I de Lacy, who died c. 1093, proving that the dedication goes back before Archbishop Thurstan's time, apparently to the reign of William I (*in tempore principis supradicti*).[40] Once more the earliest historical evidence of the dedication to Clement dates from the early Norman period, but possibilities of a pre-Conquest origin will be discussed.

The situation of the Lacy Honour of Pontefract brings us to the very heart of Norman control of Yorkshire and the North. The whole basis of the Honour of

---

Parish Churches of York. The Pictorial Evidence, The Archaeology of York Supplementary Series, 1 (York, 1998), 61.

38 D.A. Brinklow, 'Pre-Conquest Structure' in *Anglo-Scandinavian Settlement South-West of the Ouse*, ed. Joan Moulden and Dominic Tweddle, The Archaeology of York, Anglo-Scandinavian York, 8/1 (London, 1986), 57–61.

39 Richard Holmes, 'The Foundation of St Clements in the Castle of Pontefract (*Mon. Ang.*, 659, 660)', *Yorkshire Archaeological Journal*, 14 (1898), 147–57 at 149. The endowments were very valuable, consisting of tithes from various places in the honour as well as gifts of tithes from the honorial barons (W.E. Wightman, *The Lacy Family in England and Normandy 1066–1194* (Oxford, 1966), 61).

40 '*Quando Ilbertus de Laceo in honorem dei et sancte Marie, et omnium sanctorum ecclesiam beati Clementis in castello suo pro salute Willelmi regis maioris, Willelmi (filii interlined) ejus et filiorum suorum, et pro salute omnium fidelium vivorum et mortuorum in tempore principis supradicti fundavit*' (Holmes, 'The foundation', 155); Holmes deduces that there can only have been a short period of time between the listing of sub-tenants in the Foundation Charter and the list of the same land-holders in the Domesday Survey (ibid. 150).

Pontefract was its strategic position.[41] The creation of this vast landholding, mostly in West Yorkshire, but stretching across the Pennines into Lancashire, was for the purpose of maintaining control in an area of his new kingdom which caused William the Conqueror some grief. The situation of the castle of Pontefract on its sandstone bluff above the low-lying lands of the Aire valley was particularly strategic, controlling all the land routes which had to pass between the Pennine uplands and the marshes around the head of the Humber (see Fig. 14.3). It dominated the Great

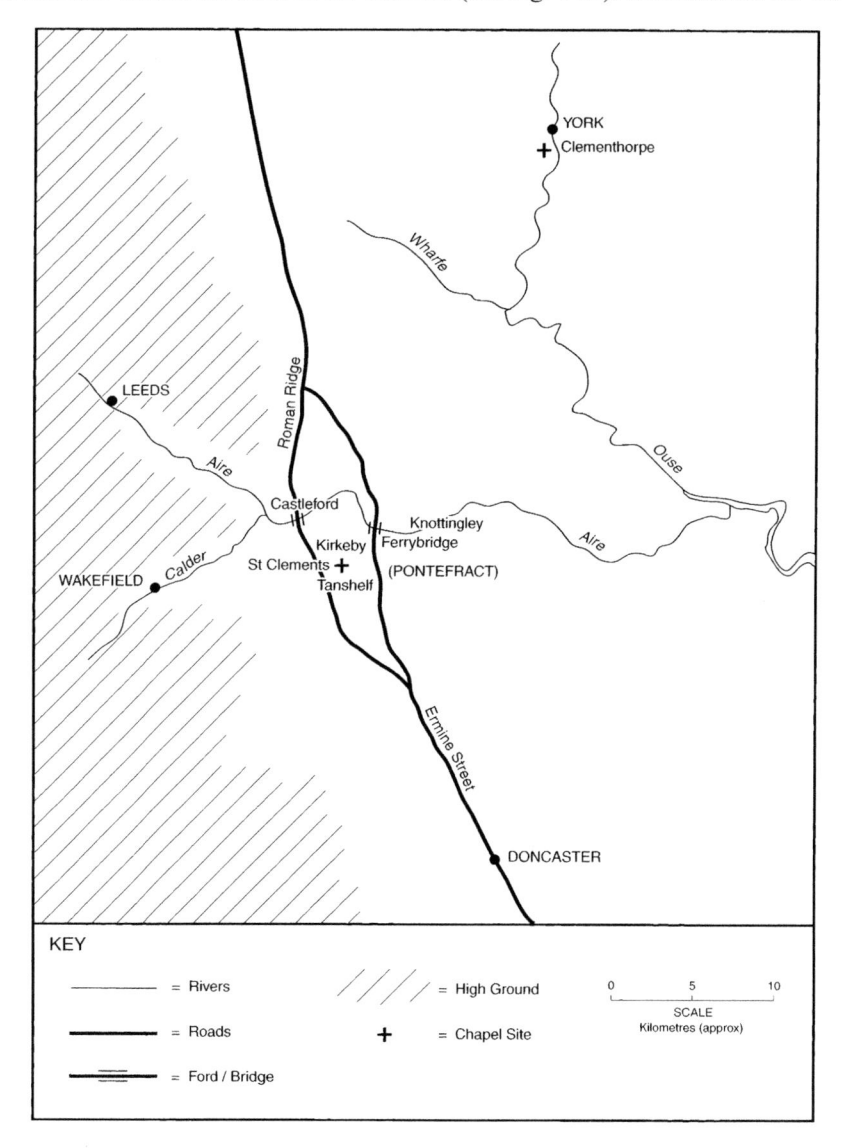

Figure 14.3   Map of routes and rivers in southern Yorkshire

---

41   Wightman, *The Lacy Family*, 19, 31.

North Road (Ermine Street), which passed nearby and crossed the Aire at Castleford, two and a half miles away. There is no mention of the castle in Domesday Book, but it was built before Ilbert died in the middle of William Rufus' reign.[42] 'The chapel, being an integral part of the building, would have been endowed formally at or soon after its completion, probably at the first assembly of the barons there.'[43]

Ilbert I was a fairly generous benefactor of existing religious houses in the north of England,[44] while his son Robert founded the Cluniac Priory of St John at Pontefract.[45] The question we have to ask is: why was St Clement chosen to be the patron of the chapel of the main Lacy stronghold, when there is no evidence to show that the Lacy family had any close association with any of the other churches dedicated to Clement in England, or indeed in Normandy?[46] It should also be noted that this appears to be the only castle chapel in the whole list of known Clement dedications in England;[47] it is quite isolated, being 26 miles south of Clementhorpe and over 50 miles north of Lincoln, where there were two churches dedicated to Clement. It was not known to Frances Arnold-Forster, for it does not appear in her list of Clement church dedications,[48] or, not being a parish church, was not considered significant enough by her to be included. Nonetheless its significance in terms of the status of the foundation is considerable (see later).

Are there similar resonances at Pontefract with regard to the well-established Clementine associations with watery locations, trading and fishing activities and the associated dangers from drowning that we have already noted in the context of Clementhorpe? Its position controlled the main road north where it crossed the River Aire, and although Pontefract Castle is not directly above the river it certainly controls the southern access to the Aire near its confluence with the Calder, where the requirements of ferrying and fording have been exceedingly important through

---

42 As argued by P. Dalton, *Conquest, Anarchy and Lordship: Yorkshire 1066–1154* (Cambridge, 1994), 67, 75–6, it seems very likely that some form of castle had been constructed by the Conqueror here well before this date.

43 Wightman, *Lacy Family*, 24.

44 Ibid., 60–61.

45 *The Chartulary of St John of Pontefract*, ed. Richard Holmes, Yorkshire Archaeological Society Record Series, 25, 30 (2 vols, Leeds, 1899–1902), I, nos. 1–7. Despite problems of authenticity with some of these charters (see *Early Yorkshire Charters*, ed. William Farrer, Yorkshire Archaeological Society Record Series Extra Series (3 vols, Leeds, 1914–1916), III, nos. 1475–9 for references to the chapel of St Clement, and especially pp. 178–9; see also *English Episcopal Acta, 20: York 1154–1181*, ed. Marie Lovatt (Oxford, 2000), 80), it is argued by Wightman, (*The Lacy Family*, 8–9) that there is a 'true tradition' behind them, probably deriving from earlier genuine charters.

46 The place from where the Lacy family originated in Normandy is supposed to be Lassy in Calvados (*Chartulary of St John*, ed. Holmes, 16); the family had some lands near Bayeux, and had some associations with Bishop Odo (Wightman, *The Lacy Family*, 60). Churches in Normandy dedicated to St Clement are all coastal, and are particularly to be found along the west coast of the Cotentin.

47 Unless the vanished church of St Clements in the Bail in the upper city of Lincoln, which appears to have been associated with the castle according to late medieval sources, could have been in origin a castle chapel.

48 Arnold-Forster, *Church Dedications*, III, 349.

the centuries.[49] Indeed the fact that the very name of Pontefract was eventually given to the castle and town nearby shows how relevant the bridge – or the lack of one! – was to the castle establishment.[50] The Conqueror is said by Orderic Vitalis to have been held up 'ad fracti pontis aquam' for three weeks in 1069 on his way north to deal with the major northern revolt (see below), and that the river was passable neither by boats nor ford.[51] There were important ferries across the Aire at both Fryston and Ferrybridge, and the place-name 'Fereia', mentioned in 1086, is pre-Conquest in origin.[52]

Fishing activities are a very relevant element here also, for the only fishery recorded in Domesday Book for the whole of west Yorkshire was at Tanshelf, a royal manor, along with three mills.[53] Some of these would have been located on the River Aire, so the fact that they are recorded under Tanshelf shows the close association between the manor and the products of the river. Moreover when Ilbert endowed the chapel of St Clement he included the tithes of the fishery in Knottingley (*decimam piscatorie Knottingleie*), which lies close to Ferrybridge.[54] This rich source of charter evidence shows that there are elements in relation to the Castle chapel which fit with the geographical situation of other Clement churches and it might be plausibly suggested that the founder of the chapel in the castle of Pontefract chose St Clement as patron firstly because of the saint's protective powers for those who undertook what was evidently a difficult crossing of a river lying athwart the main land route north, and secondly because of the river fishery which was also associated with the endowment of the chapel.

Another factor which can be added to the picture is the proto-urban status of Pontefract in 1086, for under the Domesday entry for Tanshelf are recorded the presence of 60 'lesser burgesses'.[55] The close link of Clement churches with

---

49 Margaret Faull, 'The Late Anglo-Saxon Period' in *West Yorkshire: an Archaeological Survey to A.D.1500*, West Yorkshire Metropolitan County Council (4 vols, Wakefield, 1981), I, 199.

50 There is some confusion as to where exactly this broken bridge was situated (Faull, 'The post-Roman period', 199), but it would seem most likely to have been the remains of a Roman stone bridge across the Aire at Castleford, which is the route taken by Ermine Street.

51 *The Ecclesiastical History of Ordericus Vitalis*, ed. Marjorie Chibnall (6 vols, Oxford, 1968–1980), II, 230; the text is quoted by E.A. Freeman, *The History of the Norman Conquest* (6 vols, Oxford, 1869–79), IV, 285–7. See also Dalton, *Conquest*, 11, 67.

52 *Domesday Book: a Complete Translation*, tr. Ann Williams and G.H. Martin (London, 1992), 824, 867; also Faull, 'The Late Anglo-Saxon Period', 199. Bondgate, the king's highway east of Pontefract, leading to Ferrybridge (two miles away), must have led to a ferry crossing.

53 Faull, 'The Late Anglo-Saxon Period', 190, 195; *Domesday Book*, tr. Williams and Martin, 824.

54 Holmes, 'The Foundation', 155. The fishery would have consisted of some form of weir on the river (S.A. Moorhouse, 'The Rural Medieval Landscape' in *West Yorkshire: an Archaeological Survey*, III, 746). In the fourteenth century the fishing rights of the Honour of Pontefract extended along 10 km of the River Aire below Leeds (ibid., 748).

55 *Domesday Book*, tr. Williams and Martin, p. 824; 'the only place in west Yorkshire recorded as having burgesses' (Faull, 'The Late Anglo-Saxon period', 190). The only other burghal communities in Yorkshire were York itself, which was the only urban centre in

boroughs in the Danelaw has already been mentioned, so the existence of a mercantile community at the centre of the Honour is maybe also relevant. Presumably one of the commodities traded by these lesser burgesses would have been the fish netted at the weirs along the River Aire, which they could transport by boat along the river system of the Humber estuary. If a mercantile community of traders with ships was established as 'lesser burgesses' in the castlery this would also make very good sense of the choice of Clement as patron of the castle chapel.

What is particularly striking is the very high status of the ecclesiastical foundation established by the incoming Norman lord who was incorporating the chapel within his *caput*, at the very centre of his feudal Honour.[56] It was integral to the erection of the political, commercial and ecclesiastical power structures, and Clement was considered to be a highly suitable protector to have at this extremely important Norman power centre. The constant reference to the chapel of Saint Clement in the sources[57] and the numerous grants made to it, tell us of the high regard which this foundation had in the creation of Lacy power structures in the Honour and continued to have throughout the Middle Ages.[58] But there is more to this site than a newly-established Norman *caput*, for the location had already been an extremely important strategic place, royal possession and ecclesiastical centre in pre-Conquest Northumbria, which raises issues of possible continuity of the church dedication.

Tanshelf-Kirkeby

The Normans took over an Anglo-Saxon royal vill called Tanshelf, the name of which became restricted to the western end of the town, while the castle which they built came very quickly to be called Pontefract.[59] In the main Domesday entry King Edward had held this manor TRE and Ilbert de Lacy had four ploughs in 1086.[60] This is said to be the only Anglo-Saxon royal vill for which there is evidence in late Anglo-Saxon West Yorkshire,[61] and it would appear to have been a West Saxon royal possession over a century before. It was the base for King Eadred's campaign against Northumbria and is named in the Anglo-Saxon Chronicle – the first reference to its importance – as the place where Archbishop Wulfstan I and all the councillors of

---

Yorkshire, Pocklington (15 burgesses, *Domesday Book*, tr. Williams and Martin, 788) and Dadsley near Tickhill (31 burgesses, ibid., 828): the two latter were, like Pontefract, also important centres of large Norman fiefs.

56 It was a very well endowed collegiate foundation with a dean and four prebends (Holmes, 'The Foundation', 148).

57 By contrast, the name of the saint to whom the chapel in the Lacy castle of Clitheroe was dedicated is never mentioned in the documentary sources.

58 Ian Roberts, *Pontefract Castle: Archaeological Excavations 1982–6*, Yorkshire Archaeology, 8 (Leeds, 2002), 84–8.

59 Cf. the Yorkshire *Clamores*: 'In Tanshelf and Pontefract the king 16 carucates' (*Domesday Book*, tr. Williams and Martin, 867).

60 Ibid., 825, 867.

61 Faull, 'The Late Anglo-Saxon Period', 190.

Northumbria pledged their loyalty to Eadred in 947.[62] This gives a strong indication of Tanshelf's strategic position in that it 'was surely a frontier location and a suitable place to ratify an agreement between equals rather than the submission of subjects to the ruler of the territory in which they lived'.[63] In the very next year the Chronicle records that the west Saxon army, returning south from raiding, was overtaken from behind at Castleford by the 'raiding-army that was in York' and 'a great slaughter was made there',[64] signalling again the geographical importance of the routes and fords in this particular corner of south Yorkshire.

Remarkably there were not merely two names for this frontier settlement, but three.[65] Simeon of Durham records in the twelfth century that the *villa regia* Tanshelf was also called *Puntfrait Romane Anglice vero Kirkeby*[66] although the latter is of course the Danish name ('church settlement').The name *Kirkeby* occurs sporadically between *c.* 1090 and 1440,[67] but when was it given and to which church? It must have been given to the settlement by Danish speakers, presumably in the tenth or eleventh centuries. The existence of a church in 1086 is clear from Domesday ('there is a church and a priest')[68] and recent excavations have actually exposed a late Anglo-Saxon church and burial ground on the north slope of the Castle hill (at 'The Booths') and close to the parish church of All Saints.[69] Particularly relevant to St Clement's chapel and probably an extension of that Saxon cemetery, are graves of eighth-tenth century date which have been found on the Castle promontory, giving 'some reason to suppose that the focus for the graves, certainly by the late Saxon period, was in fact a church, the predecessor of what was ultimately to become St Clement's chapel' (see Fig. 14.4).[70] The 14 Saxon burials lay in and around an early chapel which was 'a two-cell structure consisting of a nave and chancel, constructed of fine-grained sandstone ashlar',[71] remodelled in the twelfth century with a very fine

---

62 *The Anglo-Saxon Chronicles*, tr. and ed. Michael Swanton, revised edn (London, 2000), 112 s.a. 947 (D).

63 Rollason, *Northumbria*, 265. It had presumably fallen into the hands of the Wessex dynasty during their campaigns against Northumbria, and had been, just as presumably, a southern frontier base for the kings of York previously.

64 *Anglo-Saxon Chronicles*, tr. Swanton, s.a. 948 (D).

65 Armitage Goodall, *Place-Names of South-West Yorkshire*, revised edn (Cambridge, 1914), 230 also includes Domesday *Tateshale* as another name.

66 *Symeonis Dunelmensis Opera et Collectanea*, ed. Hodgson Hinde, Surtees Society, 51 (1868), 77n.

67 Faull, 'Late Anglo-Saxon period', 211.

68 *Domesday Book*, tr. Williams and Martin, 824.

69 A.H. Smith thinks that the name may have been given with reference to the Cluniac priory founded *c.*1090 (*The Place-Names of the West Riding of Yorkshire*, English Place-Name Society, 30–37 (Cambridge, 1961–3), II, 79), although admitting that a church existed there in 1086. M. Beresford, *New Towns of the Middle Ages* (London, 1967), 525, thought that All Saints (a typical Anglo-Saxon dedication: see Farmer, *Oxford Book of Saints*, 16) was the likely 'kirk' of Kirkeby. However, both of them were writing before the excavations of the pre-Conquest churches and cemeteries, which have revealed the long-standing ecclesiastical presence at The Booths and on the ridge (see following footnote).

70 Roberts, *Pontefract Castle*, 85.

71 Ibid., 75.

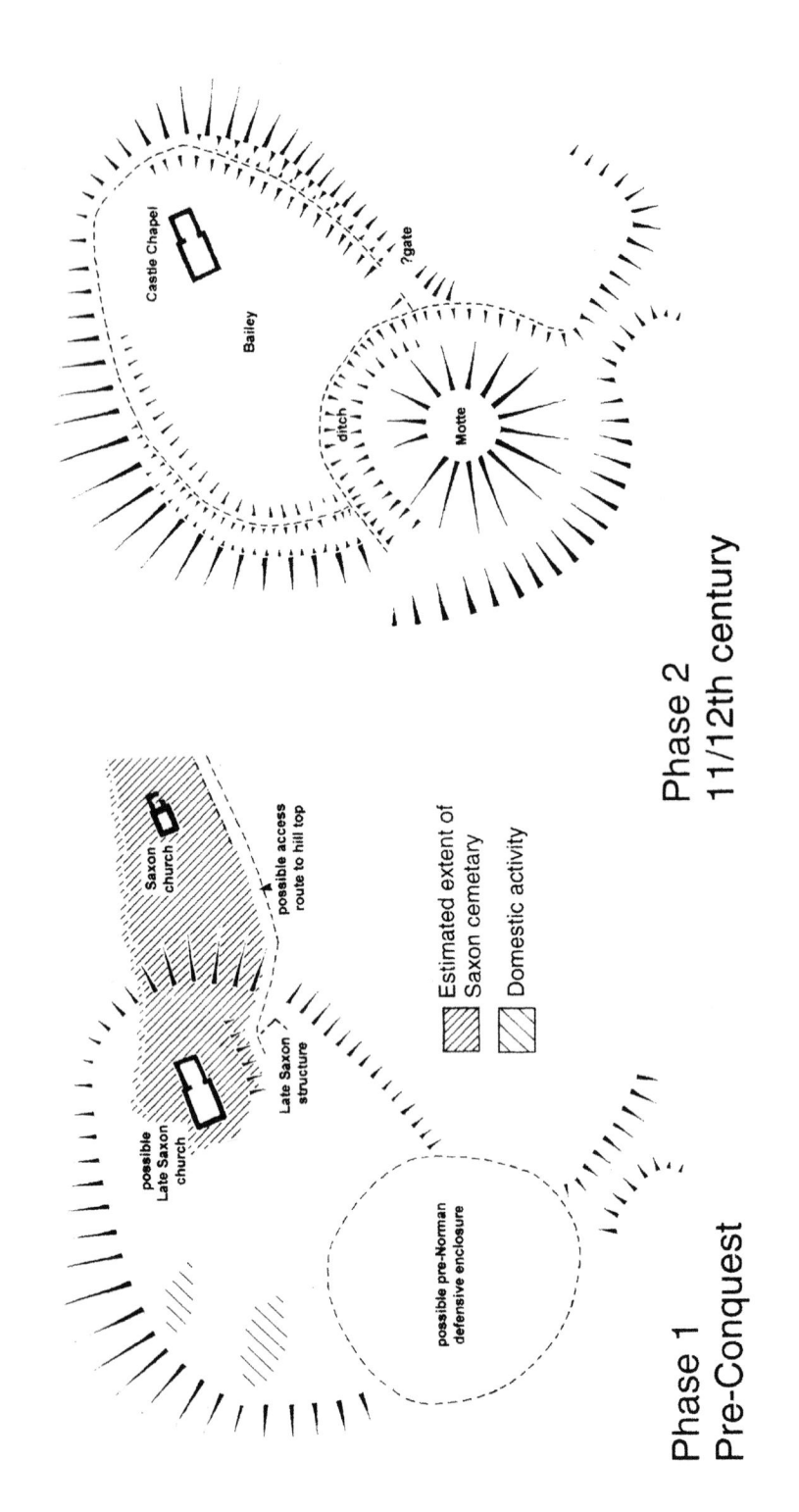

Figure 14.4 Plan of Phases 1 and 2 at Pontefract Castle from Ian Roberts, *Pontefract Castle* (Wakefield, 1990), 402

apsidal chancel made entirely of dolomitic limestone. The earlier sandstone church may have been of pre-Conquest date, for it had some typical Saxon features and the unusual location of the priest's door led the excavator to suggest that there may have been a reliquary at the east end.[72] There would seem to be convincing evidence that what sounds like a completely newly-founded and exceptionally well-endowed Norman chapel of *c.* 1090 was in fact built on an already-existing ecclesiastical site, proved by the existence of early graves and the possible accompanying two-celled stone church, the dedication of which is unknown. These may have been part of one large cemetery with the early burials at The Booths, or they may have formed a 'satellite grouping around a local focus, perhaps as kin or status groups associated with the royal palace'.[73] Whatever the relationship of the two churches and the two sets of early burials, here is archaeological evidence of a most significant pre-Conquest ecclesiastical centre, which must be the reason for the *Kirkeby* name.[74]

The position of the cemetery and early church on the ridge at the north end of the castle mount has given rise to further speculation. There is no doubt that the Church of St Clement sits awkwardly in the Norman castle enclosure, as any visitor will see (Fig. 14.5) and the excavator suggests that the de Lacy motte on the west side may have utilised an earlier Anglo-Saxon defensive position, perhaps replacing a *burh-geat* (fortified site with gatehouse)[75] and avoiding the cliff-edge location where the cemeteries and church lay. A sparse amount of archaeological evidence does point to secular settlement of Anglo-Saxon date on the castle mound. Was this the site of a pre-Conquest *burh*? If so, could it have had any commercial importance? By 1086, as we have seen, there were 60 lesser burgesses established at Tanshelf, along with three mills and a fishery, making this in some senses an important commercial centre compared with other settlement in the area.[76] Was this entirely a post-Conquest development? Maybe Ilbert was building on a pre-Conquest trading settlement; it is certainly likely that the fishery and the mills were already established in the Saxon or Anglo-Scandinavian period.[77]

This issue is crucial for the question of the date of the Saint Clement dedication. The question is whether it was given to Ilbert's castle chapel which he founded *de novo*, completely ignoring any previous ecclesiastical foundation or dedication, or whether he preferred to keep the same dedication of an already existing church, the site of which he maintained. He certainly appears to have maintained the same site, building apparently right on top of the two-cell church, which may have been of pre-Conquest date. This pointer to ecclesiastical continuity might encourage us to think that he kept Saint Clement as protector and patron. If so, why was this church in an Anglo-Saxon royal vill (or *burh)* dedicated to Clement? The relevant conditions

---

72 Ibid., 85.

73 Ibid., 401.

74 Ibid., 9. The excavator suggests (ibid., 401) that there appears to be sufficient evidence to postulate the existence of a pre-Conquest minster here.

75 Ibid., 403.

76 Ibid., 10, referring to Richard Holmes, 'Dodsworth Yorkshire Notes: the Wapentake of Osgoldcross', *Yorkshire Archaeological Journal*, 12 (1893), 42–77, at 43.

77 Faull, 'Late Anglo-Saxon period', 195–6.

Figure 14.5   The east end of St Clement's Chapel, Pontefract Castle

for the choice of a Clement dedication have already been specified – situations in which the occupation of mercantile traders put them in danger of drowning, or where travellers feared for their lives in crossing rivers on ferries or fords on foot. These dangers were present a few miles away from Tanshelf-*Kirkeby* and those Anglo-Scandinavians who gave the name of *Kirkeby* to the nearby church settlement *may* have been involved in trading, as many others were in Danelaw burhs and in York where churches dedicated to Clement also existed. But it is purely hypothetical to suggest that such traders may have existed at Tanshelf-*Kirkeby*; we can only be certain that it was a burial centre for an Anglo-Saxon population.

So far it does not appear possible to come to any conclusion as to whether the dedication to St Clement in the castle chapel of Pontefract had been given by Anglo-Scandinavian tenants of Tanshelf in the previous century, or indeed by the royal manorial lord. The evidence of the graves points to there having been a burial ground on The Booths for many centuries, but it is unlikely that a church nearby would have been dedicated to Clement for so long.[78] We have no evidence as to the circumstances of the royal vill at Tanshelf between 947 when Eadred met Archbishop Wulfstan and the Northumbrian witan there, and the evidence of Domesday Book that it belonged to King Edward in 1066. Presumably it would have been held by the earls of Northumbria, some of whom, like Eric of Lade, or Siward, may already have been

---

78   The nearby church of All Saints may be the successor to this early chapel; as noted in n. 69 the dedication was a popular one among Anglo-Saxons.

familiar with the cult of Clement in Scandinavia. But neither of them appears to have been associated with any other churches dedicated to Clement and, as is well-known, Siward dedicated his minster at Galmanho in York to the Norwegian royal martyr Olaf Haraldsson.[79] Nor, regarding the Anglo-Saxon kings' possible association, can it be said that there is any evidence that churches dedicated to Clement were located on royal estates.[80] In the absence of any positive indication as to the likelihood of a pre-Conquest date for the Clement dedication (unlike Clementhorpe, where the circumstances give a little more confidence on the matter), the possibility that it was given *de novo* by the new Norman controllers may appear more convincing. Moreover there is the dramatic situation of 1069 which can be interpreted as supplying a satisfactory explanation for the giving of this dedication.

ad Fracti Pontis aquam…Tres ebdomadas illic detinentur

Returning to the events of 1069, when William experienced a three-week delay in crossing the River Aire, it is worth pausing to consider the circumstances of this setback to his determined efforts to control the turbulent north. The resistance of the north to the Conquest 'has been told many times'[81] and the re-telling sometimes dulls an appreciation of the dramatic threat which this resistance posed to the permanency of the conquest of Anglo-Saxon England by the Normans. A few months after the successful invasion of southern England, in March 1067, the new earl who had been given authority in the north by William, Copsi, was confronted by a rebellion and murdered. His successor, Gospatric, then joined the earls Edwin and Morcar in revolt a few months later. The military campaign conducted by William in response to this situation was an impressive crackdown which saw the first castles built in an effort to control key points en route north and in York itself, the key to the north. Such an approach to the problems of Northumbria led to direct control being exercised through his immediate lieutenants rather than through native rulers. But they fared no better: the first French military commander, Robert de Commines, established himself at Durham and within a month he and his following were butchered, sparking off a co-ordinated rising. In the spring of 1069 a large force led by all the Northumbrian leaders with Edgar the Atheling, who joined them from exile in Scotland, marched south and attacked a Norman force before laying siege to York. The Conqueror led a 'lightning campaign' north and dispersed the rebels before building a second castle at York. Of course all these armed responses would have made use of the network of Roman roads, and the necessary crossing of the River Aire at Castleford in order to reach York. The situation was left in the hands of three of his closest military commanders while William returned to the safety of Winchester. But the rebels remained at large and were joined, ominously, by a Danish fleet sent by King Swein

---

79 *Anglo-Saxon Chronicles*, tr. Swanton, s.a. 1055.

80 The only historical evidence of a royal connection with a St Clement church is the recorded presence of King Edward at Mass in St Clement's Sandwich in 1046 when Earl Leofric witnessed a miraculous vision: A.S. Napier, 'An Old English Vision of Leofric, earl of Mercia', *Transactions of the Philological Society* (1908), 180–87.

81 Dalton, *Conquest, Anarchy and Lordship*, 9.

Estrithsson. On 21 September 1069 a combined assault on the castles of York ended in the slaughter of the Norman garrison and the capture of two of the commanders.

This was the situation in which the Conqueror found himself in the autumn of 1069 and the threat to the permanency of his conquest at this point was very real. He was faced by a combination of circumstances which were daunting and which needed his personal military response, for it was the threat of his presence which more than anything else appeared to demolish any sustained resistance by his opponents. When the northern rebels heard that he was coming north they appear to have abandoned any attempt to hold York against him and the Danes fled to the security of their maritime base in the Humber estuary. Two commanders were sent to Lincolnshire to engage the Danes in the Humber while William went south to Staffordshire to deal with unrest in that area. It was on his return north that he was held up at the River Aire 'which was neither fordable nor safe for navigation'[82] and he was unable to cross at the usual place.[83]

William and his forces were delayed there for three weeks and a delay of that length, probably by force of natural circumstances which he was unable to overcome, was not the sort of obstacle which William was accustomed to facing, or accepting. Orderic has detailed information about the response of those around him on the banks of the Aire: 'he rejected all advice to turn back'[84] (the easy way out); nor did he think an attempt to build a bridge was advisable, as it might have given the enemy a chance to catch them unawares.[85] Presumably he decided to dig in and wait for the conditions to improve and allow them to cross; Orderic next relates the story of the brave knight, Lisois, who, after the delay of three weeks determinedly found a fordable place, presumably further upstream, and crossed with 60 gallant knights, surviving an attack by a force on the other bank, and returning to tell William of the alternative crossing.[86] The whole Norman army then crossed at the same place and reached York traversing difficult terrain along narrow tracks, not the preferred route

---

82 *impatientem uadi nec nauigio usitatam* (Orderic, *Ecclesiastical History*, II, 230). W.E. Kapelle understands this delay to have been caused by local resistance to William, and that the north bank was held against him for three weeks (*The Norman Conquest of the North* (Chapel Hill, NC and London, 1979), 109, 117), although in a footnote he expresses uncertainty about the meaning of Orderic's text on this point.

83 This would have been either the ford at Castleford or the bridge which Stenton says 'he expected to use' but which was broken (*Anglo-Saxon England*, 3rd edn (Oxford, 1971), 604). Stenton and Douglas (*William the Conqueror* (London, 1964), 220), like Kapelle (see preceding note) consider the delay to have been due primarily to resistance from local forces.

84 Orderic, *Ecclesiastical History*, II, 230.

85 This suggests that the Norman army was ensconced in a defensible position which William was unwilling to leave for any bridge-building activity, and we can assume that the defensible position would have been on the sandstone bluff above the river plain at Tanshelf. This endorses Dalton's argument that a castle would have been constructed already at this date at Pontefract (*Conquest, Anarchy and Lordship*, 67).

86 Lisois is said to have returned to the main force the next day (so the ford he found could have been in the location of Woodlesford, ten miles upstream).

for a mounted force.[87] When they arrived at York they learned that the Danes had fled. The full details which Orderic gives of these events, the specific duration of time which he says that the Normans had to endure, the difficulties of the eventual river crossing and the march on York, as well as the fortunate outcome indicates that this was a well-remembered incident in the dramatic story of the Conqueror's conquest of the north. The safe crossing of the river is a theme which gives additional proof of his triumph over the odds, just as the safe crossing of the Channel had given evidence of the supernatural protection of the Normans at the outset of the invasion.

These dramatic incidents might therefore also provide exactly the right historical circumstances for the introduction of the Clement dedication in the stronghold which we can be certain that the Normans would have made use of from the start of their campaigns in this area, when they would have had need of this most important control point at a vital strategic location. We happen to know that William *was* appreciative of the protective powers of Saint Clement at dangerous fords when he was in a situation of military danger, for in 1047 he had given thanks at the church of Saint-Clément near Osmanville (dép. Calvados, canton Isigny-sur-Mer), after safely crossing the Passage du Grand Vey, a ford across the sands in the estuary of the River Vire. Wace in his *Roman de Rou* mentions that Duke William did this on his flight from Valognes in 1047.[88] Twenty years later he may have felt deeply grateful to St Clement for another miraculous river crossing in the very desperate situation of his campaign against the northern rebels and their Danish allies.[89] Perhaps it was the memory of this event which influenced the choice of dedication for the chapel in the castle which William granted to Ilbert de Lacy, which was one of the most important strongpoints for establishing Norman control in south Yorkshire in 1069.

Conclusion

The above discussion will have revealed exactly how difficult it is to prove anything regarding the origins of these two churches, and they serve to exemplify the wider issues regarding the foundation of St Clement churches. Both Clementhorpe and Pontefract Castle Chapel well illustrate the two strands 'Anglo-Scandinavian or Norman' posed in the question in the title to this paper. According to the evidence we have, both historical and archaeological, it can be argued that the site of the church at Clementhorpe fits into the 'Anglo-Scandinavian' context, as a church which is central to the fishing and commercial development of York in the pre-Conquest period. However, the strong archiepiscopal association gives a hint of direction from

---

87 *per silvas, paludes, montana, valles, artissimo tramite qui binos lateraliter transire non patiebatur*: Orderic, *Ecclesiastical History*, II, 230; David Hey, *Yorkshire from AD 1000* (London, 1986), 25.

88 *a grant poor et a grant ire/ passa de noit les guez de Vire/ al mostier clina Saint Clement/et preia Deu escordrement*: *Le Roman de Rou de Wace*, ed. A.J. Holden, Société des anciens textes français (3 vols, Paris, 1970, 1973), II, 23 (Part 3, lines 3675–8).

89 The savage treatment of the Northumbrians in the winter of 1069–1070 reflects William's very real fear of failure, and his determination to impose absolute authority over the north.

above over the church's establishment there as well as, possibly, over the choice of dedication.

At Pontefract the castle chapel appears firmly anchored in the Norman period of conquest in south Yorkshire, although historical evidence proves that Tanshelf was an important royal possession in the Anglo-Saxon period and excavation has shown that there was ecclesiastical presence also, which explains the additional name of *Kirkeby* at the locality. This remarkable evidence of continuity of use in this strategic place – even apparently of continuity of church site – does not mean, however, that there was continuity of church dedication. For the specific reasons which have been elaborated above, in conjunction with the evidence for the importance of the site of Pontefract castle as a symbol of Norman power and control, it seems entirely possible that the dedication to St. Clement was chosen by either the Conqueror, or his tenant-in-chief when the castle chapel was founded (or re-founded), in commemoration and recognition of the safe passage of the River Aire in 1069.[90]

---

90 It should be noted however that the foundation charter does say the church of St Clement was founded by Ilbert *in honorem dei et sancte Marie, et omnium sanctorum*. See notes 69 and 78 above for information that the nearby parish church was dedicated to All Saints.For work (forthcoming) on the St Clement project, see B.E. Crawford, *The Churches Dedicated to St Clement in Medieval England. A Hagio-Geography of the Seafarer's Saint in Eleventh-Century North Europe*, Scrinium, revue de patrologie, d'hagiographie critique et d'histoire ecclésiastique, Scripta Ecclesiastica, Série supplémentaire, 1 (St Petersburg, forthcoming).

Chapter 15

England and the Norman Myth

Nick Webber

As one element of his inaugural lecture at the University of Birmingham, Nicholas Brooks examined the role of 'national myth' in the definition of peoples, in particular the Normans and the English.[1] The Norman 'myth' of distinctiveness, reinforced in part by means of an outlandish haircut, was set alongside the English 'myth' of unity and concern over whether this myth had been effectively distinguished from historical reality. Almost 20 years later, there is still much to be said on the issue of national myth in the medieval period, not only in terms of meaning and understanding but, indeed, on subjects as fundamental as appropriateness of the term 'national'. The problem, in the main, is one of definition, as historians and others are seeking to understand the 'varieties of collective cultural identification, and the similarities and differences between ethnic and national identities'.[2] Yet if there is no immediate agreement on exactly how we should refer to the groups in question, there is more of a consensus on how we might study and understand them. The identity structures which are reflected in the 'myths' that peoples such as the Normans and English recorded (and, indeed, in their relationship to reality) retain a vital role in our examination of medieval groupings.

Many historians, including Nicholas himself, consider the role of territory an essential element in these identity structures, and a large number of descriptions and definitions of both *ethnies* (ethnically-constituted identity groups) and nations include the concept of a people historically established on a particular territory or homeland (*patria*).[3] Herwig Wolfram, for example, described a process of identity evolution in which a *gens* (people) established legitimacy by passing its name to a *patria*; only by this method could the wandering *gens* pass out of its 'origin' period and establish the beginnings of national identity. Adrian Hastings, discussing the differences between an ethnicity and a nation, indicates the 'claim' to political identity which is exercised by a nation is usually accompanied by a claim to control of a particular territory comparable to biblical Israel – every nation has a promised

---

1 Nicholas Brooks, *History and Myth, Forgery and Truth*, inaugural lecture delivered at the University of Birmingham, 23 January 1986 (Birmingham, 1986); reprinted in Nicholas Brooks, *Anglo-Saxon Myths: State and Church, 400–1066* (Cambridge, 2000), 1–19.

2 Anthony D. Smith, 'National Identities: Modern and Medieval?', in *Concepts of National Identity in the Middle Ages*, ed. Simon Forde, Lesley Johnson and Alan V. Murray, Leeds Texts and Monographs, New Series, vol. 14 (Leeds, 1995), 21–40, at 40.

3 See, for example, Nicholas Brooks, *Bede and the English*, Jarrow Lecture for 1999 (Jarrow, 2000), 5; John J. Breuilly, *Nationalism and the State*, 2nd edn (Manchester, 1993), 6; Peter Heather, *The Goths* (Oxford, 1996), 7; Anthony D. Smith, *National Identity* (London, 1991), 14; Josef Stalin, quoted in John Hutchinson and Anthony D. Smith, *Nationalism* (Oxford, 1994), 20.

land.[4] Whether or not one considers medieval peoples to have a reasonable claim to constitute nations, the importance of this concept of territory, of homeland, and of a 'promised land' or 'New Israel' is clear.

When England is considered in this framework, however, it seems readily obvious that some investigation is needed to explain how this territory was incorporated into the 'myths' of those who ruled this area. Prior to 1066, there was clearly a defined and understood kingdom of the English, established during the tenth century and which, interestingly, consciously excluded some English territories, apparently for the sake of consolidation.[5] Yet some of those Normans who crossed the Channel as part of William the Conqueror's invasion force in 1066 came to abide in England, even though they already had a homeland in Normandy.[6] It is necessary, therefore, to assess the way in which the Norman people – the *gens Normannorum* – adapted to the changes in their territorial situation following the conquest of England. Through a close examination of the portrayal of England in the Norman sources, we can understand something of the Norman attitude towards that territory and the role that it played in the constantly evolving identity, or 'myth', of the *gens Normannorum*.

From a purely political viewpoint, the position of England prior to the accession of Edward the Confessor is consistent in Norman history (and is hardly that of a promised land). The works of Dudo of St-Quentin and William of Jumièges portray good relations between Norman and English leaders (such as Rollo and Æthelstan), but this connection seemed to go no further than a recognition of mutual interests.[7] Even the tale told by Dudo, in which Rollo is given half of Æthelstan's kingdom, has no element of enduring political reality about it – Rollo returns the lands to Æthelstan within a few paragraphs.[8] Clearly, the accord between the rulers of England and Normandy was an important element in their political lives, but there is no sign during the tenth century that the Norman leaders had designs on England. Even at the end of the tenth century, when Viking fleets were using Normandy as a base from which to attack England, Richard I of Normandy was not making any bid to control England but rather reinforcing his profitable connections with Svein of Denmark.

---

4   Herwig Wolfram, *History of the Goths*, tr. Thomas J. Dunlop (Berkeley, 1988; originally published as *Geschichte der Goten*, Munich, 1979), 11; Adrian Hastings, *The Construction of Nationhood. Ethnicity, Religion and Nationalism* (Cambridge, 1997), 3, and *passim* for ideas of 'New Israel'.

5   Nicholas Brooks, 'English Identity from Bede to the Millennium', *Haskins Society Journal*, 14 (2003), 33–51, at 43–4 and 51.

6   An interesting parallel can be found in recent work by Leonard Scales, in which he indicates the growth of attachment of German immigrants to Bohemia ('At the Margin of Community: Germans in Pre-Hussite Bohemia', *TRHS*, 6th ser., 9 (1999), 327–52, in particular 335).

7   *De moribus*, 147–9, 158–60; Dudo, 30–3, 39–41; *GND*, I, 42–6, 58. For a discussion of the 'myths' on which Anglo-Saxon society was built, see Yorke, this volume.

8   *De moribus*, 159–60; Dudo, 40–41. This particular anecdote is examined in more detail below.

Indeed, this policy drove a wedge between England and Normandy to the extent that settlement had to be mediated by a papal envoy, finally producing a treaty in 991.[9]

In the eleventh century, the political destinies of England and Normandy became far more closely intertwined. The marriage of Æthelred II to Emma, daughter of Richard I and sister of Richard II, in 1002 was the first blood connection between the English and Norman ruling houses and the foundation of the later claim to the throne of William the Conqueror. Yet the Danish element to this relationship remained and, once Richard and Svein of Denmark had concluded a lasting peace, Svein invaded England, seizing the throne in 1013.[10] Æthelred and his family fled to Normandy (though Æthelred was recalled on Svein's death in 1014) and, shortly after Æthelred died in 1016, Emma married Cnut. This served to strengthen the connection between Normandy, England and Denmark, but did not detract from the good relations of the Norman leadership with the æthelings, Alfred and Edward – we are told by William of Jumièges that they were like brothers to Richard II's son, Robert.[11] The closeness of this friendship was obvious when Robert, having requested that the æthelings be allowed to return to England, called together an army and fleet to make clear his displeasure at Cnut's refusal. Unfortunately for Robert, his fleet was driven astray by bad winds, and stranded in Jersey for an extended period.[12]

After Robert's death, however, the Scandinavian element began to fade from the picture. In 1036 Alfred attempted to return to England but was captured and killed. Only a few years later, Edward was summoned back to England by Harthacnut, Cnut's heir, to be installed as his successor. As Edward was a close friend of both Robert and his son William, the personal ties here were strong, and although Emma was a strong Scandinavian sympathiser until her death in 1052, there was enough of Normandy about Edward to make him able to be regarded as a Norman candidate. In fact, the accession of Edward in 1042 marks a distinct change in the presence of England on the Norman political scene because, after many years, the Norman leaders were finally no longer intervening in the country's political destiny on behalf of others. On Edward's death, of course, the well-known events surrounding the Norman conquest of England were set in motion, and within a short period of time England had become a Norman possession. Over the following century, Normandy and England were variously united and divided under a number of rulers, prior to their reunification under Henry II in 1154.

It is clear from this political résumé that the interaction between Normandy and England was often rather more about personal relationships than it was about the territories themselves, and for this reason the territorial elements of identities can only be studied with difficulty here. In a period in which territories were particularly

---

9 The text of this treaty can be found in *Memorials of Saint Dunstan*, ed. William Stubbs, Rolls Series, 63 (London, 1874), 397–8.

10 *GND*, I, 18.

11 For extensive discussion of this subject, see Simon Keynes, 'The Æthelred in Normandy', *ANS*, 13 (1990), 173–205. Keynes also highlights the uncertainties surrounding Emma's life in the period between the death of Æthelred and her marriage to Cnut (176–7, 181–5).

12 *GND*, I, 76.

ill-defined, it proves much easier to examine groupings of people. Indeed, the terminology of the time often reinforces such a focus, particularly before the twelfth century, when kings were *reges Anglorum* rather than *reges Angliae*, for example.[13] Yet, politically, England loomed fairly large on the Norman stage, and the Normans were intervening at least indirectly in the kingdom's affairs, whether to protect potential heirs or to allow Viking raids upon it. There appears to have been no immediate interest for most of the time in obtaining the English kingdom, simply a (sensible) vested interest in the status of the country on some occasions before 1066, and consistently after it. But how then was it incorporated into the identity structure of the *gens Normannorum*?

Typically, the sparse tenth-century Norman sources provide us with little information, and do not add to our understanding of the Norman perception of England as a territory. However, certainly at the beginning of the eleventh century, and probably at the end of the tenth, Dudo of St-Quentin was recording his tale of Rollo's short-lived ownership of half of the kingdom of Æthelstan. The involvement of England in Dudo's tale does not end there, either. The reason for Rollo's initial presence in England is an aspect of a larger story – that of the journey of Rollo to Normandy, his 'promised land'. While an exile in Scandinavia, Rollo was visited by a divine voice as he lay sleeping, which told him to go to the English, where he would learn how to return to his own country as a saviour and enjoy perpetual peace. The dream was interpreted by a wise man, who said that Rollo would one day be baptised and enjoy peace when he reached the Angles. Rollo sailed for England at once, but on arrival discovered an English army awaiting him and, after two battles, put them to flight. He was then afflicted with doubt as to the proper course of action – whether to return to 'Dacia', make for Francia, or to 'afflict the English land [*Anglica terra*] with battles, and win it for himself'. At this point in time, Rollo was sent another vision, which guided him to Francia, where he was told men of different kingdoms would serve him. Therefore, having made friendly overtures to Æthelstan, who was 'holding the reins of the English kingdom', Rollo and his men wintered in England before setting out for Francia.[14]

---

13 Though the official change of title occurred in the reign of King John (Pierre Chaplais, *English Royal Documents, King John – Henry VI, 1199–1461* (Oxford, 1971), 13), the formulation *rex Angliae* appears in reliable charters as early as the reign of Henry I, and is used by Richard of Hexham, writing c.1140 (see Nick Webber, *The Evolution of Norman Identity, 911–1154* (Woodbridge, 2005), 169 n. 187).

14 *De moribus*, 144–8; Dudo, 28–32. The 'out of Scandinavia' element of the Norman origin myth bears some similarities to those Gothic and Anglo-Saxon *origines* discussed by Barbara Yorke (this vol.), though of course the Normans had good reason for such a point of origin. Both Dudo and William of Jumièges noted a Gothic connection with 'Scanza', and considered the Danes to be descended from the Goths (*De moribus*, 129; Dudo, 15; *GND* I, 14–16). As with the 'keels' of other *origines*, the 'proto-Normans' travelled in ships, though there were six of these rather than the traditional three (*De moribus*, 143; Dudo, 27; *GND* I, 32). The tale recounted by Dudo provides even more parallels, as he recorded that Rollo was the elder of two brothers; the younger, Gurim, shared the fate of Horsa, as he was slain in battle. However, they lack the semi-divine nature of those figures from other myths and, even in their Norse forms, the names *Hrolfr* and *Gormr* are not particularly alliterative

Here, apparently, England is presented as a potential homeland for Rollo and, presumably, those who travelled with him. A place in which he could enjoy peace it apparently was not, as the two battles showed and, indeed, there was no further mention of this particular vision, superseded as it was by the vision of Francia and Normandy. The purpose of England within this tale is not, therefore, immediately obvious. Certainly, it may be a literary device, as similarities can be found in later stories told of the Norman settlement in southern Italy. Both in England and in Italy, the Normans' arrival is the result of a divinely inspired journey (dream-vision/pilgrimage) and they begin by rendering assistance to their neighbours (the English and Lombards). More complex parallels are indicated by Emily Albu, based on her consideration that Dudo's account of Rollo is a deliberate analogue of *The Aeneid*. According to Albu, Rollo's journey to England is equivalent to Aeneas' false start, when he misinterprets Apollo's command. The first vision was simply urging Rollo to accept baptism and join the angels, while the second vision corrected his error of interpretation, and put him back on the right track.[15] When, later, Rollo breaks off the siege of Paris to return to England to help his ally, and Æthelstan offers half of his kingdom and goods, another classical parallel can be drawn: this time, with King Latinus' promise to share his kingdom with Aeneas.[16]

There are, of course, other possibilities, compelling as these literary and classical connections might seem. Eric Christiansen, Dudo's recent translator, reminds us of Richer's claim that Æthelstan had made a similar offer to Louis IV when Louis was in exile, and Abbo of Fleury tells of the Danes demanding half the wealth of King Edmund.[17] Dudo's tale may also have associations with the political events of the period of *c.* 994 and *c.* 1015 (his period of composition). As noted above, shortly before this Richard I and Æthelred II had been reconciled, and during this time period Emma was first made a queen (through her marriage to Æthelred) and then a refugee. This connection may have led Dudo to write of this apparent 'claim' to England – as the links between Normandy and England were reinforced by this marriage, the story may have been in circulation at the time and the peaceful relations which the marriage represented may have proven reminiscent of those which Rollo (supposedly) enjoyed with Æthelstan. In any case, it does not seem to have been written to justify Norman action pursuant to a conquest and the lateness within the composition period of Æthelred's defeat suggests it was unlikely to have been a factor in Dudo's communication of the tale.

Some last elements of Dudo's writing may provide a little further insight into the attitudes which the Normans held towards England. Though these concern the English people, rather than the land on which they lived, they do seem to complement

---

(*De moribus*, 141–3 and Dudo, 26–7 for Rollo's brother; Dudo, 187, n. 116 for the Old Norse forms. See in addition Nicholas Brooks, 'The Creation and Early Structure of the Kingdom of Kent' and 'The English Origin Myth', in Brooks, *Anglo-Saxon Myths*, 33–60 and 79–89 respectively, for further discussion of Hengist and Horsa).

15 Emily Albu, *The Normans in their Histories: Propaganda, Myth and Subversion* (Woodbridge, 2001), 15–16.

16 *De moribus*, 159–60; Dudo, 40–41, and 193, n. 178.

17 Dudo, 193, n. 178.

the tale of Rollo and Æthelstan. The first aspect is, in fact, another part of that same story. After the two battles which marked Rollo's arrival in England, Dudo reports that the 'people of that region subjected themselves to [Rollo's] authority and did fealty to him'. Later, during Rollo's siege of Paris, rebels 'renounced their fealty' and fought against Æthelstan, prompting Rollo's return to England. After the rebels were defeated, Rollo suggested that both he and Æthelstan should take hostages, so that the defeated rebels would remain 'faithful' to Æthelstan and continue in their 'fidelity' to Rollo.[18] There is, it seems, some suggestion that there were English counts who owed service, or at least faith to Rollo, and that the hostages – his 'by right' – needed to be taken to ensure continued good behaviour. However, apparently inspired to return to Francia by his dream – or perhaps by Æthelstan's suggestion that he accept baptism! – Rollo returned the hostages at the same time as he returned his half of Æthelstan's kingdom, with an injunction that they be warned against the behaviour of their sires. Rollo did, however, request that Æthelstan allow any men who wished to go with him to do so, though he politely declined Æthelstan's personal offer of aid.

Rollo is not the only Norman leader to whom Dudo attributes some form of lordship over the English. We are told that William Longsword was not someone people quarrelled with, as the Frankish rulers and Burgundian counts were 'his servants' and 'the Danes, the Flemings, the English and the Irish obeyed him'. A similar position was true for his successor, Richard I, or so the satrap Theobald claimed when attempting to arouse the ire of the French king:

> It is surely a disgrace to your authority that he gives orders to the Burgundians, accuses and upbraids the Aquitanians, rules and directs the Bretons and Normans, threatens and lays waste the Flemings, and binds himself to and conciliates the Danes and the Lotharingians and even the Saxons. The English also submit to him obediently; the Scots and the Irish are ruled under his patronage.[19]

It is, of course, unclear whether these passages refer to Englishmen within Normandy, or to the English of England, but the claims about Richard suggest the latter. There was clearly a sense, however far removed from any political reality, that the Norman leaders had some kind of control over or influence on the affairs of the English and, through this, some continued connection to or claim on England itself.

Dudo's work thus suggests a contemporary tradition of Norman interest in England. The story of Rollo and Æthelstan's friendship may have been strongly influenced by other sources (the *Aeneid*, for example) but it seems that there were elements of truth which underlay it. The analogous events reported by Richer and Abbo serve to indicate that such a story was perfectly in keeping with the expectations both of Dudo's audiences and, more importantly, his patrons. The attitude towards England portrayed in the claims of Theobald was not, therefore, unacceptable to the

---

18 *De moribus*, 146, 158–9; Dudo, 29, 39–41. The Latin term used for fealty/fidelity/faith is *fides* (*fidei* in instances 2 and 3) and *fidelitas* (*fidelitatis* in instances 1 and 4). Notably, *fides* is used with Æthelstan (*Alstemus*), and *fidelitas* with Rollo, and it is conceivable that this may be intended to reflect a difference in the nature of the bond of loyalty/faith.

19 *De moribus*, 192 and 265; Dudo, 69 and 140.

potential audience of the work, though the references may in truth have referred to Englishmen settled in Normandy.[20] Yet this attitude was not enduring, and by the time that William of Jumièges composed the *Gesta Normannorum Ducum* (during the 1050s, though it was expanded after the conquest of England), attitudes had changed significantly.[21] Dudo's tale of Rollo's initial visit to England was retold by William as an attack by a group of Danes, who defeated the English in battle. The English withdrew in disgrace, and Æthelstan sued for peace, making a pact of friendship. Though William did report that Rollo received messages from Æthelstan asking for aid against a rebellion at a later date, the battle was easily won and Rollo was not offered half a kingdom or a share of worldly possessions; instead, William wrote, he selected a large number of young men and returned to France.[22] At no point, in fact, did William make reference to the obedience of the English to the Normans leaders that is suggested in Dudo's work. Though William did record the closeness of Duke Robert and the æthelings (and Robert's consequent ire at Cnut for refusing to allow their return from exile), there is no other indication in the early parts of William's history that England was particularly important at all.[23] These changes are not insignificant. Even if William omitted the putative territorial claim of Rollo from his earlier versions, he might well have added it to his final version; Albu has noted that it 'would have given the *Gesta* a thematic unity and would have pleased King William'.[24] William's reasons for these alterations are thus ultimately revealing of Norman attitudes towards territories in general, and towards England in particular.

In the early pages of the *Gesta*, William signalled that his alteration of elements of Dudo's work was deliberate; he removed parts which seemed to him *nec ... honesti uel utilis*, in particular some of those sections dealing with Rollo's deeds prior to his arrival in Francia.[25] This was not a removal of irrelevant information, nor a deletion of tales which seemed to William to be untrue. Indeed, the political events of his day rendered any mention of a prior claim to England highly significant and, if William was clearly willing to credit (and repeat) some elements of the tales in question, there is no immediately apparent reason why he omitted the remainder. To remove information because it seemed 'neither honourable nor edifying' implies a certain sensitivity regarding that material, a sense of moral objection or, perhaps, embarrassment. This would perhaps indicate that William altered sections of Dudo's work because he considered them to be morally – that is, religiously – 'unsuitable' for his readership. Certainly, his alterations to Dudo's *Historia* have a particular focus on those events surrounding Rollo in his days as a Viking, before his baptism. Most notably, of course, this concerns the initial meeting between Rollo and Æthelstan,

---

20 Simon Keynes has suggested that the comments about Richard may reflect an attitude inspired by the presence of the æthelings at the Norman court (Keynes, 'Æthelings', 185).

21 Elisabeth M.C. van Houts, 'The *Gesta Normannorum Ducum*: a History without an End', *ANS*, 3 (1981), 106 and *GND*, I, p. xxxii.

22 *GND*, I, 32, 58–60.

23 *GND*, II, 76–8.

24 Albu, *Normans in their Histories*, 60.

25 *GND*, I, 6.

and it may be that William's distaste for Rollo's pagan deeds was stronger than his desire to please the duke to whom he dedicated his work (William the Conqueror). Alternatively, William may have made an authorial decision to omit the references to Rollo's short-lived ownership of England because the situation interfered with his portrayal of Rollo's character. Whatever the case, Albu has observed that, in the *Gesta*, the story of Rollo's aid to Æthelstan after the siege of Paris was a literary device which established Rollo's increasing Christian sympathies and concern for human obligations, and this would only be undermined if the original tale were maintained and Rollo were to refuse Æthelstan's suggestion of baptism.[26]

However, though religion was an obvious contributory element to William's alterations, the argument for religious 'decency' does not seem sufficient to explain all the changes. Although William may well have wanted to avoid a tale in which Rollo refused baptism, there was no readily apparent reason to remove Æthelstan's offer of half of his kingdom – as Dudo told it, this was not conditional upon Rollo's baptism. William's omissions elsewhere in the *Gesta*, with regard to the obedience of the English to the Norman leaders, are also not explained by the concerns of a religious man in the face of pagan tales. It is the reasoning underlying these more territorial and political concerns which allows us a clearer understanding of the Norman attitude towards England.

In his *Historia*, Dudo related that Rollo chose not to keep the half-kingdom which Æthelstan had given him because he felt he had a destiny in Francia, as foretold in his dream-vision. Normandy had been 'promised' to him and, by extension, promised as the home of the Normans. Thus Normandy was the Normans' 'New Israel' and they the chosen people, to be constituted in this land. England, on the other hand, represented something else, which had not quite achieved that high status; it was an alternative which was not good enough. Rollo was, essentially, handed a kingdom as a gift, but returned it because he saw that his destiny would take him to a better place. The actions of Rollo and his successors suggest that, while England was a place in which the Normans had a vested interest, doubtless due to its proximity, it concerned the allies of the Normans rather more than the Normans themselves. Indeed, there is almost a tradition of the Normans providing aid to those who wanted to control England. Rollo aided Æthelstan against a rebellion; Richard I provided safe harbour for Danes wishing to attack the country; Richard II and Robert the Fearless supported the æthelings in their time of need. Yet at no point, when Rollo helped Æthelstan, or when Richard II allied with the Danes, or even when Robert raised a fleet to restore the æthelings, was there any suggestion that the Normans might use this opportunity to take control of England themselves. Instead, so Dudo shows us, the Normans were content to claim vague dominance over an unspecified 'English'. There was a sense of superiority about the Norman perception of England – it was a country less than Normandy, which non-Normans might have fought over and in which Normans might have intervened, but certainly wouldn't have wanted to own.

Dudo's *Historia* thus represents a tradition in which the Normans signalled their lack of interest in the ownership of England and an explanation for William of

---

26 Albu, *Normans in their Histories*, 60. The passages in William and Dudo are referenced above.

Jumièges' alterations consequently becomes apparent. Certainly, once the Conqueror became king of England, it would have seemed senseless to portray England as something unwanted by the Normans, or something that was not worth the effort to obtain. This may explain why William did not reinsert the missing tale and comments after the conquest. Furthermore, if this was indeed a deciding factor in the presence of this tradition in the *Gesta Normannorum Ducum*, then it offers an explanation for the earlier omission after the same fashion. When Edward came to the English throne in 1042, he had Norman support, and brought Normans into the country to hold land and offices – he could be regarded as a Norman candidate.[27] The extended period which he had spent in Normandy made it easy for Normans to believe that he was Normanised enough to have named William his heir.[28] Such a promise represented a very real, if potentially insecure, claim to the throne of England and it would not do for someone who wished William to endorse his work to remind the duke of the low regard in which the country was traditionally held by his ancestors. Additionally, this Norman 'lack of interest' was probably more of a self-reassurance device than a real response to the possibility of owning England and dominating the English – before the time of William, the Normans *could not* have taken control of England and thus chose to pretend they were not interested rather than accept that they were presented with an insurmountable obstacle. As with the fashion of their great leaders, who would not enter battles they felt they could not win, so the *gens Normannorum* avoided the (for them) identity-threatening admission that someone might be beyond their ability to defeat. They believed themselves to be warriors and conquerors, they had humbled the king of Francia, and they were not prepared to enshrine England in their mythology as an unobtainable want. Normandy was their *patria* and promised land and England had been just a stop along the way.

With this in mind, it is apparent that the changes in the Norman relationship with England, initially through the connection with Edward and later due to William's conquest, would have had significant repercussions within Norman identity. In particular, the unusual situation of the Norman leader, as a king of somewhere other than the Norman *patria*, would have set those aspects of *Normannitas* associated with leadership against those associated with territory (though it should not be forgotten that King William was just as much duke of Normandy as he was king of England). In the years after William I's death, Norman perceptions were further affected by those periods in which Normandy and England were controlled by different rulers and by the intense intermingling of the *gens Normannorum* and the *gens Anglorum* within England. Careful account must therefore be taken of our post-conquest writers and their presentation of Norman regard for England after this date.

When William of Jumièges added to his work after the conquest (completing it in early 1070), he continued in the same vein as before, expanding no further on his treatment of England.[29] His coverage of the land itself remained unadorned: England was a possession, nothing more. William focussed instead on the human element, both on the *gens Normannorum* as the victorious conquerors and on Duke William

---

27 R. Allen Brown, *The Normans* (Woodbridge, 1984), 16.
28 R.H.C. Davis, *The Normans and their Myth* (London, 1976), 63.
29 *GND*, I, p. xxxv for the date.

as their leader. This lack of interest in England is paralleled in the work of William's contemporary, Guy of Amiens. In his *Carmen de Hastingae Proelio* (composed 1067 x 1070) Guy apparently did not even recognise an *Anglia*.[30] We see in his work *Gallia* and *Francia*, used interchangeably and on numerous occasions, as the homeland of the *Galli/Franci*, *Normanni*, *Cenomanni* and *Britanni*, alongside a clear sense that the title *dux Normannorum* had a territorial nature. Yet, on the English side, we see only a racial grouping of *Angli*, with almost no sense of a territorial connection at all; the land of the English is, at best, 'the kingdom'.[31]

If Guy's work seems the epitome of lack of interest, however, the *Gesta Guillelmi* of William of Poitiers is a rather different matter. In contrast to Guy's writing, the concept of England is fully evident in William's work, appearing as 'the kingdom of England' and the 'English land', for example. We are left in no doubt in the *Gesta Guillelmi* of the author's attitude towards England, however, and it was very much that of a member of the conquering side; he felt that this 'English land' should 'love [King William] and hold him in the highest respect' and 'gladly prostrate [itself] entirely at his feet'.[32] However, it was apparent that William could still appreciate the merits of England even by comparison to his own land. He wrote of England:

> This kingdom is many times richer than Gaul in its wealth of precious metals; it seems as if it should be called the granary of Ceres because of its abundance of corn, and the treasury of Arabia because of its richness of gold.[33]

It seems likely that William saw Gaul as an area which included Normandy (whereas, for him, Francia did not), and so he was, rather unusually, making a positive comparison with his own *patria*.[34]

Between the attitudes of William of Poitiers and Guy of Amiens, then, there appears to be a not insignificant gulf. From one perspective, there is an apparent lack of engagement with the concept of England; it seems not to have been an idea which Guy found useful in his writing. William of Jumièges does refer to England, but not in any great detail as a place; William of Poitiers finds it worthy of comparison with his homeland, with a sense of superiority retained through the person of Duke William. The obvious explanation for this variety is that our writers all had different

---

30 For the date, see *The Carmen de Hastingae Proelio of Guy, Bishop of Amiens*, ed. and tr. Frank Barlow, OMT (Oxford, 1999), p. xl.

31 Ibid., pp. xxiii; 45.

32 *The Gesta Guillelmi of William of Poitiers*, ed. and tr. R.H.C. Davis and Marjorie Chibnall, OMT (Oxford, 1998), 156.

33 Ibid., 168.

34 Webber, *Evolution*, 123. In the eleventh century, the term Francia only sometimes referred to the wider Frankish realm; more often, it was used to describe the area within which the *rex Francorum* could assert his authority. The contraction of royal power which occurred during the tenth century had left Francia referring only to a small bloc of land around Paris and Orléans, with some writers instead using Gaul (*Gallia*) to refer to the wider kingdom (see C. Warren Hollister, 'Normandy, France and the Anglo-Norman *Regnum*', *Speculum*, 51 (1976), 202–42, at 222–3; Jean Dunbabin, *France in the Making, 843–1180* (Oxford, 1985), 4–5; Elizabeth M. Hallam, *Capetian France, 987–1328* (London, 1980), 6; Rosamond McKitterick, *The Frankish Kingdom under the Carolingians, 751–987* (London, 1983), 18–19).

feelings about this new acquisition; the fact remains, however, that these perceptions must not only represent their own ideas, but can be expected to have some relation to the feelings of others around them – their immediate contemporaries and, of course, their intended audience. What our writers seem to be communicating, then, is uncertainty among the *gens Normannorum* regarding England, how it fitted into their world, and what this meant for *Normanitas*. As a serious issue, the fact that it generated a variety of reactions is quite understandable; what is worthy of further consideration, however, is the motivation which underlay each writers' approach.

The reaction that is perhaps most readily understood is that expressed by William of Jumièges, whose plain language serves to highlight the bland nature of his treatment when compared with the work of others. The lack of certainty we have noted above would seem reason enough for William to be tentative in expressing any opinion about the Normans' new acquisition; this combined with an unwillingness to offend the conquering duke to whom his work was addressed renders his neutrality comprehensible. In contrast, Guy of Amiens, while saying even less about England than William, is unlikely to have been following a similar thought process. Guy's is perhaps more of an active response to the situation at hand: after the conquest, the 'land of the English' had become something of a misnomer and there was no certainty that England as the eleventh-century English had understood it would continue to exist. Guy's approach may also have been coloured by a certain indifference: he was of non-Norman origin, hailing from north-eastern France, and his lack of an investment in *Normannitas* would lead one to be wholly suspect of the value of his work to this study, were it not for the possibility that it was written for Lanfranc.[35] The rather more Norman William of Poitiers, finally, seems to be representing what might be regarded as a traditional Norman approach to a conquest when he writes of England.[36] As noted, he clearly thinks of it as inferior to the conquering duke/king, and the comments on the wealth of the country, while positive, are not observations on the beauty of the land, or its prosperity, but more on the potential wealth that is available. William was, it seems, writing of the spoils of war; though he felt that England had more wealth than his own *patria*, it belonged just as much (if not more) to the *gens Normannorum*.

Apparently, then, conquest-period Norman attitudes towards England varied between indifference, and the view that it was a pot of money. From the latter viewpoint, however, the country at least had value, even if it did not command the sort of loyalty and interest that one might expect a homeland to generate. This basic divide itself may have had a logistical connection – we know that there was little opportunity for movement between England and Normandy for all but the very rich, and this would seem likely to polarise people's interests. This would lead those who dwelt in England quite naturally to seek out the best in their new home, while those in Normandy focused on the possessions and matters at hand. The 'traditionally' Norman exploitative ideology that we see in William of Poitiers, however, leads us to

---

35 The second line of the prologue to the *Carmen* features the abbreviation *L. W. salutat*, which is generally read as *Lanfrancum Wido salutat* (*Carmen*, pp. xxvii and xxv).

36 William's epithet refers solely to his schooling, rather than his origin – he was born, according to Orderic Vitalis, in Préaux (*Gesta Guillelmi*, p. xv).

suspect that the concept of a new homeland was very low on the list of considerations for these people, if it was present at all. If the *gens Normannorum* were a people destined to conquer, then England as a territory reinforced their sense of their place in the world; their dominance was only what their own myth led them to expect.

If England could be seen as an element which supported *Normannitas* after the conquest, it may not have continued to do so towards the end of the eleventh century. Were there political or historical works with a close Norman connection remaining from this period, they might help us to understand what changes in attitude took place during the later years of William I's reign, and during the separation of England and Normandy after his death. Unfortunately, we are left with a period of quiet until the early twelfth century, when we are greeted with writers who make much fuller use of territorial distinctions, sometimes to the exclusion of ethnic divisions. Writing in France, Baudri, abbot of Bourgueil, produced a lengthy piece of verse dedicated to Adela, William I's daughter, *c.* 1102. In this piece, he refers both to *Anglia* and to a *regna Anglica*, and occasionally also to a more classical *Britannia*. Though Baudri was of non-Norman origin, having been born in Meung in 1046 and schooled in Orléans, he appears to have written this piece with a Norman perspective in mind; this is suggested both by his address to Adela and his use of *hostes* to describe the English at Hastings.[37] Elsewhere, in his *Itinerarium*, he represented England not as a source of wealth, but as more of a garden than a treasury (though there is no reason to assume that this was necessarily a Norman viewpoint).[38] Eadmer, his contemporary and based in England, almost never used ethnonyms, writing instead of England and, once, 'the King's land'.[39] This limited reference is perhaps not as dispassionate as it first appears, though, and there has been some suggestion that Eadmer felt loyalties to England. However, the majority of references cited in support of this argument point more towards a sense of loyalty as an Englishman, a member of a *gens Anglorum*.[40] This would, in turn, suggest a non-Norman attitude to England by definition, but it is notable that Eadmer at no point claimed an ethnicity for himself. Furthermore, for the early twelfth century, there is perhaps less merit in the consideration that Eadmer provides a potentially non-Norman viewpoint, and more in the idea that he represents a view that was present in a mixed society.

It seems likely that the tense political nature of the time in which they wrote led Eadmer and Baudri to concentrate on territorial referents, rather than the more traditional ethnic labels, but their usage does reveal an awareness of territorial affiliation – the world could be understood in terms of places if it could not be

---

[37] For a brief summary of Baudri's life, see Shirley Ann Brown and Michael W. Herren, 'The *Adelae Comitissae* of Baudri of Bourgueil and the Bayeux Tapestry', *ANS*, 16 (1994), 55–73, at 56.

[38] Baudri of Bourgueil, *Itinerarium*, PL 166, cc. 1173–4.

[39] *Eadmeri historia novorum in Anglia*, ed. Martin Rule, Rolls Series, 81 (London, 1884), 110; *Eadmer's History of Recent Events in England*, tr. Geoffrey Bosanquet (London, 1964), 115.

[40] *Historia novorum*, 107–110; *Eadmer's History*, 111–14 for example. See R.W. Southern, *St. Anselm and his Biographer* (Cambridge, 1963), 231–2, Ann Williams, *The English and the Norman Conquest* (Woodbridge, 1995), 166–8 and Sally N. Vaughn, 'Eadmer's *Historia Novorum*: a Reinterpretation', *ANS*, 10 (1988), 259–89, at 260 on Eadmer's Englishness.

understood in terms of ethnicity.[41] During the period of separation of Normandy and England that began with William I's death, there would have been understandable difficulties labelling people as members of this or that ethnic group, if only for the potential political overtones that this might have held; dealing in territories was rather more neutral. Clearly, the concept of territorial identification was sufficiently subordinate to ethnicity that, while the latter was a charged issue, the former was not. Baudri's reference to England's fertility may indicate a further change to the concept of England in Norman, or at least French ideology, doubtless a result of the existence of a generation who had grown up considering Normandy and England to be, at least in some way, connected. If, after the conquest, England had been a object of disdain and exploitation, by this early twelfth century it had begun to have more of a homely feel. It was no *patria* for the Normans, but was perhaps becoming a place which was viewed as an acceptable alternative to home, especially, no doubt, by those for whom Normandy was not an option.[42]

As the twelfth century went on, ideas concerning England developed even further and sentiments about the country were more readily expressed. In the first half of the twelfth century, we have the work of three major writers on which to base our considerations: Orderic Vitalis, William of Malmesbury and Henry of Huntingdon. There is, of course, some debate about the ethnic affiliations of these writers and this must be kept in mind when analysing their work. Orderic Vitalis, though of mixed descent, famously referred to himself as *angligena*, leading many historians to consider him an 'English' writer, though he was more probably drawing attention only to his descent or, perhaps, to his place of birth.[43] He was writing from within Normandy and presented himself as a Norman in his *Historia Ecclesiastica*.[44] William of Malmesbury, the author of the *Gesta Regum Anglorum*, thought of himself as of mixed heritage – 'having the blood of both nations in my veins' – and

---

41 Hugh Thomas notes that England could serve as a focus for identity when Englishness was a controversial issue (Hugh M. Thomas, *The English and the Normans: Ethnic Hostility, Assimilation, and Identity, 1066–c. 1220* (Oxford, 2003), 268–9). See also Webber, *Evolution*, 139–40.

42 Robert Bartlett provides a useful summing-up of the functionality of this 'cross-channel realm', noting that England and Normandy were 'a political entity conceived of as fundamentally one' (*England under the Norman and Angevin Kings, 1075–1225* (Oxford, 2000), 11–17, quote at 11) and building on the ideas of cross-channel unity presented by David Douglas, John Le Patourel and Warren Hollister, among others (David Douglas, *The Norman Achievement, 1050–1100* (London, 1969); John Le Patourel, *The Norman Empire* (Oxford, 1976); Hollister, 'Normandy'). Evidence of the weaknesses in this structure can be found, however, both in the political sphere (David Bates, 'Normandy and England after 1066', *EHR*, 104 (1989), 851–80) and in patterns of religious patronage (Emma Cownie, *Religious Patronage in Anglo-Norman England* (London, 1998), 195).

43 For discussion of the meaning of Orderic's use of *angligena*, and Orderic's sense of Englishness, see *The Ecclesiastical History of Orderic Vitalis*, ed. Marjorie Chibnall, OMT (6 vols, Oxford, 1969–1980), I, 2; Marjorie Chibnall, *The World of Orderic Vitalis: Norman Monks and Norman Knights* (Woodbridge, 1996), 3, 8–11; Thomas, *English and Normans*, 81–2, 153–4 and 153, n. 51.

44 Webber, *Evolution*, 143.

was thus writing from a viewpoint that could potentially represent *Normannitas*.[45] Henry of Huntingdon's by-name, finally, implies an English affiliation, but it seems probable that he was of mixed descent, like Orderic and William, since he wrote that he felt ethnic kinship with Alexander of Lincoln, who was of unambiguously Norman descent, considering them to be of the same people.[46]

At first glance, Orderic's *Historia Ecclesiastica* (composed between 1114 and 1141) seems to echo the style of Baudri of Bourgueil. The only direct comments on England are short and to the point: he depicted the earls Robert of Hereford and Ralph of Norwich referring to 'the fair kingdom of England' and elsewhere mentioned 'the wealthy realm of England'.[47] Yet Orderic's attitude towards England is best illustrated by his account of the rebellion of Robert of Bellême. When Robert defeated those Normans who fought against him, Orderic wrote that they were 'put to flight in the heart of their own land'; this land in question is, notably, not Normandy but England. Apparently, from Orderic's perspective, England had almost become an extension of Normandy, the Norman heartland. This would suggest that England had achieved a position within *Normannitas* that brought it much closer to the level of Normandy than ever before. The longstanding nature of the connection between Normandy and England is made explicit elsewhere, when Orderic gives an *English* derivation for the Norman ethnonym. Such treatment implies a sense of belonging and ownership that doubtless went some way towards legitimising England as a new Norman *patria*.

William of Malmesbury's writing seems not only to support this idea, but provides perhaps the most detailed example of the changing attitudes to England and, indeed, Normandy that we have so far encountered. From the outset, we are in no doubt as to William's views on England; he referred to it as 'my country' in the early pages of his work.[48] This expression of territorial loyalty is enhanced by a highly favourable comparison with Normandy, which he described as 'dead and nearly sucked dry' and 'supported by the financial strength of England'; he longed for the day when England might 'breathe the air of that freedom whose empty shadow she has pursued so long'.[49] This parasitic presentation of Normandy seems closely in keeping with the comments of William of Poitiers in the *Gesta Guillelmi*, but from the opposite perspective – England, here, should emphatically *not* be exploited. William's loyalty to his chosen *patria* is so strong that it might suggest that he were English, were it not for his own admission of mixed heritage.[50] In fact, when he compares the *gens* Anglorum and the *gens Normannorum*, one cannot ignore the sense of Norman superiority; William apparently felt himself to be more Norman than English at heart.[51]

---

45 *GRA*, I, 424. For further discussion see Webber, *Evolution*, 148.

46 Henry, Archdeacon of Huntingdon, *Historia Anglorum*, ed. and tr. Diana Greenway, OMT (Oxford, 1996), pp. xxiii–xxvi, 4–6; also Webber, *Evolution*, 154–5.

47 Orderic, *Ecclesiastical History*, II, 312 and V, 254.

48 *GRA*, I, 14.

49 Ibid., I, 386.

50 Ibid., I, 424.

51 Webber, *Evolution*, 149–50.

With sympathies aligned in this manner, William provides a very interesting example of the extent to which England was becoming enmeshed in the sense of *Normannitas* as it existed at his time of writing (the *Gesta Regum Anglorum* was first completed around 1125, with two new editions after 1134).[52] William's work helps to clarify the relationship between ethnic and territorial identity, in that it seems to fit well with tiered identity models. Hugh Thomas comments that these two areas of identity could be uncoupled; more precisely, they were two separate aspects which sometimes worked together.[53] However, this relationship was not always simple, as can be seen from William's apparent Norman affiliation in England. Equally, Thomas draws our attention to the general idea that invaders who considered themselves Norman could be quite at home with the idea of living in England. In essence, in the first half of the twelfth century at least, it was not necessary to live in Normandy to be Norman, or in England to be English, and neither was it necessary to consider yourself English if you lived in England, or Norman in Normandy.

This separateness of the ideas of ethnicity and territory, shown particularly in the *Gesta Regum Anglorum*, allows us to see the development of an idea of homeland devoid of an ethnic context. England was, for those who lived there, apparently establishing itself quite comfortably as a *patria*. Significantly, also, Normandy itself was being displaced from this position, as David Bates has noted.[54] Those in Normandy could view England perhaps as an extension of Normandy, but in no way was it a replacement. Both of those responses are clearly comprehensible in an identity context. An element of the idea of a *patria* is a sense of home, as a locality to which one has a strong tie. That the Normans in England had begun to transfer this ideological focus from Normandy to England suggests that the strength of the tie to England was greater than that to Normandy. The fact of presence would also help to reinforce the tie, especially if it was as difficult for people to travel between the two places as it seems to have been. An import aspect of such a 'home tie' is the draw to return; if it was not possible to return to Normandy, then it was understandable that people's territorial loyalties might shift.

Notably, also, the division provides evidence that the territorial affiliations of Normans living in England did not necessarily affect their ethnicity, or their perception of their membership of the *gens Normannorum*. Indeed, the process by which some Normans came to think of themselves as English may well have been connected to the land of the English which they inhabited, but it would be to go too far to suggest that this process could have been caused by a strong territorial construct.[55] In the minds of the English, there may well have been a strongly conceived *idea* of England, but as we have noted, there is no good evidence that the Normans considered England to be anything more complex than the area of Britain owned by the king. Certainly, there seems no sense that the Normans were inheriting any spatially-defined construct of

---

52 *GRA*, I, 4–5; William of Malmesbury, *Historia Novella*, ed. Edmund King, tr. K.R. Potter, OMT (Oxford, 1998), p. xxii.
53 Thomas, *English and Normans*, 261.
54 David Bates, 'The Rise and Fall of Normandy, c.911–1204' in *England and Normandy in the Middle Ages*, ed. David Bates and Anne Curry (London, 1994), 19–36 at 30.
55 Thomas, *English and* Normans, 261–73 for discussion of the construct of England.

England from the English and they happily pushed beyond the traditional English borders, seeking to expand England rather than to conquer Wales, for example.[56] Thomas has argued that the concept of England remained largely unaffected by the conquest and while in the long term this may have been true, in the short term it appears to have been largely *ignored* by the conquest.[57] The construct of England only had value and power if people subscribed to it, and there is no real reason to believe that the Normans did so and a fair suspicion that they did not. Thus, while a strong concept of territorial loyalty may have contributed to the enduring nature of Englishness – the *gens Anglorum* were, after all, still inhabiting their *patria*, even if they felt dispossessed – such loyalties were not going to make someone English. The process of becoming English doubtless required the Normans to recognise this construct and accept it, but until they validated it with belief, it had no hold over their loyalties. William of Malmesbury's writings bear this out. It was necessary for the Normans to adopt elements of Englishness before the fact that they lived in England had any bearing on their ethnicity.

There are various elements in Henry of Huntingdon's *Historia Anglorum* which echo William of Malmesbury's work and, yet, although their final composition was separated by a relatively short period of time, a change in attitude can be noted. That change seems directly linked to the adoption or incorporation of pre-existing English perceptions concerning their *patria* and the ideology of their land. We can infer that Henry considered himself to be English from the combination of the title of his work and his expressed intention to write a history of 'our people'; yet we have already noted that this 'people' could include those who were clearly Norman and that Henry was, himself, of mixed blood.[58] He wrote between 1123 and 1154 and presented a vision of England which drew heavily on the work of Bede.[59] He lavished praise on the island on which he lived, 'formerly called Albion, later Britain, and now England', writing extensively on its fertility and abundance, its wonders, its 'excellence' and its 'pre-eminent wealth'.[60] Henry's focus was very much on the territory and he clearly had not only a strong loyalty to his homeland, but also a strong conception of the historical continuity of that homeland. Even though his history is called a *History of the English*, he notes that the English were just one of five plagues which afflicted Britain, along with the Romans, Picts and Scots (conceived of as a single plague), Danes and Normans.[61] The employment of English history was not new – William of Malmesbury had incorporated it into his *Gesta Regum Anglorum*, for example – but this explicit acceptance of a history of Britain and England as places distinct from people was unusual. Neither was Henry the only historian to reach back into the past for the distant roots of his world at this time. Geoffrey of Monmouth wrote a history of Britain which also drew heavily on Bede, showing clearly the attraction

---

56 Ibid., 263.
57 Ibid., 261–3.
58 Ibid., 4–6; above.
59 Huntingdon, pp. lxxxvi–lxxxix for Henry's use of Bede.
60 Ibid., 10–12, 18–28.
61 Ibid., 14.

of the territorial past (a focus which Bede himself had inherited from Eusebius).[62] Clearly, people who we can expect to reflect at least some Norman attitudes were incorporating a new past, and foregoing the old, as they aligned themselves with their new homeland.

This change of attitude towards history is something which has long been recognised and widely acknowledged and is often seen both as a sign of the Normans renowned adaptability and as a death knell for the *gens Normannorum*.[63] It was certainly significant in the evolution of *Normannitas*, but it does not mark a simple transition of Normans to English. Henry's attitude of inclusiveness towards Normans when he wrote of his people is doubtless symptomatic of the rather confused situation at the time that he was writing, but it is also a pragmatic and comprehensible response. If one was to deal with a world in which Normans and English lived together in England and had loyalties to that territory, while other Normans had loyalties which lay elsewhere, then simplistic descent models no longer made sense when defining ethnicities – the king of the English was not, after all, English. Indeed, what those within Henry's 'English' identity group held in common was their loyalty to a particular territory: their homeland. John Gillingham refers to the possibility that, politically, a court faction might have been identified as English, in opposition to a Norman or French faction, because 'its members, though also francophone, had their lands, interests and careers almost entirely based in England'.[64] Yet what Henry shows us is a situation which goes further than this, one in which ethnicity had become so confused that other elements of identity had become dominant, and the element with which he is dealing is that of territorial loyalty. Some Normans had accepted England as their new *patria*, and, while this acceptance may have altered their own perceptions of their *gens* membership, it had also fundamentally changed the perceptions of some members of the *gens Anglorum*. The 'construct of England', then, was not the instigator of a change in ethnic identity among the Normans who lived in England, but rather provided a common ideological referent between the native English and the Norman settlers which helped to create a sense of unity.[65]

---

62 For Geoffrey's debt to Bede, see *The Historia Regum Britannie of Geoffrey of Monmouth*, ed. Neil Wright and Julia Crick (5 vols, Cambridge, 1985–1991), I, 2; Geoffrey of Monmouth, *The History of the Kings of Britain*, tr. Lewis Thorpe (Harmondsworth, Middlesex, 1966), 53. For Bede's debt to Eusebius, see Thacker, this vol.

63 For example, both Albu, *Normans in their Histories*, 221 and Hastings, *Construction*, 171 show an appreciation of this change.

64 John Gillingham, 'Henry of Huntingdon and the Twelfth-Century Revival of the English Nation', in *Concepts of National Identity*, ed. Forde, Johnson and Murray, 75–101, at 89 (reprinted in John Gillingham, *The English in the Twelfth Century: Imperialism, National Identity and Political Values* (Woodbridge, 2000), 123–42).

65 It is worth noting that this developing attachment to and focus upon England may go some way towards explaining the 'unprecedented deluge of vituperation over the heads of the Welsh and Scots' which Gillingham has noted in Anglo-Norman histories of the late 1130s (John Gillingham, 'The Foundations of a Disunited Kingdom', in Gillingham, *English in the Twelfth Century*, 93–109, at 101–102). The Welsh and Scots of this period were not simply peoples who were at war with the English but, by invading England, had become people who were directly attacking a fundamental aspect of Englishness.

This attitude marked quite clearly a significant stage in the continued evolution of *Normannitas* and in the Norman perception of England. Indeed, what may have begun as a conceptual change when Henry began writing in the 1120s was soon to be reinforced by political events. Under Stephen, England no longer had a truly Norman king, and the political divisions during his reign meant that, once again, the terms Norman and English came to have a meaning beyond a simple ethnic denomination. In the work of historians writing towards the end of this period in England, while there may be further changes to the way that group membership was defined, the importance of territorial location and loyalty as a unifier remained. This can be seen in the identity perceptions of, for example, Richard of Hexham, writing c. 1140.[66] Even if there is some doubt as to the perceived ethnicity of these authors and, therefore, the admissibility of their views, we can see similar perceptions in the work of Geffrei Gaimar, a clearly Normannic author who wrote of England with an eye to its non-Norman past.[67]

By 1154, therefore, and the accession of Henry, another 'non-Norman' king, it seems that territory was firmly established as a referent for the identity of people in England and in Normandy, apparently from the viewpoints of both insular and continental writers. England had grown in importance from a legendary possession of Rollo to being a very real *patria* for many Norman settlers. Norman attitudes had also changed, from apparent disdain to devotion and loyalty, as England went from the proffered second choice, rejected in favour of a promised land, to a second home for Normans. For the Normans of Normandy, there were apparently ongoing attempts after the conquest to continue to ignore the relevance of England to the *gens Normannorum*, but eventually England was to be incorporated into *Normanitas* as an ideological extension of Normandy. In England, during the politically sensitive times of the late eleventh and mid-twelfth centuries, territorial loyalties became a major element in the definition of group identity. A loyalty to England, therefore, played an important part in the eventual identity transition of those Normans in England to Englishness.

---

66 Webber, *Evolution*, 167–9.
67 *Lestorie des Engles, solum la Translacion Maistre Geffrei Gaimar*, ed. T.D. Hardy and C.T. Martin, Rolls Series, 91 (2 vols, London, 1888–1889), II, pp. ix–x for Gaimar's French descent.

Chapter 16

What Happened to Ecclesiastical Charters in England 1066–c.1100?

Julia Barrow

By the time of the Norman Conquest Anglo-Saxon England could look back over a tradition of charter production lasting nearly 400 years, a tradition which Nicholas Brooks, not least through his work on the Canterbury archive, has done so much to illuminate.[1] Well over half the surviving charters of the Anglo-Saxon period are royal, but of the remainder over 200 were issued by bishops, abbots, nuns and clerics.[2] Of these, some 30 can be dated to the reign of Edward the Confessor. Output of episcopal and abbatial charters was therefore far lower than in some parts of Europe, notably France,[3] but it was not negligible: it is therefore worth asking what the impact of the Norman Conquest was on English ecclesiastical charters, both in quantity and in diplomatic forms. David Bates in his article 'The Conqueror's Charters' has pointed to the changes in output of English royal charters in the period after the Norman Conquest: low output under William I, a noticeable rise in numbers under William II (with Domesday one of the principal factors behind this) and a sharp rise under Henry I.[4] It occurred to me in 1993 when I was working on a paper on English episcopal charters over the period 700–1250 just how few bishops' charters were issued in the period 1066–1086, a scarcity most noticeable at Worcester, where a buoyant charter production over most of the tenth century and the first half of the eleventh century then came to a halt until the late 1070s and was sparse until the late 1080s.[5] The British Academy *English Episcopal Acta* series editing post-Conquest

---

1 Among which see especially N.P. Brooks, *The Early History of the Church of Canterbury* (Leicester, 1984) and Nicholas Brooks, 'Anglo-Saxon Charters: a Review of Work 1957–73; with a Postscript on the Period 1973–98', in Nicholas Brooks, *Anglo-Saxon Myths: State and Church 400–1066* (London and Rio Grande, 2000), 181–215.

2 S 1244–1428, 1488–9, 1491–2, 1499, 1523, 1526 and cf. also 1429–31, 1433–6, 1438, 1440–44, 1446–8, 1451–3, 1455–6, 1460, 1463–5, 1468, 1470–42, 1474–6, 1478, 1480.

3 Michèle Courtois, 'Remarques sur les chartes originales des évêques, antérieurs à 1121 et conservées dans les Bibliothèques et Archives de France', in *A propos des actes d'évêques: Hommage à Lucie Fossier*, ed. Michel Parisse (Nancy, 1991), 45–77.

4 David Bates, 'The Conqueror's Charters', in *England in the Eleventh Century: Proceedings of the 1990 Harlaxton Symposium*, ed. Carola Hicks (Stamford 1992), 1–15 at 14; for a discussion of charters issued by Anglo-Norman laymen and laywomen below royal rank, see Richard Mortimer, 'Anglo-Norman Lay Charters, 1066–c.1100: a Diplomatic Approach', *ANS*, 26 (2003), 153–75; see also John Hudson, 'L'écrit, les archives et le droit en Angleterre (IXe–XIIe siècle)', *Revue historique*, no. 637 (2006), 3–35.

5 Julia Barrow, 'From the Lease to the Certificate: the Evolution of Episcopal Acts in England and Wales (c. 700–c. 1250), in *Die Diplomatik der Bischofsurkunde vor 1250/ La*

episcopal *acta* is now so far advanced that comparisons between pre-and post-Conquest ecclesiastical charters can begin to be undertaken.[6] This chapter will survey briefly what happened to charters issued by English bishops and abbots (there are no extant charters of abbesses) in the three and a half decades between the Conquest and the accession of Henry I, and to compare them with equivalent charters from the reign of Edward the Confessor, and to some extent also with eleventh-century French episcopal *acta*. The aim of the exercise is essentially to find out the extent to which English beneficiaries thought it worthwhile, in the very uneasy circumstances prevailing in England between 1066 and 1087, to obtain charters from prelates, and whether, as David Bates noted in the case of royal charters, Domesday was a defining moment.[7] Other aims of the paper are to find out how leading figures in the church authenticated their charters and what this says about perceptions of their status and to survey developments in diplomatic: by 1100 charters based on the writ form were emerging as the standard type of charter in England, at the end of a 30-year process which involved adoption of both English and French diplomatic features.[8]

The charters on which this paper is based are listed in the Appendix below.[9] The principles of selection are as follows: (1) all charters issued between 1066 and 1100 by bishops of English sees and abbots of English monasteries in the first person; (2) all conventions (usually in the third person) drawn up between 1066 and 1100 in which at least one party is a bishop of an English see or an abbot of an English monastery; (3) notices in the third person recounting transactions by bishops or abbots, (4) charters issued by Bishop Odo of Bayeux for English beneficiaries; (5) charters issued by English bishops or abbots whose pontificates or abbatiates began before, but ended

---

diplomatique épiscopale avant 1250, ed. Christoph Haidacher and Werner Köfler (Innsbruck, 1995), 529–42, at 529.

6 *English Episcopal Acta* (hereafter *EEA*, cited by volume and item number), 33 volumes to date, British Academy (Oxford, 1980–2007). The volumes principally used here are the following: i, *Lincoln, 1067–1185*, ed. David M. Smith (1980); v, *York, 1070–1154*, ed. Janet E. Burton (1988); vii, *Hereford, 1079–1234*, ed. Julia Barrow (1993); xi, *Exeter, 1046–1184*, ed. Frank Barlow (1996); xviii, *Salisbury, 1078–1217*, ed. Brian Kemp (1999) and xxviii, *Canterbury, 1070–1136*, ed. Martin Brett and Joseph A. Gribbin (2004). The author is very grateful to Christopher Brooke and to Martin Brett for generously allowing her to make use of the relevant parts of two volumes in the series, ahead of publication, respectively *Worcester, 1062–1179*, ed. Mary Cheney, with C.N.L. Brooke, David M. Smith and Philippa Hoskin (now *EEA*, xxxiii (2007)) and *Rochester, 1075–1235*, ed. Martin Brett and Margaret Blount.

7 Bates, 'The Conqueror's Charters', 14.

8 Richard Sharpe, 'The Use of Writs in the Eleventh Century', *ASE*, 32 (2003), 247–91, esp. 247; Richard Sharpe, 'Address and Delivery in Anglo-Norman Royal Charters', in *Charters and Charter Scholarship in Britain and Ireland*, ed. Marie Therese Flanagan and Judith A. Green (Basingstoke, 2005), 32–52. Sharpe uses the term 'writ-charter' to refer to charters addressed to shire courts ('The Use', 249–50). Cf. also David Bates, 'The Earliest Norman Writs', *EHR*, 100 (1985), 266–84, for the introduction of writs into Normandy after 1066. David Bates, *Re-ordering the Past and Negotiating the Present in Stenton's First Century*, The Stenton Lecture 1999 (Reading, 2000), esp. 10–16, argues for the predominance of French models in England from the 1090s onwards, but I think that he seriously underrates the importance of the writ.

9 Appendix below.

after, 1100, save in those instances where the charter can be proved to have been issued after 1100. Some extraneous and late material is thus unavoidably included, but given the fluidity of contemporary diplomatic form and uncertainty about when particular diplomatic features or formulae are likely to have emerged, it seems best to take a flexible approach. Charters which have been proved to be forgeries, or which very probably are forgeries,[10] have been omitted from this survey. This does not mean, however, that all the items listed in the Appendix below are genuine. Martin Brett's work on the Rochester archive has shown the great extent of the forging activities of the monks of Rochester cathedral; charters from the Rochester archive listed below are merely those which he has not specifically been able to prove to be forged.[11] The charter of Archbishop Anselm for Chester Abbey shares the florid diplomatic of Chester's forged foundation charter, while Anselm's general confirmation to the monks of Christ Church Canterbury of properties and rights displays diplomatic forms typical of a rather later date.[12] St Nicholas' Priory, Exeter, the recipient of all the surviving charters in the name of Bishop Osbern of Exeter, was a dependency of Battle Abbey, whose capacity for forgery was enormous.[13] Selby Abbey also forged charters.[14] The charters listed in the Appendix, therefore, are not necessarily trustworthy. Here again, however, it is necessary to operate with a degree of flexibility in the hope that the work of comparing the various charters may help to elucidate the genuine and the fake.

---

10 See *EEA* volumes for comments by editors on authenticity; in addition, see the list of probable forgeries in vols. 1–30 of the series in Julia Barrow, 'Why forge Episcopal Acta? Preliminary Observations on the Forged Charters in the *English Episcopal Acta* Series', in *The Foundations of Medieval English Ecclesiastical History: Studies Presented to David Smith*, ed. Philippa Hoskin, Christopher Brooke and Barrie Dobson (Woodbridge, 2005), 18–39 at 28–36. To the list in that article should perhaps be added *EEA*, i, no. 3 (an extremely elaborate diploma of Bishop Remigius of Lincoln for Stow, no. 41 in the Appendix below), and certainly *EEA*, xi, no. 7, a supposed original for St Nicholas' Priory, Exeter in a hand of the mid-twelfth century (Tessa Webber, pers. comm.). Nos. 13–14 in the Appendix below, for the same beneficiary, are also suspect. The handwriting of no. 39 in the Appendix below is probably a decade or so later than its stated date of 20 May 1089 (Christopher Brooke, pers. comm., based on discussion with Tessa Webber and Michael Gullick).

11 *EEA Rochester*, ed. Brett and Blount, forthcoming; in general on Rochester's intense forging activity, see Martin Brett, 'Forgery at Rochester', in *Fälschungen im Mittelalter*, Monumenta Germaniae Historica (6 vols, Hanover, 1988–90), IV, 397–412.

12 See editor's reservations about these charters in notes to *EEA*, xxviii, no. 21 and no. 18. On Chester's foundation charter see Marjorie Chibnall, 'Forgery in Narrative Charters', in *Fälschungen im Mittelalter*, IV, 331–46 at 335–6: Chester's foundation charter drew not only on charters of Shrewsbury abbey but also on charters for St-Sauveur-le-Vicomte.

13 Eleanor Searle, 'Battle Abbey and Exemption: the Forged Charters', *EHR*, 83 (1968), 449–80; Stefan Dohmen, 'Exemplarische Untersuchungen zur Rechtskraft des Privilegs. Die gerichtliche Handhabung von Privilegienurkunden in England von König Stefan bis König Johann', *Archiv für Diplomatik*, 42 (1996), 33–224 at 58, 68–75; Nicholas Vincent, 'King Henry II and the Monks of Battle: the Battle Chronicle Unmasked', in *Belief and Culture in the Middle Ages: Studies Presented to Henry Mayr-Harting*, ed. Richard Gameson and Henrietta Leyser (Oxford, 2001), 264–86. On St Nicholas' Priory, Exeter, see n. 10 above.

14 Cf note to *EEA* v, no. 4; Barrow, 'Why forge Episcopal Acta?', 25, 29–30.

The list below contains 55 items, of which 41 were issued by bishops or are agreements in which at least one party was a bishop. The remaining 14 items are abbatial (it should also be noted that some of the episcopal items are conventions involving abbots). Odo of Bayeux' charters for English beneficiaries have been included because they helped to provide a model for episcopal charters in England in the post-Conquest period. Otherwise, fourteen individual bishops representing ten English sees occur in the list,[15] the most prolific being Archbishop Anselm of Canterbury (1093–1109), with eight charters[16] and Bishop Wulfstan of Worcester (1062–1095), with seven. Five individual abbots from three abbeys (Bury, Ramsey and Westminster) are represented. Bury and Westminster also figure as most prominent among the beneficiaries of surviving charters of William I[17] and it is the relative fullness of their archives in the eleventh century which explains their position here. Counting up the beneficiaries of these acts is tricky because of the number of conventions, both dispute settlements and confraternity agreements, but if we reckon the total according to archive (using the term in the sense used by the British Academy Anglo-Saxon Charters Committee)[18] it is 20: Abingdon, Bath, Le Bec, Bury St Edmunds, Christ Church Canterbury, St Augustine's Canterbury, Chester, Durham, Evesham, St Nicholas' Priory Exeter, Eynsham, Harbledown Hospital near Canterbury, Hereford, Malling, Ramsey, Rochester, Salisbury, Selby, Wells, Westminster and Worcester. This calculation reckons charters issued to, and agreements with, episcopal and abbatial tenants as part of the archive for a particular church. Examining the beneficiaries more closely allows us to see, in most cases, a close relationship between them and the bishops or abbots who issued the documents, or whose names also occur in them. Fourteen charters were issued by bishops or abbots for their cathedral or abbey communities and 15 charters for tenants of their churches.[19] Four documents record confraternities which involved the bishop or abbot's own church as well as one or more other churches.[20] Three writs issued by Abbot Gilbert of Westminster concerning the fate of outlaws were intended to protect Westminster Abbey's rights of sanctuary.[21] Only 17 charters show bishops making or confirming grants to churches other than their cathedral, and this total includes all the charters issued by Odo of Bayeux as well as many of the charters

---

15 Canterbury, Durham, Exeter, Hereford, Lincoln, Rochester, Salisbury, Wells, Worcester and York.

16 It should be noted, however, that all of Anselm's charters listed below could have been issued after 1100: see Appendix, nos. 43–6, 48–50, 54.

17 Bates, 'The Conqueror's Charters', 11, for comment on the frequency with which Bury St Edmunds and Westminster occur as beneficiaries of William I's charters; Sharpe, 'The Use of Writs', 248, 254–7 on Bury St Edmunds.

18 See N.P. Brooks, 'Anglo-Saxon Charters: Recent Work', 181, for an explanation of the use of the term 'archive' by the British Academy Anglo-Saxon charters project.

19 Appendix nos. 3, 24, 28, 34, 36–7, 39–40, 42–3, 48, 51, 53 (grantors' communities); 1–2, 10–11, 15, 18, 21–3, 27, 30–31, 35, 49, 52 (tenants).

20 Appendix, nos. 12, 16–17, 20.

21 Appendix, nos. 25–6, 29; see also Gervase Rosser, 'Sanctuary and Social Negotiation in Medieval England', in *The Cloister and the World: Essays in Medieval History in Honour of Barbara Harvey*, ed. John Blair and Brian Golding (Oxford, 1996), 57–79.

noted in the preceding paragraph as being possibly dubious.[22] The seeking out of bishops by abbeys anxious to obtain episcopal approval for their ownership of – in particular – churches and tithes did not occur in the pre-Conquest period (at that time estate churches were not as a rule separated from the manors of which they formed a part).[23] The development of this phenomenon in England has not hitherto been fully studied but was certainly quite strongly marked by *c.* 1125. The starting point, however, seems to lie in the late eleventh century, though the lack of documentation and the difficulty of establishing which acts are genuine, makes the origins of the process hard to define.[24] All in all, the pattern of situations in which charters were obtained from bishops or abbots, or in which bishops or abbots felt it appropriate to issue them, was essentially similar in the period 1066–1100 to the pattern which had prevailed before 1066: most of these documents laid down internal property arrangements for an ecclesiastical community, or regulated the granting of property to tenants. Before the Conquest grants of church property to tenants had been in the form of leases for one, two or three lives only;[25] it is worth noting that several post-Conquest grants to tenants were also limited to one life, for example Abbot Gilbert of Westminster's grant to William Baynard and Bishop Robert of Hereford's grant to Roger de Lacy.[26]

Some degree of continuity between the pre- and post-Conquest periods in the production of charters by ecclesiastics must therefore be reckoned with, but nonetheless 1066 did mark a caesura in document output. This can be appreciated most clearly by looking at the dates and dating-limits of the documents. Only 11 of the documents listed below have dates, the earliest of which is 1072 and the second earliest 1081.[27] But examining the dating-ranges of the remaining documents allows us to see that only three charters could possibly have been issued earlier than 1070. Two of these were issued by Abbot Baldwin of Bury St Edmunds and one is an agreement in which he was a party; the two former could have been issued as late as 1098 and, since their diplomatic forms are similar to ones current in the early twelfth century, this would be a more appropriate context.[28] The agreement could

---

22   Appendix nos. 4–8, 13–14, 19, 32–3, 38, 41, 44–6, 50, 54; of these, no. 41 is a charter issued by Bishop Remigius of Lincoln for Stow, a monastery under his patronage.

23   John Blair, *The Church in Anglo-Saxon Society* (Oxford, 2005), 422.

24   Appendix, nos. 13, 14 and cf. 41. The first two of these are all grants by Bishop Osbern of Exeter for the priory of St Nicholas, Exeter; other grants of churches in the name of Bishop Osbern for St Nicholas (*EEA* xi, nos. 4, 7) are likely to be forgeries. See also Barrow, 'Why forge Episcopal Acta?', 24–5.

25   Vanessa King, 'St Oswald's Tenants', in *St Oswald of Worcester: Life and Influence*, ed. Nicholas Brooks and Catherine Cubitt (London, 1996), 100–116; Barrow, 'From the Lease to the Certificate', 531–2; Francesca Tinti, 'The "Costs" of Pastoral Care: Church Dues in Late Anglo-Saxon England', in *Pastoral Care in Late Anglo-Saxon England*, ed. Francesca Tinti (Woodbridge, 2005), 27–51, at 42–7.

26   Appendix, nos. 23, 27; at least some part of no. 23, the clause dealing with aids and tithes, seems to be interpolated.

27   Appendix, nos. 11, 22–3, 27 (date miscopied by copyist), 35, 37–42.

28   Appendix, nos. 1–3.

have been issued as late as 1087.[29] Only four items in the Appendix *must* have been issued before 1080, though a total of 19 acts *could* date to before 1080.[30] This total includes the five charters of Bishop Odo and the three earliest documents of Bishop Wulfstan of Worcester, which are all confraternity agreements between Worcester cathedral priory and other monastic houses. By contrast, 14 charters were definitely issued between 1080 and 1089 and a total of 36 charters could have been.[31] Of the closely dateable items, no fewer than nine were issued between 1086 and 1089. The influence of Domesday Book is clearly marked in the output of ecclesiastical charters just as it is in royal ones.[32] Two other charters can also be considered in the context of Domesday, Bishop Gundulf of Rochester's convention with Gilbert of Tonbridge of 1085 x 1088 and Bishop Robert of Hereford's grant to Roger de Lacy of 1085, if we hypothesise that the latter item was drawn up during the opening days of the royal assembly at Gloucester at Christmas 1085 at which William I discussed the feasibility of a Domesday survey with his counsellors.[33] The Domesday survey, and perhaps even merely the anticipation that it was to take place, gave landowners sufficient security of tenure to make valid any documents which they might issue. The sudden flurry of charters dated 1089 may also result from the greater political security attained in 1088 with the expulsion of Bishops Odo of Bayeux and William of Durham from England and the strong support for William Rufus shown by the majority of the population. By contrast with the noticeable activity in the late 1080s, output which can be definitely assigned to the 1090s is low, at only four charters, though 28 items in total could date from then and of these 16 can be no earlier than 1091. Eighteen of the charters in the list below have *termini ad quem* in the twelfth century.[34] Output over 1066–1100 can therefore be summed up as (probably) non-existent 1066–1070, extremely sparse 1071–1080, but significantly more buoyant in the 1080s, especially once the Domesday Survey had been undertaken; even so, output remained low until well into the twelfth century.

Only six of the documents listed below survive in the original; these are all episcopal charters (two of Odo, one of Robert of Hereford, two of Anselm and one of Ranulf Flambard); in addition, there is a supposed original charter of Wulfstan of Worcester, quite possibly a very early remodelling of a genuine charter of his (no. 39 in the Appendix below), with a seal which may be a genuine one that had

---

29 Appendix no. 2; might this item perhaps have been connected with the Domesday Survey?

30 Appendix, nos. 10, 11, 16, 17 must be pre-1080; 1–9, 12–15, 18–19 could be pre-1080, though several of them are probably rather later.

31 Appendix, nos. 20–24, 27–8, 31–3, 35, 37–9 must have been issued between 1080 and 1089; nos. 1–9, 12–15, 18–19, 25–6, 29–30, 34, 36 could have been.

32 Bates, 'The Conqueror's Charters', 14.

33 Appendix, nos. 23–4; on Robert's probable involvement in the Domesday Survey, see Henry Loyn, 'William's Bishops: some Further Thoughts', *ANS*, 10 (1987), 223–35 at 227–9.

34 Appendix, nos. 40–42, 53 were definitely issued in the 1090s; nos. 1, 3, 12, 25–6, 29–30, 34, 36 could have been issued in the 1090s but might be earlier; nos. 40–55 can be no earlier than the 1090s.

been reattached.[35] Five of the genuine originals were authenticated by being sealed, and three seals (of Anselm and Ranulf) survive either certainly or possibly from the pre-1100 period. In addition, a probably genuine seal of Wulfstan, lost since the Second World War, was formerly attached to no. 39, and a cast taken from it survives in the Society of Antiquaries, while a seventeenth-century pen drawing with colour wash exists showing Odo of Bayeux' double seal, at that point still attached to no. 5 in the Appendix below. In each case, the method of attaching the seal was on a tongue.[36] One of Abbot Baldwin of Bury's charters, and one of Osbern's, neither surviving in the original, contain corroborative clauses referring to a seal; the use of such clauses is highly precocious in eleventh-century England, and Osbern's charter is open to doubt on other grounds as well. One of Odo's charters contains a corroboration clause referring not to a seal but to 'the sign of my hand', and similarly Remigius says he has certified his document with his own hand.[37] At all events, the frequency of seals on the surviving charters suggests that it was normal for bishops to own seal matrices in the post-Conquest period. Bishop Robert of Hereford could have had a seal for authenticating his personal correspondence, even if he did not wish to attach it to his land-grant for Roger de Lacy, which is authenticated by being a chirograph.[38] The agreement between Bishop Osmund of Salisbury and Abbot Rainald of Abingdon is described in a cartulary rubric as a chirograph, and Remigius describes his charter as a chirograph: neither document survives in the original.[39]

---

35 Appendix, nos. 4–5, 23, 48–9, 55; on the supposed original of Bishop Wulfstan, no. 39, see n. 10 above.

36 On Odo's seal see *Regesta Regum Anglo-Normannorum: the Acta of William I (1066–1087)*, ed. David Bates (Oxford, 1998), no. 74, and, for a reproduction of a seventeenth-century drawing of the seal, see *Sir Christopher Hatton's Book of Seals*, ed. L.C. Loyd and D.M. Stenton, Publications of the Northamptonshire Record Society, 15 (Oxford, 1950), no. 431 and plate VIII; for Anselm's seal, see *EEA* xxviii, p. lx and nos. 14–16, 24, with reproductions Plate I; for Ranulf's seal, see William Greenwell and Charles Hunter Blair, 'Durham Seals', part 7, *Archaeologia Aeliana*, 14 (1917), 221–91 at 230–31, no. 3110. In addition to these, the seal matrix of Bishop Peter of Chester (1075–85) survives (T.A. Heslop, 'Twelfth-Century Forgeries as Evidence for Earlier Seals: the Case of St Dunstan', in *St Dunstan: His Life, Times and Cult*, ed. Nigel Ramsay, Margaret Sparks and Tim Tatton-Brown (Woodbridge, 1992), 299–310, at plate 55d between 142 and 143; see ibid., plate 55c for a cast of the seal of Wulfstan of Worcester), and an impression of the seal of Bishop Gundulf of Rochester is attached to *Regesta Regum Anglo-Normannorum 1066–1154*, ed. H.W.C. Davis, Charles Johnson, H.A. Cronne and R.H.C. Davis (4 vols, Oxford, 1913–69), II, no. 636 of 1103. For comment on the latter, see note to *EEA* xxviii, no. 24.

37 Appendix, nos. 3 (Baldwin), 13 (Osbern), 7 (Odo) and 41 (Remigius). The wording of Osbern's charter suggests a late date of composition.

38 *EEA*, vii, no. 2. Bates, *Re-ordering the Past*, 13–14, sees this document as essentially 'French' in form. The opening words of the document, the arrangement of the witnesses' names (not in columns) and the reference to the transaction being secured 'per amicos et per pecuniam' are essentially French features; on the other hand, the reference to the grant being for one life, the use of book hand and the layout of the document, with the script parallel to the long side, strongly suggest an attempt to imitate the Worcester leases.

39 Appendix no. 38; according its wording, no. 41 was also a chirograph, but it may not be genuine.

Most of the texts listed below survive only in cartulary copies, it is true, but they were probably originally issued as single-sheet charters: one possible exception is the confraternity agreement between William of St-Calais and Abbot Vitalis of Westminster recorded in the Durham *Liber Vitae*, which may never have been issued in charter form.[40] Indeed, some monasteries, notably Shaftesbury and Gloucester, simply recorded property transactions in the immediate post-Conquest period in a brief narrative form, rather than trying to obtain charters.[41]

As far as the internal features of the documents are concerned, seven are in Old English,[42] while all the others are in Latin only. Four of the Old English texts predate the Domesday Survey; the other three must be later than 1085.[43] The small proportion of Old English texts out of the whole, and the dwindling of numbers over this period, are noticeable. In other respects, however, Anglo-Saxon traditions continued to exercise some influence over diplomatic practice. The clearest and most important example of this is the survival of the writ. No fewer than thirteen ecclesiastical charters of this period are what Richard Sharpe terms 'writ-charters', writs addressed to the personnel of one or more shire court.[44] Pre-Conquest writs of this kind issued by bishops or abbots are rare, though they do occur;[45] royal writs had been, and remained, frequent before and after 1066.[46] Ten other charters adopt the form of protocol characteristic of writs and letters – *intitulatio, inscriptio* and greeting – but nine of these have general addresses and the tenth is a letter addressed to an individual.[47] The emergence of the general address appears to have been slow – none occurs in any charter definitely dateable to before Domesday, for instance – and it should be noted that two of the charters in this category are, for other reasons, not above suspicion.[48] Richard Sharpe has noted that forms of general address begin to occur in royal charters (but not writs) under William I, but that they are few and variable. Then, under Henry I, at some point between 1106 and 1110, a fixed formula

---

40 Appendix, no. 20.

41 On Shaftesbury, see *Charters and Custumals of Shaftesbury Abbey, 1089–1216*, ed. N.E. Stacy, Records of Social and Economic History, New Series, 39 (Oxford, 2006), 63–5, and Kathleen Cook, 'Donors and Daughters: Shaftesbury Abbey's Benefactors, Endowments and Nuns c. 1086–1130', *ANS*, 12 (1990), 29–45; for Gloucester, see *Historia et Cartularium Monasterii Sancti Petri Gloucestriae*, ed. W.H. Hart, Rolls Series, 33 (London, 1863–7), I, 58–125, and comment by C.N.L. Brooke, *The Church and the Welsh Border in the Central Middle Ages* (Woodbridge, 1986), 51–65, esp. 59.

42 Appendix, nos. 5, 10–11, 16, 25, 29, 55.

43 Appendix, nos. 25, 29, 55 are later than 1085; the other four charters listed in n. 42 above are all earlier than 1086.

44 Appendix, nos. 4–6, 19, 25, 29, 33, 36, 44 (addressed to a hundred court), 46 (addressed to a lathe court), 47, 50, 55 (addressed to the thegns and drengs of Islandshire and Norhamshire); see Sharpe, 'The Use of Writs', 249–50, and Sharpe, 'Address and Delivery', 33–45.

45 *Anglo-Saxon Writs*, ed. F.E. Harmer (Manchester, 1952), nos. 3 (Latin translation) and 6.

46 *Anglo-Saxon Writs*, ed. Harmer; Sharpe, 'The Use of Writs', 247; *Regesta*, ed. Bates, 43–62.

47 Appendix, nos. 1, 3, 14, 43, 49, 51–2 have general addresses; no. 9 is addressed to a single individual.

48 Appendix no. 43 is regarded with suspicion by its editor; no. 14 is a grant to a daughter house of Battle Abbey, and its forms look late.

for a general address emerges, used in some writs.[49] It is likely that royal diplomatic formulae exercised some influence on ecclesiastical ones in this area. But while royal general addresses moved towards cataloguing the king's men according to rank and function ('*archiepiscopis, episcopis, comitibus, vicecomitibus, baronibus et omnibus fidelibus suis*'), ecclesiastical ones were less keen to stratify their audience socially. Instead, they wanted to stress unity. The word *fidelibus* would have struck episcopal clerks as being useful in religious as well as in secular contexts, and in the former it was notably inclusive – it covered all believers. Hence Abbot Baldwin of Bury's use of '*omnibus fidelibus utriusque sexus*' and '*presentibus et futuris dei fidelibus*'.[50] By the later twelfth century '*universis Cristi fidelibus*' and '*omnibus sancte matris ecclesie filiis*' were the norm for addresses in English episcopal *acta* and both these forms had begun to occur fairly often in most dioceses by just before the middle of the twelfth century.[51]

Specifically northern French influence is visible in other aspects of the documents. The form of the bishop's or abbot's title in England, though often a simple '*Gilbertus abbas*' or equivalent, was tending to include the phrase *dei gratia* by the 1080s, with the most usual form being '*Sampson dei gratia Wigornensis episcopus*' or equivalent.[52] Pre-Conquest Worcester leases, for example, had often included phrases to say that a bishop owed his office to divine permission, but *dei gratia* was not the normal expression.[53] Its adoption in England after the Conquest might have received an extra boost from the fact that Bishop Odo of Bayeux used it.[54] At Worcester, there was some attempt by Bishops Wulfstan and Samson to look back into the Anglo-Saxon past: Wulfstan favoured the term *antistes*, which Bishop

---

49 Sharpe, 'Address and Delivery', 45–6.

50 Appendix, nos. 3, 34; on the development of the general address see Sharpe, 'The Use of Writs', 249, and Sharpe, 'Address and Delivery', 45–50.

51 *EEA* i, *Lincoln, 1067–1185*, ed. David M. Smith (Oxford, 1980), p. liv; *EEA* v, p. xlv; *EEA* vi, *Norwich, 1070–1214*, ed. Christopher Harper-Bill (Oxford, 1990), p. lxii; *EEA* vii, pp. lxxi, lxxxiii–lxxxiv; *EEA* viii, *Winchester 1070–1204*, ed. M.J. Franklin (Oxford, 1993), pp. lxviii–lxix; *EEA* ix, *Bath and Wells*, ed. Frances M.R. Ramsey (Oxford, 1995), p. lxxxiii; *EEA* xi, p. xciii; *EEA* xiv, *Coventry and Lichfield 1072–1159*, ed. M.J. Franklin (Oxford, 1997), p. lviii; *EEA* xv, *London 1076–1187*, ed. Falko Neininger (Oxford, 1999); *EEA* xviii, pp. xci–xcii; *EEA* xxiv, *Durham 1153–1195*, ed. M.G. Snape (Oxford, 2002), p. lvi; *EEA* xxxi, *Ely 1109–1197*, ed. Nicholas Karn (Oxford, 2005), pp. cxxx–cxxxi; *The Acta of the Bishops of Chichester 1075–1207*, ed. Henry Mayr-Harting, Canterbury and York Society, 56 (Torquay, 1964), nos. 20, 22, 25–30, 34, 36–7, 41, 43–6, 48–53, 57–62, 65–9.

52 Appendix, nos. 1, 4, 6, 8, 9, 14, 32, 34–6, 39, 43, 45, 46, 50, 51 (forms with *dei gratia*); no. 3 (an intitulatio with *dei misericordia*); no. 53 (*munificentia Dei*). In north-eastern France, Bishop Elinand of Laon used *dei gratia* between 1055 and 1096 (*Actes des évêques de Laon des origines à 1151*, ed. Annie Dufour-Malbezin, Documents, études et répertoires, 65 (Paris, 2001), nos. 24, 28, 31, 33–6, 38–40, 42–5), though Bishop Lambert of Arras (1094–1115) preferred 'Ego Lambertus, Dei miseratione Atrebatensis episcopus': see *Les chartes des évêques d'Arras (1093–1203)*, ed. Benoît-Michel Tock, Collection de documents inédits sur l'histoire de France, Section d'histoire médiévale et de philologie, 20 (Paris, 1991), 3–31.

53 For example, Bishop Oswald of Worcester's use of *þurh Godes gyfe* (S 1299) or *largiflua dei clementia* (S 1310); in a similar vein see the opening preamble in Appendix no. 41.

54 Appendix, nos. 4, 6.

Oswald had sometimes used in his leases, and Samson had one of his charters cast entirely in hermeneutic language, including the *intitulatio* 'ego Samson munificentia dei presul'.[55]

Norman influence is also visible in the nine charters opening with the words 'Hoc/Hec est conventio' or variants thereof.[56] But, while it is clear that Norman models supplied this wording, Anglo-Saxon fore-runners may also have exercised some influence. Several late Anglo-Saxon agreements open 'Her cyð þysum gewrite þa forewearde', where the term 'foreweard' has the same meaning as *conventio*.[57] Similarly, while French influence inspires the use of notifications using parts of the verbs *scire* or *noscere* (found in 18 of the charters listed in the Appendix), the use of these phrases would not have been completely alien to Anglo-Saxon clerks used to charters opening '*Her cyth*' or '*Her swutelað*' or to writs containing the words '*and ic cuthe eow*': indeed, examples of '*Her cyth*' and '*and we kythath*' occur in a document associated with Bishop Giso and in writs of Abbot Gilbert of Westminster in the list below.[58] Both Norman and Anglo-Saxon charters could open with a date, as do three of the documents in the list below,[59] while, of the three verbal invocations which occur in post-Conquest ecclesiastical documents, one, Wulfstan of Worcester's '*On Drihtnes naman Hælendis Cristes*', is based on an invocation used by his predecessor Bishop Lyfing,[60] while the remaining two, Abbot Baldwin of Bury's '*In nomine patris et filii et spiritus sancti*' and Bishop Osmund of Salisbury's '*In nomine Sancte et individue Trinitatis*' use forms standard on the continent but which had never been used in pre-Conquest England.[61] The tiny number of verbal invocations is matched by the tiny number of arengae (four only) and no document in the list below has both a verbal invocation and an arenga.[62] In other words, the

---

55 *antistes* in Appendix, no. 37 (in which Wulfstan also uses papal terminology to refer to himself, '*servus servorum Dei*') and Hearne, *Hemingi cartularium*, II, 421–4; at one point Wulfstan refers to himself as *pontifex* (Appendix, no. 39). For Samson's charter, see Appendix no. 53.

56 Appendix, nos. 12, 17, 18, 20–24, 28, 38. For a Norman example of 1063 x 1089, see Ferdinand Lot, *Etudes critiques sur l'abbaye de Saint-Wandrille* (Paris, 1913), 80, no. 34; see also Emily Zack Tabuteau, *Transfers of Property in Eleventh-Century Norman Law* (Chapel Hill, 1988), 31–3, on *conventiones*.

57 Cf. S 1391, 1403, 1468, 1470, 1471 and, a Latin version, S 1425.

58 For examples of *scire* and *noscere* see Appendix, nos. 3, 4, 6, 19, 26, 33, 35, 46, 47, 49–51 (scire), 1, 2, 8, 13, 34, 43 (noscere); for 'Her cyth' see no. 11; for '*we kythath*' see nos. 25, 29; cf. '*Si eow eallum cuth*' in no. 5. For Norman uses of *noscere*, see Lot, *Etudes critiques*, 61–2, no. 18 ('*Noverint omnes*'), of 1035 x 1040 and 68, no. 23 ('*Notum sit*'), of 1038 x 1048.

59 For examples of Norman charters opening with dates, see Lot, *Etudes critiques*, 109, 112–14, 116–17, 119–21 (nos. 53, 57–8, 61–2, 66, all of the early twelfth century); for pre-Conquest English examples cf. S 1396–7; for post-Conquest examples see Appendix nos. 22, 27, 37.

60 Appendix, no. 16; S 1394.

61 Appendix, nos. 34, 40; for Norman examples of these or closely-related invocations, see Lot, *Etudes critiques*, 41, 52–4, 57–8, 62–7, 74–7 (nos. 10, 13, 15, 19, 20–22, 30–31).

62 Appendix, nos. 15, 41, 46, 54; the arenga in no. 41 is exceptionally long, a fully developed contemplation on the Church as the Bride of the Lamb and on cleansing through baptism.

abbots and bishops of post-Conquest England mostly did not wish to aim at a formal type of charter. There was no demand for continental diplomata and these never became popular as a model for ecclesiastical charters in post-Conquest England. Indeed, ten charters open simply with the disposition.[63] The way was thus open for bishops and abbots to move towards the writ form.

The charters are almost all evidentiary rather than dispositive, the only exceptions being injunctions (e.g. *mando*) in a few of the writs.[64] Most of the charters are confirmations or grants and the most frequently occurring verbs are *confirmare* and *concedere*; *dare*, popular in lay charters, was the verb favoured by Worcester bishops, but elsewhere ecclesiastics were more sparing with it, though sometimes using it together with *concedere* (*do et concedo*). *Tradere*, *reddere* and *donare* were hardly ever used by bishops or abbots.[65] About a fifth of the charters have clauses for the salvation of souls, a feature which is common in the charters of laymen and laywomen in England in the last three decades of the eleventh century. In both cases the souls specified commonly include not only the benefactors, but also William I, Matilda and sometimes William II (perhaps in an attempt to secure the survival of the grant if the benefactor was dispossessed at a later date). Bishops, however, might mention their predecessors rather than the king.[66] Only three of the documents refer to grants in alms and only two mention grants in perpetual or pure and perpetual alms (both these are charters of Bishop Osbern of Exeter for the Battle dependency St Nicholas' Priory in Exeter and as such not above suspicion). Grants in alms seem not to occur in lay charters in England before the 1090s, though a charter of Robert of Stafford 1088 refers to the grant itself as alms. The emergence of the term *elemosina*

---

63 Appendix, nos. 7, 10, 12, 21–2, 30–31, 48, 54. On the decline of the formal Anglo-Saxon diploma, see Charles Insley, 'Where did all the Charters go? Anglo-Saxon Charters and the New Politics of the Eleventh Century', *ANS*, 24 (2002), 109–27.

64 Appendix, no. 9 and cf. no. 51; cf. also the dispositive 'reformare decerno' in no. 41, but this document is probably suspect.

65 Appendix, nos. 13, 14, 32, 51, 54 (*confirmare*); nos. 1, 3, 4, 6, 15, 27, 30, 33, 43, 44, 46, 47, 49, 54 (*concedere*); nos. 34, 35, 52 (*dare et concedere*); nos. 37, 39, 42, 53 (*dare*); no. 5 (*tradere*); no. 49 (*reddere*); no. 8 (*donare*). *Concedere* was strongly favoured by Anselm. For lay charters see Mortimer, 'Anglo-Norman lay charters', 157 n. 18, 158 n. 21, 174 for *dare*, 155 n. 7 for *donare*, 154 n. 4 for *tradere*; for nuances in use between *dare*, *concedere* and *confirmare* in royal and private charters see Richard Sharpe, 'Give, grant, confirm: Words and Meanings in Eleventh- and Twelfth-Century Charters', forthcoming.

66 Appendix, nos. 7, 13, 22, 34, 40, 51. For examples of clauses concerning salvation of souls in lay charters of this period, see *Early Yorkshire Charters*, ed. William Farrer and C.T. Clay, 12 vols, Yorkshire Archaeological Society Record Series, Extra Series (1914–65; hereafter *EYC*), III, no. 1483, IV, nos. 2–4, IX, no. 133; *Regesta*, ed. Bates, no. 101; *Westminster Abbey Charters, 1066–c.1214*, ed. Emma Mason, London Record Society, 25 (London, 1988), no. 436; *Chronicon Abbatiae Rameseiensis*, ed. W.D. Macray, Rolls Series, 83 (London, 1886), 234; *Registrum Malmesburiense*, ed. J.S. Brewer, 2 vols, Rolls Series, 72 (London 1879–80), I, 328–9; *Feudal Documents from the Abbey of Bury St Edmunds*, ed. D.C. Douglas (London, 1932), no. 170; *The Staffordshire Chartulary, Series I*, ed. R.W. Eyton, in *Collections for a History of Staffordshire*, II, William Salt Archaeological Society, 2 (Birmingham, 1881), 178–276 at 178–85.

in ecclesiastical charters probably happened at the same time, one charter being dated 1093 and another being no earlier than 1093.[67]

The ways in which the charters close are very varied, unsurprisingly given the extreme informality of charter production in this period, but 17 of the items have sanction clauses and nearly half have witness-lists.[68] Five of the writs (not ones with witness-lists) end with farewells, a survival of the 'God eow behealde' of the Old English writs.[69] Many of the texts, however, have none of these features but close abruptly after the disposition.

By the end of the eleventh century, individuals other than the king were coming to feel more confident about their ability to issue charters and this assurance was matched by moves towards more standardised forms of charter, preserving elements of pre-1066 Norman and English features but nonetheless innovative. But it is worth pausing to dwell on the effects which the intervening period of uncertainty had on the writing and preservation of documents and a text which sums this up very nicely can be found in Winchester cathedral's fourteenth-century cartulary. In translation it runs: 'Memorandum that the monk Blacheman the goldsmith, at the request and permission of Bishop W(alkelin), that he might remain his obedientiary for ever, burnt at Bitterne a charter of the manor of Easton and altered the charter of King William [I] concerning the warren of Walkelin and fraudulently and deceitfully wrote Chichester where Porchester had previously been written, as still appears in the charter. Six months and three days later his neck was wrung by an evil spirit, and he was killed on the sea shore at Bitterne. He also stole a Bible of St Æthelwold which (Æthelwold) had ruled and written with his own hands at Glastonbury. Indeed he committed so many evil deeds that the human tongue may not narrate them, as were most clearly written and composed by the hand of Nicholas the monk of York in that same Bible'.[70]

---

67 Appendix, nos. 13, 41, 46; for lay charters, see *EYC*, IV, no. 4 and IX, no. 133, *Westminster Abbey Documents*, ed. Mason, no. 436; *The Staffordshire Chartulary*, I, no. 2. The idea of granting property in alms was imported from Normandy: on grants in alms in eleventh-century Normandy, see Tabuteau, *Transfers of Property*, 36–41.

68 Appendix, nos. 1, 7, 8, 13, 14, 21, 32, 34, 37, 39–43, 45, 53 (sanctions), and nos. 2, 3, 11, 15, 16, 18, 23–4, 27–8, 30, 34–40, 42, 48–52 (witness lists, though the names of witnesses were omitted by a copyist in the case of no. 51).

69 Appendix, nos. 9, 25–6, 29, 41 (very lengthy), 46, 55.

70 Winchester, Dean and Chapter cartulary (s. xiv ½), fo. 11, item no. 41: 'Memorandum quod Blacheman Aurifaber monachus ad rogatum et promissionem W. episcopi, ut suo perpetuo (sic for suus perpetuus) obedienciarius remaneret, combussit cartam manerii de Estone apud Byterne, et mutavit literam in Willelmi regis de warenna Walkelini episcopi, et fraude et dolo scripsit Cicestr' ubi prius scriptum erat Porcestr', sicut hactenus in eadem carta apparet. Qui post sex menses et tres dies torto collo a maligno spiritu iuxta Biterne super ripam maris interemptus est. Ipse etiam alienavit bibliam Sancti Adelwoldi quam manibus suis propriis regulavit et scripsit apud Glastoniam. Perpetravit etiam tot mala que lingua humana non sinit enarrare, sicut in dicta biblia manifestissime manu Nicholai monachi de Eboraco scripta et redacta fuerunt'. The translation is partly based on the version in A.W. Goodman, ed. *Chartulary of Winchester Cathedral* (Winchester 1927), 18, no. 41. For the writ of William I alluded to here, see *Regesta*, ed. Bates, no. 343. It is not clear whether Nicholas monk of York was a monk of Winchester originating from York, or was a monk of St Mary's Abbey in York, though perhaps the former is more probable.

Appendix

List of references to charters issued by bishops and abbots in England 1066–1100

Note: reference is only given to the most recent edition in each case, and occasionally to other recent work where this sheds light on dating or circumstances of composition. Where an original survives, this is stated; otherwise it can be assumed that the charter survives as a copy only.

1
1065 x 1098
Abbot Baldwin of Bury St Edmunds
Feudal Documents from the Abbey of Bury St Edmunds, ed. D.C. Douglas (London, 1932), no. 103.

2
1066 x 1087
Agreement between Abbot Baldwin of Bury St Edmunds and Peter, tenant of Bury St Edmunds
D.C. Douglas, 'A charter of enfeoffment under William the Conqueror', *EHR*, 42 (1927), 245–7, at 247.

3
1066 x 1098
Abbot Baldwin of Bury St Edmunds
Feudal Documents, ed. Douglas, no. 104.

4
1070 x 1082/3
Odo bishop of Bayeux and earl of Kent
(Original)
Regesta Regum Anglo-Normannorum: the Acta of William I (1066–1087), ed. David Bates (Oxford, 1998), no. 71.

5
1070 x 1082/3
Odo bishop of Bayeux and earl of Kent
(Original, Latin and Old English)
Regesta, ed. Bates, no. 74.

6
1070 x 1082/3
Odo bishop of Bayeux and earl of Kent
Regesta, ed. Bates, no. 85.

7
1070 x 1082/3
Odo bishop of Bayeux and earl of Kent
Regesta, ed. Bates, no. 86.

8
1070 x 1082/3
Archbishop Thomas I of York
Early Yorkshire Charters, ed. William Farrer and C.T. Clay, 13 vols., Yorkshire Archaeological Society Records Series, extra series (1914–1965), i, no. 41; *EEA*, v, no. 4 (calendared).

9
1070 x 1100 **or** 1109 x 1114
Archbishop Thomas (I or II) of York
EEA, v, no. 6.

10
1071 x 1080
Bishop Walcher of Durham
Durham Episcopal Charters 1071–1152, ed. H.S. Offler, Surtees Society, 179 (1968 for 1964), 1–3, no. 1.

11
29 Feb. 1072
Bishop Giso of Wells
Simon Keynes, 'Giso, bishop of Wells', *ANS*, 19 (1997), 203–71, at 262–3, App. iii.

12
1072 x 1095
Bishop Wulfstan of Worcester
The Cartulary of Worcester Cathedral Priory (Register I), ed. R.R. Darlington, Pipe Roll Society, new series, 38 (1968 for 1962–3), no. 305; *EEA*, xxxiii, no. 5.

13
1072 x 1103
Bishop Osbern of Exeter
EEA, xi, no. 5. This act is likely to be spurious: it has a corroboration clause whose wording appears to be of a date well into the twelfth century. See also n. 10 above.

14
1072 x 1103
Bishop Osbern of Exeter
EEA, xi, no. 6; cf. *EEA*, iii, no. 459. The authenticity of this act must be open to question: see n. 10 above.

15
1076 x 1085
Abbot Vitalis of Westminster
Westminster Abbey Charters 1066–c.1214, ed. Emma Mason, London Record Society, 25 (London, 1988), no. 234.

16
1077 x 16 February 1078
Bishop Wulfstan of Worcester
Diplomatarium Anglicum Aevi Sæxonici, ed. Benjamin Thorpe (London, 1865), 615–17; *Historia et Cartularium Monasterii Sancti Petri Gloucestriae*, ed. W.H. Hart, Rolls Series (London, 1863–7), III, pp. xviii–xxi; *EEA*, xxxiii, no. 7.
Dating: Ralph became abbot of Winchcombe 1077; Æthelwig abbot of Evesham may have died as late as 16 February 1078 (*The Heads of Religious Houses, England and Wales*, I, *940–1216*, ed. David Knowles, C.N.L. Brooke and Vera C.M. London, 2nd edn (Cambridge, 2001) 79, 248).

17
1077 x 1081
Bishop Wulfstan of Worcester
Worcester Cartulary, ed. Darlington, no. 304; *EEA*, xxxiii, no. 6.

18
1077 x 1087
Bishop Gundulf of Rochester
Textus Roffensis, ed. Thomas Hearne (Oxford, 1720), 212; *Registrum Roffense*, ed. John Thorpe (London, 1769), 32; forthcoming in *EEA* (Rochester) no. 10; M. Brett reports that the text is entered over an erasure, but 'there is no cogent argument from the content to suppose it seriously inaccurate'.

19
1078 x 1082/3
Bishop Odo of Bayeux
Regesta, ed. Bates, no. 135.

20
1080 x 1085
William of St-Calais, bishop of Durham
Liber Vitae Ecclesiae Dunelmensis: a Collotype Facsimile of the Original Manuscript with Introductory Essay and Notes, ed. A.H. Thompson, Surtees Society, 136 (Durham, 1923), fo. 48r; *Westminster Abbey Charters*, ed. Mason, no. 235.

21
1080 x 1087
Abbot Ailsi of Ramsey
Chronicon Abbatiae Rameseiensis, ed. W.D. Macray, Rolls Series (London, 1886), 207, no. 180 with another version 232–3, no. 238.

22
1081
Abbot Aldwine (probably in error for Ailsi) of Ramsey
Chronicon Abbatiae Rameseiensis, ed. Macray, 234, no. 240.

23
1085
Robert the Lotharingian, bishop of Hereford
(Original; chirograph).
EEA, vii, no. 2; for comment see also S. Purser, 'The origins of English feudalism? An episcopal land-grant revisited', *Historical Research*, 73 (2000), 80–92.

24
1085 x 1088
Gundulf, bishop of Rochester
EEA xxviii, no. 9

25
1085 x 1117
Abbot Gilbert of Westminster
Westminster Abbey Charters, ed. Mason, no. 239.

26
1085 x 1117
Abbot Gilbert of Westminster
Westminster Abbey Charters, ed. Mason, no. 240.

27
1086 (MS 1083, prob. in error for 1086)
Abbot Gilbert of Westminster
Westminster Abbey Charters, ed. Mason, no. 236.

28
c.1086
Bishop Wulfstan of Worcester
Domesday Book 16, Worcestershire, ed. F. and C. Thorn (Chichester, 1982), App. V, no. 5; *English Lawsuits from William I to Richard I*, ed. R.C. van Caenegem, 2 vols., Selden Society, 106–7 (London, 1990–1), I, 40, no. 15E; *EEA*, xxxiii, no. 13.

29
1086 x c.1104
Abbot Gilbert of Westminster
Westminster Abbey Charters, ed. Mason, no. 238.

30
1086 x 1107
Abbot Gilbert of Westminster
Westminster Abbey Charters, ed. Mason, no. 241.

31
c. 1087
Abbot Gilbert of Westminster
Westminster Abbey Charters, ed. Mason, no. 237.

32
1087 x 1089
Lanfranc, archbishop of Canterbury
EEA, xxviii, no. 5.

33
1087 x 1089
Lanfranc, archbishop of Canterbury
EEA, xxviii, no. 6.

34
1087 x 1098
Abbot Baldwin of Bury St Edmunds
Feudal Documents, ed. Douglas, no. 105.

35
17 June 1088 at Ramsey
Abbot Herbert of Ramsey
Chronicon Abbatiae Rameseiensis, ed. Macray, 233.

36
May 1088 x 2 August 1100
Bishop Gundulf of Rochester
Textus Roffensis, ed. Hearne, 214–15; *Registrum Roffense*, ed. Thorpe, 526; forthcoming in *EEA* (Rochester), no. 11.

37
1089
Bishop Wulfstan of Worcester
Worcester Cartulary, ed. Darlington, no. 4; *EEA*, xxxiii, no. 9.

38
14 March 1089
Bishop Osmund of Salisbury
EEA, xviii, no. 2; *The History of the Church of Abingdon*, ed. John Hudson (2 vols, Oxford, 2002–7), II, 22–5.

39
20 May 1089
Bishop Wulfstan of Worcester
(Supposed original)
Worcester Cartulary, ed. Darlington, no. 3; *EEA*, xxxiii, no. 8.

40
1091 (late January x early February)
Bishop Osmund of Salisbury
EEA, xviii, no. 3.

41
1091 (before 24 or 25 September)
Bishop Remigius of Lincoln
EEA, i, no. 3; for text see *Eynsham Cartulary*, ed. H.E. Salter, 2 vols, Oxford Historical Society, 49, 51 (Oxford, 1907–8), I, 32–5.

42
1093
Bishop Wulfstan of Worcester
Hemingi Chartularium ecclesiae Wigorniensis, ed. Thomas Hearne, 2 vols. (Oxford, 1723), II, 421–4; *EEA*, xxxiii, no. 11.

43
4 December 1093 x 21 April 1109
Anselm, archbishop of Canterbury
EEA, xxviii, no. 18, with note commenting 'the authenticity of the grant, at least in its present form, must remain in doubt'.

44
4 December 1093 x 21 April 1109
Anselm, archbishop of Canterbury
EEA, xxviii, no. 19.

45
4 December 1093 x 21 April 1109
Anselm, archbishop of Canterbury
EEA, xxviii, no. 21.

46
4 December 1093 x 21 April 1109
Anselm, archbishop of Canterbury
EEA, xxviii, no. 22.

47
February 1094 x 7 March 1108
Bishop Gundulf of Rochester
Textus Roffensis, ed. Hearne, 217–18; *Monasticon Anglicanum*, I, 165; forthcoming *EEA* (Rochester), no. 9, where editors think perhaps before 1100.

48
27 May 1095 x 21 April 1109
Anselm, archbishop of Canterbury
(Original).
EEA, xxviii, no. 16.

49
11 June 1096 x November 1097 or September 1101 x April 1103 or September 1106 x 1107
Anselm, archbishop of Canterbury
(Original)
EEA, xxviii, no. 15.

50
1096 x 1107
Anselm, archbishop of Canterbury
EEA, xxviii, no. 26.

51
8 June 1096 x 5 May 1112
Samson, bishop of Worcester
Worcester cartulary, ed. Darlington, no. 147; *EEA*, xxxiii, no. 24.

52
8 June 1096 x 5 May 1112 or 24 May 1125 x ?20 March 1150
S., bishop of Worcester (either Samson, 1096–1112, or Simon, 1125–50)
Worcester, Worcestershire County Record Office, 821 BA 3814 (Liber Albus of the bishopric), fo. 57r; ibid., 009:1 BA 2636 9 43696 (cartulary of the bishopric), fo. 57v.
EEA, xxxiii, no. 29.

53
8 June 1097 x 23 September 1097
Samson, bishop of Worcester
Hemingi chartularium, ed. Hearne, II, 426–7; *EEA*, xxxiii, no. 22.

54
1099 x 21 April 1109
Anselm, archbishop of Canterbury
EEA, xxviii, no. 12.

55
5 June 1099 x *c.* 1122
Ranulf Flambard, bishop of Durham
Durham Episcopal Charters, 1071–1152, ed. H. S. Offler, Surtees Society, 179 (Gateshead, 1968), 89, no. 18.

Nicholas Brooks:
A List of Publications

'The Unidentified Forts of the Burghal Hidage', *Medieval Archaeology*, 8 (1964), 74–90 (reprinted in *Communities and Warfare 700–1400* (London and Rio Grande, 2000), 93–113).

'Excavations at Wallingford Castle 1965: an Interim Report', *Berkshire Archaeological Journal*, 62 (1965–1966), 17–21.

'The Pre-Conquest Charters of Christ Church Canterbury', unpublished D.Phil. thesis, University of Oxford, 1968.

'The Development of Military Obligations in Eighth- and Ninth-Century England', in *England before the Conquest: Studies in Primary Sources Presented to Dorothy Whitelock*, ed. Peter Clemoes and Kathleen Hughes (Cambridge, 1971), 69–84 (reprinted in *Communities and Warfare 700–1400* (London and Rio Grande, 2000), 32–47).

'Anglo-Saxon Charters: the Work of the Last Twenty Years', *Anglo-Saxon England*, 3 (1974), 211–33 (reprinted with a postscript in *Anglo-Saxon Myths: State and Church, 400–1066* (London and Rio Grande, 2000), 181–215).

'Urban Archaeology in Scotland', in *European Towns: their Archaeology and Early History*, ed. M.W. Barley (London, 1977), 278–95.

'The Ecclesiastical Topography of Early Medieval Canterbury', in *European Towns: their Archaeology and Early History*, ed. M.W. Barley (London, 1977), 481–98 (reprinted in *Anglo-Saxon Myths: State and Church, 400–1066* (London and Rio Grande, 2000), 91–100).

N.P. Brooks and Graeme Whittington, 'Planning and Growth in the Medieval Scottish Burghs: the Example of St Andrews', *Transactions of the Institute of British Geographers*, n.s. 2 (1977), 278–95.

'St John's House: its History and Archaeology', *Annual Report and Year Book of the St Andrews Preservation Trust for 1976* (1977), 11–18.

Review of Terence Paul Smith, *The Anglo-Saxon Churches of Hertfordshire* (Chichester, 1973), in *Journal of Ecclesiastical History*, 28 (1977), 102.

N.P. Brooks and H.E. Walker, 'The Authority and Interpretation of the Bayeux Tapestry', *ANS*, 1 (1978), 1–34 and 191–9 (reprinted in *Communities and Warfare 700–1400* (London and Rio Grande, 2000), 175–218).

'Arms, Status and Warfare in Late-Saxon England', in *Ethelred the Unready: Papers from the Millenary Conference*, ed. David Hill, British Archaeological Reports, British Series 59 (Oxford, 1978), 81–103 (reprinted in *Communities and Warfare 700–1400* (London and Rio Grande, 2000), 138–61).

Review of C.R. Hart, *The Early Charters of Northern England and the North Midlands* (Leicester, 1975), in *EHR*, 93 (1978), 428–9.

'England in the Ninth Century: the Crucible of Defeat', *Transactions of the Royal Historical Society*, 5th ser. 29 (1979), 1–20 (reprinted in *Communities and Warfare 700–1400* (London and Rio Grande, 2000), 48–68).

'Abingdon', in *Lexikon des Mittelalters*, ed. Robert Auty and others (9 vols, Munich, 1977–1998), I (1977–1980), 41.

'Ælfgar', ibid., I, 179.

'Ælfgifu von Northampton', ibid., I, 179–80.

'Ælfheah', ibid., I, 180.

'Ælle', ibid., I, 181.

'Æthelberht 1', ibid., I, 187.

'Æthelnoth 1', ibid., I, 188.

'Æthelstan 1', ibid., I, 189–90.

'Æthelstan 2', ibid., I, 190.

'Æthelwine', ibid., I, 190.

'Assandun', ibid., I, 1118.

'Romney Marsh in the Early Middle Ages', in *Evolution of Marshland Landscapes*, ed. R.T. Rowley, Oxford University Department for External Studies (Oxford, 1981), 74–94.

'The Oldest Document in the College Archives: the Micheldever Forgery', in *Winchester College: Sixth-Centenary Essays*, ed. Roger Custance (Oxford, 1982), 189–228 (reprinted as 'The Micheldever Forgery', in *Anglo-Saxon Myths: State and Church, 400–1066* (London and Rio Grande, 2000), 239–74).

Latin and the Vernacular Languages, ed. Nicholas Brooks (Leicester, 1982), xi + 170 pp.

'Burh', in *Lexikon des Mittelalters*, ed. Robert Auty and others (9 vols, Munich, 1977–1998), II (1981–3), 1103.

'Byrhtnoth', ibid., II, 1169.

'Canterbury, Stadt; Kirche, Bistum und Metropole', ibid., II, 1447–54.

'Cenwalh', ibid., II, 1623.

Review of *Saints, Scholars and Heroes: Studies in Medieval Culture in Honour of Charles W. Jones*, ed. M.H. King and W.M. Stevens (Ann Arbor, MI, 1979), in *EHR*, 98 (1983), 181–2.

The Early History of the Church of Canterbury (Leicester, 1984), xiv + 402 pp.

N.P. Brooks, Margaret Gelling and D. Johnson, 'A New Charter of King Edgar', *Anglo-Saxon England*, 13 (1984), 137–55 (reprinted in *Anglo-Saxon Myths: State and Church, 400–1066* (London and Rio Grande, 2000), 217–37).

'The Organization and Achievements of the Peasants of Kent and Essex in 1381', in *Studies in Medieval History Presented to R.H.C. Davis*, ed. Henry Mayr-Harting and R.I. Moore (London and Ronceverte, 1985), 247–70 (reprinted in *Communities and Warfare 700–1400* (London and Rio Grande, 2000), 266–89).

'Warfare and International Relations, 400–1154', in *The Cambridge Historical Encyclopaedia of Great Britain and Ireland*, ed. Christopher Haigh (Cambridge, 1985), 71–7.

'Cospatric', in *Lexikon des Mittelalters*, ed. Robert Auty and others (9 vols, Munich, 1977–1998), III (1984–6), 302.

'Dover', ibid., III, 1334–5.

'Ecgfrith 2, Kg. v. Northumbrien 670–685', ibid., III, 1538–9.
'Edgar "the Ætheling"', ibid., III, 1571.
'Edith 2', ibid., III, 1578.
'Eduard d. Bekenner', ibid., III, 1583–4.
'Edwin, hl., Kg. v. Northumbrien', ibid., III, 1597–8.
'Emma 1, Kgn. v. England', ibid., III, 1886–7.
History and Myth, Forgery and Truth, Inaugural Lecture, University of Birmingham (Birmingham, 1986), 20 pp. (reprinted in *Anglo-Saxon Myths: State and Church, 400–1066* (London and Rio Grande, 2000), 1–19).
N.P. Brooks and J.A. Graham-Campbell, 'Reflections on the Viking-Age Silver Hoard from Croydon, Surrey', in *Anglo-Saxon Monetary History: Essays in Memory of R.H.M. Dolley*, ed. M.A.S. Blackburn (Leicester, 1986), 91–110 (reprinted in *Communities and Warfare 700–1400* (London and Rio Grande, 2000), 69–91.
Review of *The Anglo-Saxon Chronicle, MS B*, ed. Simon Taylor, The Anglo-Saxon Chronicle: a Collaborative Edition, gen. eds. D. Dumville and S. Keynes, 4 (Cambridge, 1983), in *EHR*, 101 (1986), 472.
'Epilogue', in *Coinage in Ninth-Century Northumbria: the Tenth Oxford Symposium on Coinage and Monetary History*, ed. D.M. Metcalf, British Archaeological Research Reports, British Series 180 (Oxford, 1987), 397–401.
Review of C.J. Arnold, *Roman Britain and Saxon England: an Archaeological Study* (London, 1984), in *EHR*, 102 (1987), 460.
'Romney Marsh in the Early Middle Ages', in *Romney Marsh: Evolution, Occupation, and Reclamation*, ed. Jill Eddison and Christopher Green, Oxford University Committee for Archaeology, Monograph 23 (Oxford, 1988), 128–59 [reworked version of 'Romney Marsh in the Early Middle Ages' (1981)], reprinted in *Anglo-Saxon Myths: State and Church 400–1066* (London and Rio Grande, 2000), 275–300.
'Evesham', in *Lexikon des Mittelalters*, ed. Robert Auty and others (9 vols, Munich, 1977–1998), IV (1987–1999), 143–4.
'Faversham', ibid., IV, 323.
'Fulford', ibid., IV, 1023.
'Godwin', ibid., IV, 1532–3.
'Gyrth', ibid., IV, 1811.
'Halfdan', ibid., IV, 1873.
'Hallamshire', ibid., IV, 1877.
'Heer, England [1], Angelsächsische Zeit', ibid., IV, 1994.
'The Creation and Early Structure of the Kingdom of Kent', in *The Origins of Anglo-Saxon Kingdoms*, ed. S.R. Bassett (Leicester, 1989) 55–74 (reprinted in *Anglo-Saxon Myths: State and Church, 400–1066* (London and Rio Grande, 2000), 33–60.
'The Formation of the Mercian Kingdom', in *The Origins of Anglo-Saxon Kingdoms*, ed. S.R. Bassett (Leicester, 1989), 159–70 (reprinted in *Anglo-Saxon Myths: State and Church, 400–1066* (London and Rio Grande, 2000), 61–77).
'Weapons and Armour', in *The Battle of Maldon, AD 991*, ed. Donald Scragg (Oxford, 1991), 208–19 (reprinted in *Communities and Warfare 700–1400* (London and Rio Grande, 2000), 162–74).

'Historical Introduction', in *The Making of England: Anglo-Saxon Art and Culture AD 600–900*, ed. Lesley Webster and Janet Backhouse, British Museum Publications (London, 1991), 9–14 (reprinted in *Anglo-Saxon Myths: State and Church, 400–1066* (London and Rio Grande, 2000), 21–31).

'Kingston on Thames', in *Lexikon des Mittelalters*, ed. Robert Auty and others (9 vols, Munich, 1977–1998), V (1991), 1159–60.

'The Career of St Dunstan', in *St Dunstan: his Life, Times and Cult*, ed. Nigel Ramsay, Margaret Sparks and Tim Tatton-Brown (Woodbridge, 1992), 1–23 (reprinted in *Anglo-Saxon Myths: State and Church, 400–1066* (London and Rio Grande, 2000), 155–80).

'Church, Crown and Community: Public Work and Seigneurial Responsibilities at Rochester Bridge', in *Warriors and Churchmen in the High Middle Ages: Essays Presented to Karl Leyser*, ed. Timothy Reuter (London, 1992), 1–20.

'Northumbria', in *Lexikon des Mittelalters*, ed. Robert Auty and others (9 vols, Munich, 1977–1998), VI (1993), 1255–7.

'Rochester Bridge, AD 43–1381', in *Traffic and Politics: the Construction and Management of Rochester Bridge AD 43–1993*, ed. Nigel Yates and James M. Gibson (Woodbridge, 1994), 1–40 (reprinted in *Communities and Warfare 700–1400* (London and Rio Grande, 2000), 219–65).

'The Anglo-Saxon Cathedral Community, 597–1070', in *A History of Canterbury Cathedral*, ed. Patrick Collinson, Nigel Ramsay and Margaret Sparks (Oxford, 1995), 1–37 (reprinted as 'The Cathedral Community at Canterbury, 597–1070', in *Anglo-Saxon Myths: State and Church, 400–1066* (London and Rio Grande, 2000), 101–54).

'The Administrative Background to the Burghal Hidage', in *The Defence of Wessex: the Burghal Hidage and Anglo-Saxon Fortifications*, ed. David Hill and Alexander Richard Rumble (Manchester, 1996), 128–50 (reprinted in *Communities and Warfare 700–1400* (London and Rio Grande, 2000), 114–37).

'The West Saxon Hidage and the "Appendix"', in *The Defence of Wessex: the Burghal Hidage and Anglo-Saxon Fortifications*, ed. David Hill and Alexander Richard Rumble (Manchester, 1996), 87–91.

St Oswald of Worcester: Life and Influence, ed. N.P. Brooks and Catherine Cubitt (London and NY, 1996), vii + 365 pp.

'Medieval European Bridges: a Window onto Changing Concepts of State Power', *Journal of the Haskins Society*, 7 (1997 for 1995), 11–29 (reprinted in *Communities and Warfare 700–1400* (London and Rio Grande, 2000), 1–31).

'The Legacy of Saints Gregory and Augustine in England', *Canterbury Cathedral Chronicle*, 92 (1998), 45–67.

Review of *The Anglo-Saxon Chronicle*, ed. M.J. Swanton (London, 1996), in *EHR*, 113 (1998), 401–402.

'Arms and Armour', in *The Blackwell Encyclopaedia of Anglo-Saxon England*, ed. Michael Lapidge, John Blair, Simon Keynes and Donald Scragg (Oxford, 1999), 45–7.

Review of Richard Marsden, *The Text of the Old Testament in Anglo-Saxon England* (Cambridge, 1995), in *American Historical Review*, 104 (1999), 234.

'Canterbury, Rome and the Construction of English Identity', in *Early Medieval Rome and the Christian West: Essays in Honour of Donald A. Bullough*, ed. Julia M.H. Smith (Leiden, 2000), 221–47.

Bede and the English, Jarrow Lecture 1999 (Jarrow, 2000), 34 pp.

Anglo-Saxon Myths: State and Church 400–1066 (London and Rio Grande, 2000), xvi + 308 pp.

'The English Origin Myth', in *Anglo-Saxon Myths: State and Church 400–1066* (London and Rio Grande, 2000), 78–89.

'Anglo-Saxon Charters: a Review of Work 1953–73, with a postscript on the period 1973–98', in *Anglo-Saxon Myths: State and Church 400–1066* (London and Rio Grande, 2000), 181–215.

Communities and Warfare 700–1400 (London and Rio Grande, 2000), xviii + 298 pp.

'Rome and Canterbury: the Limits and Myth of Romanitas', in *Roma fra Oriente e Occidente*, Settimane di Studio, 49 (2002), 797–830.

Church, State and Access to Resources in Early Anglo-Saxon England, 20th Brixworth Lecture, 2002 (Brixworth, 2003), 33 pp.

'Henry Royston Loyn 1922–2000', *Proceedings of the British Academy*, 120 (2003), 302–24.

'English Identity from Bede to the Millennium', *Haskins Society Journal*, 14 (2003), 33–51 (delivered, under the title 'English Identity from Bede to the Battle of Hastings', as the Inaugural Henry Loyn Memorial Lecture, Cardiff, 15 May 2003).

'Alfredian Government: the West Saxon Inheritance', in *Alfred the Great*, ed. Timothy Reuter (Aldershot, 2003), 153–73.

Review of *St Augustine and the Conversion of England*, ed. Richard Gameson (Stroud, 1999) in *EHR*, 118 (2003) 1350–51.

'Honorius [St Honorius] (d. 653), archbishop of Canterbury', 'Justus [St Justus] (d. 627x31), archbishop of Canterbury', 'Laurence [St Laurence, Lawrence] (d. 619), archbishop of Canterbury', 'Mellitus (d. 624), archbishop of Canterbury', 'Oswald [St Oswald] (d. 992), archbishop of York' and 'Wulfred (d. 832), archbishop of Canterbury', in *Oxford Dictionary of National Biography*, ed. H.C.G. Matthew and Brian Harrison (61 vols, Oxford, 2004), respectively XXVII, 910; XXX, 845–6; XXXII, 691; XXXVII, 751–2; XLII, 79–84; LX, 552–4.

'In Memoriam: Charles Patrick Wormald. July 9, 1947 – September 29, 2004', *Old English Newsletter*, 38 (2004), 4–6.

St Wulfstan and his World, ed. Julia S. Barrow and Nicholas Brooks (Aldershot, 2005), xix + 242 pp.

'Introduction: how do we know so much about St Wulfstan?', in *St Wulfstan and his World*, ed. Julia S. Barrow and Nicholas Brooks (Aldershot, 2005), 1–22.

Review of Guy Halsall, *Warfare and Society in the Barbarian West* (London, 2003) *EHR*, 120 (2005), 424–6.

'From British to English Christianity: Deconstructing Bede's Interpretation of the Conversion', in *Conversion and Colonisation in Anglo-Saxon England*, ed. Catherine E. Karkov and Nicholas Howe (Tempe, Arizona, 2006), 1–30.

'Rochester, A.D. 400–1066', in *Medieval Art, Architecture and Archaeology at Rochester*, ed. Tim Ayers and Tim Tatton-Brown, British Archaeological Association Conference Transactions, 28 (Leeds, 2006), 6–21.

Review of David Harrison, *The Bridges of Medieval England: Transport and Society, 400–1800* (Oxford, 2004), *EHR*, 121 (2006), 267–8.

Index

The counties used to identify English and Scottish place-names are those that existed immediately preceding the 1973–4 local government reforms.

Abba, the reeve, 97
Abbo of Fleury, abbot of Fleury (d. 1004), 148, 163
abbots, charters issued by, 229–45
Abbotsbury, abbey, 54, 66
Abingdon (Berkshire), abbey, 154, 159–60, 164–5, 232
    abbot of, *see* Rainald
acta, episcopal, *see* bishops
Adelard of Ghent, 148–53, 162
Ado of Vienne, Martyrology of, 118n
adventus Saxonum, 16, 23, 28
Ælfgifu, wife of Eadwig, 162
Ælfheah, bishop of Winchester (984–1006) and later archbishop of Canterbury (1006–12), 148–9
Ælfheah Calvus, bishop of Winchester (d. 951), 156–7
Ælfred, ealdorman, 89
Ælfric, abbot of Eynsham, homilist, 143, 154, 157, 161, 165, 192
Ælfric, archbishop of Canterbury (995–1005), 148, 150
Ælfric, *dux*, 154
Ælfstan, bishop of Rochester (d. 995), 152
Ælfweard, son of Edward the Elder, 103, 124
Ælfwig, abbot, 156
Ælfwine, abbot, 160
Ælfwold, layman, 153–4
Ælfwyn, daughter of Æthelflæd, 'Lady of the Mercians' and Æthelred, 'Lord of the Mercians', 5, 103–4, 114–15, 124
Ælle, king of Deira, father of Edwin, 142
Ælle, king of Northumbria (d. 867), 142
Ælle, supposed founder of South Saxons, 17–19, 139, 142

Aeneid, 215–16
Æsc, *see* Oisc
Æthelbald, king of the Mercians (716–57), 4, 9, 38, 78, 83, 85, 86
Æthelbald, king of the West Saxons (855–60), 121
Æthelberht I, king of Kent (d. 616), 15, 27, 69, 71, 73, 79, 96, 139
    laws of, 34n
Æthelberht II, king of Kent (725–62), 77, 79–80
Æthelberht, king of the West Saxons (860–65), 121
Æthelflæd, 'Lady of the Mercians', 2, 101–16 *passim*, esp. 102–3, 107–8, 112–16, 134
Æthelflæd, *matrona* at Glastonbury, 147
Æthelflæd the White, 162
Æthelhelm, *see* Athelm
æthelings, 110 and n, 122, 137, 207, 213, 217–18
Æthelmaer, ealdorman, 154
Æthelnoth, archbishop of Canterbury (1020–38), 82
Æthelred, archbishop of Canterbury (870–89), 89
Æthelred I, king of the West Saxons (865–71), 103, 109, 121
Æthelred II, 'the Unready', king of the English (978–1016), 3–4, 145, 148–55, 163–6, 213, 215
Æthelred, 'Lord of the Mercians' (879–911), 101, 103, 104n, 110, 111, 112, 113n, 114, 134
Æthelstan, king of the English (924–39), 5, 101–8, 113, 117, 123–6, 127–35, 137–44, 149, 156, 212, 214–18
    his fostering in Mercia, 103n, 113n, 115, 134
Æthelstan Half-King, ealdorman, 153
Æthelstan, priest, 156–7
Æthelthryth, abbess of Ely (d. 679), 71, 181n

Æthelwig, abbot of Evesham (1058–78), 243
Æthelwine, ealdorman, 153
Æthelwold, saint, bishop of Winchester (963–84), 145–6, 156–8, 164, 177, 240
  Bible said to have been copied by, 240
  cult of, 180
  Life of, *see* Wulfstan of Winchester
Æthelwold, son of King Æthelred I, 109–10, 122
Æthelwulf, ealdorman, 93
Æthelwulf, king of the West Saxons (d. 858), 80, 121, 123
Aëtius, consul (d. 454), 20–21
agriculture, 90–92, 94–5
Ailsi, abbot of Ramsey (1080–7), 243–4
Aire, river (Yorkshire, West Riding), 3, 199–202, 207–8, 210
Albion, 132
Alcuin (d. 804), 127, 176
Aldwine, abbot of Ramsey (d. 1112), 244
Alford, Michael (d. 1652), 63–5
Alfred, king of the West Saxons (871–99), 13, 19, 28, 101, 109, 112, 120–23, 127–8, 132, 138–9, 142; *see also* Anglo–Saxon Chronicle
Alfred, son of Æthelred and Emma, 213
All Saints, masses for, 181n
Alleluia, 174
alms, grants in, 239–40
Alvechurch (Worcestershire), 86
Amlaíb, *see* Olaf Guthfrithsson
Amounderness, 140
Andrew, saint, 149, 151–3, 164; *see also* Rochester
  cult of, 169–71
  masses for, 173–4, 182, 184
  octave of, 170–71, 173, 176, 184
  propers for 119–20, 126n
Angelcynn, 109, 115, 116, 127–8, 139
Angles, 23–4; *see also* East Angles
'Anglian' collection, 16–17
Anglo–Saxon Chronicle, 5, 16–19, 22–3, 27–8, 68, 71, 93, 127–31, 151–2, 177n, 203
  MS A, 103, 105, 107–9, 115
  MS B, 102–3, 104–8, 115–16
  MS C, 102–3, 104–8, 128n, 151
  B/C, 104–8

  MS D, 102, 104, 116, 151
  MS E, 151
  Chronicle of Alfred, 104, 108–9, 114 and n, 115
Angoulême sacramentary, 172n, 184
Angulsaxonum rex, title, 132
Anlaf, *see* Olaf Guthfrithsson
Annales Cambriae, 138
Anschis, 26
Anselm, archbishop of Canterbury (1093–1109), 231, 232, 234, 246–8
  seal of, 235
Ansis, 26
antiphons, 173
archbishop, consecration of, 181n; *see also* Boniface; Canterbury; York
Armes Prydein, 141
Arras, 118n
  bishop of, *see* Lambert
  Saint–Vaast, abbey, 176n
Arnold–Forster, Frances (1857–1921), 200
Asgeir the staller, 161
Ash Wednesday, *see* Lent
Ashford (Kent), 82
Ashley, W.J. (1860–1927), 34
Asser, 28
  Life of Alfred by, 19
Asterius, archbishop of Milan (but based at Genoa), 177
Astle, Thomas (1735–1803), 59, 62–3
Athelm, bishop of Wells and later archbishop of Canterbury (d. *c.* 926), 6, 117, 126, 148
Athelney, abbey, 55
Augustine, saint, archbishop of Canterbury (597–604 x 609), 21, 73, 181n, 187
Augustine, saint, bishop of Hippo (396–430), 154
Axminster (Devon), 135

B., biographer of St Dunstan, 146–50, 152
Bakewell (Derbyshire), 111
Baldwin, abbot of Bury St Edmunds (1065–98), 233, 235, 237, 238, 241, 245
Bardney (Lincolnshire), 103
Barking (Essex), abbey, 55
Barrow, G.W.S., 32–3, 36–7, 40, 43–4
basileus, as title, 141

INDEX

Bassa, mass-priest and founder of Reculver minster, 71–3
Bassett, Steven, 12, 14, 35
Bates, David, 229, 230
Bath (Somerset), abbey, 82, 97, 232
Battle (Sussex), abbey, 231, 236n, 239
Baudri, abbot of Bourgueil, 222–4
Bavaria, 33
 laws of (*Lex Bavariorum*), 33
Bayeux
 bishop of, *see* Odo
 Tapestry, 2, 3
Baynard, William, 233
Bec, abbey, 232
Bede (d. 735), 5, 16, 23–9, 71, 74, 76, 96, 127, 139, 226–7
 Ecclesiastical History by, 5, 19, 21, 23, 139, 142, 177
 Epitome by, 109
 Letter to Egbert by, 34
Benedictine Reform, in England, 145–66
benedictionals, 179–80, 182; *see also* manuscripts, BL Harley 2892
Beoley (Worcestershire), 86
Beorhtwulf, king of Mercia (840–52), 93, 96
Beowulf, 27
Berhtwald, abbot of Reculver and later archbishop of Canterbury (692–731), 72, 74–7
Bernicia, 17, 27, 131
Bible, 16–17, 28; *see also* Æthelwold, saint, bishop of Winchester
 citations,
  –, Luke 10, 1–7: 173, 174n
  –, Matt. 4, 18–22: 174n
  –, Rom. 10, 10–18, 174n
Bieda, 18
Birch, Walter de Gray, 45
Birinus, bishop of Dorchester (634–*c*. 650), saint, 7, 177
 cult of, 169–171, 174, 177–8, 180, 182, 186–8
 deposition of (3 Dec.), 170, 178–80, 182, 184, 186–7
 translation of (4 Sept.), 178–80, 188
Birmingham, university, 1–2, 11–14
bishops, 13, 168
 charters issued by, 229–48
 consecration of, 119

Bitterne (Hampshire), 240
Blacheman, monk (of Winchester) and goldsmith, 240
Blair, John, 38
Blakedown (Worcestershire), 84
Blean, forest of (Kent), 73
blessings, 178, 180
Boniface, archbishop of Mainz (d. 754), 25
boundary clause, 9, 83, 85
bracteates, 25–6
Bredehoft, Thomas, 130
Bregowine, archbishop of Canterbury (761–4), 78
Bremesbyrig, 102
Brentford (Middlesex), synod of (781), 86
Brett, Martin, 231
bretwalda, 140
Bridbury, R.A., 98
bridge service, 37–8
bridges, 2–4, 14; *see also* Rochester
Brinesford, 136
Brinsworth (Yorkshire), 135–6
Britain, British, 5, 17–18, 21, 23, 26, 127–8, 132, 134, 139–40, 144
 Roman Britain, 16, 23–4
Brittany, 175n
Broadwaters (Worcestershire), 84
Brochyl, wood of, 83, 86
Brockhill (Worcestershire), 86
Bromborough (Cheshire), 135–6
brooches, 22–4
Brooks, Nicholas, 1–15, 38, 40n, 46, 48, 71, 83, 89, 117, 119–21, 122n, 126, 127, 144, 145, 148, 162, 166, 229
Brumeford (Northumberland), 135
Brunanburh, 5, 102n, 105, 128–39, 141–4; *see also* Bromborough
Bruneswerc, 136
brytenwalda, 140
Buckfast (Devon), abbey, 54
Buckinghamshire, 96
burdens, three common, 2–4, 37; *see also trimoda necessitas*
Burghal Hidage, 2, 40
Burgred, king of Mercia (?852–873/4), 86
Burgundians, 26
burh service, 37–8
burhs, 102–3, 111, 205
burial, 22–5, 204, and see dead; *porticus*

customs and rites associated with, 21–4, 27
  female, 22–4
  ground, 38
  male, 22
  mounds, 24
  weapon-burial, 22
Burnswark (Dumfriesshire), 135–6
Burton on Trent (Staffordshire), abbey, 60, 61–5
Burton, William, 62, 65
Bury St Edmunds (Suffolk), 178
  abbey, 94, 232
  abbot of, *see* Baldwin
  tenant of, *see* Peter
Byrhtferth of Ramsey, 109n, 163

Caedwalla, king of the West Saxons (685–8), 19
Cain, 158
Caithness, 133
Calder, river, 200
calendars, 178, 182
Cambrai, 118n
Camden, William (1551–1623), 135
Cannock (Staffordshire), 85
canon law, 161–3
Canterbury (Kent), 21, 67, 73, 119–21, 148, 163, 170
  archbishops of, 232n; *see also* Ælfheah; Ælfric; Æthelnoth; Æthelred; Anselm; Athelm (Æthelhelm); Augustine; Berhtwald; Bregowine; Deusdedit; Dunstan; Jaenberht; Lanfranc; Oda; Plegmund; Theodore; Wigheard; Wulfred; (archbishop-elect)
  Christ Church, 4–8, 46, 56, 67–8, 71, 74, 75–6, 89, 126, 149, 161, 171–2, 178n, 179, 181–2, 231
  –, archive of, 8, 229, 232
  St Augustine's abbey, 68–71, 74, 76, 78–9, 94, 126, 147–8, 232
  –, abbots of, *see* Hadrian; Wulfric
Caraticos, 18, 24–5
Carolingians, 90,
  liturgical reforms of, 171, 175, 176
Carta dirige gressus, 132–3, 140, 143
Cassiodorus, 26

Castleford (Yorkshire), 200, 203, 207
Cavill, Paul, 137
Ceawlin, king of the West Saxons, 139
cemeteries, *see* burial, cremation
cento, 129n
Cenwald, bishop of Worcester (929–57), 102n, 143–4
Ceolfrith, son of Cyneberht, 83, 86
Cerdic, 16–19, 23–4
Cerdices ford, 18
Cerne, abbey, 143
Chadwick, H.M. (1870–1947), 28
Channel, 209
chants, liturgical, 168–70, 173–4, 178n, 188
Chaplais, Pierre (1920–2006), 46–7
Charente, river, 157
Charford (Hampshire), 18
Charlemagne, emperor (d. 814), 175n
Charles the Straightforward, king of the West Franks (898–923, d. 929), 125
Charles-Edwards, Thomas, 35, 41
charters, 8–9, 13–14; *see also* abbots; bishops
  Anglo–Saxon, 36, 45–66, 141, 229
  S 8: 70, 74–6, 78
  S 24: 80
  S 29: 74, 78
  S 31: 70, 77–8
  S 38: 70
  S 59: 93n
  S 62: 93n
  S 64: 84n
  S 86: 78
  S 87: 78
  S 88: 78
  S 89: 9, 58, 83–7
  S 91: 78
  S 92: 4, 38, 53
  S 98: 78
  S 103a: 78
  S 103b: 78
  S 109: 93n
  S 134: 81
  S 143: 78
  S 160: 81
  S 167: 81
  S 180: 83n
  S 204: 97n
  S 206: 93n

INDEX

S 212: 86
S 215: 94n
S 298: 97n
S 385: 94n
S 407: 141
S 412: 141n
S 413: 141n
S 416: 141n
S 417: 141n
S 418: 141n
S 419: 141n
S 422: 141n
S 425: 141n
S 426: 141n
S 427: 141
S 429: 141n
S 430: 141n
S 431: 141n
S 434: 141n
S 435: 141n
S 436: 141n
S 437: 141n
S 438: 141n
S 445: 141n
S 446: 141n
S 497: 74n
S 501: 49
S 512: 74n
S 545: 64–5
S 546: 74, 81–2
S 553: 60
S 554: 62, 64
S 646: 81
S 676a: 53
S 705a: 55
S 712a: 52–3
S 726: 86
S 731: 58
S 745: 158
S 794a: 53
S 798: 51
S 863: 65
S 875: 49
S 885: 152, 164
S 891: 164–5
S 893: 152, 164
S 904: 55
S 937: 165
S 1030: 51, 60

S 1182: 80n, 94n
S 1195: 97n
S 1197: 97n
S 1254: 93n
S 1255: 93n
S 1257: 84, 86
S 1260: 93n
S 1261: 93n
S 1262: 93n
S 1264: 70, 80
S 1267: 80
S 1272: 93n
S 1273: 93n
S 1279: 94n
S 1280: 94n
S 1281: 94n
S 1282: 94n
S 1283: 94n
S 1285: 94n
S 1287: 94n
S 1288: 94n
S 1299: 237n
S 1310: 237n
S 1379: 57
S 1390: 82
S 1391: 238n
S 1394: 238n
S 1396: 238n
S 1397: 238n
S 1403: 238n
S 1404: 236n
S 1411: 83–4, 86
S 1412: 93n
S 1415: 94n
S 1416: 94n
S 1421: 94n
S 1425: 238n
S 1427: 236n
S 1429: 58
S 1430: 93n
S 1436: 70, 80–81
S 1437: 97n
S 1440: 97n
S 1444: 94n, 95n
S 1468: 238n
S 1470: 238n
S 1471: 238n
S 1508: 81–2, 89n
S 1612: 70, 78

S 1861: 51
  forged charters, 231; *see also* forgery
Cheddar (Somerset), 166
Chelsea, synod of (816), 92–3, 96
Chertsey (Surrey), abbey, 71
Chester, 103
  abbey of, 231, 232
  bishop of, *see* Peter
Chichester (Sussex), 18, 240
Chilmington (Kent), 82
chirograph, 235
Christ, cult of, 174
Christianity, 24–5, 28
Chronicle of Æthelweard, 114–15, 137, 142
Chronicle of the Church of York, 155–6
churches,
  field, 38
  minster, 38; *see also* Reculver
  parish, 233; *see also* Reculver
Churchill (Worcestershire), 84
Cissa, 18
Clamores, 157
Clark, Cecily (1926–92), 152
Cledemuth, 103
Clement, saint, 3, 191–3; *see also*
    Osmanville; Rome
  churches in Denmark and Norway
    dedicated to, 193–4
  churches in England dedicated to,
    189–94, 196, 201
  cult of, 191–4
  feast of, 192
  Letter to Corinthians by, 192
  wells associated with, 193
Clementhorpe, 189–90, 194–8, 207, 209;
    see also York
  inquisition into (1106), 196
  nunnery of, 197–8
Clonmacnoise, Annals of, 138
Cnut, king of the English (1016–35), 3, 150,
    177, 213
  laws of, 39
  sons of, 150; *see also* Harthacnut
Coenwulf, king of Mercia (796–821),
    80–81, 83
Coke, Sir Edward (1552–1634), 60, 62
Cole, 94
Coleman, hagiographer, 156–7

collectars, Durham, *see* manuscripts,
    Durham, Cathedral Library, A. IV. 19
  Wulfstan Portiforium, *see* manuscripts
    CCCC 391
Collectio Canonum Hibernensis, 161–2
collects, 173, 176–7, 181–2
Commune sanctorum, 169, 170–71, 173
  masses for, 173–4, 182, 185
confessors, masses for, 170–71, 173–4,
    175–6, 185
confraternity, agreements of, 232, 234, 236
Conquest, Norman, 9, 92, 85, 150, 229, 230
Constantine II, king of Scots (900–52), 128,
    130, 133–4, 137–8, 140
Constantinople, 26
Conybeare, J.J. (1779–1824), 42
Cookley (Worcestershire), 84, 85, 86
Copsi, earl of Northumbria (1067), 207
Corbie, abbey, 118n
Cornish, Cornwall, 133
coronation, 6, 121
  ordines for, 6, 117–26
  –, 'Erdmann', 123
  –, First Anglo-Saxon *Ordo*, 118–23
  –, Second Anglo-Saxon *Ordo*, 117–26
  –, 'Seven Forms', 123
costume, 22
Cotton, Sir Robert (1571–1631), 56–7
courts, and history–writing, 101, 105n,
    108–9, 111, 113
Crawford Charters, 59
cremation, 21–2
Crisanthus and Daria, saints, cult of, 171n
Cronne, Harry, 11
cross
  Holy Cross, Good Friday veneration of,
    168n
  stone, *see* Reculver
Crowland (Lincolnshire), 178
crown, 124; *see also* coronation
cursing, liturgical, 8, 146, 154–66
Cuthbert, saint (d. 687), cult of, 181n
Cuthred, son of Cynegils, king of the West
    Saxons, 177n
Cwoenthryth, daughter of Coenwulf, 80
Cydela, 85
Cydelanmynster, *see* Kidderminster
Cymen, 18

Cyneberht, companion of King Æthelbald of Mercia, 9, 83, 84, 85
Cynegils, king of the West Saxons (611–?642), 177
Cynric, 16–17, 23
Cyril and Methodius, saints, mission in the Crimea, 193

Dalrymple, David, Lord Hailes (1726–92), 43
Danelaw, 32, 134
Danes, 131, 144, 213, 217–18
Daniel, bishop of Winchester (c. 705–44), 25
Davis, R.H.C. (1918–91), 2, 11
dead, and living, masses for, 171–2, 175, 186
Deira, 131
Deneberht, bishop of Worcester (d. 822), 83
Deneheah, abbot of Reculver, 78
Denewulf, bishop of Winchester (d. 908), 95
Denmark, 21, 90, 213, 217–18
Derby, 102, 112
Dering, Sir Edward (1598–1644), 52, 56–7, 66
Deusdedit, archbishop of Canterbury (655–64), 71
devil, appearance by, 147
D'Ewes, Sir Simonds (1602–50), 57
Dewick, E.S., 158–60
Dickinson, Tania, 23
Dingesmere, 130, 137
Dodsworth, Roger (d. 1654), 52, 198
Domesday Book, 32, 159, 199, 200–203, 206, 230, 234
Don valley (Yorkshire), 136
Dorchester on Thames (Oxfordshire), 177–8; *see also* Birinus
drengs, 236n
Dublin, 130, 134
    Norse of, 128, 134
Dudo of St-Quentin, 2, 212, 214–18
Dugdale, William (1605–86), 52
Dumville, David, 159
Dunnottar (Kincardineshire), 133n
Dunstan, archbishop of Canterbury (959–88), 8, 13, 39, 71, 81, 145–57, 161–3, 166
    Life of, *see* B.
Dunwalhus pincerna, 80
Dunwaling land, 80, 82
Durham, 207; *see also* Simeon of Durham
    bishops of, 232n; *see also* Flambard, Ranulf; Walcher; William of Saint-Calais
    cathedral, 232
    collectars, *see* manuscripts, Durham, Cathedral Library, A. IV. 19
    Liber Vitae of, 236

Eadberht (I), king of West Kent (725–48), 77–9
Eadberht (II), king of Kent (active c. 762 x 764), 77–9
Eadberht (III) (Eadberht Praen), king of Kent (c. 796–798), 79n
Eadburg (of Winchester), saint, 159
Eadgifu, daughter of Edward the Elder, 125
Eadmer, biographer of St Anselm (d. in or after 1126), 145, 153, 222
Eadmund, *see* Edmund
Eadred, king of the English (946–55), 143, 147, 149, 203, 206
Eadric (d. 686), king of Kent, 74, 76, 96
Eadric Streona (d. 1017), 39
Eadwig, king of the English (955–9), 147–9, 162, 164
ealdormen, 36
Ealdred, archbishop of York (1061–9), 155
Ealhhun, bishop of Worcester (d. 869 x 872), 93
Ealhmund, king of Kent (d. 785), 79
Ealhswith, wife of Alfred (d. 902), 101, 103, 104, 106, 109–10, 112
Eamont, 132–3, 140
Eanwulf, ealdorman, 93
Eardwulf, king of West Kent (d. before 762), 77
East Angles, 17, 27, 127
    king of, *see* Rædwald
Easter, vigil for, 168n
Easton, manor of (Hampshire), 240
Eastry (Kent), 80, 82
Ecclefechan (Dumfriesshire), 136
eccles names, 37
Ecgberht, king of Kent (d. 779 x 784), 71–2, 74, 79
Ecgberht, king of the West Saxons (d. 802–39), 79–80, 139–40
Ecgfrith, king of Mercia (796), 5–6
Ecgwine, bishop of Worcester (d. 717), 163

Edgar, ætheling, 207
Edgar, king of the English (959–75), 145, 148–9, 162, 164
  laws of, 39
  wives of, 39, 145; *see also* Æthelflæd the White
Edinburgh Review, 43
Edith, queen, wife of Edward the Confessor (d. 1075), 191–2
Edmund, king of the English (939–46), 82, 128, 130–31, 137, 143–4, 145, 147–9, 166
Edward the Confessor, king of the English (1042–66), 161, 202, 206, 212–13, 219, 229, 230
Edward the Elder, king of Wessex (899–924), 10, 95, 103, 107–15, 117, 120–22, 124–6, 128, 130, 132, 138, 143
Edward the Martyr, king of the English (975–8), 145, 155, 162
  Passio of, 145
Edwin, earl of Mercia (d. 1071), 207
Edwin, king of Northumbria (616–33), 139
Egbert Pontifical, 118n
Egil Skallgrimsson, 142
Egils Saga, 134–6, 141
Elinand, bishop of Laon (1055–96), 237n
Ellesmere (Shropshire), 84
Elmham, Thomas (d. in or after 1427), 78
Ely (Cambridgeshire), abbey, 81, 161, 172; *see also* Æthelthryth; *Liber Eliensis*
Emma, queen, wife of Æthelred 'the Unready' and then of Cnut, 213, 215
England, English, 127, 131, 211–28
  king of the English, *see* Æthelred 'the Unready'; Æthelstan; Cnut; Eadred; Eadwig; Edgar; Edmund; Edward the Confessor; Edward the Martyr; Harthacnut; Henry I; Henry II; William I; William II
English identity, 28–9, 127, 139
Enville (Staffordshire), 85
Eorcenberht, king of Kent (640–64), 71
Eric of Lade, earl of Northumbria, 206
ethnicity, 211–28
ethnogenesis, 15, 20
Evesham (Worcestershire), abbey, 163, 232
  abbot of, *see* Æthelwig
excommunication, 146

Exeter, 119, 133n
  bishops of, 232n; *see also* Osbern
  St Nicholas' priory, 231, 232, 233n, 239
Exultet, Easter vigil prayer, 168n
Eynsham (Oxfordshire), abbey, 232
  abbot of, *see* Ælfric

family,
  politics, 110–12 and n, 113
  structure, 41–2
Farndon (Cheshire), 103
Faversham (Kent), 79
feretrum, see reliquary
ferries, 200–201
Ferrybridge (Yorkshire), 201
fields, common, 92
Finglesham (Kent), 25, 27
  belt-buckle from, 27
Fisher, D.J.V., 39
fishery, 196–7, 201, 205
Fiskerton (Lincolnshire), 191
Five Boroughs, 131, 190
Flambard, Ranulf, bishop of Durham (1099–1128), 234, 247
  seal of, 235
Flemings, 82
Fleury, abbey, 157–8; *see also* Abbo of Fleury
fords, 200–201
Fordwich (Kent), 78
forgery, 11–12; *see also* charters
Formosus, pope (891–6), 123
Forth, Firth of, 32, 36, 43
fortuna, 26
Francia, 75, 90, 117–18, 122–3, 171, 175–6; *see also* Carolingians
  Frankish coins (Merovingian), 73
  Frankish dress, 23
Fraxinetum, *see* Garde–Freinet
Fresnot(us), monk of Reculver, 82
Frisia, 34, 43
Frome (Somerset), 141
Fulder, tenant of church of Worcester, 94
fyrd service, 37–8

Gaimar, *see* Geffrei Gaimar
Garde-Freinet, 120n
garnets, gold and garnet jewellery, 27
Geats, 27

Geffrei Gaimar, 136, 228
Gellone sacramentary, 175n, 184
genealogies, 16–18, 25–8
Geoffrey of Monmouth (d. 1154/5), 141, 226–7
Gerefa, 97
Germani, 16
Germanus, monk, 158
Germany, 16, 20–25, 27–8, 40–41
Gewisse, 18–19, 25, 28
Ghent, *see* Adelard of Ghent
    abbey of St Peter's, 157
Gilbert, abbot of Westminster (d. 1117), 232, 233, 238, 244–5
Gilbert of Tonbridge, 234
Gildas, 19–21, 28–9
    De Excidio Britanniae by, 19–20, 28
Giso, bishop of Wells (1061–88), 238, 242
Givehard, dean of Reculver minster, 82
Gladstone, W.E., 42
Glastonbury (Somerset), abbey, 54, 60, 81, 97, 147–9, 153–4, 159–60, 240
    abbot of, *see* Dunstan
Gloucester, 103, 234
    abbey, 236
Good Friday, veneration of the Holy Cross on, 168n
Gospatric, earl of Northumbria (1067–8), 207
Gospel-book, 69; *see also* Reculver
Goths, 20, 26–8
grave-goods, 24; *see also* burial
'Great Army', 3
Great North Road, 199–200
Great Stour, river (Kent), 72, 74, 78
Gregory I (the Great), pope (590–604), 20, 139
    Pastoral Care by, 96
Gregory, bishop of Tours (d. 594), 27
Gretsch, Mechthild, 159
Griffith, Michael, *see* Alford, Michael
Grimbald, saint, cult of, 174
Grimm, Jacob (1785–1863), 34
Gullick, Michael, 231n
Gumley, Synod of (749), 4, 38
Gundulf, bishop of Rochester (1077–1108), 234, 243, 244, 245, 247
    seal of, 235n
Guthfrith, son of Sihtric, 132
Guy of Amiens, 220–21

Gwent, 132

Hadrian, abbot of St Peter and St Paul (St Augustine's), Canterbury (d. 710), 71–2, 76
Hadrian I, pope (772–95), 175n
Hædde, bishop of Winchester (676–705), 177
Hägermann, Dieter, 90
Haimeric, priest and notary, 82
Hampshire, 17–19, 32
Hamwic, 73
Hanmer (Cheshire), 84
Harbledown (Kent), hospital, 232
Härke, Heinrich, 22
Harley, Sir Robert (1579–1656), 58
Harthacnut, king of the English (1040–42), 213
Harvey, P.D.A., 97
Hatton, Sir Christopher (d. 1670), 52, 58
Heahberht, abbot of Reculver, 77
helmets, 4, 124
Helmholz, Thomas, 162
Hengist, 1, 16–19, 25–8, 141
Henry I, king of the English (1100–35), 9, 229, 230, 236
Henry II, king of the English (1154–89), 213, 228
Henry of Huntingdon (*c*. 1088–*c*. 1157), 223–4, 226–7
Herbert, abbot of Ramsey (1087–90/91), 245
here, 33
Hereford, 133
    bishops of, 232n; *see also* Robert the Lotharingian
    cathedral, 232
heriraita, 33
heriot, 4
Herne (Kent), 73, 82
Hertford, council of (672), 20
Heruli, 26
High Easter (Essex), 161
High Weald (Kent), 76
Higham Upshire (Kent), 77, 82
Hillborough (Kent), 67–8
Hilton, Rodney (1916–2002), 11
Hincmar, archbishop of Rheims (845–82), 119, 121
Historia Brittonum, 19
Hlothhere (d. 685), king of Kent, 74, 96

and Eadric, laws of, 34n
Hoath (Kent), 73, 82
Holland, Joseph (d. 1605), 51
Holy Cross, *see* cross
Holy Spirit, 147–8
Homans, G.C., 34
Honorius I (d. 638), pope, 177
Hopkins, William (1647–1700), 58
Horsa, 1, 16–19, 25–8, 141
horseshoe, 40
Hugh fitz Baldric, 159
Humber, estuary, 3, 134, 136, 139, 189, 202, 208
hundred court, 236n
Husmerae, 83
Hwaetred, abbot of Reculver, 79
Hwicce, charters of, 36

Ida, king of Bernicia, 27
identity, ethnic, 15–29, 127, 211–28
Ine, king of the West Saxons (688–726), 16
  lawcode of, 33, 36
Ingram, James (1774–1850), 42
inhumation, *see* burial
invocations, liturgical, 178
Ireland, 33, 35, 41
Irminric, king of Kent, 15, 27
iron-mining, 76
Islandshire (Northumberland), 236n
Ismere House (Worcestershire), 84–5; *see also* Stour in Ismere
Israel, Children of, 29
Italy, 75
Iudoc, saint, cult of, 174, 181n

Jaenberht, archbishop of Canterbury (765–92), 5
jewellery, 22–4, 27
John XIV or XV, pope, 154
John of Worcester, *Chronicon* by, 131–2, 134, 136, 143
John, Eric, 34, 38
Johnson, Ann, 129
Jolliffe, J.E.A., 32, 36–7
Jones, S.R.H., 90, 91
Jordanes, 20, 26
  Getica by, 26
Jutes, 17–19, 23–5, 27

Kasten, Brigitte, 90, 91
keels, 20
Kemble, John Mitchell (1807–57), 34–5, 39, 42, 45
Kent, 1, 4, 12, 15, 17–19, 23–9, 32, 34, 67–8, 76–7, 80, 120
  earl of, *see* Odo of Bayeux
  female dress in, 23
  kings of, 70, 77; *see also* Æthelberht; Æthelberht II; Eadberht; Eadberht II; Eadberht III (Eadberht Praen); Eadric; Ealhmund; Eardwulf; Ecgberht; Hlothhere; Irminric; Oswine; Wihtred
  –, genealogy of, 26
  laws of, 33
  minsters of, 6–7; *see also* Reculver
Ker, Neil (1908–82), 159
Kidderminster (Worcestershire), 84, 85, 86
Kiev, 194
kingdoms, 24
Kingston on Thames (Surrey), 122n, 126
Kingswinford (Worcestershire), 86
Kinver, wood of (Staffordshire), 83, 85, 86
Kirkeby (*Kirkeby*) (Yorkshire), 203, 205–6, 210
Knaresborough (Yorkshire), 42
Knottingley (Yorkshire), 201

Lacy, family, 200
  –, honour of, in Yorkshire and Lancashire, 198, 202
Lacy, Ilbert I de, 198, 200, 202, 205, 209
Lacy, Ilbert II de, 198
Lacy, Robert de, 200
Lacy, Roger de, 233, 234, 235
Lambert, bishop of Arras (1094–1115), 237n
Lanalet Pontifical, 118n
Lancing (Sussex), 18
land, tenure of, 41
Landrecht, 42
Lanfranc, archbishop of Canterbury (1070–89), 245
Lantfred, hagiographer, 154
Laon, bishop of, *see* Elinand
Lapidge, Michael, 133n, 140, 146, 160
lathe, 32
  court, 236n
Le Neve, Peter (1661–1729), 58

lease, leasehold, 9, 90, 93–6, 98–9, 233, 235n, 237
lectionaries, 174
Lehnrecht, 42
Leicester, 102, 112
Leicestershire, 31, 36
Leland, John (d. 1552), 67–70, 135
Lennard, Reginald (1885–1967), 98
Lent, 157
Leo, pope (? VII, 936–9), 157
Leofgifu of London, 191
Leofric Missal, 118, 126n; *see also* manuscripts, Bodl., Bodley 579
lessons, liturgical, 168–9, 173–4
    Epistle, 174n
    Gospel, 174n
Lex Saxonum, 33
Leyser, Karl (1920–92), 139
Liber Eliensis, 161; *see also* Ely
Lichfield, see of, 5–6
Lincoln, 200
    bishops of, 232n; *see also* Remigius
Lincoln's Inn, 31
Lincolnshire, 207
Lisois, knight, 208
litanies, 178, 182
literacy, 5, 89, 92, 95–7
Little, Lester, 157
Lombards, 26
London, 78, 94, 112, 152–3
    St Paul's, 54, 155
Lothian, 43
Louis III, king of the West Franks (d. 882), 144
Louis IV, king of the West Franks (936–54), 117, 123–4
Loyn, H.R., 31
Lucy, saint, cult of, 169–71, 174
    masses for, 173, 182, 185
Ludwigslied, 144
Lyfing, bishop of Worcester (d. 1046), 238
Lyminge (Kent), 76

McDougall, Ian, 135
Machutus (Machlonus), saint, 159
Maegla, 18
Magna Carta, 10, 57
Magyars, 120n
Maitland, F.W. (1850–1906), 31–2, 41

Maldon (Essex), battle of, 4
    Battle of Maldon, poem, 4
Malling, 232
Malmesbury (Wiltshire), 70; *see also* William of Malmesbury
Mannus, 16
manorialisation, 36
manuscripts,
    BL Add. 82931: 64
    BL Arundel 60: 178n
    BL Cotton Otho A i: 53
    BL Cotton Tiberius A iii: 170, 178n. 181n, 188
    BL Cotton Tiberius A vi: 104
    BL Cotton Tiberius B i, 104: 128n
    BL Cotton Tiberius B iv: 104
    BL Cotton Tiberius A iii: 104n
    BL Cotton Titus D xxvii: 160, 178n
    BL Cotton Vitellius A xviii (Vitellius Sacramentary): 178n, 179–80, 181n, 182n, 184, 186–8
    BL Harley 2892 (Canterbury Benedictional): 179n, 181, 184, 187
    BL Harley 4660: 58
    BL Royal 1 E vi: 69
    BL Royal 2 B v: 158–9
    BN, lat. 943: 162
    BN, lat. 2291: 176n
    BN, lat. 12050: 176n
    BN, lat. 987: 179n, 181, 187
    Bodl., Bodley 579 (Leofric Missal): 176–7, 184
    Bodl., Bodley 718: 162
    Bodl., Digby 39: 183n
    Bodl., Digby 63 (S.C. no. 1664): 178n
    Bodl., Douce 296 (S.C. no. 21870): 178n
    CCCC 140: 156
    CCCC 146 (Samson Pontifical): 179n, 181, 187
    CCCC 286: 69
    CCCC 391 (Wulfstan Portiforium): 176, 178n, 179–80, 182n, 184, 187–8
    CCCC 422: 178nn
    Durham, Cathedral Library, A. IV. 19 (Durham Collectar): 175n
    Düsseldorf, Landes– und Stadtbibliothek, D1: 176n
    Le Havre, BM 330 (New Minster missal): 173–4, 179–82, 184, 186–8

London, Society of Antiquaries, MS 154*: 175n
New York, Pierpont Morgan Library, 926: 178n, 188
Oslo, Rijksarkivet, Lat. fragm. 209 + 239: 168–88
Oslo, Rijksarkivet, Mi. 1: 167n, 168n
Rouen, BM, Y. 6 [274] (missal of Robert of Jumièges): 171–2, 176–7, 179n, 180–84, 186–7
Stockholm, Kammararkivet,Mi. 1: 168n, 177–8n
Vatican, Reg. lat. 112: 178n
Vatican, Reg. lat. 316: 171n
Marian office, 158–61
'mark theory', 34–5
Markgenossenschaften, 34
Martin I, pope (649–55), 157
martyrology, *see* Ado of Vienne
martyrs, masses for, 170
Martyrs, Four Crowned, mass of, 118n
Mary, saint, 153, 158–61
Matilda, queen, wife of William I (d. 1083), 239
Medway, estuary, 3
Mercia, Mercians, 5, 12, 17, 70, 79, 93, 114–16, 117, 120, 124, 126, 127–8, 130–1, 134, 137–8
    kings of, 76–7, 79, 81; *see also* Æthelbald; Beorhtwulf; Burgred; Coenwulf; Ecgfrith; Offa
Mercian Register, 5, 101, 102n
'mere' as a place–name element, 84
Mersey, 135
Micheldever (Hampshire), 8
Midlands, 37
    West Midlands, 33
milites, 82
mills, 74, 92
Milton Abbas (Dorset), 54
Minster-in-Thanet (Kent), 71, 76, 78, 80
missals, 168, 170, 173; *see also* Leofric Missal; Robert of Jumièges, missal of; Winchester, New Minster, missal of
missionaries, 167–8, 177, 183
monks, masses for, 171–2, 176, 185
Morcar, earl of Northumbria, 207
Morfe, forest (Staffordshire), 83, 85, 86

Morfe Hall (Staffordshire), 85
Morfe House (Stafforshire), 85
Morfeheath (Staffordshire), 85
Moses, Prayer of, 165; *see also* Ælfric of Eynsham
murrain, 151–2
music, liturgical, 170, and see chants; neumes
myth, 1–2, 211–28; *see also* origin legends

Nailor, C.C., 67
Namier, Sir Lewis (1888–1960), 39
Natan leaga, see Netley
Natanleod, 18
Nedenes (Norway), 168
Netley (Hampshire), 18
neumes, musical notation, 170, 173–4, 183n
Nicholas, monk of York (or Nicholas of York, monk), 240
nobility, 43
Norhamshire (Northumberland), 236n
Normandy, Normans, 2, 200, 211–28; *see also* Conquest, Norman
Normannitas, 211–28
Norsemen, 130, 134–8, 142, 144
North Foreland, *see* Thanet
Northumbria, Northumbrians, 12, 17, 27, 32, 127, 132–3, 138, 140, 142, 178n, 189–90, 203, 207; *see also* Bernicia; Deira
    coins from, 73
    earls of, *see* Copsi; Eric of Lade; Gospatric; Morcar; Robert de Commines; Siward
    kings of, *see* Ælle; Edwin; Oswald; Oswiu
Norway, 36, 194
notation, *see* neums
Nottingham, 93, 111
Noyon, 118n
nuns and nunneries, 110 and n

oaths, 132–3
Oda, archbishop of Canterbury (941–58), 71, 81, 161–2
Odin, 25–6; *see also* Woden
Odo, bishop of Bayeux (1049–97), 230, 232, 234, 235, 237, 241–2, 243
    seal of, 235
Oeric, 26

Offa, king of Mercia (757–96), 4, 5, 38, 80, 83, 84
office, offices, liturgical, 178n, 181n, 183n
  rhymed, 178n, 188
Oisc, 18, 26–7
Olaf Guthfrithsson (Anlaf, Amlaíb), 128, 130–31, 133, 137–8, 143
Olaf Haroldsson, saint, king of Norway, 194, 207
oral tradition, 16, 26, 28
Orchard, Nicholas, 118–21
Orderic Vitalis (d. *c*. 1142), 201, 208–9, 223–4
ordinations, 181n
ordo, *see* coronation
Ordulf, magnate, 154
origin legends, 1–2, 15–29
Orkney, 133
Osbern, bishop of Exeter (1072–1103), 231, 233n, 235, 239, 242
Osbern, monk of Christ Church Canterbury and hagiographer, 145, 149–51, 153, 155
  Life of St Dunstan by, 149–51
Osburh, mother of Alfred, king of Wessex, 19
Osgar, monk, 157
Oslo, 168n
Osmanville, church of St Clement in, 209
Osmund, bishop of Salisbury (1078–99), 235, 238, 245
Osric, ealdorman, 93
Ostphalia, 33
Oswald, archbishop of York (961–92) and bishop of Worcester (971–92), saint, 8, 13, 145, 158, 237n, 238
Oswald, king of Northumbria, saint (634–42), 103, 139, 177
Oswine, king of Kent, 76
Oswiu, king of Northumbria (651–75), 139
Otford (Kent), 79
Ottonian court, 143
Ouse, river, 189
Owain, king of Strathclyde, 128
Oxford, 43, 112
  university, 34, 42
  –, Rawlinson chair of Anglo–Saxon at, 42

papyrus, 75
Parrett, river (Somerset), 93

Passage du Grand Vey, 209
Paul, saint and apostle, 147, 153
Peers, C.R. (1868–1952), 68
Penrith (Cumberland), 132
Pentecost, 163–4
Peter, bishop of Chester (1072–85), 235n
Peter (*Petrus*), cleric, author of *Carta dirige gressus*, 132, 133n, 143
Peter, saint and apostle, 153, 192
Peterborough, 172
  abbey, 191
Petheram, John (1807–58), 42
Phillipps, Sir Thomas (1792–1872), 59–60
Pictish Chronicle, 138
Picts, 142
plague, 71
Plegmund, archbishop of Canterbury (890–923), 5, 117–21, 123, 126
pōl (place-name element), 84
Pontefract (Yorkshire), 3, 189–90, 198–206, 209–10
  All Saints' church in, 203
  The Booths in, 203, 206
  castle, 198–210
  –, chapel of St Clement in, 189, 198, 200–207, 209–10
  cemetery, 203–5
  priory of St John (Cluniac), 200
pontifical, see Egbert; Lanalet
  Samson pontifical, see manuscripts, CCCC 146
Porchester (Hampshire), 240
Port, 17–19, 25
porticus, 68–9, 79
Portsmouth (Hampshire), 18
Postan, Michael (1899–1981), 98
postcommunion, 182
prayers, 168–9, 173–4, 178; *see also* blessings; collects; postcommunion; prefaces; secrets
prefaces, 173, 175, 179–80, 182–3
priests, masses for, 171–2, 175–6, 183, 185–6
Prise, Sir John (d. 1555), 50, 65
prophecy, 146–66
Psalter, 158

Rackham, Oliver, 37
Rædwald, king of the East Angles, 139

Rainald, abbot of Abingdon (1084–97), 235
Ralph, abbot of Winchcombe (1077–93), 243
Ramsey (Huntingdonshire), abbey, 50–51, 153, 232
  abbot of, *see* Ailsi; Aldwine; Herbert
Ratoldus, Sacramentary of, 126n
Ravenna, Cosmographer of, 26
Reading (Berkshire), 43
Rectitudines Singularum Personarum, 97
Reculver (Kent), church of, 7, 67–82
  –, abbots of, *see* Bassa; Berhtwald; Deneheah; Heahberht; Hwaetred
  –, carved stone cross at, 68, 81
  –, charters concerning, 8, 70–71, 74–82
  –, dean of, *see* Givehard
  –, Gospel-book formerly at, 68
  –, monks of, *see* Fresnot(us) and Tancrad; *see also* Haimeric
Rees, W., 32
Reformation (Scandinavian), 167
Regularis Concordia, 158, 168n
Regulbium, 67, 72–3
reliquaries, 177
Remigius, bishop of Lincoln (1067–92), 231n, 233n, 235, 246
Repton (Derbyshire), 94
Resting Places of Saints, 156
Rheims, 119
  archbishop of, *see* Hincmar
Rhine, river, 157, 193
Richard I, duke of Normandy (942–96), 212, 215, 216, 218
Richard II, duke of Normandy (996–1026), 213, 218
Richard of Hexham, 228
Ridley, Cecilia, 42
rings, as part of regalia, 125
Robert I (the Fearless), duke of Normandy (1027–35), 213, 218
Robert de Commines, 207
Robert of Jumièges, missal of, *see* manuscripts, Le Havre, BM Y. 6 [274]
Robert the Lotharingian, bishop of Hereford (1079–95), 233, 234, 235, 244
Robert of Stafford, 239
Robertson, Eben William (1815–74), 4, 31–44
Robertson, William (1721–93), 43

Rochester, 77, 150–52, 154, 164–5; *see also* Andrew, saint
  bishops of, 232n; *see also* Ælfstan; Gundulf
  bridge, 3, 14
  cathedral, 7–8, 71, 231,
  cathedral archive, 231, 232
  see of, 150–51
rod, as part of regalia, 125
Rollo, count of Rouen, 212, 214–18
Roman Britain, *see* Britain
Rome, 6, 7, 120, 123, 126, 163
  church of San Clemente in, 193
  Roman empire, 24–5
Rosenwein, Barbara, 90
Ross, Sir William Charles (1794–1860), 31n

Sachsenspiegel, 33, 42
sacramentaries, 179; *see also* Angoulême; Gellone; manuscripts, BL Cotton Vitellius A xviii; Winchcombe traditions of,
  –, Frankish (Eighth-Century Gelasian), 171–2, 175–6
  –, Gregorian, 171–2, 182–3
  –, *Hadrianum*, 175, 184
  –, mixed Gregorian, 171, 175–7, 183
  –, Old Gelasian, 171n, 184
  –, Supplemented Gregorian, 175–6, 183–4
St Albans (Hertfordshire), abbey, 54, 178n
St-Amand, 118n
St Andrews (Fife), 13, 138
  university of, 1, 9–10
St-Bertin, abbey, 82
St Gall, 69
St Nicholas-at-Wade (Kent), 74
St-Riquier (Centula), 69
St-Sauveur-le-Vicomte, abbey, 231n
St-Vaast, *see* Arras
St-Wandrille, abbey, 157
Salisbury (Wiltshire), bishops of, 232n; *see also* Osmund
  cathedral, 232
salt, 4, 74
Samson, bishop of Worcester (1096–1112), 237–8, 247–8
Saracens, 120n
Sarre (Kent), 73–4, 78, 82
Saucourt, battle of, 144
Sawyer, Peter, 2, 31, 47–8

Saxonia, 133, 140
Saxons, 23–4, 26–7, 140; *see also Lex Saxonum*
  East, kings of, 77
  South, 17–19
  West, 17–19, 23, 28, 80, 126, 127–8, 130, 134, 137–8; *see also* Wessex; West Saxon Gospels
Say, William, 50
Scandinavia, 20, 23, 25–8, 167–8
Scergeat, 102
Scotland, Scots, 31–3, 36, 40, 43, 128, 130, 132–4, 137, 142, 207
  king of, *see* Constantine II
scripts,
  Anglo-Caroline minuscule, Style IV, 170
  majuscule, 170
  minuscule, 170
  rustic capitals, 170
seals, 235
secrets, 173, 176n, 177–8, 181–2
Selby (Yorkshire), abbey, 231, 232
Selden, John (1584–1654), 60, 66
Sergius III, pope (904–11), 123
Severn, river, 85
Shaftesbury (Dorset), abbey, 236
Sharpe, Richard, 230n, 236
Sheldwich (Kent), 79–80, 82
Shelsley Beauchamp (Worcestershire), 86
Sherborne (Dorset), diocese of, 120
shire, 32–3, 37, 40
  court, 236
Shirlet, forest (Shropshire), 85
Shrewsbury, abbey, 231n
Sidonius, 20
Sihtric, king of York (d. 927), 102, 132, 140
Simeon of Durham, 133n, 203
Sims-Williams, Patrick, 83
Siward, earl of Northumbria (d. 1055), 206–7
Skara (Sweden), 168n
skeletons, 22
Smyth, Alfred, 137
soke, 32
Solway Firth, 136
Somers, John, Baron Somers (1651–1716), 59
Spelman, Sir Henry (d. 1641), 56, 64
Staffordshire, 208
Stenton, Sir Frank (1880–1967), 31–2, 38, 86

Stevenson, W.H. (1858–1924), 38
stirrup, 40
Stour, river (Warwickshire), 84
Stour, river (Worcestershire), 83–5
Stour in Ismere (Worcestershire), 9, 83–7
Stow (Lincolnshire), 231n, 233n
Strathclyde, king of, *see* Owain
Stubbs, William (1825–1901), 31, 38, 42
Stuf, 17–19
Sture, *see* Stour in Ismere
Sturry (Kent), 74
Suger, abbot of St-Denis (1122–51), 95
Sulcard of Westminster, 150–52, 154
sulungs, 73–4, 76
Sutton Hoo, ship burial at, 24, 27
Svein, *see* Swein
Swaefheard, king of Kent (689–92), 77
Sweden, 25, 27
Swein I Forkbeard, king of Denmark and of the English (d. 1014), 212–13
Swein II Estrithsson, king of Denmark, 207–8
Swithhun, saint, cult of, 154, 168n, 177n, 180, 181n
sword, royal, 125
Syme, Sir Ronald (1903–89), 39

Tacitus
  Germania by, 16
Tamar, river, 133n
Tamworth (Staffordshire), 102, 103
Tancrad, monk of Reculver, 82
Tanner, Thomas (1674–1735), bishop of St Asaph, 52
Tanshelf (Yorkshire), 201–3, 205–6, 210
Tardebigge (Worcestershire), 86
Tate, Francis (1560–1616), 51
Tavistock (Devon), abbey, 154
Taylor, H.M. (1907–95), 69
Tennyson, Alfred (1809–92), 128
Thanet (Kent), 72, 82; *see also* Minster-in-Thanet
Textus Roffensis, 3
Thames, river, 189
thane, see thegns
Theel-Land, 34
thegns, 33, 236n
Theodore, archbishop of Canterbury (668–90), 71–2, 74–6

Theodoric, king of the Ostrogoths (d. 526), 26
Theodric, son of Ida of Bernicia, 27
Thingwall (Cheshire), 137
Thomas I, archbishop of York (d. 1100), 242
Thomas II, archbishop of York (d. 1114), 242
Thomson, Rodney, 150
'thorpe' as a place-name element, 196
thrymsas, 73
Thurstan, archbishop of York (1119–40), 196–8
Tiber, river, 123
tithes, 233
tolls, toll-stations, 73–4, 78
towns, history of, 12–13
trade, 27, 73–4, 201
Tribal Hidage, 40, 84, 96
trimoda necessitas, 37–8
Trinity Board of Navigation, 67
Turner, Derek, 123

Uecta, 18; *see also* Wight
Ulster, Annals of, 138
Upstreet (Kent), 74
urbanism, *see* towns

Valognes, 209
vespers, liturgical office, 178n, 181n
Vikings, 2, 70, 90, 91, 149, 151, 166, 212, 214, 217; *see also* Norsemen
vills, 33, 40
  royal, 32
Vinheiðr, battle of, 134, 142
Vire, river, 209
Virgin Mary, cult of, 174
virgins, masses for, 170–71, 174–5, 182, 185
Vitalian, pope (657–72), 71
Vitalis, abbot of Westminster (1076–1085?), 151, 236, 243
Vitellius sacramentary, see manuscripts, BL Cotton Vitellius A xviii
Vortigern, 1
votives, 175, 181n, 186
  masses for, 171–2, 176
  pro temptatione carnis, 172n

Walcher, bishop of Durham (1071–80), 242
Wales, Welsh, 33, 35, 93, 132–3
Walkelin, bishop of Winchester (1070–98), 240
  warren of, 240
Walker, H.E., 3
Walker, Simon, 129, 139, 142–4
Wallop (Hampshire), 32
Wanley, Humfrey (1672–1726), 53, 54, 59, 64
Wantsum channel (Kent), 72–4, 80
warfare, 12
warriors, 22
warships, 20
weapons, *see* burial
Webber, Tessa, 231n
Weever, John (d. 1632), 69
Wells (Somerset), bishops of, 119, 126, 232n; *see also* Athelm; Giso
  cathedral, 119–20, 232
Werferth, bishop of Worcester, 106n
wergeld, 40
Wertermorum, 133n
Wessex, 2, 80, 93, 130, 134, 143, 177; *see also* Gewisse; Saxons, West
  dioceses of, 120; *see also* Dorchester; Sherborne; Wells; Winchester
  kings of, 70–71, 80–81, 130, and see Æthelred I; Æthelwulf; Alfred; Caedwalla; Ceawlin; Cynegils; Edward the Elder; Ine
  –, genealogy of, 28
Westminster, abbey, 151, 155, 232; *see also* Sulcard
  abbot of, *see* Gilbert; Vitalis
  sanctuary, 232
Westphalia, 33
West Saxon Gospels, 156
Wherwell (Hampshire), abbey, 55
White, Lynn (1907–87), 40
Wigheard, archbishop-elect of Canterbury (d. 668), 71
Wight, Isle of, 17–19
Wihtgar, 17–19, 25
Wihtred (d. 725), king of Kent, 76–7, 96
  lawcode of, 77
Wihtwara, 17, 18
William Longsword, count of Rouen (d. 942), 216
William I, king of the English (1066–87), 3, 155, 198–9, 201, 207–10, 212–13, 217–20, 222–3, 239
  charters issued by, 229, 232, 236, 240

William II, king of the English (1087–1100), 155, 200, 234, 239
  charters issued by, 229
William of Jumièges, 212–13, 218–21
William of Malmesbury (d. in or after 1142), 133n, 134, 150–51, 153–7, 161, 166, 223–6
William of Poitiers, 220–21, 224
William of Saint-Calais, bishop of Durham (1081–96), 234, 236, 243
Williams, Howard, 21–2
Wimborne, 110
Winchcombe (Gloucestershire), abbey, 81, 243
  abbot of, see Ralph
  annals of, 81
  sacramentary of, 175n, 177n
Winchester, 149, 156, 163–4, 166, 168, 177–8, 180–82, 207; see also Wulfstan of Winchester
  bishops of, see Ælfheah; Ælfheah Calvus; Æthelwold; Daniel; Denewulf; Walkelin; see also Birinus, bishop of Dorchester
  College, 9
  diocese of, 120
  Hyde abbey, 64; see also New Minster
  –, missal of, see manuscripts, Le Havre, BM 330
  New Minster, 124, 158–60, 178–9; see also Hyde abbey
  Nunnaminster, 159–60
  Old Minster, 3, 141, 164–5, 177–8, 240
Wippedesfleot, 18
Wirral (Cheshire), 137
Witham, river (Lincolnshire), 191
Wlencing, 18
Woden, 1, 16, 25, 26, 27
Wolverley (Worcestershire), 84–6
women, in chronicles, 101, 102, 108n, 109, 116n
  clothing of, 22–4
  of Mercian royal families, 103 and n, 110, 112; see also Æthelflæd; Ælfwyn; Ealhswith
Wood, Michael, 125, 136, 141–2
woodland, 86–7; see also Brochyl; Kinver; Morfe

Woolf, Alex, 20–21, 120
Worcester, 8, 13, 57–9, 83, 94, 131, 143–4, 153, 155, 179–80, 229, 232, 234; see also John of Worcester
  bishops of, 232n, 239; see also Cenwald; Deneberht; Ealhhun; Ecgwine; Lyfing; Oswald; Samson; Werferth; Wulfstan, saint
Worcester College, Oxford, 31
Wormald, Patrick (1947–2004), 117, 122n, 124
writ, 230, 236, 239, 240
writ-charter, 236
Wulferd, 86
Wulfred, archbishop of Canterbury (805–32), 80, 120
Wulfric, abbot of St Augustine's, Canterbury, 148
Wulfstan I, archbishop of York (931–56), 202, 206
Wulfstan II, archbishop of York (the Homilist; d. 1023), 161–2
Wulfstan, saint, bishop of Worcester (1062–95), 8, 13, 155–6, 176, 232, 234, 237, 242, 243, 244; 245; 246
  seal of, 235
Wulfstan of Winchester, *Life of St Æthelwold* by, 146, 156

yeomanry, yeomen, 43, 92
York, 44, 133–4, 142, 155, 190, 194–8, 203, 207–9, 240; see also Clementhorpe
  archbishops of, 194, 197–8, 232n; see also Ealdred; Oswald; Thomas I; Thomas II; Thurstan; Wulfstan I; Wulfstan II
  –, *Rights and Customs of the*, 196
  –, shire of, 194
  Guildhall, 197
  king of, see Sihtric
  Old Baile castle, 197
  shipwrights in, 196
  trading zone in, 194–6
Yorkshire, 209